# KILLER CHILI

Library of Congress Control Number: 2006939951

ISBN-10: 1-932855-60-2
ISBN-13: 978-1-932855-60-9

Cover photograph: Jupiterimages

*Killer Chili: Savory Recipes from North America's Favorite Restaurants* is produced by becker&mayer!, Bellevue, Washington.
www.beckermayer.com

Design: Kasey Free
Editorial: Kate Perry
Image Coordination: Stephanie Anderson and Lisa Metzger
Production Coordination: Shirley Woo

10  9  8  7  6  5  4  3  2  1

Manufactured in China.

Chronicle Books LLC
680 Second Street
San Francisco, California 94105

www.chroniclebooks.com

# KILLER CHILI

STEPHANIE ANDERSON

*Savory Recipes from North America's Favorite Restaurants*

# CONTENTS

# INTRODUCTION

One of the best things about chili—besides the delicious, mouthwatering flavors—is its versatility and adaptability; playing with the spices and cooking techniques in each recipe is at the very heart of making chili. Even if two chili recipes match on paper, the ingredients usually end up a tad "adjusted" by the time the concoction reaches the bowl. The makings vary from one enthusiast to another, and from region to region, and with as many different ingredients as you can use in chili comes as many (or more) opinions about what makes the "best" chili. Creators of Texas-style chili, for instance, firmly and unequivocally eschew beans and any vegetables (except chile peppers, of course); Cincinnati chili more closely resembles an Italian bolognese sauce; both East Coast and Midwestern chili tends to be a bit sweet and contains beans, meat, and tomatoes.

Self-proclaimed chiliheads go to great lengths to prove they know all there is about chili. H. Allen Smith,

a prolific author considered by many to be the official chili oracle, claimed in his aptly titled manifesto "Nobody Knows More About Chili Than I Do," published in *Holiday* magazine in 1967, that he and his brother did not speak for more than a year after a falling-out over their antithetical views on chili making. Smith also wrote that had he known about Lyndon Johnson's opinions on chili, he would not have voted for him in 1964. I doubt very much that tomato soup ever inspired anything close to that.

While different varieties of chili are made all over the world, the fare is inextricably linked to the culture and history of the Lone Star State; in fact, it's the official state dish. Devotees widely believe that chili was invented in Texas, perhaps due to its proximity to Mexico. Texas saw the very first chili parlors, small, family-owned joints that whipped up and served nothing but Texas-style bowls of chili, dubbed "chili con carne." The competitive spirit surrounding chili was

likely born in these establishments, as each one had its own closely guarded secret recipe.

Due to the chili craze in Texas, chili parlors opened up in many corners of the United States (and some even in Canada), but most of these ventures have since closed. The ones that do still exist, however, maintain an essential secrecy around their recipes. Take Cincinnati, Ohio, for example. Cincinnati-style chili is a far cry from the Texan variety, but Ohioans are just as fanatical. This type of chili was reportedly invented by Greek immigrants, and is much thinner than the traditional chili con carne made popular in Texas. Cincinnati chili includes some unexpected flavors—allspice, cloves, cinnamon, and cocoa—alongside more traditional chili spices, such as garlic, cumin, cayenne, and chili powder.

You will be hard-pressed to find a Cincinnati chili parlor that will provide you with a recipe, however. Apparently, the almost two hundred chili parlors in Cincinnati have an agreement with one another not to share their recipes, which is why you won't find one in this book; but no chili book is complete without at least a mention of Cincinnati chili and its cult-like status.

Luckily, many other restaurants across the U.S. and Canada were more than happy to share their secrets with me. Traditionalists will be pleased to find recipes for real Texas chili from the Cosmos Café in Houston and Clark's Outpost in Tioga, Texas. Many of the recipes in *Killer Chili* are refreshingly innovative, such as the bison chili from Meriwether's in St. Louis, the sun-dried tomato and chorizo chili from the Sherwood House Restaurant in Canmore, Alberta, and the catfish and red bean chili from the Crown Restaurant in Indianola, Mississippi. There are also several healthy, hearty vegetarian recipes for cooks who want to omit meat from their chili.

I hope these recipes inspire you to have fun and to experiment in your own kitchen, not just with chili but with anything you cook!

# CHILI 101

## Chile Peppers

The thing that makes chili chili is, of course, the chile pepper. Chile peppers are any of the hot varieties from the capsaicin-producing *Capsicum* genus, which is a member of the nightshade family. They are beloved all over the world and are a major component of not only Tex-Mex cooking, but also Thai, Indian, Chinese, Indonesian, Korean, South American, Caribbean, and other cuisines. Each kind of chile is different from the next, from the smoky chipotle to the deceptively delicate-sounding Scotch bonnet, one of the hottest chiles in the world. Their shapes and colors vary, too, and if you are lucky enough to have access to farmers' markets or specialty grocery stores, you know the sight of a rainbow of chile peppers is a real treat.

What chiles have in common with one another is their heat, and it's that same heat that elevates what might otherwise be just beef or vegetable stew into the chili stratosphere. The chemical compound capsaicin, naturally occuring in chiles, is quite fascinating. When you ingest a chile, the capsaicin sends a pain sensation to the brain, which releases feel-good endorphins, the body's natural painkillers. Not only that, capsaicin is hydrophobic, which means that drinking water is ineffective in quelling the heat; reach for milk or a piece of buttered bread instead. Alcoholic beverages work, too, which is perhaps why beer is often the preferred accompaniment to chili.

While all chiles pack a punch, the degree of that punch and the flavor they imbue vary. The Scoville scale, created by chemist Wilbur Scoville in 1912, specifically measures the heat of chile peppers by determining the amount of capsaicin present in each pepper. Chiles are assigned a range of Scoville heat units (SHUs). For instance, Tabasco sauce, made from the Tabasco chile, has between 600 and 800 SHUs. The hottest chile in the world, the Dorset Naga, has between 800,000 and almost two million SHUs. Nearly every recipe for chili that you'll encounter will use chili powder in addition to or in place of the actual peppers. Typically, chili powder is made from dried ground chiles, usually the ancho variety, plus cayenne pepper, cumin, and other spices. When a recipe calls for peppers, it's good to know what you're dealing with before you start. Here's a (very) brief primer on some of the chiles and sweet peppers used in the recipes in this book:

**Bell pepper** (0 SHUs): Sweet, with no heat.

**New Mexico red** (500-2,500 SHUs): Also known as Anaheim; very mild.

**Poblano** (1,000–1,500 SHUs): Very mild; one of the most popular chiles grown in Mexico. Anchos are dried poblanos.

**Pasilla** (1,000–4,000 SHUs): Mild to medium-hot; chilacas are a fresh variety of pasillas, and chile negros are a dried variety.

**Jalapeno** (2,000–8,500 SHUs): One of the most popular chiles. Chipotles are smoked, dried jalapenos, often packed in adobo sauce.

**Cayenne** (30,000–50,000 SHUs): Moderately hot; most often dried and ground.

**Serrano** (10,000–23,000 SHUs): A very "meaty" Mexican variety; moderately hot.

**Habanero** (100,000–350,000 SHUs): One of the world's hottest chiles, with a fruity aroma and flavor; cultivated in Mexico's Yucatan peninsula, parts of Latin America, and the American Southwest.

**Scotch bonnets** (100,000–350,000 SHUs): One of the world's hottest chiles and a derivative of the habanero; found in the Caribbean.

Always wash your hands in hot, soapy water after handling chile peppers. Better yet, wear rubber gloves.

Chiles can cause immediate skin irritation for some people, and the oils from the peppers stay on your hands for longer than you realize, so be sure you've scrubbed away every last trace before getting your fingers near your eyes and other delicate body parts. The area at the base of the stem and the seeds are the most potent parts of chile peppers, and most recipes say to remove them. Unless you're a culinary daredevil, it's not a step you want to forget.

## Beans

Many recipes call for dried beans, which must be soaked overnight. (Canned beans are often a fine substitute in a pinch.) If you forgot or don't have time to soak dried beans overnight, follow these instructions from Mary Ellen Hope, owner of Bishop's Chili in Chicago, to cook them more quickly:

> Boil 2 large pots of water. Place the dried beans in a separate large stockpot. Pour one pot of boiling water over the beans and stir. Let them soak until the water cools, then drain, leaving the beans in the stockpot. Add the second pot of boiling water to the beans, soak until water cools, and drain the beans.

Cooked beans are usually added to chili close to the end of the cooking process; if they cook too long, they can disintegrate into a mushy mess.

## General Cookin' Tips

Famous chili aficionado H. Allen Smith believed that all "civilized" chili cooks make chili in an iron kettle, but that's just not practical in most kitchens. However, you should definitely use a large, heavy pot for most of the recipes in *Killer Chili*. While many of the recipes are scaled back from their original restaurant-size forms, most still make a gallon of chili or more—perfect for a large group or for leftovers. Chili can be eaten as a side dish or an entrée, and serving sizes vary, but for our purposes, each serving is approximately one cup, a standard entrée size. With anything you cook, always use the best ingredients you can find and afford—it really makes a difference. It's a common misconception that soups, particularly those that utilize a lot of ingredients as chili does, are just a means of ridding the refrigerator of leftovers, and that the quality of the ingredients doesn't matter. With anything you cook or bake, the sum will only be as good as its parts.

Chili takes some time between the soaking, the chopping, and the simmering, but it's worth it. Don't cut the cooking time short if you want the best result. If the instructions say to let the chili simmer for three hours, let it simmer for three hours. Chili is the gift that keeps on giving, too; it will taste even better a day or a few days after you've made it, as the time allows all of the flavors to really meet and mingle. If you have leftover chili, it freezes and reheats beautifully.

Chili is a great way to experiment with ingredients you may not use often, or at all. Make a pact with yourself: If you can't quickly find a certain chile, spice, or cut of meat, search for it. Visit ethnic grocery stores you pass on your way home from work but never go to. Introduce yourself to your neighborhood butcher and request the cut you need rather than grabbing the first available pre-wrapped item in the case. Throw away spices that are too old (yes, they age, too) and replace them with new ones. Order a high-quality chili powder or another spice online or from a specialty foods shop. With a little bit of time and effort, you'll be well on your way to being a modern-day chili queen (or king)!

# DRY DOCK RESTAURANT & TAVERN

## PORTLAND, MAINE

A Portland staple since 1983, the Dry Dock Restaurant & Tavern actually has two docks that overlook the scenic working waterfront. Located at the eastern end of busy Commercial Street in the Old Port section of the city, the Dry Dock is a favorite with locals and tourists.

Like all coastal New England towns, Portland is known for its plentiful seafood. Menus abound with local catches, and the Dry Dock is no exception. Diners can feast on peel-and-eat shrimp, a Maine crabmeat roll, fried clams, fried haddock, lobster and crabmeat clubs, and the famous shrimp Bloody Mary. There's plenty for land-

lubbers to enjoy, too, including filet mignon, superb burgers, and Reuben and corned-beef sandwiches. Chowders and chili are another delicious draw for diners hoping to ward off the coastal chill.

Developed by Dry Dock cook Shirley Tubbs, Shirley's Chili is a fairly traditional, hearty chili with ground beef, tomato, and beans. Dry Dock manager Jeannine LaRochelle explains that the secret behind it is that they allow individual or groups of ingredients to cook and simmer awhile before adding more ingredients. The process of layering flavors creates a well-spiced, dynamic chili that scintillates on the palate.

# Shirley's Chili

1 pound ground chuck

1 tablespoon kosher salt

1 tablespoon freshly ground black pepper

1 green bell pepper, seeded and diced

1/2 red bell pepper, seeded and diced

2 jalapeno peppers, seeded and diced

1 large white onion, diced

4 large or 6 small cloves garlic, minced

2 bay leaves

1 tablespoon dried oregano, crumbled

1 teaspoon dried basil, crumbled

5 tablespoons chili powder

2 tablespoons ground cumin

1/2 teaspoon ground red pepper

One 28-ounce can tomatoes, diced

One 28-ounce can tomato sauce

One 28-ounce can red kidney beans, drained and rinsed

Diced onions, shredded cheddar cheese, tortilla chips (optional)

Heat a heavy 4½-quart saucepan on medium-low heat until hot, then add the ground chuck and half of the salt and black pepper. (You should use salt and pepper throughout the cooking process when adding the ingredients.) Add the bell peppers, jalapenos, onion, and garlic to the beef and sauté until the beef is cooked through, 10 to 15 minutes. Add the bay leaves, spices, and remaining salt and pepper, stir well, and cook for 4 to 5 minutes. Add the tomatoes, tomato sauce, and kidney beans. Stir, then simmer for 2 hours. During the last 30 minutes of cooking, check the seasoning and add more salt and black pepper if needed.

Serve in a crock with diced onions, melted Cheddar cheese, and tortilla chips, if desired. *Serves 12.*

## GENERAL COOKIN' TIP

★ Be sure to cook the spices for 4 to 5 minutes before adding the tomatoes, tomato sauce, and kidney beans, to cook off the rawness of the spices.

# MAINE DINER

## WELLS, MAINE

**N**ew England carries the unfortunate stigma of being, to put it delicately, a little less hospitable than other parts of the country. Whoever came up with that stereotype clearly never made it to the Maine Diner, where friendliness is next to godliness. Myles Henry and his two brothers opened the diner in 1983 with a simple plan to serve good, home-cooked food in a clean, friendly atmosphere. It seemed like a winner of an idea, but it took several years for it to catch on with customers. Once people tried the Maine Diner, though, it became an instant favorite, and since the early '90s, has maintained its reputation for being bustling—and serving good, home-cooked food in a clean, friendly atmosphere. It's not uncommon for Boston residents to make the seventy-mile drive north once a week or more, even on their lunch hours. Even the *Today* show crew made the trek.

Along with meat loaf, potpie, and a score of seafood dishes (it is Maine, after all), Maine Diner's chili is a popular constant on the menu. Like much of the food served at the diner, the recipe hails from Henry's mother, though it's been "tweaked" a bit. "For a non–Tex-Mex restaurant," Henry says, "we have great chili." His secret? "Chili is like pizza," he says. "There are so many way to make it. The key for us is to make it in small batches, and make it often."

# Maine Diner Chili

1 pound ground chuck

1 small onion, coarsely chopped

1 clove garlic, minced

1 tomato, diced

1 48-ounce can chili con carne

1 48-ounce can kidney beans, drained

$\frac{1}{3}$ cup prepared horseradish

2 cups water

$\frac{1}{2}$ teaspoon salt

$\frac{1}{2}$ teaspoon freshly ground black pepper

1 tablespoon dried thyme, crushed

1 teaspoon chili powder

$\frac{1}{2}$ teaspoon red pepper flakes

1 dash Tabasco sauce

In a large, heavy pot, sauté the ground chuck over medium heat until cooked through, 10 to 15 minutes. Drain and return to the pot. Add the onion and garlic, then add all the remaining ingredients and stir. Cook over low heat for 3 hours, stirring occasionally. *Serves 8.*

## GENERAL COOKIN' TIP

★ This chili is even better reheated the next day—and the day after that!

# GOURMET CAFÉ

## GLENS FALLS, NEW YORK

Every neighborhood should have a restaurant like the Gourmet Café in Glen Falls. Owner and chef Francis Willis and his wife, Tracy, have created a casual, cozy spot and a menu with fresh salads, soups, panini, and other fare, most of which Willis prepares on a long table in the dining room. Donning crisp chef's whites, Willis surrounds himself with bowls of vegetables, spices, meats, and other ingredients, and has several sauté pans going on a series of tabletop gas burners. Diners watch Willis toss, turn, and flip their food, and during warmer months, patrons can sample Willis' creations at an outdoor sidewalk table.

Willis' main priority is giving his customers what they want, and true to form, his versatile Southwestern Black Bean Chili can easily become vegetarian if you delete the beef and broth and use more beans. Just add 1 cup dried kidney beans, 1 cup lentils, and 1 cup green split peas to the black and Great Northern beans. Soak the beans and the split peas (but not the lentils) in cold water for at least 8 hours, though overnight is preferred, then follow the rest of the original recipe for a delicious, meat-free meal.

# Southwestern Black Bean Chili

1½ cups dried black beans

1 cup dried Great Northern beans

¼ cup olive oil

2 tablespoons minced garlic

1 large white onion, diced

1 green bell pepper, seeded and diced

1 red bell pepper, seeded and diced

2 pounds lean ground beef

¼ cup hot chili powder

¼ cup mild chili powder

2 teaspoons ground cumin

2 teaspoons ground coriander

1 teaspoon cayenne pepper

1 teaspoon red pepper flakes

1 teaspoon freshly ground black pepper

2 tablespoons sugar

1 tablespoon dried oregano, crumbled

1 tablespoon kosher salt

4 cups (16 ounces) dark beer, preferably stout or porter

2 cups beef broth

Two 28-ounce cans diced tomatoes

One 28-ounce can tomato purée

Shredded Cheddar cheese, diced red onion, and sour cream for garnish

Pick over and rinse the beans. Soak the beans in a large pot filled with cold water for at least 8 hours or preferably overnight; do not drain. Transfer the pot to the stove. Cook the beans slowly over medium heat until tender, about 1 hour. Drain the beans and set aside.

In a large, heavy pot, heat the olive oil over medium heat and sauté the garlic, onion, and peppers until slightly soft. Add the beef and sauté until fully cooked. Add the spices, sugar, oregano, and salt and stir until they start to stick to the bottom of the pan. Add the beer and stir, cooking until the volume of beer reduces by half. Add the beef broth and the diced and puréed tomatoes and stir thoroughly. Add the cooked beans, reduce the heat to low, and simmer for 2 hours. Serve in bowls, topped with the cheese, onion, and sour cream. *Serves 6 to 8.*

# PORTSMOUTH BREWERY

## PORTSMOUTH, NEW HAMPSHIRE

The iconic '80s sitcom *Cheers* taught us that bars are not just for drinking, but for community and friendship building, as well. Pushing that concept just a bit further are brewpubs, where visitors can meet, mingle, and actually get to watch—not just taste—beer brewing right before their eyes. Microbrews and the brewpubs that serve them are known for being inventive and often a bit irreverent, and the Portsmouth Brewery in New Hampshire is typical in that regard.

After working as head brewer at the Northampton Brewery in Massachusetts, owner Peter Egelston brought his brewing know-how to the Granite State.

Portsmouth and its sister company, Smuttynose Brewing Company, now produce a variety of brews, including Black Cat Stout, "Wild Thang" Wild Rice Ale, and Old Brown Dog Ale. Many of the restaurant's dishes are made with beer, including the brewery's chili, which uses Smuttynose's Old Brown Dog Ale. But non–New Hampshire residents shouldn't despair—a different brand or variety will make a fine substitute. When you think about it, beer and chili are about as perfect a match as peanut butter and jelly. Hot and spicy foods practically beg for a cold, frosty beer to be consumed on the side; the Portsmouth Brewery just cuts to the chase and adds some to the pot.

# Portsmouth Brewery Chili

1 tablespoon canola oil

1 pound ground chorizo sausage

1 pound lean ground beef

2 cups diced onions

2 cups diced green bell peppers

1/4 cup minced garlic

One 48-ounce can chopped tomatoes

1 tablespoon ground cumin

1 tablespoon ground coriander

1 tablespoon chili powder

1 teaspoon cayenne pepper

1 teaspoon kosher salt

12 ounces Smuttynose Old Brown Dog Ale or another English brown ale

4 cups cooked kidney beans, drained

In a large, heavy pot, heat the oil over medium heat. Add the meat, and brown. Add the onion, pepper, and garlic and simmer until soft. Add the tomatoes, seasonings, and ale. Simmer for 1 to 1½ hours, stirring occasionally to keep the chili from sticking to the pot. Add the kidney beans and stir before serving. *Serves 8 to 10.*

## GENERAL COOKIN' TIP

★ If you want a spicier chili, double the amount of cayenne pepper.

★ For a thicker chili, add tomatoes slowly until chili reaches the desired consistency.

# ROSEBUD DINER

## ── SOMERVILLE, MASSACHUSETTS ──

Located in a restored historic diner car in Somerville, a Boston suburb, the Rosebud Diner was added to the National Register of Historic Places in 1999. This listing is appropriate; one of the reasons visitors love the Rosebud so much is that it's barely changed since its 1941 opening. After more than sixty years, the diner is still full of chrome, swiveling counterstools, and old-fashioned comfort food delivered quickly to the tables by sassy, sharp-tongued servers. Over the years the menu has changed a bit to keep up with the times; veggie burgers certainly weren't standard fare in the '40s! The diner also has a full bar to accommodate those looking to indulge in a Bloody Mary with their scrambled eggs and home fries.

Another relatively new feature is Tom Norton, who started cooking at the Rosebud in 1999. He developed his chili recipe about twenty years ago, however, and brought it with him to the diner. Like everything at the Rosebud Diner, Norton's recipe is neither fussy nor fancy, but don't let the simple recipe fool you—Norton's chili is a savory treat. The chef and part-time musician debuted his chili years ago at a local annual music festival, where hundreds of hungry fans and musicians gobbled the stuff up, and it's now a continual bestseller at the diner. He urges home cooks to practice his "trial-and-error" technique with the recipe, as well, particularly when it comes to the spices, the amounts of which are listed "to taste."

# Rosebud Chili

2 $\frac{1}{2}$ pounds ground beef

3 $\frac{2}{3}$ cups canned red kidney beans, drained

3 $\frac{2}{3}$ cups canned baked beans, drained

2 stalks celery, chopped

$\frac{1}{2}$ large white onion, chopped

$\frac{1}{2}$ cup sliced jalapeno chiles

$\frac{1}{2}$ large red bell pepper, seeded and chopped

$\frac{1}{2}$ large green bell pepper, seeded and chopped

6 $\frac{1}{2}$ cups diced fresh tomatoes

Ground cumin to taste

Chili powder to taste

Seasoned salt to taste

Freshly ground black pepper to taste

Dash of Tabasco sauce, or to taste (optional)

In a large, heavy pot, combine the beef with just enough water to cover it. Bring to a simmer over medium heat and cook until browned. Drain. Add the beans, celery, onion, chiles, peppers, and tomatoes and cook until tender. Season with the cumin, chili powder, seasoned salt, and pepper. For added spice, add a dash (or more) of Tabasco. *Serves 10 to 12 people.*

# VANILLA BEAN CAFÉ

## —— POMFRET, CONNECTICUT ——

Chili and vanilla beans don't often find themselves mentioned in the same breath, but people are certainly talking about the chili at the Vanilla Bean Café. Locals in Pomfret, Connecticut, have known about the eatery's chili for years, but those outside this small town really started to take notice after the New York *Times* wrote about it. The café has also received accolades from other prestigious publications, including the Boston *Globe* and *Yankee* magazine, which called it "one of the outstanding reasons to visit New England."

Owner Barry Jessurun and his family opened the Vanilla Bean Café in 1989 in a restored, early-nineteenth-century barn. Back then, the café seated only sixteen people, but since then has expanded its capacity to fit ninety people inside and forty outside. Their philosophy for their restaurant, as laid out when they started the place, was to "create a place where we would feel comfortable and serve food that we would want to eat. If we wouldn't eat it, we certainly wouldn't serve it." Easily surpassing this standard, the menu is chock-full of inventive, delightful fare.

The Vanilla Bean cooks its chili slowly for several hours to allow the array of flavors to meld. This chili uses two kinds of meat—lean ground beef and spicy chorizo sausage—to make the soup a perfect hearty, satisfying choice for lunch or a light supper.

# Award-Winning Chili

2 pounds lean ground beef

2 teaspoons plus 1½ tablespoons chili powder

½ teaspoon plus ½ tablespoon ground cumin

2 teaspoons black pepper

½ teaspoon cayenne pepper, or to taste

2 drops Tabasco sauce

2 links fresh smoked Mexican chorizo sausage

1 tablespoon minced Jalapeno chile

3 cloves garlic, minced

1 onion, chopped

4 stalks celery, chopped

½ red bell pepper, seeded and chopped

½ green bell pepper, seeded and chopped

One 16-ounce can tomato sauce

One 28-ounce can tomato purée

One 28-ounce can diced tomatoes

One 16-ounce can kidney beans, drained

In a large, heavy skillet, combine the ground beef with the 2 teaspoons chili powder, the ½ teaspoon cumin, the black pepper, cayenne pepper, and Tabasco sauce. Cook over medium heat until the meat is browned. Drain, reserving 3 tablespoons of the fat.

Slice the chorizo in half lengthwise and cut into bite-size pieces. In a large, heavy pot, cook the chorizo over medium-high heat for 4 to 5 minutes. Add the 1½ tablespoons chili powder, the ½ tablespoon cumin, the jalapeno, garlic, onion, celery, bell peppers, and reserved fat. Cook until the vegetables are tender. Add the tomato products, reduce the heat to medium, and cook for 15 to 20 minutes, stirring occasionally. Stir in the cooked beef and kidney beans and simmer for 2 hours. Serve in crocks with tortilla chips, shredded Cheddar cheese, and scallions, if desired. *Serves 10 to 12.*

## GENERAL COOKIN' TIP

★ Chili is known and loved for its versatility. It freezes very well, so any leftovers can be stored in the freezer for up to 6 months and reheated when desired.

NORTHEASTERN U.S.
KILLER CHILI

# MAREMMA

## NEW YORK, NEW YORK

After one glance at the recipe for chef Cesare Casella's chili, you know you're in for something new. The Tuscan chef delights in catching diners off-guard, piquing their interest, if not their suspicion, and then delivering inventive, unexpected dishes that pack a wallop. He's been doing it for years at his Manhattan restaurant, Maremma. The name comes from a cattle-breeding region on the Tuscan coast in Italy, and the whole eatery is an homage to cowboys. Pictures of Tuscan cowboys adorn the walls, and old-time country tunes wail throughout the dining room. When he's not in the kitchen, Casella often roams about his restaurant wearing—you guessed it—cowboy boots. And the requisite bull's horns are mounted on the wall.

Advocates of Texas bowls of red or Cincinnati five-ways might pooh-pooh this chili for its lack of traditional chili qualities, but whatever you may think, it all comes down to one thing: This chili is tasty. It has strong Italian influences, including fresh rosemary and sage, pancetta, and fennel seeds—beloved flavors in Mediterranean cooking. But Casella blends those with garam masala (a spice most often found in Indian cuisine), coffee, chocolate, and more traditional chili ingredients, such as beef, tomatoes, and chili powder. This is cooking (and eating!) at its best, when the food becomes more than a meal and is elevated to an experience.

# Cesare Casella's Tuscan Chili

1 red onion, quartered

1 small carrot, chopped

1 jalapeno chile, chopped

1 tablespoon chopped fresh rosemary

1/2 tablespoon chopped fresh sage

2 stalks celery, chopped

4 cloves garlic

2 ounces pancetta, chopped

8 strips bacon

3 tablespoons olive oil

2 pounds beef chuck or skirt steak, cut into 1-inch strips

Salt and freshly ground pepper to taste

1 tablespoon garam masala

One 16-ounce can tomato purée

1/2 teaspoon ground cumin

1/2 teaspoon fennel seed

1 1/2 tablespoon chili powder

1 small potato, peeled and cut into 1/2-inch cubes

2 cups water

1 cup brewed dark-roast coffee

5 cups beef broth

2 cups canned red or kidney beans, drained

3/4 ounce unsweetened chocolate, chopped

Freshly grated Parmesan cheese for garnish

1 small white onion, coarsely chopped

1 avocado, peeled, pitted, and coarsely chopped

Preheat the oven to 400°F. In a food processor, chop the onion, carrot, jalapeno, rosemary, sage, celery, garlic, and pancetta. Place the bacon on a sided baking sheet and bake in the oven until crisp, about 15 minutes. Remove, dry with paper towels, and set aside. In a large, heavy saucepan, combine the olive oil and chopped-vegetable mixture and cook over medium-high heat for 10 minutes.

In a large bowl, season the meat with the salt, pepper, and garam masala. Add to the saucepan and cook for 12 minutes, stirring occasionally. Add the tomato purée, cumin, fennel seed, chili powder, potato, and water. Cover and simmer for 20 minutes. Add the coffee and 2 cups of the beef broth and cook for another 20 minutes, stirring constantly. Add the beans and 1 cup of the beef broth and simmer for 30 minutes. Add the remaining 2 cups broth and simmer for 15 minutes. Add the chocolate and cook for another 20 minutes, stirring occasionally. Crumble the bacon. Serve the chili garnished with the Parmesan, crumbled bacon, onion, and avocado. *Serves 6.*

# MAIN STREET EURO-AMERICAN BISTRO & BAR

## PRINCETON, NEW JERSEY

**M**ain Street was first established as a high-end catering business in 1984 in the Kingston neighborhood, at the north end of Princeton. In 1992, owner Sue Simpkins expanded it to include the bistro and bar, and Princetonians think of Main Street as their "kitchen away from home." The clientele of Main Street is as eclectic as the menu, with Princeton students and professors, New York commuters, and local businesspeople making up a corps of regular patrons. "It's a place where neighbors gather," Simpkins says. "It's really comfortable; it's not glitzy, not city-chic, and not chain fastfood. You know you're going to run into friends, and you know you're going to have good food. A good loaf of bread, a good bottle of wine, how can you lose with that?"

Part of that good food is Main Street's chili, which started out on the catering menu twenty-five years ago and has now become a fixture on the bistro menu. "It's a well-established chili in this neighborhood," Simpkins says. "There are no miraculous secret ingredients, but it's a combination of parts." Like the bistro, the chili could perhaps be described as Euro-American, with its use of sweet Italian sausage and Burgundy wine. The American part? Simpkins' own herb concoction, a special blend of ground fiery chiles and mild peppers, herbs, and spices, which she brought with her when she moved to Princeton from Seattle, and aptly named Wild West Chili Spice.

# Main Street Chili

Olive oil for browning
$\frac{1}{2}$ pound sweet Italian sausage
$2\frac{1}{2}$ pounds ground beef
3 onions, chopped
1 clove garlic, minced
One 28-ounce can peeled plum tomatoes
One 6-ounce can tomato paste
$\frac{1}{4}$ cup Burgundy or other dry red wine
2 tablespoons fresh lemon juice
$\frac{1}{3}$ cup Wild West Chili Spice (see tip)
1 teaspoon salt
$\frac{1}{4}$ cup minced fresh parsley
$\frac{1}{4}$ cup minced fresh dill
$1\frac{1}{2}$ cups beef broth
One 16-ounce can kidney beans, drained
Sour cream and shredded cheddar cheese (optional)

In a large, heavy pot, heat the oil over medium heat and brown the sausage and beef. Drain well. Crumble the beef, cut the sausage into $\frac{3}{8}$-inch pieces, and return to the pan. Add the onions and cook over medium heat until the onions are translucent. Add all the remaining ingredients. Cover and simmer over low heat for 30 minutes.

Serve with sour cream, shredded Cheddar cheese, and wedges of warm corn bread, if desired. *Serves 10.*

## GENERAL COOKIN' TIP

★ Main Street Wild West Chili Spice can be purchased through Main Street's website (www.mainstreetprinceton.com), but you can use the following recipe to make a zesty substitute: $\frac{1}{4}$ cup chili powder, 3 tablespoons ground cumin, 1 tablespoon dried basil, 1 tablespoon dried oregano, $1\frac{1}{2}$ teaspoons ground black pepper, and 2 teaspoons salt. Mix together. Store unused seasoning in a covered jar.

# SALAMANDRA

## — CARLISLE, PENNSYLVANIA —

Salamandra is one of those great neighborhood restaurants that are hard to leave. Between the cheery goldenrod-colored walls hung with paintings by local artists, the smell of freshly baked bread, and the warm glow emanating from the wood-fired brick oven in the back section of the tiny bistro, it's no wonder Salamandra's regulars have been coming for lunch or dinner once a week or more for years. Nothing here is too over-the-top or overdone; it's simple food made with super-fresh ingredients. Owner and chef Sally Powers, who creates each menu with co-chef Quentin Zell, is an advocate of minimalist cooking and believes that unfussy dishes using high-quality ingredients equal a better meal.

Salamandra's food firmly falls into the Italian category, but Zell has the freedom to experiment and dabble, and the customers love it when he does. One of Zell's most popular chilis features grilled chicken and poblano chilis. Poblanos are green, fairly mild, and heart-shaped, and they're usually stuffed with meat or cheese in the Mexican dish *chiles rellenos*. Here the peppers blend beautifully with the strong, fresh flavors of garlic, onion, cumin, chili powder, tomato, and fresh cilantro.

# Poblano and Grilled Chicken Chili

3 tablespoons olive oil

1 large red onion, finely chopped

3 poblano chiles, seeded and finely chopped

3 garlic cloves, minced

One 16-ounce can chopped tomatoes, with juice

2 tablespoons dark chili powder

$1/2$ teaspoon ground cumin

1 tablespoon minced fresh cilantro

Salt and freshly ground pepper to taste

7 ounces canned kidney beans, rinsed and drained

7 ounces canned black beans, rinsed and drained

10 to 12 ounces skinless, boneless chicken, grilled and cut into small cubes

2 cups chicken broth

1 tablespoon tomato paste

5 green onions, finely chopped

1 cup shredded Gruyère cheese

In a large, heavy saucepan, heat the oil over medium heat. Add the onion and poblanos. Cook for 3 to 4 minutes, stirring occasionally, until the onion just softens. Add the garlic and continue cooking until the onion begins to color. Add the tomatoes with their juice, chili powder, cumin, and cilantro. Bring just to a boil, reduce the heat, cover, and simmer for 10 minutes. Season with salt and pepper. Add the kidney beans, black beans, and grilled chicken. Stir in the chicken broth and tomato paste. Cover and continue simmering for 30 to 40 minutes, stirring occasionally, until the vegetables are tender. Taste and adjust the seasoning. Serve hot, topped with the green onions and shredded cheese. *Serves 6 to 7.*

## GENERAL COOKIN' TIPS

★ Have all your ingredients assembled and prepared before you start cooking. It makes your time in the kitchen more enjoyable and less rushed.

★ If you have time, roast or smoke the poblanos to add a bit more kick.

# SIDECAR BAR & GRILLE

## —— PHILADELPHIA, PENNSYLVANIA ——

The Sidecar Bar & Grille in downtown Philadelphia is a quintessential neighborhood bar. Located on the corner of Twenty-second and Christian Streets, the building looks modest from the outside, but owners Adam and Jennifer Ritter have created a sleek, urban-chic watering hole inside. Local papers have touted the Sidecar as one of the city's best-kept secrets, for both its food and its cocktails. Adult libations are certainly the biggest draw here, including the Sidecar the bar is named for, fashionable martinis, and old-school Pabst Blue Ribbon.

Another crowd-pleaser is the chili, developed by chef Richard Freedman. "People dig it," he says. "And if you're the cook, it's nice because it doesn't take all day, you can freeze some for next time, and it still tastes like it came from the Rio Grande on a chuck wagon." Freedman stresses that his recipe, like all recipes, is a guideline, and that cooks should experiment with the ingredients at will. For instance, if you prefer a bit of smokiness, add a tablespoon of chipotle powder. Or add a few tablespoons of stone-ground cornmeal to the sautéed vegetables for a thicker, stick-to-your-ribs texture. You can substitute pinto or black beans for kidney beans, or venison or wild boar for the beef. For an extra kick, add a shot (or so) of tequila with the beer.

# Sidecar Bar & Grille Chili

1 tablespoon corn, peanut, or canola oil

1 large green bell pepper, diced

1 large yellow onion, diced

3 tablespoons minced garlic

1 tablespoon ground cumin

1 tablespoon cayenne pepper

3 tablespoons chili powder

1 tablespoon ground ancho chile

3 tablespoons adobo seasoning

2 tablespoons salt

1 tablespoon freshly ground black pepper

3 pounds ground beef

2 cups lager

One 28-ounce can crushed tomatoes

One 28-ounce can kidney beans, rinsed and drained

Sour cream, shredded cheddar cheese, sliced green onion, and chopped fresh
cilantro (optional)

In a large, heavy pot, heat the oil over medium-low heat and sauté the bell pepper, onion, garlic, and seasonings until tender. Form the ground beef into large, thin burgerlike patties and sear in batches in a smoking hot iron skillet until the meat is very dark brown. Flip over and sear the other sides. Then break up the meat a bit and brown the inside of the patties. Using a slotted spoon, transfer the cooked meat to the pot. Drain and discard as much fat as you can from the skillet before you add another batch of beef.

Once all the beef is seared and in the pot, add the lager, cover, and bring to a boil. Add the tomatoes and reduce the heat to a simmer. Add the kidney beans and simmer for about 20 minutes. Taste and adjust the seasoning. Serve in bowls with tortilla chips and top with shredded Cheddar cheese, sour cream, sliced green onion, and fresh cilantro, if desired. *Serves 11.*

## GENERAL COOKIN' TIP

★ If you plan on freezing your chili, cool it to room temperature before transferring it to the freezer to prevent bacterial growth.

# CAFÉ LATTE

## ST. PAUL, MINNESOTA

Don't let the name fool you. Patrons at Café Latte can enjoy much, much more than just coffee. This Twin Cities eatery serves a huge variety of fresh food, beverages—including the lattes, of course—and desserts in an open, airy cafeteria-style setting. It also houses a gallery, with rotating exhibits of paintings, sculptures, pottery, wood carvings, and other artwork throughout the year.

Patrons can pick up gourmet boxed lunches with sandwiches of dilled egg salad, smoked turkey, tuna salad, or baked ham; fresh fruit or vegetable salads; and sweet chocolate hearts for dessert. Café Latte starts baking bread for their sandwiches—organic sourdough, whole-wheat, ten-grain, and rye—in the middle of the night to get ready for the morning rush. For dinner, people can dine on hand-crafted fresh-baked pizzas, complemented by an array of well-priced wines. There's even daily afternoon tea, complete with finger sandwiches, desserts, and a pot of tea—as close to Great Britain as you can get in Minnesota.

Café Latte also channels the American Southwest with its chicken salsa chili, which features chicken breasts and a variety of vegetables and spices, and is finished with the fresh zing of lime and cilantro. Hominy, which is made from dried corn kernels, thickens the chili and adds an earthy flavor.

# Chicken Salsa Chili

3 tablespoons olive oil

1 pound boneless, skinless chicken breasts, cut into 1-inch pieces

1 1/2 cups chopped yellow onions

1/2 teaspoon red pepper flakes

1 tablespoon minced garlic

2 teaspoons minced jalapeno chile

1 1/2 cups chicken broth

3 tablespoons chili powder

One 28-ounce can whole tomatoes, broken up, with juice

One 28-ounce can tomato purée

Two 15-ounce cans dark red kidney beans, drained

One 15-ounce can hominy, drained

1/3 cup chopped fresh cilantro

2 tablespoons fresh lime juice

Chopped red onion, sour cream, shredded cheddar cheese, tortilla chips (optional)

In a large, heavy pot, heat the olive oil over medium heat and sauté the chicken until opaque throughout. Add the onions, reduce the heat to medium-low, and cook for 3 minutes, or until the onions are tender. Add the pepper flakes, garlic, jalapeno, chicken broth, chili powder, tomatoes, tomato purée, beans, and hominy. Simmer for 15 to 20 minutes, until everything is incorporated and the chili thickens to the desired consistency.

To serve, add the cilantro and lime juice, and adjust the seasoning to taste. Ladle the chili into bowls; if desired, top with sour cream, chopped red onions, shredded Cheddar cheese, and tortilla chips. *Serves 2 to 3.*

MIDWESTERN U.S. ★ KILLER CHILI

# FAMOUS DAVE'S

## MINNEAPOLIS, MINNESOTA

Dave Anderson first fell in love with ribs as a kid in Chicago. His father brought the succulent meat home in his lunch pail, and it was love at first bite for the young boy. In the twenty-five years that followed, Anderson searched high and low for the country's best barbecue, tasting smoked meat at thousands of rib joints in the barbecue capitals of Memphis, Kansas City, Texas, the Carolinas, and his native Chicago. His destiny was clear: He needed to open a place of his own.

The first Famous Dave's opened in 1994 in the small lakeside town of Hayward, outside Minneapolis. Visitors from the Twin Cities began traveling to Famous Dave's

BBQ Shack in droves, and eventually convinced him to open a restaurant in Minneapolis. More than a decade later, Famous Dave's is now an institution, not just as a barbecue joint but also as a hoppin' blues club.

Famous Dave's has done an exceptional job translating its barbecue greatness to its other forte, chili. They won't reveal the recipes for their Steak & Burger Seasoning or BBQ sauce, but you can buy the concoctions directly from their website, www.famousbbq.com. Vibrant and exciting, their chili has a staggering blend of flavors and textures. Treat your family and friends to it, and you'll become famous for chili, too.

# Famous Dave's Route 66 Truck Stop Chili

3 pounds lean coarse-ground beef

2 teaspoons Famous Dave's Steak & Burger Seasoning (see page 32)

5 tablespoons chili powder

1 teaspoon coarse-ground black pepper

4 teaspoons ground cumin

2 teaspoons Maggi seasoning

1 tablespoon dried basil

1 teaspoon garlic powder

1 cup chopped celery

1 cup chopped onion

1 cup chopped green bell pepper

1 large jalapeno chile, seeded and minced

Two 16-ounce cans hot chili beans with broth

One 22-ounce can tomato juice

One 15-ounce can diced tomatoes with juice

One 15-ounce can tomato purée

One 10-ounce can beef broth

3 tablespoons Famous Dave's BBQ Sauce (see page 32)

2 tablespoons Kahlúa liqueur

2 tablespoons Worcestershire sauce

Shredded cheddar cheese, chopped onion (optional)

In a large, heavy pot, combine the ground beef, Steak & Burger Seasoning, chili powder, black pepper, cumin, Maggi seasoning, basil, and garlic powder and mix well. Cook over medium heat until the ground beef begins to turn a crusty brown, stirring frequently. Add the celery, onion, green pepper, and jalapeno. Cook until the vegetables are tender, stirring frequently. Add the chili beans, tomato juice, tomatoes, tomato purée, broth, BBQ sauce, Kahlúa, and Worcestershire sauce and mix well. Simmer to your desired consistency, stirring occasionally. Ladle into bowls and serve with shredded Cheddar cheese, chopped onion, corn bread and/or crackers, if desired. *Serves 6 to 8.*

MIDWESTERN U.S. · KILLER CHILI

# BAR ABILENE

## MINNEAPOLIS, MINNESOTA

You might expect a place called Bar Abilene to be located in Texas, not Minnesota, and that's the idea. The restaurant describes itself as a "Texas margarita grill," and its logo features a letter A that looks straight from the hot end of a branding iron.

Though it may not feel like Texas outside in the dead of a harsh Minnesota winter, Bar Abilene conjures up a true Lone Star experience. Guacamole is made tableside by the servers, and the bartenders whip up a mean margarita—twenty-five different varieties, in fact. The cuisine is dubbed "cowboy fusion," and includes cayenne-dusted calamari with arugula, wasabi, and smoked-tomato aioli, combining Asian, Southwestern, and Mediterranean flavors on one plate.

The menu changes seasonally, but an assortment of inventive quesadillas, tacos, seafood, and burgers are always available.

What Tex-Mex restaurant would be complete without chili? Bar Abilene's rendition is not exactly Texasstyle—there are beans and tomatoes involved—but it features ground beef, poblano and chipotle chiles, beer, and a ton of spices. Some of the other ingredients, such as tamarind pulp, ancho purée, and masa harina, are perhaps not items you typically keep in your pantry, but a visit to a Latino specialty store or through the ethnic-food aisles of your grocery store should do the trick. You can also order them from a variety of online purveyors.

# Bar Abilene Chili

3 tablespoons canola oil

2 pounds ground beef

1$\frac{1}{4}$ tablespoons minced garlic

1$\frac{1}{4}$ tablespoons chili powder

1$\frac{3}{4}$ tablespoons ground cumin

$\frac{1}{4}$ teaspoon ground coriander

1 teaspoon cayenne pepper

$\frac{1}{4}$ teaspoon dry mustard

1$\frac{3}{4}$ tablespoons paprika

3$\frac{3}{4}$ teaspoons salt

$\frac{1}{8}$ teaspoon freshly ground black pepper

$\frac{1}{2}$ cup ancho purée

2$\frac{1}{2}$ cups Guinness beer

2$\frac{1}{4}$ cups chicken broth

1$\frac{3}{4}$ cups salsa roja (red salsa)

5$\frac{1}{2}$ tablespoons tamarind pulp

2 cups cooked black beans, drained

1 tablespoon molasses

3 to 4 chipotle chiles, minced

1 poblano chile, finely chopped

4 cups canned chopped tomatoes

$\frac{2}{3}$ cup masa harina

In a large, heavy pot, heat 2 tablespoons of the oil over medium heat and brown the beef. Add the garlic and all the herbs and spices, stirring to combine. Make a small "well" in the meat, add the remaining 1 tablespoon oil, and fry the ancho purée for about 2 minutes. Stir in the beer and cook to reduce for 10 minutes. Add the broth and salsa roja and simmer for 20 minutes. Add the tamarind pulp, beans, and molasses and simmer for 2 hours.

Stir in the chiles, tomatoes, and masa harina and bring to a boil. Stir to blend, then serve. *Serves 4 to 6.*

# AMY'S CAFÉ

## — MADISON, WISCONSIN —

Chili is heralded for its filling, stick-to-your-ribs heartiness, and vegetarian chili can be—and often is—just as gratifying as its meaty counterparts. Plus, as a meal, you can't get more versatile: Chili can contain almost anything you want to eat.

The vegetarian chili at Amy's Café in Madison, Wisconsin, is both versatile and hearty. Amy's is not a vegetarian restaurant, but its menu boasts pleasing meatless options, including a Mediterranean platter of house-made hummus and tabbouleh. In the meat-less-but-not-exactly-healthy category is the Wisconsin take on fried mozzarella: fried cheese curds.

What separates vegetarian chili from vegetable stew? The spices, of course. Amy's chili features the standard chili flavors—cumin, chili powder, and cayenne pepper—combined with chili beans, roasted red peppers, onions, and your choice of fresh vegetables. Be sure to add vegetables with the longest cooking times to the pan first and those with the shortest cooking times last.

07/03/2019

An INN–Reach request has been placed on the following item:

Shelving      ccmor

Call Number:   641.823 ANDERSON

Volume:

Author:    Anderson, Stephanie.

Title:     Killer chili : savory recipes from North

Barcode:    31901044845347

Record#:    i28503041

Owning Library:1500 ST. MARY'S ROAD

         MORAGA, CA 94556

Please pull this item and send it to the patron at the library location listed below:

Name:    **LARSON, PAULINE**

Patron Type:    LINK+ Undergrad

Institution:    **91** – Sunnyvale Public

Delivery Stop:    **91** – Circulation Desk

Pickup At:    **Circulation Desk**

# Amy's Café Vegetarian Chili

¼ cup olive oil

2 small onions, chopped

1 tablespoon minced garlic

2 tablespoons chopped fresh parsley

1 teaspoon dried oregano

1 teaspoon dried basil

½ cup roasted red bell pepper

1 tablespoon ground cumin

1 tablespoon chili powder

Pinch of cayenne pepper

4 cups chili sauce

3 cups cooked chili beans

1 cup cooked kidney beans

3 cups mixed chopped vegetables (such as green beans, broccoli, mushrooms, bell peppers, and corn kernels)

In a large, heavy pot, heat the oil over medium heat. Add the onions, garlic, parsley, oregano, basil, and red pepper and sauté until tender, 5 to 10 minutes. Add the cumin, chili powder, cayenne pepper, chili sauce, and beans and heat through.

While the bean mixture cooks, put the vegetables in a medium saucepan. Add enough water to cover the vegetables and simmer over medium heat until almost tender, 10 to 15 minutes. Drain and add to the bean mixture. Bring to a boil, then reduce the heat to medium-low and simmer for 15 minutes. *Serves 6 to 8.*

# BISHOP'S FAMOUS CHILI

## WESTMONT, ILLINOIS

The Windy City may have the Sears Tower, but the Chicago suburb Westmont has Bishop's Chili. In 1925, Mary Bishop was cooking chili at legendary Ole's Chili, but got fired after making changes to the recipe. Out of work, Bishop opened her own chili joint on Chicago's west side. Her son, George, joined his mother's venture, and his business savvy helped the meager chili parlor expand into other parts of Illinois, including Forest Park and Westmont. Eventually George's daughters married, and their husbands wanted to continue the Bishop chili legacy.

Currently, only the Westmont location remains open, but the business is still a family operation; Mary Bishop's great-granddaughter, Mary Ellen Hope, now runs the business. And they're still making the same recipe that Grandma Bishop created more than eighty years ago, and serving it in a few different ways: in chili mac (chili over spaghetti), on hot dogs, in tamales, and by itself in a bowl.

That said, the folks at Bishop's Chili were a little hesitant to give up their family secret. Hope, though, decided to craft a recipe that is very much like the original Bishop's Chili—you'll have to travel to Westmont, Illinois, for the real thing. Whether you've tasted the original Bishop's Chili or not, this delicous version will not disappoint.

# "I Can't Believe It's Not Bishop's Chili" Chili

1 pound boneless choice beef bottom roast, cut Into $\frac{1}{2}$-inch dice

$\frac{1}{2}$ pound lean boneless pork trimmings or boneless end-cut pork roast, cut into $\frac{1}{2}$-inch dice

2 tablespoons salt

1 or 2 ancho chiles

6 japone chiles (small dried red peppers)

1 pound white onions, cut into small chunks

2 tablespoons garlic powder

2 tablespoons chili powder

5 pounds dried pinto beans, soaked overnight, rinsed, and drained

In a large stockpot, combine the beef, pork, and salt and add water to cover. Bring to a boil. Skim off any foam, cover, and reduce the heat to a simmer. Cook for 2 hours. Meanwhile, soak the ancho and japone chiles in just enough warm water to cover them.

In a food processor, process the onions to a coarse purée. Empty into a bowl and add the garlic powder and chili powder. Drain the ancho and japone chiles, purée them in the food processor, and add to the onion mixture.

Drain the meat. Purée the pork in the food processor and add to the onion mixture. Return to the stockpot and stir. Add the rinsed beans, cover, and simmer for 2 hours, or until the beans are soft, stirring often to prevent burning. Water may be added if needed. Purée the cooked beef in the food processor and add to the chili.

Let the chili cool to room temperature, then cover and refrigerate overnight. Reheat over low heat to serve. *Serves 8.*

# BIG BOPPER'S

## MARBLEHEAD, OHIO

When a restaurant's logo features a flaming chile pepper, you know you're in for a serious bowl of chili. And at Big Bopper's, they do it up right. Owner Ken Kostal developed his Island Heat Chili recipe over twenty years ago, after seeing an advertisement for a chili cook-off in Cleveland, where he competed and took the grand prize. Turns out he had a secret weapon: a family recipe of his manager at the time. "It was either his mom's or grandmother's," Kostal says.

Since then, Kostal has become somewhat of a chili guru, enjoying fame and acclaim in chili circles all over the country; he's racked up more awards and honors for his chili than he can count. He used to split his time between Big Bopper's and trekking to chili contests in every corner of the United States, but now he sticks closer to home. Still, he runs nine charity cook-offs in Ohio and is a judge at the world championship. "I took the avenue of being the chili chairman," he says.

With chili as amazing as his, he can call himself whatever he wants. Kostal describes his Island Heat as "not too spicy, with good flavor." And he gladly shares his chili philosophy: Real chili does not have beans in it—serve them on the side if you must; chili should be cooked slowly; and it's good with and on anything, including nacho chips, potato skins, burgers, and omelets. Chili is also perfect just by itself.

# Island Heat Chili

5 pounds ground beef

8 cups water

2 cups tomato paste

4 cups chopped onions

1 1/2 teaspoons minced garlic

2 1/2 teaspoons Worcestershire sauce

8 1/2 tablespoons chili powder

5 teaspoons ground cumin

1 tablespoon salt

5 teaspoons freshly ground black pepper

1 teaspoon red pepper flakes

1 1/4 teaspoons ground allspice

Sour cream, minced jalapenos, and shredded cheddar cheese (optional)

In a large, heavy skillet, brown the meat in batches over medium heat. Drain off all the fat. Transfer the meat to a large, heavy pot. Stir in the water, tomato paste, onions, garlic, 7 1/2 tablespoons of the chili powder, and all the other remaining ingredients. Bring to a simmer and cook for 2 1/2 hours. Stir in the remaining 1 tablespoon chili powder and cook 30 minutes to 1 hour longer, or until the desired consistency is reached. Serve with beans, sour cream, minced jalapenos, and shredded Cheddar cheese, if desired. *Serves 15.*

## GENERAL COOKIN' TIP

★ The chili will start out thin, but will thicken as it cooks.

MIDWESTERN U.S.

KILLER CHILI

# MARKET STREET GRILL

## WABASH, INDIANA

Indiana is mostly known for basketball, race cars, and John Mellencamp, but the Hoosier State also produces some mighty fine chili. Some of the best in the state can be found in the small town of Wabash, at the Market Street Grill.

Owner Bill Gerding—or "Wild Bill," as he's known on the chili circuit—professes a deep love and reverence for chili. He's been making it for more than twenty-five years and has competed in—and won—cook-offs all over the country. Now a chili emeritus of sorts, he serves as an organizer and judge. A member of the International Chili Society, Gerding has some pretty strong opinions about the do's and don'ts of good chili. Beans? Yes. Tomatoes? Yes. Macaroni? No.

His award-winning Indiana Red utilizes beans and tomatoes, and both ground chuck and round steak—typical for Midwestern chili—as well as beer, onions, peppers, kidney beans, and lots of spices, including garlic powder, cumin, and paprika. As a nod to the cowboys and ranch hands of yore, Gerding and his staff serve the chili in miniature black iron kettles. While the Indiana red isn't knock-your-socks-off spicy, it does have a kick, and Gerding aptly urges on his menu, "If you're looking for wimpy, order corn flakes."

# Wild Bill's World-Famous Indiana Red "Chili with an Attitude"

1/4 cup canola oil

2 1/2 pounds coarse-ground chuck

1 1/4 pounds round steak, cut into 1/2-inch dice

1/4 cup hot chili powder

1 1/2 tablespoons ground cumin

1/2 tablespoon paprika

3/4 teaspoon garlic powder

3/4 teaspoon black pepper

1 1/2 tablespoons salt

1/2 tablespoon sugar

3/4 cup beer

3/4 cup water

3 cups tomato sauce

6 cups diced tomatoes

6 cups cooked dark red kidney beans with broth

1 1/4 cups diced onions

3/8 cup diced green bell pepper

In a large, heavy pot, heat the oil over medium heat and brown the meat. Mix the spices, salt, sugar, beer, and water together, then add to the pot with the meat and oil. Reduce the heat to low and cook for 5 minutes. Add the tomato sauce, tomatoes, beans and broth, onions, and bell pepper. Simmer for 4 hours, stirring occasionally to prevent sticking.

Place the chili pot into an ice bath to cool. Cover and refrigerate overnight.

Before serving, remove the film of oil floating on top of the chili and discard. Reheat the chili and serve. *Serves 12.*

# THE PAINTED GIRAFFE CAFÉ

## — ST. LOUIS, MISSOURI —

Granted, most people don't go to zoos to eat, and why should they? Zoo food typically means hot dogs and soft pretzels served from a cart, a necessity to maintaining one's energy when flitting from the lemurs to the cheetahs to the reptiles. The Painted Giraffe Café at the St. Louis Zoo, however, has raised the bar. Chef—yes, an actual chef!—Jerry Chollet creates quick bites that are adult, kid, and palate friendly. Hot dogs are available, but so are Thai turkey wraps, meatball sandwiches, BLTs on croissants, fish and chips, and a great chili.

Painted Giraffe's food helped propel the St. Louis Zoo to the No. 1 spot in *Zagat* and a listing in *Parenting* magazine's survey of the best zoos in the United States. The café opened in 1988, and Chollet took over the reins at the upscale cafeteria a few years later. The chili—house made, like the rest of their soups and desserts—is not too spicy but full of zesty, savory flavor, and home cooks will appreciate its simple ingredients and preparation. It's the perfect chili to serve to a large number of hungry guests.

# Painted Giraffe Café Chili

5 pounds ground beef

1$\frac{1}{4}$ cups diced onion

$\frac{2}{3}$ cup diced green bell pepper

Two and a half 28-ounce cans diced tomatoes, with juice

Two 40-ounce cans kidney beans, with juice

8 cups rich beef broth

2 teaspoons garlic powder

1$\frac{1}{2}$ teaspoons red pepper flakes

2 teaspoons freshly ground black pepper

3 tablespoons ground cumin

$\frac{1}{2}$ bay leaf

2 teaspoons dried oregano

2$\frac{1}{2}$ tablespoons chili powder

2$\frac{1}{2}$ teaspoons salt

In a large, heavy pot, brown the meat in batches over medium heat. Drain and discard all but $\frac{1}{4}$ cup of the fat. Transfer the meat to a bowl. In the same pot, sauté the onion and pepper in the reserved beef fat until tender. Add the tomatoes and kidney beans and stir well. Add the broth and spices, reduce the heat to low, and cook for 2 to 3 minutes. Add the cooked meat. Bring to a boil, then reduce the heat to low and simmer for 30 to 45 minutes, skimming the fat from the surface as needed. *Serves 14.*

## GENERAL COOKIN' TIP

★ This chili is not too thick, so oyster crackers complement it well to make a great meal.

# MERIWETHER'S

## ST. LOUIS, MISSOURI

The food at Meriwether's, a fine-dining restaurant in the Missouri History Museum, is so delicious that even the Food Network has taken notice. Named for Meriwether Lewis, of the Lewis and Clark expedition, which passed through Missouri on its famous journey, the restaurant was dubbed one of the country's Best Museum Restaurants by the Network's show *Best Of*. After a day of discovery in the museum, which houses the original Louisiana Purchase document, a replica of Charles Lindbergh's famous airplane *The Spirit of St. Louis*, and personal items once belonging to William Clark, Chuck Berry, Tina Turner, Miles Davis, Charles Lindbergh, and Scott Joplin, history buffs can rest and refuel in Meriwether's.

Instead of the usual ground beef, Meriwether's chili recipe calls for ground bison meat. The restaurant uses Missouri-raised buffalo, but bison farms are cropping up in nearly every corner of the United States and Canada. It's worth the effort to find and support local farms, if possible. Buffalo was once a free-roaming species that survived solely on prairie grasses, so look for meat that comes from free-range or grass-fed bison versus grain fed for a product that's more natural and healthier. Bison is tender and lean—great in burgers and fantastic in chili. The combination of the meat, two kinds of beans, and a mélange of spices and vegetables will become a favorite in no time, making your home the new place where the buffalo roam.

# Bison Chili

2 to 3 tablespoons canola oil

$\frac{1}{2}$ cup diced onion

$\frac{1}{2}$ poblano chile, roasted, seeded, and diced (optional)

1 stalk celery, diced

$\frac{1}{2}$ cup diced red bell pepper

2 tablespoons minced garlic

1$\frac{1}{4}$ pounds ground bison meat

4 tablespoons dark chili powder

$\frac{1}{2}$ tablespoon ground cumin

1 teaspoon cayenne pepper

52 ounces canned diced tomatoes

52 ounces canned kidney beans

52 ounces canned black beans

$\frac{3}{4}$ cup tomato juice

In a large, heavy pot, heat the canola oil over medium heat and sauté the onion, chile, celery, bell pepper, and garlic until the onion is translucent. Add the meat and cook until brown. In a small bowl, mix together the chili powder, cumin, and cayenne and add to the meat and vegetables. Add the tomatoes, beans, and tomato juice. Simmer for 40 minutes, stirring occasionally, and serve. *Serves 10.*

# ESKIMO JOE'S

## STILLWATER, OKLAHOMA

Eskimo Joe's is the quintessential college-town hangout; even *The Sporting News* and *Sports Illustrated* deemed it one of the top college sports bars in the country. Conveniently located just one block from Oklahoma State University's campus, its wall are hung with huge televisions to facilitate game-day crowds, and of course, they serve a lot of beer.

One thing that sets Eskimo Joe's apart from other college sports bars, however, is that the food is very good. No pathetic pizza or stale nachos here—the fare is a bit more sophisticated than that. Dishes include a pecan smoked-pork shoulder sandwich, a variety of chicken sandwiches called "fowl things," and chili, which is piled onto hot dogs, nachos, burgers, and that Midwest and Southern favorite, Fritos pie—a mound of Fritos corn chips smothered with onions, tomato, and cheese in addition to the chili.

Eskimo Joe's recipe is a perfect game-day chili. It's tasty, with a bit of bite from the green chiles, and couldn't be easier to make. It can easily be doubled for bigger crowds, and you can serve it by itself or as a topping for other foods.

# Eskimo Joe's World-Famous Chili

3 pounds ground beef

Two 4-ounce cans peeled whole green chiles

One 10-ounce can diced tomatoes with green chiles

One 10-ounce can spicy chili beans

Two 8-ounce cans tomato sauce

$3/4$ cup chopped green bell pepper

$3/4$ cup chopped onion

$1/4$ cup chili powder

1 tablespoon seasoned salt

1 tablespoon ground cumin

2 teaspoons dried oregano, crumbled

1 tablespoon freshly ground black pepper

$1/2$ teaspoon red pepper flakes

1 teaspoon salt

$1 1/4$ cups water

In a large, heavy skillet, brown the meat over medium heat. Add all the remaining ingredients and simmer until the vegetables are tender, about 1 hour, until the chili reaches 165°F. *Serves 4.*

## GENERAL COOKIN' TIP

★ After browning the meat, you can put all the ingredients in a slow cooker on low for about 8 hours, instead of simmering the mixture on the stove.

# VIA CUCINA

## WASHINGTON, DISTRICT OF COLUMBIA

Residents of the metropolitan Washington, D.C., area are lucky enough to have six Via Cucina market-cafés to choose from, though the Pennsylvania Avenue location was the first. Each café offers incredibly fresh and flavorful Mediterranean-style breakfast and lunch options. They emphasize the merging of the European-style marketplace and café, where people can have their pick of ripe produce and freshly baked breads, then find those same ingredients at the corner bistro in a salad, soup, sandwich, or pastry.

One inventive item on the Via Cucina menu is White Turkey Chili. It uses two kinds of turkey—turkey breast slices and ground turkey—for a real punch of flavor and texture. Combined with the turkey are the bite of jalapeno chiles and Tabasco, the smooth nuttiness of pearl barley, two types of beans, and subtle flavors of dried marjoram and summer savory, a sweet, mild herb perfect for meat dishes. This chili is a lighter alternative to standard red chilis, but it's just as satisfying.

# White Turkey Chili

2 tablespoons canola oil

$1/2$ cup finely chopped onion

$1\frac{1}{2}$ tablespoons minced garlic

4 teaspoons ground cumin

1 pound turkey breast slices, cut into $1/2$-inch dice

$1/2$ pound ground turkey

3 cups chicken broth

$1/4$ cup pearl barley

2 tablespoons minced jalapeno chile

1 teaspoon dried marjoram

1 teaspoon dried summer savory

One 15-ounce can cannellini or Great Northern beans, drained and rinsed

One 15-ounce can chickpeas (garbanzo beans), drained and rinsed

Several dashes Tabasco sauce

Salt and pepper to taste

Chopped green onions, shredded Cheddar cheese, and sour cream for garnish

In a large, heavy saucepan, heat the oil over medium heat. Add the onion and garlic and sauté until tender, about 5 minutes. Add the cumin and stir until fragrant, about 30 seconds. Add the diced and ground turkey and sauté until no longer pink, about 4 minutes. Add the broth, barley, jalapeno, marjoram, and summer savory. Cover and simmer, stirring occasionally, until the barley is almost tender, about 40 minutes. Add the cannellini and chickpeas. Simmer, uncovered, until the barley is tender and the chili is thick, about 15 minutes. Season with the Tabasco sauce, salt, and pepper. Serve with the green onions, cheese, and sour cream. *Serves 4.*

SOUTHERN U.S. KILLER CHILI

# THE ROOST

## LEXINGTON PARK, MARYLAND

Contrary to what its name implies, poultry does not rule the Roost—ham does. Diners love the "old ham" sandwich, which may sound a bit unappetizing to the uninitiated, but is actually succulent. The St. Mary's County ham sandwich, crammed with kale and other veggies, is another specialty. And owner Bill Harris and his fellow Roost-ers are no slouches when it comes to cooking up some mighty fine chili, too.

Located in Lexington Park, Maryland, about sixty miles south of Washington, D.C., the Roost has enjoyed a loyal following for decades. Harris describes

Roost devotees as "a cult, but a good cult." He should know; before he bought the place, he'd been coming to the Roost since his teenage years. The décor is old-fashioned and quaint, qualities that infuse the menu. Most of the recipes are simple and venerable; some are as many as fifty years old. The chili recipe has been around for more than twenty-five years, Harris says. Though he calls the recipe "pretty basic," people adore the results. It's the perfect example of East Coast–style chili: a little bit sweet, a little bit hot, but chunky, satisfying, and full of flavor.

# The Roost Chili

2½ pounds ground beef
½ large onion, diced
½ tablespoon dried oregano, crumbled
6 cups crushed tomatoes
6 tablespoons chili powder
2 tablespoons garlic powder
1½ cups ketchup
½ teaspoon red pepper flakes
6 cups cooked dark red kidney beans

In a large, heavy pot, sauté the beef, onion, and oregano until brown. Add all the remaining ingredients and simmer for about 1 hour, or until the chili reaches the desired consistency. Serves 15.

## GENERAL COOKIN' TIP

★ Bill Harris recommends using Schreiber- or McCormick-brand spices.

SOUTHERN U.S.
KILLER CHILI

# BISTRO 301

## — LOUISVILLE, KENTUCKY —

Formerly known as Deke's Marketplace Grill, Bistro 301 provides inventive lunch and dinner offerings to the Louisville masses. It's been a downtown staple for years, and rightfully so. The menu is, as expected, composed of bistro-style dishes, and favorites include tortellini diablo, with chicken and Cajun sausage in a red pepper–cream sauce, and an Asian chopped salad. Plus, Bistro 301 offers Kentucky's favorite, a "hot Brown sandwich," made of roasted turkey and laden with bacon, a rich Mornay sauce, and grated Parmesan.

Diners dig Bistro 301's vegetarian Southwest Vegetable Chili. It's a cornucopia of fresh veggies: three kinds of bell peppers, onion, tomato, squash, and eggplant. The addition of black beans and some hot spices makes this chili so satisfying and so flavorful, you won't miss the meat. Besides being healthy and delicious, the best part of Bistro 301's chili is that it's quick and easy to prepare. The brunt of the work comes from dicing the vegetables, but the rest is a snap and takes under an hour.

# Southwest Vegetable Chili

2 to 3 tablespoons canola oil

1 cup diced red bell pepper

1 cup diced yellow bell pepper

1 cup diced green bell pepper

1 cup diced yellow onion

1 cup diced yellow squash

1 cup diced eggplant

1 cup diced tomato

3 cups tomato sauce

1 cup cooked black beans

$1/4$ cup minced jalapeno chile

$1/4$ cup chipotle chile purée

3 tablespoons chili powder

1 tablespoon ground cumin

Salt and freshly ground pepper to taste

In a large, heavy skillet, heat the oil and sauté the peppers, onion, squash, eggplant, and tomato until the onion is translucent. Add all the remaining ingredients and simmer for 30 to 45 minutes. *Serves 4.*

SOUTHERN U.S. KILLER CHILI

# WILLY B'S GOURMET SMOKEHOUSE

## FRANKLIN, TENNESSEE

Bill Bayersdorfer, owner of Willy B's, knows food. As an infant, the Kentucky native ate so much and so often, his mother took him to a doctor to find out what was wrong with him. As a teenager, he put away six meals a day without ever getting fat. He helped his mother make pancakes on Saturday mornings, and especially loved cooking over campfires during Boy Scout camping trips.

Little did he know then that cooking over an open flame would eventually become his career. In the summer of 1993, Bayersdorfer began selling barbecue from an old New York City–style street cart in downtown Louisville, Kentucky. Just six weeks later, his ribs were voted the best in the Kentuckiana region. Since then, the business has relocated from the street cart to a stationary location in Tennessee, and the accolades continue to pour in. Bayersdorfer and his barbecue have been featured on the Food Network, in the New York *Times*, and on the *Today* show.

While the barbecue at Willy B's gets most of the acclaim, the chili is certainly not to be missed. (Neither is the decadent World-Famous Brownie.) Bayersdorfer's tips for the perfect chili? Use the finest, freshest ingredients you can find. He also suggests using lean meats and dark red kidney beans, which have a more robust flavor than the lighter ones. Lastly, be patient. "If the recipe says to simmer for two hours or four hours, do that," Bayersdorfer says. And, "Like any soup, it's best if it sits for a day, to give the ingredients an opportunity to marry."

# Willy B's Red Chili

1½ pounds lean ground chuck

1 pound lean spicy bulk sausage

1 pound onions, chopped

1½ tablespoons minced garlic

3 cups tomato juice

12 cups chopped tomatoes with juice

¼ cup chili powder, mixed with 6 cups water

2½ tablespoons ground cumin

2 tablespoons salt

¾ teaspoon cayenne pepper

12 cups cooked dark red kidney beans

In a large, heavy pot, brown the chuck and sausage over medium heat. When the meat is halfway cooked, add the onions and garlic and continue to sauté until the onions are translucent. Add the tomato juice, tomatoes, chili powder liquid, cumin, salt, and cayenne pepper and thoroughly stir to blend and incorporate all the flavors and seasonings. Simmer for 1 hour. Add the beans and simmer for 30 minutes. Serve. *Serves 15 to 20.*

## GENERAL COOKIN' TIP

★ To make the chili spicier, marginally increase the amount of cayenne pepper.

# SWEET AND SAVORY BAKE SHOP & CAFÉ

## WILMINGTON, NORTH CAROLINA

**A**s soon as the weather turns warm, East Coasters hear the call of the seashore, and many of the most popular summertime sand-and-sea meccas are located in the Carolinas. Besides its proximity to the ocean, Wilmington, North Carolina, is a tourist haven due to its immortalization in classic films—both versions of *Cape Fear*, and *Blue Velvet*—and teeny-bopper TV shows like *Dawson's Creek* and *One Tree Hill*. The town has the distinction of being nestled between the Cape Fear River and the mighty Atlantic. There's water, water everywhere, so it's fitting that

Dave Herring, owner of the Sweet and Savory Bake Shop & Café, calls his chili Saltwater Chili.

There's actually no saltwater in the chili, but it's full of seafood, namely shrimp, crabmeat, and clams. Herring tasted and cooked a multitude of different chili styles during the course of his "culinary travels" in New Mexico, Colorado, Georgia, New York, and much of the rest of the United States. Of his Saltwater Chili, he says, "All I've done is substitute the meat with seafood. The final product is just like regular chili. It's got the roasted chiles, the chili powder, everything else."

# Saltwater Chili

2 tablespoons olive oil

1 large onion, chopped

1 tablespoon garlic, chopped

2 tablespoons canned green chile peppers, chopped

1 tablespoons jalepeno pepper, seeded and chopped

1 teaspoon red pepper flakes

$\frac{1}{4}$ teaspoon salt

$\frac{1}{4}$ teaspoon pepper

1 tablespoon Italian seasoning

1 tablespoon ground cumin

1 green bell pepper, seeded and chopped

1 red bell pepper, seeded and chopped

1 cup canned steamed clams, chopped

$\frac{1}{2}$ pound fresh shrimp, peeled and deveined, then chopped

1 cup canned or steamed claw crabmeat

$1\frac{1}{2}$ cups diced tomatoes with juice

$1\frac{1}{2}$ cups canned red kidney beans with broth

$1\frac{1}{2}$ cups cooked Great Northern beans with broth

3 tablespoons chili powder

In a large, heavy pot, heat the olive oil over medium heat. Add the onion and garlic and sauté until the onion is translucent. Add all the remaining ingredients, except the tomatoes, beans, and chili powder. Stir well. Add the tomatoes, beans, and chili powder. Cook for about 30 minutes, until the shrimp is pink and everything else is thoroughly heated. Taste and adjust the seasoning. Serve. *Serves 6.*

## GENERAL COOKIN' TIP

★ Wait until close to the end of the cooking process to add the chili powder so the ingredients don't stick to the bottom of the pot and give the chili a burnt taste.

# ATLANTA FISH MARKET

## ATLANTA, GEORGIA

The Atlanta Fish Market is not really a market, but a restaurant. The moniker is a bit of a misnomer, but the freshness that the word "market" implies is no misrepresentation. Voted Best Seafood Restaurant by *Atlanta* magazine, the place, which resembles an old train station, feels welcoming and comfortable, and the menu is outstanding. It's printed twice a day to make sure customers have their pick of the freshest fish. Executive chef Robert Holley was trained in French provincial cuisine, but his talents work beautifully in a Southern seafood spot. His selections include a variety of sushi, and feature such unusual fish as Indian River redfish, Arctic char, and Caribbean triggerfish.

Holley's Cape Cod Seafood Chili is one of his more inventive recipes. It includes several standard chili ingredients—jalapenos, chili powder, kidney beans, and tomatoes—but instead of using beef or pork, Holley utilizes scallops, shrimp, and cod. The concoction teases the palate with a combination of flavors and textures. The result is an utterly satisfying and unforgettable chili.

# Cape Cod Seafood Chili

3 tablespoons olive oil

1 onion, diced

2 jalapeno chiles, seeded and diced

2 red bell peppers, seeded and diced

1 green bell pepper, seeded and diced

1 yellow bell pepper, seeded and diced

6 garlic cloves, minced

2 tablespoons salt

2 tablespoons chili powder

1 teaspoon freshly ground black pepper

1 teaspoon red pepper flakes

3 bay leaves

1 teaspoon ground allspice

6 tablespoons tomato paste

1 cup (8 ounces) bottled clam juice

$3^1/_2$ cups crushed tomatoes

One 15-ounce can kidney beans

4 ounces dark chocolate, chopped

$^1/_2$ cup chopped fresh cilantro

$^1/_2$ cup chopped fresh parsley

$1^1/_2$ pounds bay scallops

$1^1/_2$ pounds bay (cocktail) shrimp

One 6- to 8-ounce cod fillet, cut into chunks

In a large, heavy pot, heat the olive oil over medium heat. Add the onion, chiles, peppers, and garlic and sauté for 2 to 3 minutes. Add the salt, chili powder, black pepper, red pepper, bay leaves, and allspice and stir well. Add the tomato paste and stir for 2 minutes. Add the clam juice and crushed tomatoes and bring to a simmer. Add the beans, chocolate, cilantro, and parsley.

Taste for seasoning and add more if necessary. Add the scallops, shrimp, and cod and cook for 3 to 5 minutes, or just until the scallops and cod are opaque throughout. *Serves 6 to 8.*

# THE CROWN RESTAURANT

## INDIANOLA, MISSISSIPPI

B. B. King may be this tiny Mississippi Delta town's most famous resident, but thanks to Evelyn Roughton—or Miss Evelyn, as her employees call her—catfish is Indianola's most famous food. In 1976, Roughton and her husband, Tony, opened an antiques shop with a small tearoom, which served just lunch and afternoon tea. In the late '90s, however, the Roughtons relocated and expanded their business to incorporate the Crown Restaurant and the connecting Taste of Gourmet gift shop, now located on the town's main street.

Catfish is king at the Crown—and all over the Delta, where the farm-raised catfish industry first began. In 1997, Roughton and her husband penned the cookbook *The Classic Catfish*, and there's little else on the menu besides the whiskered fish, but the preparations of it are mind-bogglingly varied: pâté, casserole, poached au gratin, rolls, Florentine, and pies. Roughton's smoked catfish pâté has won international acclaim, and she and the Crown have been featured on CNN and the Food Network, and in *Southern Living* and the Washington *Post*. A favorite recipe of Roughton's is her Red Bean and Catfish chili, of which she says, "Mmmm, you wouldn't believe how good it smells when you're cooking it."

# Red Bean & Catfish Chili

2 tablespoons canola oil

1 large onion, minced

3 garlic cloves, minced

2 tablespoons chili powder

1 teaspoon ground cumin

$1/2$ teaspoon ground coriander

1 teaspoon ground cinnamon

1 teaspoon dried oregano, crumbled

$1/2$ teaspoon cayenne pepper

One 16-ounce can diced tomatoes with juice

1 large green bell pepper, seeded and diced

One 16-ounce can kidney beans, drained and rinsed

$1/2$ teaspoon salt

Freshly ground pepper to taste

1 pound catfish fillets, diced

In a large, heavy saucepan, heat the oil over medium heat and sauté the onion, garlic, chili powder, cumin, coriander, cinnamon, oregano, and cayenne pepper for 2 to 3 minutes, stirring constantly. Add the tomatoes and juice, green pepper, kidney beans, salt, and pepper. Stir for 1 minute. Add the diced catfish fillets and gently stir into the chili. Reduce the heat to low and simmer for 15 minutes. Serve immediately. *Serves 2 to 3.*

# CLARK'S OUTPOST BARBECUE RESTAURANT

## TIOGA, TEXAS

Texas is one of two key chili epicenters in the United States (Cincinnati is the other). Fans of Lone Star State chili, which traditionally includes beef and chile peppers but not tomatoes or beans, claim that their particular style is the only real chili. As they say, don't mess with Texas—particularly when it comes to the very heated and long-running debate over which style of chili reigns supreme.

Located fifty miles north of Dallas, Clark's Outpost Barbecue Restaurant in Tioga, as the name implies, is best known for its slow-cooked barbecue, but the chili here is the real deal, at least by Texas standards. Tioga is proud of taking things slow, and eight hours are needed to smoke the restaurant's ribs and three days to smoke its brisket.

Clark's Outpost chili involves a good deal of time, too, but the recipe is about as pared down as it gets— just beef, onions, chiles, herbs, and some water. It gets its flavor from long simmering and from chipotle chile peppers, which are warm and smoky, not lightning-bolt hot. Canned chipotles are packed in Mexican adobo sauce, a deep-red, piquant concoction of ground chiles, vinegar, and herbs. This chili requires time, but it's well worth the wait.

# Beef Chili with Chipotles & Cilantro

2 pounds lean ground beef

2$\frac{1}{4}$ cups chopped onions

3 tablespoons ground cumin

3 tablespoons chili powder

1$\frac{1}{2}$ tablespoons garlic powder

1 tablespoon minced canned chipotle chile in adobo sauce (see tip)

2$\frac{1}{2}$ cups water, plus more as needed

1 cup minced fresh cilantro

Salt and freshly ground pepper to taste

Shredded Cheddar cheese and sour cream for garnish

In a large, heavy Dutch oven, sauté the beef and 2 cups of the chopped onions over high heat, stirring often and breaking up the meat with back of a spoon, until the beef is cooked through, about 10 minutes. Add the cumin, chili powder, garlic powder, and chipotle and sauté for 3 minutes. Mix in the 2$\frac{1}{2}$ cups of water and $\frac{1}{2}$ cup of the cilantro. Reduce the heat to medium-low. Partially cover and cook for 1$\frac{1}{2}$ hours, adding more water by $\frac{1}{4}$ cupfuls if the chili becomes dry. Season with salt and pepper. Mix the remaining $\frac{1}{2}$ cup cilantro into the chili. Ladle into bowls and garnish with Cheddar cheese, sour cream, and the remaining $\frac{1}{4}$ cup chopped onion. *Serves 6.*

## GENERAL COOKIN' TIP

★ If you can't find canned chipotle chiles in your market, you can purchase them at Latin American groceries, specialty foods stores, and online.

SOUTHERN U.S.
KILLER CHILI

# COSMOS CAFÉ

## HOUSTON, TEXAS

What makes chili chili? Answers vary from region to region and even person to person, but traditionally, combining chile peppers, some form of meat, and spices and cooking it all in a pot qualifies. The Cosmos Café may call their blend green chile soup, but this is about as chili as chili can be.

Texas is known for its chili and its music, and revelers can enjoy both at the Cosmos Café. The joint regularly hosts an eclectic lineup of live rockabilly, Western swing, R&B, and more, while the menu boasts Reuben sandwiches, house-made potato chips, and, of course, its award-winning green chile chili. Most of the soup's flavor comes from pork butt and poblano chiles—almost four pounds of pork and 1½ pound of chiles, to be precise. Depending on which part of North America you inhabit, these green chile peppers, sometimes mistakenly called pasillas, can be purchased in supermarkets or Latino markets. In this recipe, poblanos are roasted for additional smokiness and depth of flavor, rounding out the delicious, traditional chili.

# Green Chile Soup

1½ pounds poblano chiles (about 6 large chiles)

3¾ pounds boneless pork butt (pork shoulder), trimmed and cut
   into 1-inch pieces

Salt and freshly ground pepper to taste

3 tablespoons all-purpose flour

3 tablespoons canola oil

3 cups coarsely chopped onions

6 large garlic cloves, minced

1 tablespoon dried oregano, crumbled

1 tablespoon ground cumin

5 cups chicken broth

One 14-ounce can diced tomatoes with juice

Char the chiles over a gas flame or under a broiler until blackened on all sides. Enclose in paper bag and let stand for 10 minutes. Peel and seed the chiles and cut into 1-inch pieces. Put the pork in a large bowl. Sprinkle with salt and pepper. Add the flour and toss to coat the pork.

In a large, wide pot, heat 2 tablespoons of the oil over high heat. Working in batches and adding more oil as needed, cook the pork until brown on all sides, about 6 minutes per batch. Use a slotted spoon to transfer the pork to a large bowl. Reduce the heat to medium. Add the onions to the pot and stir until tender, about 6 minutes. Add the garlic, oregano, and cumin and stir for 2 minutes. Return the cooked pork and any accumulated juices to the pot. Add the broth, chiles, and tomatoes with juice and bring to a boil. Reduce the heat and simmer, uncovered, stirring occasionally, until the chili thickens and the meat is very tender, about 2 hours. Taste and adjust the seasoning. *Serves 6.*

## GENERAL COOKIN' TIP

★ For an authentic Tex-Mex experience, serve the chili with warm corn tortillas and bowls of chopped fresh cilantro, chopped green onions, and sour cream for garnish.

SOUTHERN U.S. KILLER CHILI

# HOWLEY'S RESTAURANT

## — WEST PALM BEACH, FLORIDA —

Since its inception in 1950, Howley's Restaurant has been one of West Palm Beach's most beloved dining spots. Patrons have been happily feasting on their sandwiches, cocktails, and all-day breakfast, including a massive egg sandwich that boasts two fried eggs, bacon or sausage, cheese, ham, and French fries packed into a kaiser roll. In 2005, the diner underwent a renovation that maintained its quirky, kitschy retro style while adding some more modern improvements, like a dancing hula-girl lamp and a new sign out front that declares Howley's motto: "Cooked in sight, must be right."

Chili is one of many things that Howley's does right. It's meaty and spicy, with two different kinds of chile peppers. A word of caution: Habanero and Scotch bonnet peppers are two of the hottest peppers in the world; jalapenos are mild in comparison. These spicy chiles can be found in most supermarkets, but plan accordingly if you prefer your food a bit less *caliente*. The seeds in chile peppers pack a wallop, so one way to lower heat is to scrape them out and discard them before dicing. Howley's chef Greg Schiff suggests passing around bowls of sour cream, guacamole, salsa, and chopped onions as garnishing possibilities.

# Howley's Chili

**2 red bell peppers, seeded and diced**

**2 green bell peppers, seeded and diced**

**2 whlte onions, diced, plus diced onion for garnish**

**$\frac{1}{3}$ cup canola oil**

**1 habanero or Scotch bonnet chile, seeded and diced**

**1 jalapeno chile, seeded and diced**

**3 pounds ground beef**

**Salt to taste**

**Freshly ground black pepper to taste, plus 1 tablespoon**

**1 tablespoon ground cumin**

**2 tablespoons Worcestershire sauce**

**5 cups crushed tomatoes**

**2 tablespoons cayenne pepper**

**3 tablespoons chili powder**

**2 tablespoons garlic powder**

**4 cups cooked red kidney beans**

**6 to 8 dashes Tabasco sauce**

**Sour cream, guacamole, and salsa for garnish**

In a large, heavy pot, cook the bell peppers and 2 onions, covered, over medium-low heat, stirring occasionally, until tender. Add the oil and stir. Reduce the heat, add the chiles, and stir until the onions are translucent and the chiles are soft. Stir in the ground beef, salt, pepper to taste, cumin, and Worcestershire sauce. Cook until the meat is browned. Add the tomatoes and simmer for 30 minutes. Add the cayenne, the 1 tablespoon black pepper, the chili powder, and garlic powder. Add the kidney beans and Tabasco. Stir and add more seasonings, if desired. Cover and cook for at least 45 minutes. Let the chili stand for 20 minutes before serving. Serve in bowls and garnish with the sour cream, diced onion, guacamole, and salsa. *Serves 12.*

# WORLD CLASS CHILI

## SEATTLE, WASHINGTON

World Class Chili is everything a great chili restaurant should be: It's fun, occasionally a little raucous, unpretentious, a tad boastful, and devoted to chili as if it were manna from heaven. One look at the mural depicting God giving man a bowl of chili, and you know you've come to the right place— and that's before you've sampled the chili.

Chili is part of owner Joe Canavan's family lore. He credits his grand-uncle Bill with bestowing on him his knowledge of chili cooking, and for motivating him to open his place in Seattle's Pike Place Market. Each day, Canavan and his crew serve at least four different varieties of chili, including a traditional Texas beef chili; a California-style chicken chili; a Cincinnati chili spiced with cinnamon, cloves, and chocolate; and a vegetarian lentil chili. The chili comes in "Texas-sized" or "Alaska-sized" bowls, and can be ordered in larger quantities for sizeable gatherings. Patrons can choose to have it with corn bread, tortilla chips, or crackers, and over pinto beans, black beans, brown rice, or seashell pasta.

In World Class Chili's vegetarian chili, the meat is replaced with lentils. Canavan does make a concession for meat-lovers, however, and suggests serving the chili over hot links or chorizo sausage, particularly the kind made at neighboring Uli's Famous Sausage. Vegetarians, fear not: Other than the serve-with-sausage option at the end, this recipe is completely free of any meat products.

# World Class Vegetarian Chili

1$\frac{1}{2}$ tablespoons corn or peanut oil

1 small white onion, finely chopped

1 stalk celery, finely chopped

1 carrot, finely chopped

4 cloves garlic, minced

4 tablespoons chili powder

1 teaspoon cayenne powder

1 teaspoon black pepper, or more to taste

1 jalapeno chile, slits cut in skin

3 pounds lentils

1 teaspoon sugar

2 teaspoons ground cumin

1 tablespoon salt

1 teaspoon fresh lime juice

8 hot links, chorizo, or other spicy sausage, cooked and sliced (optional)

In a large, heavy pot, heat the oil over medium-high to high heat and cook the onion, celery, carrot, and garlic for 3 to 4 minutes. Add 2 tablespoons of the chili powder, $\frac{1}{2}$ teaspoon of the cayenne, the black pepper, and jalapeno. Immediately add the lentils, stir, and then add cold water to cover the lentils by 1 inch. Bring to a boil, cover, and reduce the heat to a high simmer. In 25 minutes, check the lentils—they should be almost tender—and add a bit more water if necessary. Bring back to boil, then add the sugar, remaining 2 teaspoons chili powder, and the cumin. Cook at a high simmer for 10 minutes, then add the salt and the remaining 1$\frac{1}{2}$ teaspoons cayenne. Squeeze in the lime juice and cook for another 5 minutes. Let the chili sit for 10 minutes, and then serve over the sausage, if desired. *Serves 8.*

## GENERAL COOKIN' TIPS

★ For a more interesting presentation, cut 8 acorn squash in half, scoop out the seeds, and slice a piece off the bottom of each piece so it sits flat in a roasting pan. Add $\frac{1}{2}$ inch of water to the pan and bake the squash in a preheated 400°F oven for 1 hour, or until tender. Ladle the chili into the squash and enjoy!

★ For an extra-interesting flavor, substitute 2 tablespoons ground ancho chile for the chili powder.

# COUGAR RANCH BED & BREAKFAST LODGE

## MISSOULA, MONTANA

One reason people love chili so much is because it's one of the most versatile dishes ever invented. There are so many can-dos when it comes to chili, and so few don't-even-think-its; a perfect example is the chili from the Cougar Ranch Bed & Breakfast Lodge in Missoula, Montana, where guests can enjoy luxurious accommodations in a rustic, gloriously gorgeous setting. The ranch, like most everything in Big Sky Country, is sprawling, covering a 160-acre expanse of wilderness.

Instead of the usual beef, pork, or even chicken, Cougar Ranch's chili is made with elk, for an unexpected and unusual treat. Elk is lower in fat than even poultry and fish, and packed with protein. And it also happens to be delicious and less "gamey" than other wild game. Elk is a fairly standard provision in the western United States and in parts of Canada, but a real rarity most everywhere else. Never fear—the wonders of the Internet make it a snap to order elk meat shipped right to your door. Once you have the ground elk meat in hand (it browns just like ground beef), the rest of Cougar Ranch's recipe is fairly straightforward and hearty, with a touch of cocoa richness.

# Hearty Elk Chili & Beans

1 pound dried red or pinto beans

2 pounds ground elk

2 garlic cloves, minced

1 large onion, chopped

1 green bell pepper, seeded and chopped

2 tablespoons all-purpose flour

One 28-ounce can tomatoes with juice

One 16-ounce can tomato sauce

1 cup water, plus more as needed

1/4 teaspoon salt

1/4 teaspoon freshly ground pepper

2 tablespoons ground cumin

1 tablespoon unsweetened baking cocoa

2 to 4 tablespoons chili powder

In a large, heavy pot, combine the beans with 4 cups of water and bring to a boil. Turn off the heat, cover the pot, and soak the beans for 3 hours. Drain, cover the beans with water, and bring to a boil. Turn the heat down and simmer the beans while preparing the rest of the ingredients.

In a large, heavy skillet, sauté the elk just until the meat is almost completely cooked. Add the garlic, onion, and green pepper and sauté until the onion is translucent. Add the flour and stir until the mixture forms a paste. Add the tomatoes with their juice, the tomato sauce, and the 1 cup water and stir until well mixed. Add the salt, pepper, cumin, cocoa, and chili powder. Bring to a boil and simmer for 15 minutes. Add to the simmering beans and continue simmering until the beans are tender, about 1 1/2 hours. Add water as needed during cooking to ensure that there is enough liquid to cover the beans and meat. Stir often, and serve when the chili reaches the desired taste and consistency. *Serves 5 to 6.*

WESTERN U.S. · KILLER CHILI!

# UPTOWN CAFÉ

## — BUTTE, MONTANA —

Since owners Barb Kornet and Guy Graham opened Uptown Café in 1985, the residents of the historic mining town of Butte have delighted in the restaurant's innovative big-city offerings. The décor is elegant yet comfortable, complete with walls adorned with work from regional artists and romantic lighting. Just as the Uptown's motto says, it's "civilized dining in the wild, wild West."

The Uptown Café has attracted scores of fans since its inception, including the *New York Times Magazine,* *Gourmet, Outside,* and renowned travel-and-food writers Jane and Michael Stern. The menu options include artichoke ravioli, beef Wellington, cioppino, and a blackened halibut steak for dinner, and a variety of sandwiches, pastas, soups, and other comfort foods for lunch. The Uptown serves its fantastic beef-and-pork chili for lunch every Monday, with a hunk of corn bread smothered in butter and honey; shredded Cheddar or Monterey jack cheese, diced onions, and sour cream also make delicious accompaniments, if you so desire.

# Uptown Café Chili

¾ pound ground beef

¾ pound ground pork

1 cup finely diced yellow onions

1 red bell pepper, seeded and finely diced

1 green bell pepper, seeded and finely diced

1 teaspoon minced garlic

4 teaspoons good-quality chili powder

1 teaspoon cumin seeds

1 teaspoon ground cumin

1 teaspoon coarse-ground black pepper

1 bay leaf

⅛ teaspoon cayenne pepper

1 beef bouillon cube

One 28-ounce can diced tomatoes in purée

Two 12-ounce cans good tomato juice, such as Campbell's

One 24- to 28-ounce can red kidney beans, drained and rinsed

In a heavy 6-quart pot, combine the ground beef, ground pork, onions, peppers, garlic, chili powder, cumin seeds, ground cumin, black pepper, bay leaf, and cayenne pepper. Cook over medium heat until the ground meats are thoroughly cooked and the onions are soft, stirring often to break up the meat. Add the bouillon cube, tomatoes in purée, and tomato juice. Bring to a boil, then reduce the heat and simmer for 1 hour, stirring often. Add the kidney beans and cook until the beans are heated through. Remove the bay leaf, skim any fat from the top of the chili, and serve. *Serves 8 to 10.*

# BAKERY BAR

## PORTLAND, OREGON

Cakes may be king at Portland's Bakery Bar—even the eatery's motto proclaims, "Eat cake!"—but the place is not just for sweet treats. Here you can have your lunch—and eat cake, too. According to co-owner Jocelyn Barda, the Bakery Bar has become a gathering spot for "a lively mix of Portland residents," including local artists and designers, businesspeople, rowers exiting the Willamette River, and parents and kids who need a treat after a day adventuring at the nearby Oregon Museum of Science and Industry.

Sugar cravings can be conquered with cupcakes, cream puffs, pear-ginger caramel pie, and one of several decadent "cakes for two." Patrons looking for a non-dessert lunch can choose from fresh salads, soups, and sandwiches, including one overflowing with roasted vegetables and a delicate egg salad made with Dijon mustard, green onions, celery, and fresh basil. The Bakery Bar also serves homemade soups, and Portland residents love the chili. Made with lean ground turkey, it's a bit lighter than its beef counterparts, but it's definitely not a wimpy chili. Packed with spices (including cinnamon and thyme), tomatoes, garlic, beans, and a touch of brown sugar for sweetness, this chili might just make you forget to save room for dessert.

# Bakery Bar Turkey Chili

2 tablespoons olive oil

1 1/4 cups chopped onion

5 cloves garlic, minced

1 1/2 pounds ground dark-meat turkey

3/4 teaspoon salt

1 tablespoon dried thyme, crumbled

2 tablespoons ground cumin

1/4 cup chili powder

1 tablespoon ground cinnamon

1 tablespoon brown sugar

1 teaspoon cayenne pepper

Two 28-ounce cans whole tomatoes with juice, puréed in a food processor

1 bay leaf

Two 15-ounce cans pinto beans, drained

One 12-ounce can tomato paste

1 cup water

Shredded sharp cheddar cheese, chopped red or green onion,
   sour cream (optional)

In a heavy 8-quart pot, heat the olive oil over medium-low heat. Add the onion and garlic and cook until soft and beginning to brown. Add the ground turkey and cook until browned, stirring the meat frequently to break it up. Add the salt, thyme, cumin, chili powder, cinnamon, brown sugar, and cayenne, stirring well to combine, and cook for 3 minutes.

Add the tomatoes and juice, bay leaf, pinto beans, tomato paste, and water, stirring well to combine. Bring to a boil, then reduce the heat and simmer on low heat for 60 to 90 minutes, stirring occasionally. Remove the bay leaf. Serve with shredded sharp Cheddar cheese, chopped red or green onions, and sour cream, if desired. *Serves 10.*

## GENERAL COOKIN' TIP

★ Adding the spices to the meat mixture before the liquids are added helps to bring out their full flavor.

# THE DUNDEE BISTRO

## — DUNDEE, OREGON —

Located in the middle of Oregon wine country in the northern Willamette Valley, the Dundee Bistro is a wine- and food-lover's paradise. The restaurant was founded in 1999 by one of Oregon's premier winemaking clans, the Ponzi family. The Dundee Bistro is actually one-third of the town of Dundee's Culinary Center, which also includes the Ponzi Wine Bar and Your Northwest, a specialty store selling regional foods and crafts.

The Ponzis modeled the Dundee Bistro after small, intimate eateries they've visited in wine regions all over the world, places where patrons can unwind and enjoy perfectly paired food and wine. Chef Jason Stoller Smith has created an exciting menu, which includes dishes, such as local Kumamoto oysters, roasted butternut squash soup with chanterelles, and Oregon petrale sole with spinach risotto, made with many organic and locally grown ingredients.

Chef Smith also gives traditional chili a creative Pacific Northwest touch. This creamy, savory chili features cannellini beans, fresh herbs, and the delicate, slightly sweet meat of Dungeness crab. These shellfish are readily available on the West Coast; other kinds of lump crabmeat may be substituted.

# White Bean Chili with Dungeness Crab

2 pounds dried cannellini beans

$1/3$ cup olive oil

3 yellow onions, diced

1 small can peeled green chiles, drained and diced

1 tablespoon minced garlic

3 tablespoons ground cumin

$1/3$ cup chopped fresh cilantro

2 tablespoons chopped fresh oregano

$1/2$ teaspoon cayenne pepper

1 teaspoon ground cloves

1 whole ham hock

3 quarts chicken broth

$1^1/2$ cups shredded Monterey jack cheese

3 cups sour cream

2 pounds fresh Dungeness crabmeat, picked over for shells

$1/4$ cup sliced bacon, cooked crisp, and croutons for garnish

Pick over and rinse the cannellini beans. In a large pot, cover the beans with 3 inches of water and soak overnight. Drain.

In a large, heavy pot, heat the oil over medium-high heat. Sauté the onions, chiles, and garlic until the onions are translucent. Add the cumin, cilantro, oregano, cayenne, and cloves. Add the drained beans, ham hock, and chicken broth and cook until the beans are tender, 2 to 3 hours. Add the cheese, stirring until well mixed. Add the sour cream, stirring until well mixed. Add the crabmeat, and stir well. Crumble the bacon. Top each serving with bacon and croutons. *Serves 12.*

# NORTH COAST BREWING COMPANY

## FORT BRAGG, CALIFORNIA

The North Coast Brewing Company in Fort Bragg, California, founded in 1988, holds the distinction of being one of the very first brewpubs in America. Located on the Mendocino coast, North Coast started out small and local. It now brews a variety of ales that reach thirty-six states—a lucky break for non-Californians. The beers, including Old Rasputin, Brother Thelonius, Blue Star, and PranQster Ale, are packed with flavor—a far cry from the watered-down brews coming from the bigger guys.

At some brewpubs, the food is an afterthought, but North Coast doesn't believe you have to sacrifice the quality of one for the other. Visitors who need something a bit more substantial than just beer in their bellies can order food at their Tap Room & Grill. What could go better with a pint than fresh Pacific oysters, Brazilian-style deep-sea scallops, wild-mushroom ravioli, porterhouse steaks, and beer's best friend, chili? The brewery's Route 66 Chili—named for the famous highway spanning the western United States—is so beloved that it was featured in *Bon Appetit* magazine. It's a combination of two chili types: Texas red and New Mexico green, and features pork butt, two kinds of chiles, and, not surprisingly, a bottle of amber ale.

# Route 66 Chili

3 pounds boneless pork butt (pork shoulder), trimmed and cut into 1-inch pieces

All-purpose flour for dredging

$1/2$ cup olive oil

$3/4$ cup chopped onion

4 poblano chiles, seeded and chopped

$1/4$ cup minced garlic

One 28-ounce can diced tomatoes with juice

Two 19-ounce cans enchilada sauce

One 12-ounce bottle amber ale

One 7-ounce can diced green chiles

1 tablespoon ground cumin

1 tablespoon chili powder

Sour cream and sliced green onions for garnish

Dredge the pork in the flour to coat, shaking off the excess. In a large, heavy pot, heat $1/4$ cup of the olive oil over medium-high heat. Working in batches, brown the pork on all sides, about 8 minutes for each batch. Use a slotted spoon to carefully transfer the cooked pork to a large bowl. Add the remaining $1/4$ cup olive oil to the pot. Add the onion and sauté until translucent, about 4 minutes. Add the poblano chiles and garlic and sauté for 2 minutes. Mix in the pork, tomatoes with juice, enchilada sauce, ale, green chiles, cumin, and chili powder. Simmer over low heat, stirring occasionally, for about 1 hour, until the meat is tender and the chili thickens slightly. Serve with sour cream and sliced green onions. *Serves 8.*

WESTERN U.S. ★ KILLER CHILI

# GLOBAL CHILI COMPANY

## BOULDER, COLORADO

When owner Kyle Thomas, a former banker, lived in Singapore in the 1990s, he and his family invited friends to spend Thanksgiving with them. The day after Thanksgiving, instead of simply reheating leftover turkey, vegetables, and cranberries, Thomas put them all together, added Thai and Malaysian chile peppers, and made chili. Thomas' turkey chili was so divine that two visiting Colorado friends suggested he open chili kiosks at ski resorts in the States. Nearly a decade later, Thomas and his family moved back to the United States and took their friends' advice, opening Global Chili Company in downtown Boulder in 2005.

Rather than focusing on one type of chili, the menu at Global Chili Company, as its name implies, paints a broader brushstroke, reflecting the varied countries, cultures, and cuisines Thomas has experienced in his travels. Thomas envisions his restaurant as being much more than just a place to grab a bowl of chili; the eatery urges patrons to "think global and eat local."

Global Chili's menu features nearly every kind of chili under the sun, from gumbolike New Orleans style to Thai style with mangos and coconut milk. The Sedona chili blends chicken, sweet and russet potatoes, carrots, bacon, beans, and tomatoes with a plethora of spices and chile peppers. Thomas admits, "It takes some time, but so do most things worth doing."

# Sedona Chili

1 teaspoon cayenne pepper

1 tablespoon ground cumin

1 teaspoon dried oregano

2 teaspoons paprika

1 1/3 pounds boneless chicken thighs, rinsed and diced

1 ancho chile

1 pasilla chile

1 dried New Mexico red chile

3 tablespoons light olive oil

2 chipotle peppers in adobo sauce

2/3 pound carrots, peeled and diced

1/3 pound russet potatoes, peeled and diced

1/3 pound sweet potatoes, peeled and diced

1 teaspoon salt

1/3 tablespoon freshly ground black pepper

1/4 pound cooked bacon, crumbled, 2 tablespoons fat reserved

2 cups chicken broth

1 1/3 cups diced yellow onions

2 tablespoons minced garlic

One 28-ounce can canned diced tomatoes with juice

1 cup cooked black beans, drained

1 cup canned white Northern beans

1 bottle Sam Adams beer

3 tablespoons packed brown sugar

2 cups water

2 1/2 cups fresh or frozen corn kernels

Chopped bell peppers and sour cream for garnish

Preheat the broiler. Mix the cayenne, cumin, oregano, and paprika together and place half in a self-sealing plastic bag; reserve the rest. Toss the chicken in the bag until coated. Refrigerate for at least 30 minutes. Toss the chiles in 1/2 tablespoon of the olive oil. Broil on a baking sheet, turning until they are puffed on all sides, about 5 minutes. Allow them to cool, and, using gloves, stem, seed, and tear them into pieces. Combine with the chipotle peppers, purée in a food processor, and set aside.

Preheat the oven to 3/5°F. Toss the carrots and potatoes in 1 1/2 tablespoons of olive oil, salt, and pepper. Place on oiled baking sheets and roast until golden brown, about 1 hour, turning after 30 minutes. In a Dutch oven, cook the bacon and remove when browned. Then cook the chicken in the reserved bacon fat in batches. Discard the fat. Shred the chicken and set aside. Increase the heat to medium-high and add the remaining 1 tablespoon olive oil. Add the onions and garlic and cook for about 5 minutes. Add the tomatoes with juice, chili purée, beans, beer, sugar, and remaining spice mixture and cook for 20 minutes. Add the chicken broth and stir. Remove half the mixture from the Dutch oven and purée in a food processor with the water. Return the purée to the dutch oven. Add the reserved cooking liquid and simmer for 10 minutes. Stir in the corn and bake for 3 hours, checking every hour. Stir in the chicken and serve. *Serves 12 to 15.*

WESTERN U.S. ★ ★ KILLER CHILI

# TAYLOR'S AUTOMATIC REFRESHER

## SAN FRANCISCO, CALIFORNIA

Taylor's Automatic Refresher harkens back to the days of the American roadhouse, and while their food is comfortably old-fashioned, it's also undoubtedly modern. Fish and chips made with mahimahi, and heavenly espresso or white pistachio milkshakes complement their hamburgers—made from all-natural, grass-fed California Angus beef—and ahi tuna burgers with wasabi mayonnaise.

In 1999, brothers Joel and Duncan Gott renovated an old drive-in in St. Helena, California. The first location won acclaim from renowned wine critic Robert Parker, who declared the double cheeseburger his "most memorable meal of 1999." The second location, inside San Francisco's Ferry Building, opened in 2004.

A gigantic red neon sign demanding EAT hangs over the counter at the San Francisco spot—not that the diners really need the extra encouragement. This food, especially their chili, is the real San Francisco (and St. Helena) treat. Their seriously fantastic chili is warm, hearty, and packs a bit of a punch with beer—San Francisco's very own Anchor Steam.

# Taylor's Automatic Refresher Chili

1 ½ pounds ground beef

1 yellow onion, diced

1 red bell pepper, seeded and diced

1 green bell pepper, seeded and diced

3 cloves garlic, minced

⅓ cup ground coriander

⅓ cup ground cumin

1 ½ cups (12 ounces) Anchor Steam beer

1 bay leaf

¾ cup (6 ounces) chipotle chiles in adobo sauce, puréed in a blender

⅓ cup chili powder

1 ½ cups (12 ounces) diced tomatoes

1 ½ cups (12 ounces) kidney beans, drained

Salt to taste

Shredded Cheddar cheese and chopped green onions, for garnish

In a large, heavy skillet, brown the beef over medium heat. Drain and discard all but 1 tablespoon of the fat. Transfer the meat to a bowl. In the same skillet, heat the reserved fat over medium heat and sauté the onion, peppers, and garlic until soft. Add the coriander, cumin, beer, and bay leaf and simmer for 3 minutes. Add the beef, puréed chipotle chiles, and chili powder. Add the tomatoes, beans, and salt. Reduce the heat to low and simmer for 45 minutes to 1 hour. Remove from the heat and let cool. Refrigerate overnight. Reheat. Remove the bay leaf. Serve the chili with the shredded cheese and onions. *Serves 4.*

# THE KITCHEN FOR EXPLORING FOODS

## ——PASADENA, CALIFORNIA——

For more than twenty years, Peggy Dark, owner of the Kitchen for Exploring Foods, has experimented with all sorts of flavors, textures, and ingredients that keep her customers begging for more. The Kitchen has received a Zagat Award of Distinction, and has been featured on *Today* and in *Gourmet* magazine. It's grown into one of the top catering companies in Los Angeles, and its Gourmet-To-Go location is Pasadena gourmands' idea of paradise. A large glass case is packed with salads, sandwiches, baked goods, fresh fruit, and roasted veggies, and patrons can pick up boxed lunches to go. The demand for these boxed lunches, however, is so high that customers must order at least four days in advance.

Regular customers keep their fingers crossed on a daily basis that Dark and her staff will offer their White Chicken Chili. It's a creamy, utterly decadent chili that features navy beans, mild green chiles, chunks of chicken, Monterey jack cheese, and sour cream, and serving it with salsa adds the extra kick of fresh tomatoes.

# White Chicken Chili

1 cup dried navy beans, picked over and rinsed

8 tablespoons (1 stick) unsalted butter

1 large onion, chopped

$^1/_4$ cup all-purpose flour

$^3/_4$ cup chicken broth

2 cups half-and-half

1 teaspoon Tabasco sauce, or to taste

$1^1/_2$ teaspoons chili powder

1 teaspoon ground cumin

$^1/_2$ teaspoon salt, or to taste

$^1/_2$ teaspoon freshly ground white pepper, or to taste

Two 4-ounce cans peeled whole green chiles, drained and chopped

5 boneless, skinless chicken breast halves, cooked and cut into $^1/_2$-inch pieces

$1^1/_2$ cups shredded Monterey jack cheese

$^1/_2$ cup sour cream

Fresh cilantro and salsa for garnish

In a medium pot, soak the beans overnight in enough cold water to cover the beans by 2 inches. Drain the beans in a colander and return to the pot with fresh cold water, covering the beans by 2 inches. Cook the beans at a bare simmer on very low heat until tender, about 1 hour, and drain in a colander.

In a medium skillet, melt 2 tablespoons of the butter over medium heat and cook the onion until softened. In a large, heavy pot, melt the remaining 6 tablespoons butter over medium low heat and whisk in the flour to make a roux. Cook the roux, whisking constantly, for 3 minutes. Stir in the onion and gradually add the broth and half-and-half, whisking constantly. Bring the mixture to a boil, then reduce the heat to low and simmer, stirring occasionally, for 5 minutes or until thickened. Stir in the Tabasco, chili powder, cumin, salt, and white pepper. Add the beans, chiles, chicken, and cheese. Increase the heat to medium-low and cook, stirring frequently, for 20 minutes. Stir in the sour cream. Garnish with the cilantro and salsa. *Serves 4 to 6.*

WESTERN U.S.
KILLER CHILI

# TEAKWOODS BAR & GRILL

## SCOTTSDALE, ARIZONA

If ever there were a quintessential neighborhood watering hole, then Teakwoods Bar & Grill is the place. The Scottsdale tavern prides itself on being a favorite spot of Scottsdale residents to eat, drink, chat, and catch a game on one of the bar's two dozen televisions. The beer selection is impressive, with a mix of stalwart favorites like Pabst Blue Ribbon and Guinness alongside smaller upstarts, such as Fat Tire from Colorado. Teakwoods even pours hometown brews like Kilt Lifter Scottish-Style Ale from Tempe, Arizona's Four Peaks Brewery.

Open for lunch and dinner (and, of course, happy hour), Teakwoods boasts a menu that ups the ante on pub grub. Diners can dig into fresh salads, five different kinds of hot dogs, lavosh, gyros, a slew of burgers and other sandwiches, and Uncle Tom's Moose Dip, which features sausage, black beans, cheese, and fresh jalapenos. Teakwoods also has a sumptuous chili on the menu, replete with tomatoes, onions, peppers, pinto and kidney beans, and ground beef. Made by chef Erik Olsen, this dish is best washed down with your favorite local beer.

# Teakwoods Chili

Canola oil for sautéing
1/2 white onion, diced
1 red bell pepper, seeded and diced
1 green bell pepper, seeded and diced
1 3/4 pounds ground beef
76 1/2 ounces canned tomato strips
5 15-ounce cans tomato sauce
1/2 tablespoon freshly ground black pepper
3/4 teaspoon onion powder
2 tablespoons minced garlic
3/4 cup chili powder
1/4 tablespoon salt
Two 28-ounce cans kidney beans
Two 28-ounce cans pinto beans

In a large, heavy pot, heat the oil over medium heat and sauté the onion and bell peppers until the onion is translucent. Add the ground beef and cook until brown. Add the tomato strips, tomato sauce, black pepper, onion powder, garlic, chili powder, salt, and beans and mix thoroughly. Reduce the heat to low and simmer for 3 hours. Serve. *Serves 20.*

# WILD BILL'S SALOON

## BANFF, ALBERTA

Wild Bill's is aptly referred to as "Banff's legendary saloon." Its namesake was a real-life Western adventurer, but not the one you may be thinking of: Canada's version was named Wild Bill Peyto, not Cody. As the story goes, Peyto was born in England and immigrated to Canada in 1886. He settled in Banff and became a trail guide in the harsh Alberta wilderness, leading the very first group to climb Mt. Assiniboine. He later joined the Canadian Mounted Police, and is still considered to be one of western Canada's leading self-taught naturalists, hunters, geologists, and all-around outdoorsmen.

The eponymous Banff saloon is an homage not only to Wild Bill Peyto, but to Alberta's past and present cowboy ethos. Patrons can not only enjoy a good, hearty meal and a cold beer, but hear live bands, do the two-step in the dance hall, take in the majestic view on the patio, watch a football game, and even rope a calf. The décor is just as rugged as the terrain outdoors, with lots of wood, stone, and taxidermy. The food can best be described as Tex-Mex, and any such restaurant worth its salt has to have good chili. The smoky, zesty Wild Billy Chili is made with high-quality Alberta beef, two kinds of beans, chipotle chiles, dark beer, and tomatoes.

# Wild Billy Chili

1 1/2 pounds ground beef
1/4 cup canola oil
3 onions, diced
1 green bell pepper, seeded and diced
1 red bell pepper, seeded and diced
1/4 cup minced garlic
1/4 cup red pepper flakes
1/4 cup chili powder
2 tablespoons ground cumin
2 tablespoons ground coriander
1 tablespoon dried oregano, crumbled
1 cinnamon stick
1/2 can beer (the darker, the better)
1 tablespoon diced canned chipotle chiles
Four 14-ounce cans crushed tomatoes
One 14-ounce can red kidney beans
One 14-ounce can black beans
1 tablespoon liquid smoke
2 tablespoons Frank's RedHot Original Cayenne Pepper Sauce or other hot sauce
Salt and freshly ground black pepper to taste

Preheat the oven to 450°F. Put the ground beef in a large roasting pan and place in the oven. Bake, stirring occasionally to break up the meat, until the meat has started to brown, 20 to 40 minutes. Drain the cooked beef in a colander in the sink.

While the beef is cooking, in a large, heavy pot, heat the oil over medium-high heat. Add the onions and cook, stirring occasionally until they start to caramelize. Add the peppers and garlic and cook until soft. Add the spices, stir, and turn off the heat. Let sit for 5 to 10 minutes to release the flavor from the spices.

Return the pot to medium-high heat and add the beer, stirring to scrape up the browned bits from the bottom. Add all the remaining ingredients and the drained beef. Stir well and bring to a simmer, taking care not to burn the bottom. Simmer for 1 hour. Remove the cinnamon stick and add salt and pepper. *Serves 10 to 15.*

# THE OLD COPPER KETTLE RESTAURANT & PUB

## — FERGUS, ONTARIO —

If the thought of an old copper kettle conjures images of an English granny serving tea and cakes next to a crackling fire, your version is pretty close to the version in Fergus, Ontario. The Old Copper Kettle feels as cozy and comfortable as tea at your granny's might—if your granny also served nearly a dozen draft beers and hosted monthly Celtic and bluegrass jams.

The small town of Fergus is known for its annual summer truck show—reportedly the largest in North America—and for its Scottish Festival and Highland Games, where revelers don kilts, listen to pipe-and-drum music, and throw heavy stones and hammers. Located on St. Andrew Street, the town's primary thoroughfare, the Old Copper Kettle prides itself on being an authentic British Isles–style pub and a home away from home for a strong expatriate contingent. The original pine floors and tin ceiling date back to the 1870s, and tea is served every afternoon. The menu, which exclusively features homemade dishes crafted from local ingredients, includes typical pub fare, such as bangers and mash, shepherd's pie, and Cornish pasties, along with sandwiches, salads, and soups.

Chili may seem an odd choice for a British pub in Canada, but it fits well with the stick-to-your-ribs traditional U.K. dishes. This recipe is simple, with a relatively short list of ingredients, but a creamy, country-style ale gives the chili a depth of flavor and is perfect for serving alongside it. The Old Copper Kettle uses an ale from Wellington Brewery in neighboring Guelph, Ontario, but any malty, full-bodied ale will work in its place.

# Wellington County Pub Chili

**4 tablespoons canola oil**
**2 onions, chopped**
**5 tablespoons chili powder**
**3 garlic cloves, minced**
**2 tablespoons tomato purée**
**2 pounds ground beef**
**1 bay leaf**
**One 28-ounce can tomatoes**
**2 cups Wellington County Ale or other malty ale**
**One 28-ounce can kidney beans, drained**
**Shredded aged Cheddar cheese for garnish**

In a large, heavy pot, heat 1 tablespoon of the oil over medium heat and sauté the onions until soft. Add the chili powder, garlic, tomato purée, the remaining 3 tablespoons oil, and the ground beef in small batches, browning and stirring it in with the onions and spice. Add the bay leaf and tomatoes. Add the ale and simmer for 1 hour. Add the kidney beans and simmer for 15 minutes. Remove the bay leaf. Serve in individual bowls. Top with shredded aged Cheddar cheese. *Serves 6 to 8.*

## GENERAL COOKIN' TIP

★ As with most chili, this is best cooked the day before and then reheated.

# THE DISH & THE RUNAWAY SPOON

## EDMONTON, ALBERTA

Life is full of mysteries worth pondering: Is there life on Mars? How does Donald Trump get his hair to do that? And whatever happened to the dish and the spoon after they ditched that cat and fiddle and ran away together? We may never know the answers to those other burning questions, but it appears that the nursery-rhyme tableware relocated to Canada.

Fans of Edmonton's favorite bistro, the Dish (and its sister catering company, the Runaway Spoon), use words such as "funky," "eclectic," and "quirky" to describe the atmosphere of the place. Owner Carole Amerongen and her crew, not surprisingly, take old favorites and re-imagine them in fresh, inventive ways. Menu offerings include Parmesan and spinach risotto cakes, a mango-curry chicken wrap, a deep-dish sweet potato shepherd's pie, and a rustic lamb stew. Even their chili is perked up, as they've substituted bison for standard beef or pork, and added three types of beans, herbed tomato sauce, and a slew of veggies and spices. It's so good, you'll be over the moon, too.

# The Dish Bison Chili

1 cup dried pinto beans

1 cup dried black beans

Canola oil for sautéing

2 cups sliced onions

$\frac{1}{2}$ tablespoon minced garlic

1 cup diced green bell peppers

5 ounces button mushrooms, sliced

$1\frac{1}{4}$ pounds ground bison

$\frac{1}{2}$ cup fresh or frozen corn kernels

$2\frac{1}{4}$ cups tomato sauce with basil and oregano

Two 28-ounce cans chopped tomatoes

10 ounces canned kidney beans, drained

$\frac{3}{4}$ teaspoon red pepper flakes

2 tablespoons chili powder

1 tablespoon ground cumin

$\frac{1}{2}$ tablespoon ground coriander

$\frac{3}{4}$ tablespoon minced chipotle chiles in adobo sauce (add more for a spicier chili)

$\frac{1}{2}$ tablespoon salt

$\frac{1}{2}$ tablespoon freshly ground pepper

$1\frac{1}{2}$ tablespoons fresh lime juice

2 tablespoons packed brown sugar

Shredded Cheddar cheese, sour cream, and fresh cilantro for garnish

Pick over and rinse the beans. In a large saucepan, soak the beans overnight in water to cover by 2 inches.

In a large, heavy pot, heat the oil over medium heat and sauté the onions, garlic, peppers, and mushrooms until the onions are translucent. Add the ground bison and brown. Add the corn, tomato sauce, and tomatoes. Cook for 1 hour. Add the spices, salt, pepper, lime juice, and sugar, reduce the heat to low, and simmer for 1 hour. Drain the soaked beans and add to the pot along with the kidney beans. Cook for 1 hour. Garnish with Cheddar cheese, a dollop of sour cream, and cilantro and serve. *Serves 8.*

# THE BOILER HOUSE RESTAURANT

## — TORONTO, ONTARIO —

If you're a fan of industrial-chic design and wildly innovative cuisine, then Toronto's Boiler House is for you. Located in an old two-story warehouse in the hip, historic Distillery District, the chophouse features a twenty-two-foot-long wine rack, hardwood floors, and hand-carved timber tables. Coveys of smaller, more intimate dining spaces dot the open space.

The Boiler House has garnered awards since its inception, due in no small part to the masterful styling of executive chef Jason Rosso. *USA Today* praised the restaurant's "big-city sophistication [and] small-town charm." The Boiler House's dishes, which include an East Coast cod and green onion cake with sour-pickle relish and citrus butter, and a grilled bone-in New York strip steak with vanilla-scented sweet potatoes and goat cheese–sage glacé, push the culinary envelope; it's steak and seafood dressed to the nines.

Rosso first made his adventurous lobster chili at Peller Estates Winery in Ontario's Niagara region, and even graciously shared his recipe with Canada's Food Network. It's lobster and chili unlike you've ever tasted them before: together. For this dish, Rosso makes his own homemade chili powder, which you can keep to use in other recipes. Pair this chili with a bottle of semi-dry Riesling, a Sauvignon Blanc, or a Gewürztraminer for a truly decadent dinner.

# Lobster Chili

**Homemade Chili Powder**

   6 tablespoons paprika

   2 tablespoons ground turmeric

   1 tablespoon red pepper flakes

   1 teaspoon ground cumin

   1 teaspoon dried oregano, crumbled

   $1/2$ teaspoon cayenne pepper

   $1/2$ teaspoon garlic powder

   $1/2$ teaspoon salt

   $1/4$ teaspoon ground cloves


1 tablespoon olive oil

3 shallots, minced

2 cloves garlic, minced

2 stalks celery, finely chopped

1 yellow bell pepper, seeded and finely chopped

One 15-ounce can kidney beans, drained

$1/4$ cup tomato paste

1 cup fish or lobster stock, or as desired

Two $1^1/4$-pound lobsters, cooked, shelled, and diced

$1/2$ cup heavy cream


For the chili powder: Combine all the spices in a coffee or spice grinder and blend to a fine powder. You will not need all of the chili powder, but it keeps very well in a jar for another use.

In a heavy, medium pot, heat the olive oil over medium heat. Add the shallots, garlic, celery, and yellow pepper and sauté for 6 minutes. Add the kidney beans, 3 tablespoons of the chili powder, and the tomato paste and cook for 5 minutes, stirring constantly. The mixture will seem very thick, so add the stock to thin it out to your desired consistency. (You may need to add a little water to thin it down, as well.) Cook the chili base for 10 minutes, stirring constantly. Add the diced lobster meat and cream. Cook for about 1 minute, or until the lobster is heated through. Taste and adjust the seasoning. *Serves 6.*

# MUDDY WATERS SMOKEHOUSE & BLUES

## WINNIPEG, MANITOBA

Muddy Waters Smokehouse & Blues touts itself as "the place that loves to party," and you have to trust that a restaurant that encourages its guests to sign their names on its walls means business. Besides that, it may well be the closest thing to the Deep South in Canada. Located in Winnipeg's the Forks market, Muddy Waters serves up both authentic and admittedly "not-so-authentic" Southern favorites and hospitality.

As the name implies, ribs are the main event here. Manitobans can feast on all things ribs to their hearts'

content: fried rib tips, pulled rib meat nachos, a smoked rib meat sandwich, and barbecued chicken and rib combo platters. One of the few non-rib items on the menu is the Muddy Waters Chili, which combines ground beef, tomatoes, kidney beans, and a sharp, tasty blend of spices. The real kicker comes at the end, when the entire concoction is poured into a casserole dish, layered with shredded Monterey jack or Cheddar cheese and baked for a few minutes in the oven. The result is a gooey, cheesy delight sure to fill you up.

# Muddy Waters Chili

1 tablespoon canola oil

1 pound ground beef

1 green bell pepper, seeded and diced

1 yellow onion, diced

2 stalks celery, diced

1 jalapeno chile, minced

2 cloves garlic, minced

$1/2$ teaspoon ground cumin

2 teaspoons chili powder

$1/2$ teaspoon cayenne pepper

1 tablespoon packed brown sugar

$1/2$ teaspoon dry mustard

16 ounces canned kidney beans, drained

16 ounces crushed tomatoes

2 plum (Roma) tomatoes, diced

Salt and freshly ground pepper to taste

$1/2$ cup shredded Monterey jack or Cheddar cheese

Snipped fresh chives for garnish

Preheat the oven to 375°F. In a large, heavy skillet heat the oil over medium heat and brown the beef. Add the green pepper, onion, celery, jalapeno, and garlic and sauté until slightly tender. Mix all the dry ingredients together in a separate bowl. Add to the beef mixture and stir thoroughly to avoid lumps. Cook until the vegetables are tender, about 10 minutes. Add the kidney beans, crushed tomatoes, diced tomatoes, and salt and pepper and bring to a boil. Reduce the heat to low and simmer for 1 hour, stirring occasionally. Place in a casserole dish, top with the cheese, and bake for 5 to 6 minutes, or until the cheese is melted. Garnish with the chives and serve. *Serves 4 to 6*

# THE SHERWOOD HOUSE RESTAURANT

## ———— CANMORE, ALBERTA ————

If your idea of perfection includes mountain vistas, roaring fireplaces, and log cabins, you need look no further than Canmore, Alberta. Situated in the Canadian Rockies, the area is a tourist hotspot, well known for its glorious skiing and snowboarding, hiking, rock-climbing (and even dog-sledding), and its postcard-perfect scenic beauty.

After a long day navigating the slopes or gallivanting across mountainous terrain, visitors can relax and refuel at the Sherwood House Restaurant, which looks and feels like a big, cozy log cabin, complete with the requisite stone fireplace and wood, wood everywhere. Guests have been visiting this alpine retreat for nearly a century to dine on authentic Canadian cuisine, hear live music, and warm up with a drink at the bar. The menu is game-heavy: venison, ostrich, and bison feature prominently alongside rainbow trout and Alberta beef. Chili is a must for its substance and heat, but the Sherwood House's variety does things a little differently. This chili recipe combines the traditional ground beef, kidney beans, and spices with chorizo sausage, sun-dried tomatoes, and potato for a unique flavor and texture.

# Sun-Dried Tomato & Sausage Chili

2 tablespoons olive oil

1 red onion, diced

1½ pounds ground beef

11 ounces chorizo sausage, chopped

4 tomatoes, diced

¼ cup oil-packed sun-dried tomatoes, drained and chopped

1 russet potato, peeled and diced

One 6-ounce can tomato paste

One 6-ounce can kidney beans, drained

1 garlic clove, minced

3 tablespoons chili powder

¼ teaspoon red pepper flakes, or to taste

1 teaspoon packed brown sugar

1 tablespoon dried oregano, crumbled

1 tablespoon ground cumin

1 cup water

Salt and freshly ground black pepper to taste

In a large, heavy pot, heat the oil over medium heat and sauté the onion. Add the beef and sausage and brown. Add all the remaining ingredients and reduce the heat to medium-low. Cover and simmer for 1½ hours. Season with salt and pepper. *Serves 6.*

## GENERAL COOKIN' TIP

★ Instead of the red pepper flakes, you can substitute minced green chile, such as jalapeno or serrano.

# McSORLEY'S SALOON & GRILL

## TORONTO, ONTARIO

McSorley's Saloon & Grill is one of those places that doesn't take itself too seriously, from the beer and hockey paraphernalia covering nearly every free centimeter of wall space, to the contents of its menu. Vegetarian dishes are marked with the McSorley's take on the iconic no-smoking symbol—a bone in a circle with a slash through it—and many of the dishes have wacky names: Take the All-Day Hangover Breakfast or the Kabob's Your Uncle, for instance. The best part is that the food doesn't just have a sense of humor, it tastes great, too. While much of it is standard bar-and-grill fare, the McSorley's menu includes some unexpectedly transcontinental items, such as pad Thai, pot stickers, and samosas.

McSorley's gives bar chili a good (and healthy) make-over, as well. Its vegetarian chili is a veritable garden patch of veggies: corn, onion, sweet peppers, tomatoes, beans, garlic, celery, chickpeas, and fresh cilantro, with the surprise kick of fresh ginger. It's served with nacho chips, and owner Simon Hamlon swears it's the best veggie chili ever made. So good, in fact, that you'll make no bones about forgetting its meat-free designation.

# McSorley's Wonderful Veggie Chili

Olive oil for sautéing

2 large carrots, peeled and chopped

1 large white onion, chopped

2 stalks celery, chopped

1 red bell pepper, seeded and chopped

1 green bell pepper, seeded and chopped

1 clove garlic, minced

$1\frac{1}{2}$-inch piece fresh ginger, minced

2 bay leaves

1 teaspoon dried thyme

1 teaspoon dried rosemary

1 teaspoon cayenne pepper

2 tablespoons chili powder

One 28-ounce can plum tomatoes

One 19-ounce can kidney beans, drained

One 19-ounce can chickpeas (garbanzo beans), drained

One $5\frac{1}{2}$-ounce can tomato paste

2 cups frozen corn kernels

$\frac{1}{2}$ cup chopped fresh cilantro

2 dashes Frank's RedHot Sauce or other hot sauce

In a large, heavy saucepan, heat the oil over medium heat and sauté the carrots, onion, celery, peppers, garlic, and ginger for 10 minutes. Add the bay leaves, thyme, rosemary, cayenne, and chili powder. Add the tomatoes, beans, chickpeas, tomato paste, and corn and simmer for 20 minutes. Remove the bay leaves. Add the cilantro and hot sauce. Serve. *Serves 4.*

# OH! CANADA

## CALGARY, ALBERTA

Like its neighbor to the south, Canada is a melting pot of diverse people from all corners of the globe speaking different languages, practicing different customs, and eating different foods. Canadian cuisine, though certainly influenced by English and French culinary traditions, is equally influenced by other European, Asian, African, and Latin foods. That said, Canadians are certainly proud of their own culinary heritage. Oh! Canada Restaurant & Bar wears that pride on its sleeve (or, at least, on its sign). Located in the Nexen Tower in downtown Calgary, Oh! Canada specializes in Canadian cuisine. The menu, with dishes prepared by Oh! Canada's "kitchen prime minister," Scott Sprouse, features such enticing edibles as a Green Party salad, the Gretzky smoked-turkey sandwich, the Tragically Hip Alberta beef sandwich, and Newfie Fish & Chips.

Oh! Canada also serves some remarkable chili. While it doesn't have a funky name or feature distinctly Canadian ingredients, it is its own melting pot of flavors and spices. Want to "eat, drink, and be Canadian," as Oh! Canada's motto urges? Serve this chili while watching your favorite hockey team on the tube or after a day on the ice.

# Oh! Canada Chili

3 pounds ground beef sirloin

2 tablespoons extra-virgin olive oil

2 large yellow onions, finely chopped

10 garlic cloves, minced

2 cups fresh or frozen corn kernels

$\frac{1}{4}$ cup red pepper flakes

2 tablespoons ground cumin

1 tablespoon chili powder

16 ounces canned kidney beans, drained and rinsed

16 ounces canned chickpeas (garbanzo beans), drained and rinsed

16 ounces canned whole tomatoes with juice

16 ounces canned tomato purée

$\frac{1}{2}$ cup warm water

1 teaspoon seasoned salt (preferably Lawry's)

1 tablespoon freshly ground black pepper

Shredded aged Cheddar cheese and sliced green onions for garnish

In a large, heavy skillet, heat the olive oil over medium heat and brown the beef. Drain the fat and reserve the meat.

In a clean large, heavy skillet, heat the remaining 1 tablespoon of olive oil over medium-high heat and cook the onions and garlic until the onions are translucent. Add the corn, cooked sirloin, and all of the seasonings. Give it a quick stir and add the beans, whole tomatoes with juice, and tomato purée. Reduce the heat to medium-low and simmer for 2 hours, adjusting the consistency with the water. Season with the salt and pepper. Garnish with the shredded Cheddar and green onions and serve with corn bread, if desired. *Serves 6 to 8.*

# THE STILL BAR & GRILL

## KITCHENER, ONTARIO

One-half of Ontario's Twin Cities, Kitchener boasts at least one thing that its sister city, Waterloo, doesn't have: the Still Bar & Grill. And what does the Still have that other bar-grill establishments in the area don't have? The largest patio in the bi-city area, its own nightclub, and an outdoor beach volleyball court, for starters.

With so much going on under one roof, you might assume that the food would be an afterthought, a mere edible napkin of sorts to soak up the Tequila Poppers and Cowboy Cocktails, but you would be wrong. It's not health food, but it's good food. Of particular note is the Still Chili, which gets extra-special attention on Cowboy Thursdays, when Twin City urban cowboys (and girls) come out to eat, drink, and be merry. Try whipping this chili up the next time a herd of friends moseys on over to your place; it's super quick, super easy, and super tasty. It can be thrown together on a whim too, as you probably already have all the ingredients, and the dish takes only a few minutes to cook.

# The Still Chili

1 large onion, diced

1 large red bell pepper, seeded and diced

1 large green bell pepper, seeded and diced

11 pounds lean ground beef

12 cups chili sauce

12 cups tomato-based pasta sauce

12 cups cooked kidney beans

$1/2$ beef bouillon cube dissolved in $1/2$ cup water

Cayenne pepper, to taste

In a large, heavy pot, combine the onion, peppers, and ground beef and brown over medium-high heat. Add the sauces, kidney beans, dissolved bouillon cube, and cayenne and stir to combine. Simmer for 10 minutes, then serve. *Serves 15.*

## GENERAL COOKIN' TIP

★ The dissolved bouillon cube can be replaced with $1/2$ cup beef broth.

# TOMATO FRESH FOOD CAFÉ

## ── VANCOUVER, BRITISH COLUMBIA ──

"Fresh" has become such a buzzword in the restaurant world that it barely manages to catch diners' eyes anymore. In Vancouver, lovers of good food have the good fortune of the Tomato Fresh Food Café, where "fresh food" isn't just a catchphrase, but a mission. Owner James Gaudreault, along with his wife, Star Spilos, and chef James Campbell, opened the café in the early '90s with the intention of creating a cozy, comfortable, and affordable place where people could enjoy fresh, delicious, innovative meals made from local and mostly organic ingredients. Sound simple? It is, and that's exactly the point—it's a fuss- and fad-free approach to food. Vancouver residents have taken notice, and the Tomato Fresh Food Café is now a favorite fixture on Cambie Street. Many patrons frequent the bright, cheery café several times a week, and *Vancouver* magazine voted it the Best Neighbourhood Restaurant in 2003. Gaudreault and Spilos even penned their own cookbook of recipes from the restaurant, called *As Fresh as It Gets*, in 2006.

# Tomato Fresh Food Café Vegetarian Chili

$1/4$ cup plus 6 tablespoons olive oil

1 unpeeled eggplant, cut into $1/2$-inch dice

2 onions, finely diced

4 garlic cloves, minced

1 jalapeno chile, minced

1 cup button mushrooms, quartered

2 small green bell peppers, seeded and finely diced

1 cup V-8 vegetable juice

One 28-ounce can chopped plum tomatoes

2 cups finely diced fresh plum tomatoes

2 tablespoons ground ancho chile

1 tablespoons ground cumin

1 teaspoons ground fennel

1 tablespoon freshly ground black pepper

1 tablespoon salt

1 cup canned dark red kidney beans, drained and rinsed

1 cup canned garbanzo beans (chickpeas), drained and rinsed

$1/2$ cup fresh dill, chopped

$1/2$ cup fresh Italian flat-leaf parsley, chopped

1 tablespoon fresh oregano, chopped

1 tablespoon fresh basil, chopped

2 tablespoons fresh lemon juice

1 cup shredded Cheddar or Monterey Jack cheese

In a large skillet, heat the $1/4$ cup olive oil over medium heat. Add the eggplant and sauté until almost tender. Using a slotted spoon, transfer to a large bowl. In the same skillet, heat the 6 tablespoons olive oil over low heat. Add the onions, garlic, jalapeno, mushrooms, and bell peppers. Sauté until softened, about 10 minutes. Add the sautéed eggplant, V-8 juice, canned and fresh plum tomatoes, ground ancho chile, cumin, fennel, black pepper, and salt. Cook, uncovered, stirring ocasionally, for 30 minutes. Add the kidney and garbanzo beans, dill, parsley, oregano, basil, and lemon juice. Cook for another 15 minutes. Stir well, taste, and adjust the seasonings. Serve topped with the shredded Cheddar or Monterey jack cheese. *Serves 8 to 10.*

# INDEX

## ACKNOWLEDGMENTS

Thanks to all the chefs and restaurant owners who generously shared their chili recipes, photographs, and stories to make this book possible.

Thanks and love to Scott, the Andersons, the Witmers, and all of my family and friends. Thanks also to the faculty, administration, staff, and students at Shippensburg University.

Thanks to everyone at becker&mayer! Extra-special thanks to Kate Perry, Kasey Free, Lisa Metzger, Shirley Woo, and Kjersti Egerdahl.

Thanks to everyone at Chronicle Books.

## RESOURCES

Chili Appreciation Society International, International Chili Society, The Food Network, Jane & Michael Stern, *Gourmet*, *Bon Appetit*, Epicurious.com, and National Public Radio.

## IMAGE CREDITS

All interior photographs are courtesy of each respective restaurant, except for the following: page 6 (right): Saint Louis Zoo; page 7 (center image): © becker&mayer!; page 14: Jim MacNeill; page 26: Luke Nerone/Juke Photographers; page 44: Saint Louis Zoo; page 54: © becker&mayer!; page 58: © becker&mayer!; page 64: © becker&mayer!; page 66: © becker&mayer!; page 76: Jocelyn Barda; page 84: © becker&mayer!; page 86: © becker&mayer!

# OTHER TASTY COOKBOOKS IN THE *Killer* SERIES

Spanning from east to west, Texas to Toronto, and countless spots in between, the acclaimed *Killer Ribs* serves up smokin' recipes for the most succulent sauces, spiciest rubs, and juiciest ribs you've ever tasted. From tangy, slow-roasted baby backs and sweet pineapple loin-back pork ribs to zesty black pepper beef ribs and citrus-laden alligator ribs, every delicious region is represented. Whether you're a seasoned barbecue enthusiast or a hungry greenhorn, you'll be inspired to create these tempting dishes cooked up by award-winning chefs from every corner of the continent.

$16.95 ISBN-10: 1-932855-37-8; ISBN-13: 978-1-932855-37-1

*Killer Pies* presents fresh-baked recipes from award-winning restaurants in North America. These passionate pie masters have shared their fail-proof methods for producing flaky perfection, and their advice will have you baking the most unforgettably delightful versions of America's tried-and-true dessert. Create Florida's classic Key Lime or sink your teeth into peach-blackberry perfection as they do in the Northeast. Craft the heartland's favorite sour cream raisin or treat yourself to Canada's renowned maple-walnut. Stuffed with the ripest homegrown and professional recipes from New Hampshire to Arizona and everywhere in between, *Killer Pies* is sure to stir up your inner filling and leave you licking your fork with satisfaction!

$16.95 ISBN-10: 1-932855-57-2; ISBN-13: 978-1-932855-57-9

TO ALL OF YOU WITH TATTERED BOOKS . . .
WE CAN'T THANK YOU ENOUGH!

KAREN BRIMACOMBE HELEN MILES

MARY HALPEN VAL ROBINSON

LINDA JACOBSON JOAN WILSON

# FOREWARNING

ONCE UPON A TIME, A SENIOR BOOK EDITOR LOOKED AT "THE BEST OF BRIDGE", OUR FIRST COOKBOOK, AND SAID "THIS BOOK WILL HAVE A LIFE OF TWO DECADES". UNBELIEVABLE! SHE WAS RIGHT!! "THE BEST OF BRIDGE" (COMMONLY REFERRED TO AS "THE RED ONE") IS NOW 22 YEARS OLD AND HAS SOLD NEARLY 1,000,000 COPIES.

TODAY, ALL THE KIDS WHO WERE RAISED ON BEST OF BRIDGE RECIPES ARE COOKING FOR THEMSELVES AND ASKING FOR A COLLECTION OF THEIR FAVORITES. SO ARE THEIR PARENTS. OUR NEW CUSTOMERS WANT TO KNOW "WHICH BOOK DO I BUY FIRST?"

YOU'RE HOLDING THE ANSWER - A COLLECTION OF YOUR FAVORITE RECIPES FROM ALL SIX BEST OF BRIDGE COOKBOOKS. WE'VE UPDATED LOTS OF THE RECIPES TO INCLUDE MORE FRESH INGREDIENTS AND LOW-FAT SUBSTITUTIONS AND INCLUDED MORE OF OUR NEW FAVORITES COLLECTED OVER THE PAST 3 YEARS. THE JOKES ARE NEW AND THE RECIPES WORK!

"THE LADIES OF THE BRIDGE" PROMISE YOU SIMPLE RECIPES WITH GOURMET RESULTS. WE KNOW YOU'LL HAVE FUN IN THE KITCHEN WITH "THE BEST OF THE BEST AND MORE"!

# TABLE OF CONTENTS

# FRONT COVER RECIPE

ASPARAGUS VINAIGRETTE (PAGE 161)

## MUFFINS

Jalapeño Corn Muffins
Phantom Rhubarb Muffins
Sunshine Muffins
Super Blueberry Lemon Muffins
Apple Bran Muffins
Banana Muffins
Cheddar Apple Muffins

## BREADS

Best-Ever Banana Bread
"Land of Nod" Cinnamon Buns
Cranberry Scones
Flaky Freezer Biscuits
Yorkshire Pudding
Pita Toasts
Baguette Sticks

## BRUNCHES

Relatively Low-Fat Granola
Swiss Apple Quiche
French Toast Raphael
Mediterranean Pie
Christmas Morning Wife Saver
Southwest Brunch Bake
Huevos Rancheros
Eggs Olé!
Weekend Spouse Saver
Stampede Casserole
Mexican Strata
Scotty's Nest Eggs
Vegetable Frittata

# JALAPEÑO CORN MUFFINS

| | |
|---|---|
| ½ CUP FLOUR | 125 mL |
| 1 TBSP. BAKING POWDER | 15 mL |
| ½ TSP. SALT | 2 mL |
| 1½ CUPS YELLOW CORNMEAL | 375 mL |
| 2 EGGS | |
| 1 CUP FAT-FREE SOUR CREAM | 250 mL |
| 1 CUP GRATED LIGHT CHEDDAR CHEESE | 250 mL |
| 10 OZ. CAN CREAMED CORN | 284 g |
| ¼ CUP SEEDED & CHOPPED JALAPEÑO PEPPERS | 60 mL |
| ½ CUP BUTTER OR MARGARINE, MELTED | 125 mL |

SIFT FLOUR, BAKING POWDER AND SALT TOGETHER. ADD CORNMEAL, EGGS, SOUR CREAM, CHEESE, CREAMED CORN, JALAPEÑO PEPPERS AND BUTTER; MIX WELL. SPRAY MEDIUM MUFFIN TINS OR USE PAPER LINERS AND FILL WITH MIXTURE. BAKE AT 450°F (230°F) FOR 15-20 MINUTES. MAKES ABOUT 18 MEDIUM MUFFINS.

HOW DO YOU EXPLAIN COUNTERCLOCKWISE TO A CHILD WITH A DIGITAL WATCH?

# — PHANTOM RHUBARB MUFFINS —

*WHAT DO YOU MEAN THEY'RE GONE? - AGAIN?*

## RHUBARB MUFFINS

| | |
|---|---|
| ½ CUP FAT-FREE SOUR CREAM | 125 mL |
| ¼ CUP VEGETABLE OIL | 60 mL |
| 1 LARGE EGG | |
| 1⅓ CUPS FLOUR | 325 mL |
| 1 CUP DICED RHUBARB | 250 mL |
| ⅔ CUP BROWN SUGAR | 150 mL |
| ½ TSP. BAKING SODA | 2 mL |
| ¼ TSP. SALT | 1 mL |

## BROWN SUGAR CINNAMON TOPPING

| | |
|---|---|
| ¼ CUP BROWN SUGAR | 60 mL |
| ¼ CUP CHOPPED PECANS | 60 mL |
| ½ TSP. CINNAMON | 2 mL |
| 2 TSP. MELTED BUTTER | 10 mL |

TO MAKE MUFFINS: BLEND TOGETHER SOUR CREAM, OIL AND EGG. SET ASIDE. IN ANOTHER BOWL, STIR REMAINING INGREDIENTS TOGETHER AND COMBINE WITH SOUR CREAM MIXTURE. MIX JUST UNTIL MOISTENED. FILL 12 LARGE MUFFIN CUPS ⅔ FULL.

TO MAKE TOPPING: COMBINE ALL INGREDIENTS AND SPOON ONTO EACH MUFFIN. BAKE AT 350°F (180°C) FOR 25-30 MINUTES.

*IF YOU THINK YOU'RE TOO SMALL TO HAVE AN IMPACT, TRY GOING TO SLEEP WITH A MOSQUITO IN THE ROOM.*

# SUNSHINE MUFFINS

*SO QUICK YOU WON'T BELIEVE IT!!*

| | |
|---|---|
| 1 ORANGE | |
| ½ CUP ORANGE JUICE | 125 mL |
| 1 EGG | |
| ¼ CUP OIL | 60 mL |
| 1½ CUPS FLOUR | 375 mL |
| ¾ CUP SUGAR | 175 mL |
| 1 TSP. BAKING POWDER | 5 mL |
| 1 TSP. BAKING SODA | 5 mL |
| 1 TSP. SALT | 5 mL |
| ½ CUP RAISINS (OPTIONAL) | 125 mL |
| ½ CUP CHOPPED NUTS (OPTIONAL) | 125 mL |

CUT ORANGE INTO 8 PIECES. PUT CUT-UP ORANGE (THAT'S RIGHT - THE WHOLE ORANGE), ORANGE JUICE, EGG AND OIL IN BLENDER. BLEND UNTIL SMOOTH. ADD FLOUR, SUGAR, BAKING POWDER, BAKING SODA AND SALT. BLEND. ADD RAISINS AND NUTS. BLEND JUST UNTIL MIXED. POUR MIXTURE INTO MUFFIN TINS AND BAKE AT 375°F (190°C) FOR 15-20 MINUTES. MAKES 16 MEDIUM MUFFINS.

UPDATE: TRY THIS RECIPE WITH DRIED CRANBERRIES.

DID YOU HEAR ABOUT THE NEW GARLIC DIET? YOU DON'T ACTUALLY LOSE ANY WEIGHT, BUT YOU LOOK THINNER FROM A DISTANCE.

# SUPER BLUEBERRY LEMON MUFFINS

THESE WILL DISAPPEAR AS QUICKLY AS YOU MAKE THEM!

## BLUEBERRY LEMON MUFFINS

| | |
|---|---|
| 2 CUPS FLOUR | 500 mL |
| ½ CUP SUGAR | 125 mL |
| 1 TBSP. BAKING POWDER | 15 mL |
| ½ TSP. SALT | 2 mL |
| RIND OF 1 LEMON | |
| 1 EGG | |
| 1 CUP MILK | 250 mL |
| ½ CUP BUTTER, MELTED | 125 mL |
| 1 CUP FRESH OR FROZEN BLUEBERRIES | 250 mL |

## LEMON BUTTER TOPPING

| | |
|---|---|
| ¼ CUP MELTED BUTTER | 60 mL |
| 2 TBSP. LEMON JUICE | 30 mL |
| ½ CUP SUGAR | 125 mL |

TO MAKE MUFFINS: MIX FLOUR, SUGAR, BAKING POWDER, SALT AND LEMON RIND IN LARGE BOWL. BEAT EGG IN MEDIUM BOWL; ADD MILK AND BUTTER. ADD EGG MIXTURE TO DRY INGREDIENTS. STIR UNTIL JUST MIXED (BATTER WILL BE LUMPY). STIR IN BLUEBERRIES. FILL MUFFIN PANS ⅔ FULL; BAKE AT 375°F (190°C) FOR 20 MINUTES.

TO MAKE TOPPING: COMBINE MELTED BUTTER AND LEMON JUICE. MEASURE SUGAR IN SEPARATE DISH. DUNK TOPS OF SLIGHTLY COOLED MUFFINS INTO LEMON BUTTER AND THEN SUGAR.
MAKES 16 MEDIUM MUFFINS.

# APPLE BRAN MUFFINS

A SPICY VARIATION OF AN OLD FAVORITE. KEEP THE BATTER IN THE REFRIGERATOR SO YOU CAN BAKE FRESH MUFFINS DURING THE WEEK.

| | |
|---|---:|
| 4 CUPS FLOUR | 1 L |
| 3 CUPS NATURAL BRAN | 750 mL |
| 2 TSP. BAKING POWDER | 10 mL |
| 2 TSP. BAKING SODA | 10 mL |
| 2 TSP. CINNAMON | 10 mL |
| 1 TSP. SALT | 5 mL |
| 1/4-1/2 TSP. NUTMEG | 1-2 mL |
| 1 CUP PACKED BROWN SUGAR | 250 mL |
| 3/4 CUP MARGARINE, ROOM TEMPERATURE | 175 mL |
| 3 EGGS | |
| 14 OZ. CAN UNSWEETENED APPLESAUCE | 398 mL |
| 1 1/2 CUPS BUTTERMILK | 375 mL |
| 1/2 CUP MOLASSES | 125 mL |
| 1 CUP RAISINS | 250 mL |
| 1 MEDIUM APPLE, PEELED, CORED & CHOPPED | |

STIR TOGETHER FLOUR, BRAN, BAKING POWDER, BAKING SODA, CINNAMON, SALT AND NUTMEG. IN SEPARATE BOWL, CREAM TOGETHER SUGAR AND MARGARINE. BEAT IN EGGS 1 AT A TIME UNTIL FLUFFY. STIR IN APPLESAUCE, BUTTERMILK, MOLASSES, RAISINS AND APPLE. ADD TO FLOUR MIXTURE AND STIR JUST UNTIL DRY INGREDIENTS ARE MOISTENED (BATTER SHOULD STILL BE LUMPY). STORE IN COVERED CONTAINER IN THE REFRIGERATOR FOR UP TO 5 DAYS. TO BAKE, PREHEAT OVEN TO 375°F (190°C) SPOON BATTER

# APPLE BRAN MUFFINS

CONTINUED FROM PAGE 12.

INTO GREASED OR PAPER-LINED MUFFIN CUPS. BAKE 15-20 MINUTES, UNTIL TOOTHPICK INSERTED INTO CENTER OF MUFFIN COMES OUT CLEAN. MAKES 30 LARGE MUFFINS.

# BANANA MUFFINS

ANOTHER RECIPE FOR ALL THOSE OVERRIPE BANANAS. VERY MOIST. GREAT FOR THE LUNCH BOX!

| | |
|---|---|
| ½ CUP BUTTER OR MARGARINE | 125 mL |
| 1 CUP SUGAR | 250 mL |
| 2 EGGS | |
| 1 CUP MASHED RIPE BANANAS | 250 mL |
| 1½ CUPS FLOUR | 375 mL |
| 1 TSP. NUTMEG | 5 mL |
| 1 TSP. BAKING SODA | 5 mL |
| 2 TSP. HOT WATER | 10 mL |
| 1 TSP. VANILLA | 5 mL |

CREAM BUTTER AND SUGAR. ADD EGGS AND BANANAS. MIX WELL. STIR IN FLOUR AND NUTMEG. DISSOLVE SODA IN HOT WATER, ADD TO BANANA MIXTURE. STIR IN VANILLA. FILL GREASED MUFFIN TINS ½ FULL. BAKE AT 350°F (180°C) FOR ABOUT 20 MINUTES, OR UNTIL GOLDEN BROWN.
MAKES 24 MEDIUM MUFFINS.

# CHEDDAR APPLE MUFFINS

AN AWARD WINNER!

| | |
|---|---|
| 3 CUPS FLOUR | 750 mL |
| 2/3 CUP SUGAR | 150 mL |
| 4 TSP. BAKING POWDER | 20 mL |
| 1 TSP. SALT | 5 mL |
| 1 TSP. CINNAMON | 5 mL |
| 2 CUPS GRATED CHEDDAR CHEESE | 500 mL |
| 2 EGGS | |
| 1 CUP APPLE JUICE | 250 mL |
| 1/2 CUP BUTTER OR MARGARINE, MELTED | 125 mL |
| 2 CUPS PEELED, FINELY CHOPPED APPLES | 500 mL |

PREHEAT OVEN TO 375°F (190°C). COMBINE FLOUR, SUGAR, BAKING POWDER, SALT AND CINNAMON IN LARGE BOWL. MIX IN CHEESE. BEAT EGGS IN MEDIUM BOWL. ADD APPLE JUICE; STIR IN BUTTER AND APPLE. ADD ALL AT ONCE TO FLOUR MIXTURE. STIR JUST UNTIL MOISTENED. FILL GREASED MUFFIN TINS. BAKE FOR 25-30 MINUTES. MAKES 2 DOZEN MEDIUM MUFFINS.

THE ONLY THING WRONG WITH DOING NOTHING IS THAT YOU NEVER KNOW WHEN YOU'RE FINISHED.

# BEST-EVER BANANA BREAD

DAY-O! HEY MISTER TALLYMAN - TALLY THIS ONE!

| | |
|---|---|
| 1 CUP BUTTER | 250 mL |
| 2 CUPS SUGAR | 500 mL |
| 3 CUPS MASHED RIPE BANANAS | 750 mL |
| (6 BANANAS) | |
| 4 EGGS, WELL BEATEN | |
| 2½ CUPS FLOUR | 625 mL |
| 2 TSP. BAKING SODA | 10 mL |
| 1 TSP. SALT | 5 mL |
| 1 TSP. NUTMEG | 5 mL |

PREHEAT OVEN TO 350°F (180°C). CREAM BUTTER AND SUGAR UNTIL LIGHT AND FLUFFY. ADD BANANAS AND EGGS AND BEAT UNTIL WELL MIXED. MIX DRY INGREDIENTS AND BLEND WITH BANANA MIXTURE, BUT DO NOT OVERMIX. POUR INTO 2 LIGHTLY GREASED LOAF PANS OR A BUNDT PAN. BAKE 55 MINUTES TO 1 HOUR; TEST FOR DONENESS (TOOTHPICK INSERTED IN MIDDLE COMES OUT CLEAN) AND COOL ON RACK FOR 10 MINUTES BEFORE REMOVING FROM PANS. FREEZES BEAUTIFULLY.

HINT: FREEZE OVERRIPE BANANAS IN THEIR SKINS IN A PLASTIC BAG.

THE DIFFERENCE BETWEEN A TAX COLLECTOR AND A TAXIDERMIST IS THE TAXIDERMIST LEAVES THE HIDE.

# "LAND OF NOD" CINNAMON BUNS

WHO WOULD THINK YOU COULD BE THIS ORGANIZED SO EARLY IN THE A.M. !!

| | |
|---|---:|
| 20 FROZEN DOUGH ROLLS | |
| 1 CUP BROWN SUGAR | 250 mL |
| ¼ CUP VANILLA INSTANT PUDDING | 60 mL |
| 1-2 TBSP. CINNAMON | 15-30 mL |
| ¾ CUP RAISINS (OPTIONAL) | 175 mL |
| ¼-½ CUP MELTED BUTTER | 60-125 mL |

BEFORE YOU PUT THE CAT OUT AND TURN OFF THE LIGHTS, GREASE A 10" (25 cm) BUNDT PAN AND ADD FROZEN ROLLS. SPRINKLE WITH BROWN SUGAR, PUDDING POWDER, CINNAMON AND RAISINS. POUR MELTED BUTTER OVER ALL. COVER WITH A CLEAN, DAMP CLOTH. (LEAVE OUT AT ROOM TEMPERATURE) TURN OUT THE LIGHTS AND SAY GOODNIGHT!

IN THE MORNING, PREHEAT OVEN TO 350°F (180°C) AND BAKE FOR 25 MINUTES. LET SIT FOR 5 MINUTES AND THEN TURN OUT ON A SERVING PLATE. NOW, AREN'T YOU CLEVER?

GAS PRICES ARE SO HIGH I ASKED FOR TWO DOLLARS WORTH AND THE ATTENDANT SPRAYED A LITTLE BEHIND MY EAR.

# CRANBERRY SCONES

| | |
|---|---|
| ¾ cup buttermilk or plain yogurt | 175 mL |
| 1 egg | |
| 2¾ cups flour | 675 mL |
| 4 tsp. baking powder | 20 mL |
| ½ tsp. baking soda | 2 mL |
| ½ tsp. salt | 2 mL |
| ½ cup butter or margarine | 125 mL |
| 1 cup coarsely chopped cranberries (fresh or frozen) | 250 mL |
| ½ cup sugar | 125 mL |
| rind of 1 orange | |
| 1 tbsp. butter, melted | 15 mL |
| ¼ cup icing sugar | 60 mL |

Preheat oven to 375°F (190°C). Beat buttermilk and egg in small bowl and set aside. In large bowl, measure flour, baking powder, baking soda and salt. Cut in butter until mixture resembles small peas. Mix in cranberries, sugar and orange rind. Add buttermilk mixture and stir until soft dough forms. Using your hands, form dough into a large ball and place on floured surface. Pat out to 1" (2.5 cm) thickness. Cut in 4" (10 cm) rounds. Place on ungreased cookie sheet and bake scones for 15-20 minutes. While still warm, brush with butter and sprinkle with icing sugar. Makes 8 large scones.

Why do we call it a TV set when you get only one?

# FLAKY FREEZER BISCUITS

THESE WONDERFUL BISCUITS CAN BE BAKED IMMEDIATELY OR FROZEN AND BAKED AS NEEDED.

| | |
|---|---|
| 1 TBSP. YEAST (1 PKG.) | 15 mL |
| 2 TBSP. SUGAR | 30 mL |
| 1/4 CUP WARM WATER | 60 mL |
| 5 CUPS FLOUR | 1.25 L |
| 3 TBSP. SUGAR | 45 mL |
| 1 TBSP. BAKING POWDER | 15 mL |
| 1 TSP. BAKING SODA | 5 mL |
| 1 TSP. SALT | 5 mL |
| 1 CUP BUTTER OR MARGARINE | 250 mL |
| 2 CUPS BUTTERMILK | 500 mL |

IN A SMALL BOWL COMBINE YEAST AND SUGAR IN WATER. SET ASIDE FOR 10 MINUTES. IN A LARGE BOWL MIX FLOUR, SUGAR, BAKING POWDER, SODA AND SALT. CUT IN BUTTER TO FORM A CRUMBLY MIXTURE. STIR IN YEAST MIXTURE AND BUTTERMILK. MIX JUST ENOUGH TO HOLD DOUGH TOGETHER. ROLL DOUGH 3/4" (2 cm) THICK ON FLOURED SURFACE. CUT OUT BISCUITS WITH THE TOP OF A GLASS OR A CUTTER. PRICK TOPS WITH FORK. FREEZE SEPARATELY ON COOKIE SHEET. AFTER BISCUITS ARE FROZEN, STACK AND WRAP WELL. BEFORE BAKING THAW AND LET RISE UNTIL DOUBLED IN SIZE (ABOUT 30 MINUTES). BAKE AT 425°F (220°C) FOR 15 MINUTES ON A LIGHTLY GREASED COOKIE SHEET.
MAKES 3-4 DOZEN.

ALTERNATIVE: GRATED CHEDDAR CHEESE MAY BE ADDED TO SOFT DOUGH FOR FLAKY CHEESE BISCUITS.

# YORKSHIRE PUDDING

A FAVORITE WITH ROAST BEEF DINNER! MAKE WHILE ROAST IS RESTING. (WHICH IS MORE THAN YOU GET TO DO!)

| | |
|---|---|
| 1 CUP FLOUR | 250 mL |
| 1/2 TSP. SALT | 2 mL |
| 1/2 CUP MILK | 125 mL |
| 2 EGGS, BEATEN | |
| 1/2 CUP WATER | 125 mL |
| MELTED BUTTER OR OIL | |

IN A BLENDER MIX FLOUR, SALT, MILK, EGGS AND WATER. BLEND WELL AND LEAVE AT ROOM TEMPERATURE FOR 1 HOUR. EVERYTIME YOU WALK BY - GIVE IT A WHIRL! WHEN ROAST IS DONE, REMOVE FROM OVEN AND COVER WITH FOIL TO KEEP WARM. PREHEAT OVEN TO 400°F (200°C). POUR 1 TBSP. (15 mL) BEEF DRIPPINGS, MELTED BUTTER OR OIL INTO 8 MEDIUM MUFFIN TINS. PLACE IN OVEN UNTIL BUBBLING HOT. (WATCH CLOSELY BECAUSE YOU DON'T WANT THE BUTTER TO BURN.) REMOVE FROM OVEN AND POUR BATTER INTO HOT BUTTER. BAKE AT 400°F (200°C) FOR 20 MINUTES AND THEN AT 350°F (180°C). FOR 10 MINUTES LONGER. YORKSHIRE WILL PUFF UP AND BE HOLLOW INSIDE. SERVE IMMEDIATELY WITH GRAVY.

THE WAR BETWEEN THE SEXES WILL NEVER BE WON. THERE IS TOO MUCH FRATERNIZING WITH THE ENEMY.

## PITA TOASTS

| | |
|---|---|
| 3/4 CUP BUTTER | 175 mL |
| 2 TBSP. FINELY CHOPPED FRESH PARSLEY | 30 mL |
| 1 TBSP. CHOPPED CHIVES | 15 mL |
| 1 TBSP. LEMON JUICE | 15 mL |
| 1 LARGE GARLIC CLOVE, MINCED | |
| 6 PITA ROUNDS | |

PREHEAT OVEN TO 450°F (230°C). CREAM TOGETHER FIRST 5 INGREDIENTS, COVER; SET ASIDE FOR AT LEAST 1 HOUR. CUT PITA ROUNDS INTO 4 WEDGES AND SEPARATE LAYERS. SPREAD EACH PIECE WITH SOME OF THE BUTTER MIXTURE. ARRANGE ON A LARGE BAKING SHEET IN 1 LAYER. BAKE FOR 5 MINUTES, UNTIL LIGHTLY BROWNED AND CRISP. MAKES 48 TOASTS. SERVE WITH YOUR FAVORITE DIPS OR IN PLACE OF GARLIC TOAST OR ROLLS.

## BAGUETTE STICKS

GREAT SERVED WITH PASTA OR A STEAMING BOWL OF SOUP.

| | |
|---|---|
| 1 BAGUETTE | |
| 1/2 CUP BUTTER, SOFTENED | 125 mL |
| 3 TBSP. PARMESAN CHEESE | 45 mL |
| 2 LARGE GARLIC CLOVES, MINCED | |
| 1/4 CUP CHOPPED FRESH PARSLEY | 60 mL |

CUT BAGUETTE INTO THIRDS. CUT EACH PIECE INTO 4 BREADSTICKS. MIX REMAINING INGREDIENTS AND SPREAD ON STICKS. BROIL UNTIL BROWNED. MAKES 12 STICKS. PICTURED ON PAGE 153.

# RELATIVELY LOW-FAT GRANOLA

EXCELLENT SERVED OVER YOGURT - OR JUST FOR NIBBLIES.

| | |
|---|---|
| 4 CUPS LARGE FLAKE OATMEAL | 1 L |
| 1 CUP SLICED ALMONDS | 250 mL |
| ½ CUP SUNFLOWER SEEDS | 125 mL |
| ½ CUP WHEAT GERM | 125 mL |
| ½ TSP. CINNAMON | 2 mL |
| ½ CUP BROWN SUGAR | 125 mL |
| ⅓ CUP HONEY | 75 mL |
| RIND & JUICE OF 1 LEMON | |
| RIND & JUICE OF 1 ORANGE | |
| 2 CUPS FINELY CHOPPED DRIED FRUIT | 500 mL |
| (CRANBERRIES, APRICOTS, PEACHES, BANANA CHIPS, APPLES) | |

IN A LARGE BOWL, COMBINE OATMEAL, ALMONDS, SUNFLOWER SEEDS, WHEAT GERM AND CINNAMON. IN A SAUCEPAN, COMBINE BROWN SUGAR AND HONEY AND BRING TO BOIL. REMOVE FROM HEAT AND ADD LEMON AND ORANGE RIND AND JUICE. TOSS LIQUID MIXTURE WITH DRY MIXTURE. SPRAY A LARGE, EDGED BAKING SHEET WITH COOKING SPRAY. SPREAD WITH GRANOLA AND BAKE AT 300°F (150°C) FOR 30 MINUTES, STIRRING EVERY 10 MINUTES, UNTIL GOLDEN BROWN. COOL. ADD DRIED FRUIT AND STORE IN AIRTIGHT CONTAINER. MAKES ABOUT 7 CUPS (1.75 L).

A BRAIN IS A WONDERFUL ORGAN; IT STARTS THE MOMENT YOU GET UP AND DOESN'T STOP UNTIL YOU GET TO THE OFFICE.

# SWISS APPLE QUICHE

FULL MARKS! YOU CAN TAKE THIS ONE TO THE BANK. MAKES 2 QUICHES.

## PASTRY SHELLS

| | |
|---|---|
| 1 CUP FLOUR | 250 mL |
| ½ CUP WHOLE-WHEAT FLOUR | 125 mL |
| 1½ TSP. SUGAR | 7 mL |
| ½ CUP BUTTER | 125 mL |
| 1 EGG YOLK | |
| 3 TBSP. ICE WATER | 45 mL |

## FILLING

| | |
|---|---|
| 3 MEDIUM TART GREEN APPLES, PEELED & FINELY CHOPPED | |
| 8 GREEN ONIONS, THINLY SLICED | |
| ¼ TSP. NUTMEG | 1 mL |
| ½ TSP. CURRY POWDER | 2 mL |
| 2 TBSP. BUTTER | 30 mL |
| 4 CUPS GRATED GRUYÈRE CHEESE | 1 L |
| 1 CUP WHIPPING CREAM | 250 mL |
| 4 EGGS LIGHTLY BEATEN | |
| ½ CUP DRY VERMOUTH OR DRY WHITE WINE | 125 mL |
| ¼ TSP. COARSELY GROUND PEPPER | 1 mL |

PASTRY SHELLS: SIFT TOGETHER THE FLOURS AND SUGAR, CUT IN THE BUTTER UNTIL MIXTURE RESEMBLES COARSE MEAL. BEAT EGG YOLK WITH ICE WATER AND STIR INTO FLOUR MIXTURE UNTIL DOUGH IS FORMED, ADDING ADDITIONAL WATER, 1 TSP. (5 mL) AT A TIME, IF NEEDED. FORM DOUGH INTO 2 BALLS AND FLATTEN SLIGHTLY. WRAP IN WAXED PAPER AND CHILL FOR 1 HOUR.

# SWISS APPLE QUICHE

CONTINUED FROM PAGE 22.

PREHEAT OVEN TO 425°F (220°C). ROLL OUT DOUGH ON FLOURED SURFACE. PLACE IN 2, 9" (23 cm) PIE PLATES OR QUICHE PANS AND CRIMP EDGES. PRICK BOTTOMS LIGHTLY WITH A FORK AND BAKE ON LOWER RACK OF OVEN FOR 15 MINUTES. CHECK AND COVER EDGES WITH FOIL IF TOO BROWN. RETURN TO OVEN AND BAKE AN ADDITIONAL 5 MINUTES. REMOVE FROM OVEN AND COOL.

FILLING: PREHEAT OVEN TO 375°F (190°C). COMBINE APPLES, GREEN ONIONS, NUTMEG AND CURRY. SAUTÉ IN BUTTER FOR 3-5 MINUTES, OR JUST UNTIL SOFT. COOL. SPOON INTO COOLED PIE SHELLS AND TOP WITH GRATED CHEESE. COMBINE CREAM, EGGS, VERMOUTH AND PEPPER. POUR SLOWLY OVER CHEESE. REDUCE HEAT TO 350°F (180°C). BAKE QUICHES ON MIDDLE RACK FOR 35-45 MINUTES, OR UNTIL FIRM AND GOLDEN. WATCH THAT PASTRY EDGES DON'T GET TOO BROWN. COVER IF NECESSARY. REMOVE FROM OVEN AND COOL ON A RACK FOR 15 MINUTES. EACH QUICHE SERVES 8.

TOO BAD THAT ALL THE PEOPLE WHO KNOW HOW TO RUN THE COUNTRY ARE BUSY DRIVING TAXICABS AND CUTTING HAIR.

# FRENCH TOAST RAPHAEL

A GREAT BRUNCH DISH TO BE PREPARED THE NIGHT BEFORE!

| | |
|---|---|
| 6 CUPS WHITE BREAD, CRUSTS REMOVED CUT INTO 1" (2.5 cm) CUBES | 1.5 L |
| 6 OZ. CREAM CHEESE, CUT INTO SMALL CUBES | 170 g |
| 6 EGGS, WELL-BEATEN | |
| 1 CUP MILK | 250 mL |
| 1/2 TSP. CINNAMON | 2 mL |
| 1/3 CUP DARK MAPLE SYRUP | 75 mL |

PLACE HALF THE BREAD IN A GREASED 8" (20 cm) SQUARE PAN. DOT CHEESE ON TOP. COVER WITH REMAINING BREAD. COMBINE REMAINING INGREDIENTS AND POUR OVER ALL. COVER WITH PLASTIC WRAP AND REFRIGERATE OVERNIGHT. IN THE MORNING, REMOVE PLASTIC AND BAKE IN PREHEATED 375°F (190°C) OVEN FOR 45 MINUTES. IT WILL BE PUFFY AND GOLDEN. SERVE IMMEDIATELY WITH EXTRA MAPLE SYRUP AND CRISP BACON. SERVES 6.

IF BANKERS CAN COUNT, WHY DO THEY HAVE EIGHT WINDOWS AND FOUR TELLERS?

# MEDITERRANEAN PIE

IMPRESSIVE, EASY TO MAKE & TASTES TERRIFIC!

| | |
|---|---|
| 2 SMALL ONIONS, CHOPPED | |
| 2 GARLIC CLOVES, MINCED | |
| 2 TBSP. BUTTER OR MARGARINE | 30 mL |
| 3-10 OZ. PKGS. FROZEN SPINACH, THAWED & SQUEEZED DRY | 3-283 g |
| 2-14 OZ. PKGS. FROZEN PUFF PASTRY, ROLLED TO 1/8" (3 mm) | 2-397 g |
| 3/4 LB. BLACK FOREST HAM, SLICED | 365 g |
| 1 LB. MOZZARELLA CHEESE, GRATED | 500 g |
| 2 RED PEPPERS, SEEDED & DICED | |
| 8 EGGS, BEATEN | |
| 1 EGG, BEATEN | |

SAUTÉ ONIONS AND GARLIC IN BUTTER. STIR IN SPINACH. LINE A 10" (25 cm) SPRINGFORM PAN WITH PASTRY, MAKING SURE IT OVERLAPS THE SIDES. LAYER 1/2 THE HAM, 1/2 THE CHEESE, 1/2 THE RED PEPPER, 1/2 THE SPINACH MIXTURE INTO THE PIE SHELL. POUR IN 1/2 THE BEATEN EGGS. REPEAT ALL LAYERS, PAN WILL BE FULL. COVER WITH PASTRY AND PINCH THE EDGES TO SEAL. TRIM EXCESS PASTRY AND SLASH THE TOP TO ALLOW STEAM TO ESCAPE. BRUSH TOP CRUST WITH BEATEN EGG. BAKE AT 400°F (200°C) FOR 15 MINUTES, REDUCE HEAT TO 350°F (180°C) AND BAKE FOR 45 MINUTES. IF THE CRUST BECOMES TOO BROWN, COVER LIGHTLY (DON'T SEAL) WITH FOIL. COOL THE PIE FOR 15 MINUTES AND REMOVE SPRINGFORM. THIS IS A SURE-FIRE HIT! SERVES 10.

# CHRISTMAS MORNING WIFE SAVER

A CANADIAN TRADITION - DON'T WAIT FOR CHRISTMAS! MAKE BREAKFAST THE NIGHT BEFORE AND ENJOY YOUR MORNING.

| | |
|---|---|
| 16 SLICES WHITE BREAD, CRUSTS REMOVED | |
| SLICES OF CANADIAN BACK BACON OR HAM | |
| SLICES OF SHARP CHEDDAR CHEESE | |
| 6 EGGS | |
| ½ TSP. PEPPER | 2 mL |
| ½-1 TSP. DRY MUSTARD | 2-5 mL |
| ¼ CUP MINCED ONION | 60 mL |
| ¼ CUP FINELY CHOPPED GREEN PEPPER | 60 mL |
| 1-2 TSP. WORCESTERSHIRE SAUCE | 5-10 mL |
| 3 CUPS MILK | 750 mL |
| DASH TABASCO | |
| ¼ LB. BUTTER | 125 g |
| SPECIAL "K" OR CRUSHED CORNFLAKES | |

PUT 8 PIECES OF BREAD IN A 9 x 13" (23 x 33 cm) BUTTERED GLASS BAKING DISH. ADD PIECES TO COVER DISH ENTIRELY. COVER BREAD WITH THINLY SLICED BACON. TOP WITH SLICES OF CHEDDAR CHEESE. COVER WITH SLICES OF BREAD. IN A BOWL, BEAT EGGS AND PEPPER. ADD MUSTARD, ONION, GREEN PEPPER, WORCESTERSHIRE, MILK AND TABASCO. POUR OVER BREAD, COVER AND REFRIGERATE OVERNIGHT. IN THE MORNING, MELT BUTTER AND POUR OVER TOP. COVER WITH CRUSHED SPECIAL "K" OR CORNFLAKES. BAKE AT 350°F (180°C) UNCOVERED, 1 HOUR. LET SIT 10 MINUTES BEFORE SERVING. SERVE WITH FRESH FRUIT AND "LAND OF NOD" CINNAMON BUNS (PAGE 16). SERVES 8.

# SOUTHWEST BRUNCH BAKE

|  |  |
|---|---|
| 4 cups frozen shredded-style hash brown potatoes | 1 L |
| 15 oz. can black beans, rinsed & drained | 425 mL |
| 1 cup frozen whole kernel corn | 250 mL |
| 1 red pepper, chopped | |
| ½ cup chopped onion | 125 mL |
| 2 cups shredded Monterey Jack cheese | 500 mL |
| 2 tbsp. chopped fresh cilantro | 30 mL |
| 8 eggs | |
| 1¼ cups milk | 300 mL |
| ½ tsp. salt | 2 mL |
| ¼ tsp. cayenne pepper | 1 mL |

Spray 7 x 11" (18 x 28 cm) baking dish with cooking spray. Mix potatoes, beans, corn, red pepper and onion in baking dish. Sprinkle with cheese and cilantro. Beat eggs, milk, salt and cayenne pepper until well blended. Pour evenly over potato mixture. Cover and refrigerate at least 2 hours but no longer than 24 hours. Heat oven to 350°F (180°C) and bake, uncovered, 55-60 minutes, or until knife inserted in center comes out clean. Let stand 5 minutes before cutting. Serves 6-8. Serve with sliced fresh tomatoes or salsa and jalapeño corn muffins (page 8).

The only substitute for good manners is fast reflexes.

# HUEVOS RANCHEROS

POACHED EGGS - SOUTHWESTERN STYLE

## CHILI SAUCE

| | |
|---|---|
| 2 TBSP. VEGETABLE OIL | 30 mL |
| 1 CUP FINELY CHOPPED ONION | 250 mL |
| 1 CUP FINELY CHOPPED RED OR ANAHEIM PEPPER | 250 mL |
| 2 GARLIC CLOVES, MINCED | |
| 28 OZ. CAN CHOPPED TOMATOES | 796 mL |
| 1 TSP. SUGAR | 5 mL |
| SALT & PEPPER TO TASTE | |
| 1/4 TSP. CRUSHED HOT PEPPER FLAKES (OPTIONAL) | 1 mL |
| 1 CUP GRATED CHEDDAR CHEESE | 250 mL |

4-8" (20 cm) FLOUR OR CORN TORTILLAS
8 EGGS (FOR POACHING)

## GARNISH:
SALSA, SOUR CREAM, GRATED CHEDDAR, GUACAMOLE, CANNED BLACK BEANS, RINSED & DRAINED

TO PREPARE SAUCE: IN A DEEP FRYING PAN, HEAT OIL; SAUTÉ ONION, PEPPER AND GARLIC UNTIL SOFT. ADD TOMATOES AND SEASONINGS; SIMMER 20 MINUTES. ADD CHEESE; HEAT AND STIR UNTIL MELTED AND WELL BLENDED.

WRAP TORTILLAS IN FOIL AND HEAT IN OVEN. HEAT BEANS.

TO POACH EGGS: BREAK EGGS INTO BUBBLING SAUCE AND POACH 3-5 MINUTES TO DESIRED DONENESS. PLACE EGGS AND CHILI SAUCE ON TORTILLAS AND PASS THE GARNISHES. SERVES 4.

# EGGS OLÉ!

EASY, COLORFUL AND OF COURSE, DELICIOUS!

| | |
|---|---|
| 12 EGGS | |
| 1/4 CUP WATER | 60 mL |
| SALT & PEPPER TO TASTE | |
| 3 TBSP. BUTTER - AND THEN | 45 mL |
| 3 TBSP. BUTTER | 45 mL |
| 1 CUP SLICED MUSHROOMS | 250 mL |
| 1/2 CUP CHOPPED GREEN ONION | 125 mL |
| 1/2 CUP COARSELY CHOPPED GREEN PEPPER | 125 mL |
| 1/2 CUP COARSELY CHOPPED RED PEPPER (NOTHING'S TOO GOOD FOR YOUR GUESTS) | 125 mL |
| 1/2 CUP COARSELY CHOPPED ZUCCHINI | 125 mL |
| 1/2 CUP COARSELY CHOPPED TOMATOES | 125 mL |
| 1/4 CUP GREEN CHILIES (OPTIONAL) | 60 mL |
| SALT AND PEPPER TO TASTE (AGAIN) | |
| 1/2 LB. MONTEREY JACK CHEESE, GRATED | 250 g |
| SALSA, MILD OR HOT | |

BEAT EGGS AND WATER TOGETHER. SEASON WITH SALT AND PEPPER. MELT THE FIRST BUTTER IN FRYING PAN AND ADD EGG MIXTURE. SCRAMBLE JUST UNTIL MOIST. PLACE IN LARGE OVENPROOF DISH; KEEP WARM IN 150°F (65°C) OVEN. MELT THE OTHER BUTTER IN FRYING PAN; SAUTÉ ALL VEGGIES TILL TENDER. SEASON WITH SALT AND PEPPER. SPOON OVER EGGS, SPRINKLE WITH GRATED CHEESE AND BAKE AT 300°F (150°C) OVEN UNTIL CHEESE MELTS. SERVE WITH LOTS OF SALSA. GOOD FOR 6. CARAMBA!

# WEEKEND SPOUSE SAVER

HAVE THE SEÑOR MAKE THIS MEXICAN MARVEL - THE NEXT BRUNCH FAVORITE.

|  |  |
|---|---|
| 3-4 OZ. CANS MILD GREEN CHILIES, CHOPPED | 3-115 g |
| 6 CORN TORTILLAS, IN 1" (2.5 cm) STRIPS | |
| 2 LBS. HOT ITALIAN SAUSAGE, CASING REMOVED, COOKED, DRAINED | 1 kg |
| 2½ CUPS GRATED MONTEREY JACK CHEESE | 625 mL |
| ½ CUP MILK | 125 mL |
| 8 EGGS | |
| ½ TSP. SALT | 2 mL |
| ½ TSP. GARLIC SALT | 2 mL |
| ½ TSP. ONION SALT | 2 mL |
| ½ TSP. CUMIN | 2 mL |
| ½ TSP. FRESHLY GROUND PEPPER | 2 mL |
| PAPRIKA TO SPRINKLE | |
| 2 LARGE RIPE TOMATOES, SLICED | |
| SALSA & SOUR CREAM FOR CONDIMENTS | |

THE NIGHT BEFORE, GREASE A 9 x 13" (23 x 33 cm) CASSEROLE; LAYER ½ THE CHILIES, ½ THE CORN TORTILLAS, ½ THE COOKED SAUSAGE, AND ½ THE CHEESE. REPEAT LAYERS. IN A MEDIUM BOWL, BEAT MILK, EGGS, SALT, GARLIC SALT, ONION SALT, CUMIN AND PEPPER. POUR OVER CASSEROLE INGREDIENTS. SPRINKLE WITH PAPRIKA. COVER WITH PLASTIC WRAP AND REFRIGERATE OVERNIGHT. HOORAY - IT'S THE FOLLOWING DAY, AND YOU'RE READY! PREHEAT OVEN TO 350°F (180°C). PLACE TOMATOES OVER

## WEEKEND SPOUSE SAVER

CONTINUED FROM PAGE 30.
TOP OF CASSEROLE. BAKE 1 HOUR, OR UNTIL SET
IN CENTER AND SLIGHTLY BROWNED AT EDGES.
LET SIT 5 MINUTES BEFORE SERVING. PASS THE
SALSA AND SOUR CREAM. SERVE WITH A TRAY
OF SLICED FRESH FRUIT. MAGNIFICO! SERVES 10.

## STAMPEDE CASSEROLE

ROUND UP THE COWPOKES - THIS BRUNCH IS A
MUST. IT'S EASY TO DO - BUT THEY'LL THINK
YOU'VE FUSSED!

| | | |
|---|---|---|
| 1½ LBS. BULK PORK SAUSAGE | 750 | g |
| 3-4 OZ. CANS GREEN CHILIES, DRAINED | 3-115 | g |
| 1 LB. CHEDDAR CHEESE, GRATED | 500 | g |
| 1 LB. MONTEREY JACK CHEESE, GRATED | 500 | g |
| 9 EGGS, BEATEN | | |
| 1 CUP MILK | 250 mL | |
| 2 TBSP. FLOUR | 30 mL | |
| PAPRIKA | | |

BROWN SAUSAGE AND DRAIN WELL. SPLIT CHILIES
AND REMOVE SEEDS. SAVE ⅓ OF THE CHILIES
AND CUT IN THIN STRIPS. LAYER SAUSAGE WITH
CHEESES AND REMAINING ⅔ OF CHILIES IN A
GREASED 9 X 13" (23 X 33 cm) GLASS BAKING
DISH. BEAT EGGS, MILK AND FLOUR TOGETHER
UNTIL WELL-BLENDED. POUR OVER LAYERED
MIXTURE. DECORATE TOP WITH STRIPS OF CHILIES
IN A LATTICE-WORK PATTERN. SPRINKLE WITH
PAPRIKA AND BAKE AT 350°F (180°C) FOR
45 MINUTES. SERVES 12.

# MEXICAN STRATA

*OLÉ! - ANOTHER WIFE-SAVER AND A GREAT MAKE AHEAD!*

| | |
|---|---|
| 16 SLICES WHITE BREAD, TRIMMED | |
| 4 LARGE RIPE TOMATOES, SLICED | |
| 1 MEDIUM ONION, SLICED & SEPARATED | |
| 2-4 OZ. CANS CHOPPED GREEN CHILIES, DRAINED | 2-113 g |
| 1½ CUPS GRATED CHEDDAR OR MONTEREY JACK CHEESE | 375 mL |
| 7 EGGS | |
| 3½ CUPS MILK | 875 mL |
| ½ TSP. SALT | 2 mL |
| ½ TSP. GARLIC SALT | 2 mL |
| ½ TSP. GROUND CUMIN | 2 mL |
| ½ TSP. CHILI POWDER | 2 mL |

PLACE 8 SLICES OF BREAD IN BOTTOM OF BUTTERED 9 x 13" (23 x 33 cm) PAN. ARRANGE TOMATO SLICES, ONION RINGS AND GREEN CHILIES OVER BREAD. SPRINKLE ⅔ OF THE CHEESE OVER ALL. TOP WITH REMAINING SLICES OF BREAD. BEAT EGGS, MILK AND SEASONINGS, POUR OVER BREAD (LIQUID SHOULD COME TO TOP OF PAN). IF MORE LIQUID IS NEEDED, ADD MIXTURE OF 1 EGG AND ½ CUP (125 mL) MILK. SPRINKLE REMAINING CHEESE OVER TOP. COVER WITH FOIL AND REFRIGERATE OVERNIGHT. REMOVE FROM REFRIGERATOR 1 HOUR BEFORE BAKING FOR A LIGHTER AND FLUFFIER DISH. PREHEAT OVEN TO 350°F (180°C). BAKE, UNCOVERED, FOR 1 TO 1½ HOURS, OR UNTIL KNIFE INSERTED IN CENTER

## MEXICAN STRATA

CONTINUED FROM PAGE 32.

COMES OUT CLEAN. ALLOW TO STAND 5 MINUTES BEFORE SERVING. SERVE WITH PICANTE SALSA OR PICALILLI. SERVES 8.

WHY DO PSYCHICS HAVE TO ASK YOUR NAME?

## SCOTTY'S NEST EGGS

ONE OF OUR FAVORITE BACHELORS LOVES TO WHIP THIS UP. - UPDATE - SCOTTY IS NOW MARRIED AND WE THINK THIS RECIPE DID IT!

### EACH NEST

2-3 THIN SLICES BLACK FOREST HAM
1 EGG
1 TBSP. CREAM                           15 mL
1 HEAPING TBSP. GRATED SWISS CHEESE    25 mL
SPRINKLE OF DRIED BASIL
ENGLISH MUFFIN

PREHEAT OVEN TO 350°F (180°C). GREASE LARGE MUFFIN TINS. LINE WITH HAM AND BREAK EGG OVER TOP. ADD CREAM AND SPRINKLE WITH CHEESE AND BASIL. BAKE 12-15 MINUTES. SERVE ON HALF A TOASTED ENGLISH MUFFIN. (PLACE WATER IN ANY UNUSED MUFFIN CUPS TO PREVENT DAMAGE.)

# VEGETABLE FRITTATA

| | |
|---|---|
| 1 TBSP. VEGETABLE OIL | 15 mL |
| 1 CUP BROCCOLI FLORETS, CUT INTO BITE-SIZED PIECES | 250 mL |
| 1/2 CUP SHREDDED CARROT | 125 mL |
| 1/2 CUP CHOPPED ONION | 125 mL |
| 1/2 RED PEPPER, CHOPPED | |
| 4 EGGS | |
| 1/4 CUP MILK | 60 mL |
| 1 TBSP. CHOPPED FRESH PARSLEY | 15 mL |
| 1/4 TSP. SALT | 1 mL |
| 1/4 TSP. TABASCO | 1 mL |
| 3/4 CUP GRATED CHEDDAR CHEESE | 175 mL |
| 1 TBSP. GRATED PARMESAN CHEESE | 15 mL |

HEAT OIL IN A MEDIUM-SIZED FRYING PAN. COOK BROCCOLI, CARROT AND ONION ABOUT 5 MINUTES, STIRRING FREQUENTLY, UNTIL BROCCOLI IS TENDER-CRISP. ADD RED PEPPER AND STIR. BEAT EGGS, MILK, PARSLEY, SALT AND TABASCO UNTIL BLENDED. POUR MIXTURE OVER VEGETABLES. SPRINKLE WITH CHEESES AND REDUCE HEAT TO LOW. COVER AND COOK UNTIL EGGS ARE SET IN THE MIDDLE, 5-10 MINUTES. CUT INTO WEDGES. SERVES 4. (PICTURED ON PAGE 136.)

ONE OF THE ADVANTAGES OF GETTING OLD IS THAT YOU CAN SING IN THE BATHROOM WHILE YOU ARE BRUSHING YOUR TEETH.

# BEVERAGES

Eggnog Supreme

Winter Punch

Marguaritas Mucho Grande

# OTHER GOOD THINGS

Never-Fail Blender Hollandaise

Roasted Orange Pepper and Corn Salsa

Papaya Salsa

Kiwi Salsa

Pickled Onions

Cranberry Pear Chutney

Green Tomato Relish

B.L.'s Best Mustard Pickles

# EGGNOG SUPREME

THIS IS A BEST OF BRIDGE CHRISTMAS TRADITION.

| | |
|---|---|
| 12 EGG YOLKS | |
| 1 CUP SUGAR | 250 mL |
| 7/8 CUP BRANDY (OKAY! USE THE WHOLE CUP) | 205 mL |
| 1 1/3 CUPS RYE OR RUM | 325 mL |
| 2 CUPS HALF & HALF CREAM | 500 mL |
| 12 EGG WHITES | |
| 3 CUPS WHIPPING CREAM | 750 mL |
| NUTMEG FOR GARNISH | |

IN A LARGE BOWL, BEAT EGG YOLKS AND SUGAR TOGETHER UNTIL LEMON COLORED AND THICK. ADD BRANDY, RYE OR RUM AND CREAM. BLEND WELL. CHILL FOR SEVERAL HOURS. BEAT EGG WHITES UNTIL STIFF. BEAT WHIPPING CREAM IN LARGE BOWL AND FOLD IN EGG WHITES. FOLD INTO EGG YOLK MIXTURE. POUR INTO A LARGE PUNCH BOWL. SPRINKLE WITH GRATED NUTMEG. ENJOY! SERVES A CROWD.!.

THE REAL REASON THAT MOUNTAIN CLIMBERS TIE THEMSELVES TOGETHER IS TO KEEP THE SENSIBLE ONE FROM GOING HOME.

# WINTER PUNCH

A HOT TODDY FOR: AFTER SKATING, AFTER SKIING, AFTER SNOWBOARDING, AFTER TREE CHOPPING OR WHILST SAP GATHERING.

| | |
|---|---|
| 2 CINNAMON STICKS | |
| 16 WHOLE CLOVES | |
| 6 CUPS APPLE JUICE | 1.5 L |
| 2 CUPS CRANBERRY COCKTAIL | 500 mL |
| 4 OZ. CINNAMON HEARTS (RED HOTS) | 125 g |
| 1 TSP. ANGOSTURA BITTERS | 5 mL |
| 1 CUP RUM | 250 mL |

TIE CINNAMON STICKS AND CLOVES IN CHEESE-CLOTH. IN A LARGE POT COMBINE REMAINING INGREDIENTS, EXCEPT RUM. PLACE CHEESECLOTH BAG IN MIXTURE AND SIMMER FOR 45 MINUTES. ADD RUM. SERVES 8.

# MARGUARITAS MUCHO GRANDE

OVER THE RIDGE WITH THE BEST OF BRIDGE.

| | |
|---|---|
| ¾ CUP FROZEN LIMEADE | 175 mL |
| ¾ CUP WATER | 175 mL |
| ¾ CUP TEQUILA | 175 mL |
| ⅓ CUP TRIPLE SEC | 75 mL |
| ICE TO FILL BLENDER | |

POUR ABOVE INGREDIENTS INTO BLENDER AND BLEND UNTIL FROTHY. MAKES 6 DRINKS. OLÉ!

# NEVER-FAIL BLENDER HOLLANDAISE

| | |
|---|---|
| 1 CUP BUTTER | 250 mL |
| 4 EGG YOLKS | |
| 1/4 TSP. EACH: SALT, SUGAR, TABASCO & DRY MUSTARD | 1 mL |
| 2 TBSP. FRESH LEMON JUICE | 30 mL |

HEAT BUTTER TO A FULL BOIL, BEING CAREFUL NOT TO BROWN. COMBINE ALL OTHER INGREDIENTS. WITH BLENDER TURNED ON HIGH, SLOWLY POUR BUTTER INTO YOLK MIXTURE IN A THIN STREAM UNTIL ALL IS ADDED. KEEPS WELL IN REFRIGERATOR FOR SEVERAL DAYS. WHEN REHEATING, HEAT OVER HOT (NOT BOILING) WATER IN TOP OF DOUBLE BOILER. MAKES ABOUT 1 1/4 CUPS (300 mL) OF SAUCE.

ELEMENTARY SCHOOL OBSERVATIONS:

SOCRATES WAS A FAMOUS GREEK TEACHER WHO DIED FROM AN OVERDOSE OF WEDLOCK.

SIR FRANCIS DRAKE CIRCUMCISED THE WORLD WITH A 100-FOOT CLIPPER.

ONE OF THE CAUSES OF THE AMERICAN REVOLUTIONARY WAR WAS THAT THE ENGLISH PUT TACKS IN THEIR TEA.

# ROASTED ORANGE PEPPER AND CORN SALSA

GOOD ON TACOS AND FAJITAS.

| | |
|---|---|
| 3 YELLOW PEPPERS, HALVED AND SEEDED | |
| ½ CUP CHICKEN BROTH | 125 mL |
| ½ TSP. CUMIN | 2 mL |
| SALT AND PEPPER TO TASTE | |
| 19 OZ. CAN KERNEL CORN | 540 mL |
| ¼-½ TSP. HOT RED PEPPER FLAKES | 1-2 mL |

PLACE PEPPER HALVES CUT-SIDE DOWN ON A COOKIE SHEET. BROIL UNTIL SKINS ARE BLACKENED AND PUFFED. LEAVE SKINS ON AND PLACE PEPPERS IN SAUCEPAN, ADD CHICKEN BROTH AND COOK, UNCOVERED, 10 MINUTES. PURÉE WITH CUMIN, SALT AND PEPPER. ADD CORN AND PEPPER FLAKES. STORE IN REFRIGERATOR. MAKES 2 CUPS (500 mL).

# PAPAYA SALSA

GREAT WITH GRILLED PORK CHOPS OR CHICKEN.

| | |
|---|---|
| 1 RIPE PAPAYA, SEEDED & DICED | |
| ¼ CUP CHOPPED RED ONION | 60 mL |
| 1 TBSP. FINELY CHOPPED JALAPEÑO PEPPER | 15 mL |
| 1 TBSP. CHOPPED FRESH CILANTRO | 15 mL |
| JUICE OF 1 LIME | |
| 1 TSP. LIQUID HONEY | 5 mL |
| SALT & PEPPER TO TASTE | |

COMBINE ALL INGREDIENTS AND CHILL. SERVES 4.

# KIWI SALSA

REFRESHING! SERVE WITH GRILLED CHICKEN OR FISH.

| | |
|---|---|
| 2 TBSP. LIME JUICE | 30 mL |
| 1 TBSP. OLIVE OIL | 15 mL |
| 1 JALAPEÑO PEPPER, SEEDED & MINCED | |
| 1 TSP. HONEY | 5 mL |
| 1 GARLIC CLOVE, MINCED | |
| 1 TSP. CURRY | 5 mL |
| 1 TSP. CUMIN | 5 mL |
| ¼ TSP. HOT RED PEPPER FLAKES | 1 mL |

6 KIWI FRUIT, PEELED & DICED
1 SMALL ONION, PEELED & DICED

MIX MARINADE INGREDIENTS IN SMALL BOWL. ADD KIWI AND ONION. STIR AND LET STAND AT ROOM TEMPERATURE FOR AT LEAST 1 HOUR. REFRIGERATE UNTIL READY TO SERVE. MAKES 2 CUPS (500 mL).

REMEMBER THE GOOD OLD DAYS WHEN IT COST MORE TO RUN A CAR THAN TO PARK IT?

# PICKLED ONIONS

GREAT WITH ROAST BEEF SANDWICHES. SERVES A CROWD.

| | |
|---|---|
| 4 LARGE YELLOW ONIONS, THINLY SLICED | |
| 1½ CUPS WHITE VINEGAR | 375 mL |
| 1½ CUPS WATER | 375 mL |
| 1 CUP WHITE SUGAR | 250 mL |
| ¼ CUP FRESH LEMON JUICE | 60 mL |
| ¼ TSP. TABASCO SAUCE | 1 mL |
| 1 TSP. SALT | 5 mL |
| ½ TSP. SEASONED PEPPER | 2 mL |
| 2 GARLIC CLOVES, MINCED | |
| 1 CUP SOUR CREAM (FAT-FREE IS OKAY) | 250 mL |
| 1 TSP. CELERY SEED | 5 mL |

COMBINE ALL INGREDIENTS, EXCEPT SOUR CREAM AND CELERY SEED. MARINATE OVERNIGHT. BEFORE SERVING, DRAIN AND STIR IN SOUR CREAM AND CELERY SEED. PLACE IN A PRETTY BOWL - THERE'S NOTHING BEAUTIFUL ABOUT AN ONION!

IF CONVENIENCE STORES ARE OPEN 7 DAYS A WEEK, 365 DAYS A YEAR, WHY ARE THERE LOCKS ON THE DOORS?

# CRANBERRY PEAR CHUTNEY

THIS CHUTNEY IS PACKED WITH WONDERFUL FLAVORS.

| | | |
|---|---|---|
| 2 CUPS WATER | 500 mL | |
| 1 CUP RAISINS | 250 mL | |
| 2 CUPS SUGAR | 500 mL | |
| 2 TBSP. WHITE WINE VINEGAR | 30 mL | |
| 1 CUP ORANGE JUICE | 250 mL | |
| 2 TBSP. GRATED ORANGE ZEST | 30 mL | |
| 2 TBSP. SLIVERED FRESH GINGER | 30 mL | |
| 6 CUPS CRANBERRIES, FRESH OR FROZEN | 1.5 L | |
| 2 PEARS, PEELED, CORED, CHOPPED | | |
| 1 CUP TOASTED SLIVERED ALMONDS | 250 mL | |

BOIL WATER AND ADD RAISINS. REMOVE FROM HEAT AND LET STAND 20 MINUTES. DRAIN, RESERVING ½ CUP (125 mL) LIQUID. ADD SUGAR AND VINEGAR TO RAISIN WATER. HEAT IN SAUCEPAN UNTIL SUGAR DISSOLVES. INCREASE HEAT AND BOIL, WITHOUT STIRRING, UNTIL SYRUP TURNS GOLDEN BROWN, ABOUT 15 MINUTES. ADD ORANGE JUICE, ZEST, GINGER AND CRANBERRIES AND COOK ABOUT 10 MINUTES. STIR IN RAISINS, PEARS AND ALMONDS. POUR INTO STERILIZED JARS AND KEEP REFRIGERATED. MAKES ABOUT 6 CUPS (1.5 L).

IF ALL THE WORLD IS A STAGE, WHERE DOES THE AUDIENCE SIT?

# GREEN TOMATO RELISH

YOU MADE IT YOURSELF? - AREN'T YOU WONDERFUL DEAR!

| | |
|---|---|
| 7½ LBS. GREEN TOMATOES, THINLY SLICED | 3.25 kg |
| 5 GREEN PEPPERS, QUARTERED, SEEDED & SLICED | |
| 4 RED PEPPERS, QUARTERED, SEEDED & SLICED | |
| 4 LARGE ONIONS, HALVED & SLICED | |
| 1 CUP SALT | 250 mL |
| 4 CUPS VINEGAR | 1 L |
| 6 CUPS SUGAR | 1.5 kg |
| 1 TSP. CINNAMON | 5 mL |
| 1 TSP. GROUND CLOVES | 5 mL |
| 1 TBSP. TURMERIC | 15 mL |
| 2 TBSP. MIXED PICKLING SPICES | 30 mL |

PLACE SLICED TOMATOES, PEPPERS AND ONIONS IN A LARGE POT. COVER WITH SALT AND LET STAND OVERNIGHT. DRAIN AND RINSE WELL. RETURN TO POT AND ADD REMAINING INGREDIENTS. BRING TO A BOIL, REDUCE TO SIMMER AND COOK UNTIL DESIRED CONSISTENCY, APPROXIMATELY 30 MINUTES. PUT IN STERILIZED PINT (500 mL) JARS AND SEAL. DELICIOUS SERVED WITH EVERYTHING! MAKES APPROXIMATELY 12 PINT (500 mL) JARS.

WHAT WAS THE BEST THING BEFORE SLICED BREAD?

# B.L.'S BEST MUSTARD PICKLES

2 BUNCHES CELERY
3 LARGE CUCUMBERS
6 LARGE ONIONS
1 LARGE CAULIFLOWER
12 MEDIUM GREEN TOMATOES
2 RED PEPPERS
½ CUP PICKLING SALT — 125 mL

## MUSTARD DRESSING

| | |
|---|---|
| 8 CUPS WHITE SUGAR | 2 L |
| ⅔ CUP DRY MUSTARD | 150 mL |
| 1 TBSP. TURMERIC | 15 mL |
| 2 TBSP. CELERY SALT | 30 mL |
| 2 TBSP. CURRY POWDER | 30 mL |
| 1 CUP FLOUR | 250 mL |
| 2 CUPS MALT VINEGAR | 500 mL |
| 4 CUPS WHITE VINEGAR | 1 L |

CHOP ALL VEGETABLES AND MIX IN A LARGE POT
OR ROASTER. COVER WITH PICKLING SALT AND
LET STAND 1 HOUR. DRAIN OFF 2 CUPS (500 mL)
OF LIQUID. MIX DRY INGREDIENTS TOGETHER IN A
SAUCEPAN. ADD VINEGARS AND BOIL GENTLY
UNTIL THICKENED. POUR OVER VEGETABLES. COOK
FOR 10 MINUTES. COOL ANOTHER 10 MINUTES. POUR
INTO STERILIZED JARS. MAKES APPROXIMATELY
10-12 PINT (500 mL) JARS.

THE TROUBLE WITH CLASS REUNIONS IS THAT OLD
FLAMES HAVE BECOME EVEN OLDER.

# APPETIZERS

Antipasto
Year-Round Spinach Dip
Sun-Dried Tomato Dip
Hummus
Pesto Torte
Charred Pepper & Feta Dip
Layered Crab Dip
Mexicana Antipasto
Zippy Crab and Artichoke Dip
Brandy Cheese Spread
Ruth's Chokes
Hot Artichoke Dip
Artichoke Nibblers
Hot Cheese Spread
Brandy-Nut Brie
Brie with Sun-Dried Tomatoes
Cocktail Crisps
Asparagus Roll-Ups
French Blankets
Pasadena Pinwheels
Smoked Salmon Quesadillas
Stacked Pizza
Curried Chicken Triangles
Samosas in Phyllo
Chicken Satay with Spicy Peanut Dipping Sauce
Buffalo Chicken Wings
Hot 'N' Spicy Wings
Jelly Balls
Shrimp 'N' Beer

# ANTIPASTO

A DELICIOUS APPETIZER TO SERVE DURING THE FESTIVE SEASON. A GREAT GIFT TO ADD TO A CHRISTMAS BASKET. IT'S A LOT OF CHOPPING BUT DON'T USE A FOOD PROCESSOR!!

| | |
|---|---|
| 1 CUP OLIVE OIL | 250 mL |
| 1 LARGE CAULIFLOWER, CUT INTO BITE-SIZED PIECES | |
| 2 LARGE GREEN PEPPERS, CHOPPED | |
| 2-10½ OZ. CANS SLICED RIPE OLIVES, CHOPPED | 2-294 mL |
| 16 OZ. JAR GREEN OLIVES WITH PIMIENTO, CHOPPED | 500 mL |
| 2-13 OZ. JARS PICKLED ONIONS, CHOPPED | 2-375 mL |
| 2-10 OZ. CANS MUSHROOM STEMS & PIECES | 2-284 mL |
| 48 OZ. JAR MIXED PICKLES, CHOPPED | 1.5 L |
| 2-48 OZ. BOTTLES KETCHUP | 2-1.5 L |
| 15 OZ. BOTTLE HOT KETCHUP | 450 mL |
| 2-2 OZ. CANS ANCHOVIES, CHOPPED (OPTIONAL) | 2-55 g |
| 3-4½ OZ. CANS SOLID TUNA, CHOPPED | 3-113 g |
| 3-4 OZ. CANS SMALL SHRIMP | 3-113 g |

DRAIN ALL JARS AND CANS. PUT ALL INGREDIENTS, EXCEPT THE FISH, INTO A LARGE DUTCH OVEN. BRING TO A BOIL THEN SIMMER FOR 20 MINUTES, STIRRING OFTEN. POUR BOILING WATER OVER ALL THE FISH TO RINSE. DRAIN AND ADD TO MIXTURE. GENTLY STIR AND SIMMER FOR ANOTHER 10 MINUTES. POUR INTO

## ANTIPASTO

CONTINUED FROM PAGE 46.

STERILIZED JARS USING NEW LIDS. PROCESS. SERVE WITH CRACKERS.

TO PROCESS: PLACE JARS ON RACK IN LARGE, DEEP POT. ADD WATER THREE QUARTERS OF THE WAY UP THE JARS. COVER AND BRING WATER TO BOIL. SIMMER FOR AT LEAST 20 MINUTES. LET COOL. LIDS WILL POP AS THEY COOL. TIGHTEN LIDS AND STORE IN COOL PLACE. MAKES 16-18, 8 OZ. (250 mL) JARS OF ANTIPASTO.

## YEAR-ROUND SPINACH DIP

| | |
|---|---|
| 1 CUP MAYONNAISE | 250 mL |
| 1 CUP SOUR CREAM | 250 mL |
| 10 OZ. PKG. FROZEN CHOPPED SPINACH | 283 g |
| (WELL SQUEEZED!) | |
| 8 OZ. CAN WATER CHESTNUTS, CHOPPED | 236 mL |
| 1½ OZ. KNORRS VEGETABLE SOUP MIX (1 PKG.) | 40 g |
| ½ CUP CHOPPED GREEN ONION | 125 mL |
| 1 ROUND LOAF OF BREAD, RYE, PUMPERNICKEL OR WHITE | |

COMBINE ALL INGREDIENTS, EXCEPT BREAD AND MIX WELL. CHILL SEVERAL HOURS OR OVERNIGHT. SERVE IN A HOLLOWED-OUT ROUND LOAF OF BREAD. CUT SCOOPED OUT BREAD INTO CUBES AND SERVE WITH DIP. YOU'LL NEED SOME CRACKERS TOO!

# SUN-DRIED TOMATO DIP

KEEP THESE INGREDIENTS ON HAND AND PRESTO - AN INSTANT APPETIZER!

| | |
|---|---|
| 8 OZ. LIGHT SPREADABLE CREAM CHEESE | 250 g |
| 2 TBSP. MAYONNAISE | 30 mL |
| 1 TSP. LEMON JUICE | 5 mL |
| 1/4 CUP FINELY CHOPPED SUN-DRIED TOMATOES (RECONSTITUTED IF DRIED) | 60 mL |
| 1/4 CUP FRESH BASIL, CHOPPED | 60 mL |
| 2 GARLIC CLOVES, MINCED | |

MIX CREAM CHEESE, MAYONNAISE AND LEMON JUICE TOGETHER IN A BOWL. ADD TOMATOES, BASIL AND GARLIC AND MIX WELL. LET SIT FOR AT LEAST 1 HOUR BEFORE SERVING. SERVE WITH CRACKERS OR BAGEL CHIPS.

LOGIC IS WHEN YOU COME TO THE CONCLUSION THAT EITHER YOU'RE GAINING WEIGHT OR THE HOLES IN YOUR BELT ARE HEALING UP.

Samosas in Phyllo, page 66

Shrimp 'N' Beer, page 72

# HUMMUS

A MIDDLE EASTERN DIP - YUMMUS MAKE.

| | |
|---|---|
| 3 GARLIC CLOVES, MINCED | |
| 19 OZ. CAN CHICK-PEAS (GARBANZO BEANS) DRAINED | 540 mL |
| ¼ CUP TAHINI (SESAME SEED PASTE)* | 60 mL |
| 3 TBSP. LEMON JUICE | 45 mL |
| 1 TBSP. VEGETABLE OIL | 15 mL |
| 2 TBSP. WATER OR CHICK-PEA LIQUID | 30 mL |
| 1 TSP. CUMIN | 5 mL |
| ½ TSP. SALT | 2 mL |

IN FOOD PROCESSOR (OR BLENDER) MINCE GARLIC. ADD CHICK-PEAS, TAHINI, LEMON JUICE, OIL, WATER, CUMIN AND SALT; PROCESS UNTIL SMOOTH. TASTE AND ADJUST SEASONING IF NECESSARY. TRANSFER TO SERVING BOWL. MAKES ABOUT 1½ CUPS (375 mL). SERVE WITH WARM PITA BREAD FOR DIPPING.

* IF YOU'RE OUT OF TAHINI - PEANUT BUTTER MAKES A GOOD SUBSTITUTE.

FOOD IS AN IMPORTANT PART OF A BALANCED DIET.

## PESTO TORTE

A GREAT MAKE-AHEAD FOR A CROWD!

| | | |
|---|---|---|
| 12 OZ. CREAM CHEESE, ROOM TEMPERATURE | 340 | g |
| 3 OZ. CHÈVRE (GOAT CHEESE) | 85 | g |
| ½ CUP PESTO | 125 | mL |
| 10 SUN-DRIED TOMATOES IN OIL, DRAINED & SLIVERED | | |
| ¼ CUP PINE NUTS | 60 | mL |
| FRESH BASIL FOR GARNISH | | |

LINE A SMALL BOWL WITH PLASTIC WRAP, LEAVING SOME OVERLAPPING THE EDGES. SET ASIDE. IN ANOTHER BOWL, BEAT CHEESES TOGETHER UNTIL VERY SMOOTH. SPREAD A LAYER OF CREAMED MIXTURE IN BOTTOM OF BOWL. TOP WITH A LAYER OF PESTO. SPREAD THIS WITH ANOTHER LAYER OF CHEESE MIXTURE, THEN TOP WITH SOME SUN-DRIED TOMATOES AND A SPRINKLING OF PINE NUTS. REPEAT LAYERS ENDING WITH CHEESE MIXTURE AND A FEW PINE NUTS. FOLD UP PLASTIC WRAP AROUND TORTE AND GENTLY PRESS TO COMPRESS LAYERS. REFRIGERATE UNTIL READY TO SERVE. UNWRAP TOP OF MOLD, LIFT OUT OF BOWL AND INVERT ONTO A PLATE. GARNISH WITH PINE NUTS AND FRESH BASIL. SERVE WITH CRACKERS OR BAGUETTE SLICES.

THE NICE THING ABOUT EGOTISTS IS THAT THEY DON'T TALK ABOUT OTHER PEOPLE.

# CHARRED PEPPER & FETA DIP

MAKE THIS THE DAY BEFORE YOU NEED IT!

| | | |
|---|---:|---|
| 3 LARGE RED PEPPERS | | |
| 6 OZ. FETA CHEESE | 170 | g |
| 2 TBSP. PINE NUTS | 30 | mL |
| 1 TBSP. OLIVE OIL | 15 | mL |

TO CHAR PEPPERS: CUT PEPPERS IN THIRDS AND REMOVE SEEDS. PLACE CUT-SIDE DOWN ON COOKIE SHEET. BROIL UNTIL SKINS ARE BLACKENED AND PUFFED. PUT PEPPERS IN A COVERED CASSEROLE AND LET STAND FOR 10 MINUTES TO STEAM. REMOVE AND PEEL. PLACE ALL INGREDIENTS IN FOOD PROCESSOR AND BLEND. REFRIGERATE UNTIL READY TO SERVE. SERVE WITH CRACKERS OR FRESH VEGETABLES.

# LAYERED CRAB DIP

LAST MINUTE COMPANY? NO PROBLEM!

| | | |
|---|---:|---|
| 8 OZ. CREAM CHEESE, SOFTENED | 250 | g |
| 1 TBSP. GRATED ONION | 15 | mL |
| 1 TBSP. WORCESTERSHIRE SAUCE | 15 | mL |
| 1½ TSP. LEMON JUICE | 7 | mL |
| ½ CUP CHILI OR COCKTAIL SAUCE | 125 | mL |
| 7 OZ. CAN CRAB MEAT | 198 | g |
| 2 TBSP. CHOPPED PARSLEY | 30 | mL |

MIX CHEESE, ONION, WORCESTERSHIRE SAUCE AND LEMON JUICE TOGETHER. SPREAD IN A SHALLOW SERVING DISH. SPREAD CHILI SAUCE OVER TOP. DRAIN AND RINSE CRAB AND SPREAD OVER CHILI SAUCE. SPRINKLE WITH PARSLEY. SERVE WITH ASSORTED CRACKERS.

# MEXICANA ANTIPASTO

BANDITOS STEAL FOR THIS!

| | |
|---|---|
| 8 OZ. CREAM CHEESE | 250 g |
| DASH GARLIC POWDER | |
| ½ CUP SOUR CREAM (FAT-FREE IS FINE) | 125 mL |
| 1 LARGE AVOCADO, MASHED | |
| ¼ TSP. LEMON JUICE | 1 mL |
| 1 TOMATO, FINELY CHOPPED | |
| 4 OZ. CAN GREEN CHILIES | 114 mL |
| 5 SLICES BACON, COOKED CRISP & DICED | |
| 3-4 GREEN ONIONS, CHOPPED | |
| ¼ CUP SLICED RIPE OLIVES | 60 mL |
| ¼ CUP SLICED STUFFED GREEN OLIVES | 60 mL |
| 8 OZ. BOTTLE TACO SAUCE (HOT) | 250 mL |
| 1 CUP GRATED CHEDDAR CHEESE | 250 mL |

COMBINE CHEESE, GARLIC AND SOUR CREAM AND USE AS THE FIRST LAYER IN A 9" (23 CM) PIE PLATE. COMBINE AVOCADO, LEMON JUICE, TOMATO AND GREEN CHILIES FOR THE SECOND LAYER. SPRINKLE ON BACON, GREEN ONION AND OLIVES. SPREAD TACO SAUCE OVER ALL AND SPRINKLE WITH GRATED CHEDDAR. REFRIGERATE. SERVE WITH CORN CHIPS OR TACO CHIPS. SERVES 10-12 - HOPEFULLY.

PATIENCE IS THE ABILITY TO LET YOUR LIGHT SHINE AFTER YOUR FUSE HAS BLOWN.

# ZIPPY CRAB AND ARTICHOKE DIP

| | | |
|---|---|---|
| 8 OZ. CREAM CHEESE, ROOM TEMPERATURE | 250 | g |
| 1/2 CUP MAYONNAISE | 125 | mL |
| SALT & PEPPER TO TASTE | | |
| 7 OZ. CAN CRABMEAT, WELL DRAINED | 198 | g |
| 6 OZ. JAR MARINATED ARTICHOKE HEARTS, DRAINED & CHOPPED | 170 | g |
| 1/4 CUP SLICED GREEN ONION | 60 | mL |
| 1/2 CUP DICED RED PEPPER | 125 | mL |
| 1/2 CUP DICED CELERY | 125 | mL |
| 1/4 CUP FINELY CHOPPED PARSLEY | 60 | mL |
| 1 TSP. LEMON JUICE | 5 | mL |
| 1 TSP. TABASCO | 5 | mL |

BEAT CREAM CHEESE IN LARGE BOWL UNTIL SMOOTH. ADD MAYONNAISE, BEAT UNTIL WELL BLENDED. FOLD IN ALL REMAINING INGREDIENTS. SERVE WITH CRACKERS OR TOASTED BAGUETTE SLICES.

# BRANDY CHEESE SPREAD

THE LONGER STORED - THE BETTER TASTING!

| | | |
|---|---|---|
| 1/2 CUP BUTTER, SOFTENED | 125 | mL |
| 3 CUPS GRATED CHEDDAR CHEESE | 750 | mL |
| 1 TBSP. SESAME SEEDS | 15 | mL |
| 2 TBSP. BRANDY | 30 | mL |

BLEND TOGETHER, COVER AND REFRIGERATE UNTIL 1/2 HOUR BEFORE SERVING. YUMMY ON CRACKERS! MAKES 2 CUPS (500 mL).

## RUTH'S CHOKES

QUICK AND EASY.

| | |
|---|---|
| 14 OZ. CAN ARTICHOKE HEARTS | 398 mL |
| 1/2 CUP MAYONNAISE | 125 mL |
| 1/2 CUP GRATED PARMESAN CHEESE | 125 mL |

PLACE ARTICHOKE HEARTS ON COOKIE SHEET. YOU MAY HAVE TO TRIM THEM SO THEY WILL STAND UP. MIX PARMESAN CHEESE IN MAYONNAISE AND TOP EACH ARTICHOKE WITH 1 TSP. (5 mL) OF MIXTURE. PUT UNDER BROILER FOR ABOUT 2 MINUTES, OR UNTIL TOP IS BROWNED. WATCH CONSTANTLY. SERVES 4-6.

NOTE: IF LARGE ARTICHOKES ARE USED, CUT IN HALF AND REST ON SIDES TO BROIL.

## HOT ARTICHOKE DIP

IF YOU LOVE IT - SERVES 1! OTHERWISE SERVES 6.

| | |
|---|---|
| 14 OZ. CAN ARTICHOKE HEARTS, DRAINED & CHOPPED | 398 mL |
| 1/2 CUP FRESHLY GRATED PARMESAN CHEESE | 125 mL |
| 1 CUP MAYONNAISE | 250 mL |
| 1 GARLIC CLOVE, MINCED | |
| DASH LEMON JUICE | |

MIX ALL INGREDIENTS. BAKE AT 350°F (180°C) FOR 10 MINUTES. SERVE WITH CRACKERS.

# ARTICHOKE NIBBLERS

| | | |
|---|---|---|
| 2-6 OZ. JARS MARINATED ARTICHOKE HEARTS | 2-170 | g |
| 1 SMALL ONION, FINELY CHOPPED | | |
| 1 GARLIC CLOVE, MINCED | | |
| 4 EGGS, BEATEN | | |
| 1/4 CUP FINE DRY BREAD CRUMBS | 60 | mL |
| 1/4 TSP. SALT | 1 | mL |
| 1/4 TSP. EACH PEPPER, OREGANO & TABASCO SAUCE | 1 | mL |
| 2 CUPS GRATED SHARP CHEDDAR CHEESE | 500 | mL |
| 4 OZ. JAR PIMIENTO | 115 | g |
| 2 TBSP. SNIPPED PARSLEY | 30 | mL |

DRAIN LIQUID FROM 1 JAR OF ARTICHOKE HEARTS AND DISCARD. DRAIN LIQUID FROM THE OTHER JAR INTO FRYING PAN. ADD ONION AND GARLIC AND SAUTÉ. CHOP ARTICHOKES INTO QUARTERS. COMBINE EGGS, CRUMBS, SALT, PEPPER, OREGANO AND TABASCO. STIR IN CHEESE, PIMIENTO AND ARTICHOKES. ADD ONION MIXTURE. POUR INTO 9" (23 cm) SQUARE BUTTERED BAKING DISH. SPRINKLE WITH PARSLEY AND BAKE AT 325°F (160°C) FOR 30 MINUTES, OR UNTIL LIGHTLY SET. CUT IN 1" (2.5 cm) SQUARES.

I'M APPROACHING THE AGE OF 40 FROM A LOT OF DIFFERENT DIRECTIONS - ESPECIALLY FROM THE MIDDLE AND THE BACK SIDE.

# HOT CHEESE SPREAD

| | |
|---|---:|
| 3 CUPS GRATED SHARP CHEESE | 750 mL |
| 1/2 CUP CHOPPED RIPE OLIVES | 125 mL |
| 1 MEDIUM ONION, CHOPPED | |
| 1 CUP MAYONNAISE | 250 mL |
| 1/2 TSP. CURRY POWDER | 2 mL |
| 1 SMALL GARLIC CLOVE, MINCED | |
| DASH OF PAPRIKA | |

MIX CHEESE, OLIVES AND ONION TOGETHER. ADD MAYONNAISE, CURRY POWDER, GARLIC AND PAPRIKA. SPOON INTO A JAR AND STORE IN REFRIGERATOR. TO SERVE, SPREAD ON SMALL RYE BREAD OR CRACKERS. HEAT UNDER BROILER UNTIL CHEESE MELTS.

# BRANDY-NUT BRIE

WHAT COULD BE EASIER?

| | |
|---|---:|
| 1/4 CUP BROWN SUGAR | 60 mL |
| 1/4 CUP PECANS OR CASHEWS, CHOPPED | 60 mL |
| 1 TBSP. BRANDY OR WHISKY | 15 mL |
| 7 1/2 OZ. ROUND BRIE CHEESE | 235 g |
| CRACKERS | |

GET READY . . . STIR TOGETHER SUGAR, NUTS AND BRANDY. SCORE THE TOP OF THE CHEESE AND PLACE ON AN OVENPROOF PLATTER. BAKE AT 400°F (200°C) FOR 4-5 MINUTES, UNTIL CHEESE IS SOFTENED. MOUND SUGAR MIXTURE OVER CHEESE AND BAKE 2-3 MINUTES MORE UNTIL SUGAR IS MELTED. SERVE WARM WITH CRACKERS.

# BRIE WITH SUN-DRIED TOMATOES

YOU CAN USE ANY SIZE ROUND OF BRIE - ADJUST THE INGREDIENTS TO FIT THE "ROUND".

| | | |
|---|---|---|
| 7½ OZ. ROUND BRIE CHEESE | 235 | g |
| 4 OZ. SUN-DRIED TOMATOES IN OIL, DRAINED & FINELY CHOPPED | 115 | g |
| 2-3 GARLIC CLOVES, MINCED | | |
| 2 TBSP. CHOPPED FRESH PARSLEY | 30 mL | |

SCORE THE TOP OF THE CHEESE. MIX TOMATOES AND GARLIC; PILE GENEROUSLY ON CHEESE. SPRINKLE WITH PARSLEY. (IT'S NOT NECESSARY TO REMOVE RIND FROM CHEESE.) HEAT IN A 350°F (180°C) OVEN UNTIL CHEESE BEGINS TO MELT. SERVE WITH BAGEL CHIPS OR CRACKERS.

# COCKTAIL CRISPS

OUR FAVORITE COCKTAIL COOKIE - FREEZES WELL.

| | | |
|---|---|---|
| 1 CUP BUTTER | 250 mL | |
| 8 OZ. PKG. IMPERIAL CHEESE (SHARP COLD PACK CHEDDAR CHEESE) | 250 | g |
| DASH OF SALT | | |
| ¼ TSP. CAYENNE PEPPER OR TABASCO | 1 mL | |
| ¼ TSP. WORCESTERSHIRE SAUCE | 1 mL | |
| 1½ CUPS FLOUR | 375 mL | |
| 4 CUPS RICE KRISPIES | 1 L | |

CREAM BUTTER AND CHEESE TOGETHER. ADD SEASONINGS. BEAT IN FLOUR THEN ADD RICE KRISPIES. MIX WELL. SHAPE INTO BALLS. PRESS DOWN WITH A FORK WHICH HAS BEEN DIPPED IN COLD WATER. BAKE AT 350°F (180°C) FOR 15-20 MINUTES, UNTIL LIGHTLY BROWNED. MAKES ABOUT 4 DOZEN.

# ASPARAGUS ROLL-UPS

A GREAT APPETIZER TO MAKE AHEAD AND FREEZE.

| | |
|---|---|
| 2 WHITE SANDWICH LOAVES | |
| 8 OZ. ROQUEFORT CHEESE | 250 g |
| 8 OZ. CREAM CHEESE | 250 g |
| 1 TBSP. MAYONNAISE | 15 mL |
| 1 EGG | |
| 36 FRESH ASPARAGUS SPEARS, SNAP OFF ENDS | |
| ½ CUP BUTTER, MELTED | 125 mL |

CUT CRUSTS OFF BREAD AND ROLL EACH SLICE FLAT WITH A ROLLING PIN. COMBINE CHEESES, MAYONNAISE AND EGG IN BLENDER AND SPREAD ON BREAD. TOP WITH 1 ASPARAGUS SPEAR AND ROLL UP. BRUSH WITH MELTED BUTTER, CUT INTO 3 PIECES AND PLACE ON UNGREASED COOKIE SHEET. (AT THIS POINT YOU MAY LAYER ROLLS BETWEEN WAXED PAPER AND PLACE IN AN AIRTIGHT CONTAINER AND FREEZE.) BAKE AT 350°F (180°C) FOR ABOUT 15 MINUTES, OR UNTIL LIGHTLY BROWNED. MAKES ABOUT 9 DOZEN.

HEAT MAKES OBJECTS EXPAND AND COLD MAKES THEM CONTRACT. THAT'S WHY THE DAYS ARE LONGER IN THE SUMMER AND SHORTER IN THE WINTER.

# FRENCH BLANKETS

A QUESADILLA WITH A FRENCH TWIST . . .
QUELLE SURPRISE!

DIJON MUSTARD
4-10" (25 cm) FLOUR TORTILLAS
6 OZ. BRIE CHEESE, RIND REMOVED,          170 g
     ROOM TEMPERATURE
1 BUNCH FRESH SPINACH LEAVES, STEMS
     REMOVED
OLIVE OIL

## AIOLI *

½ CUP MAYONNAISE                          125 mL
1 GARLIC CLOVE, MINCED
1 TSP. LEMON JUICE                        5 mL

SPREAD A THIN LAYER OF DIJON ON 1 TORTILLA.
SPREAD BRIE ON SECOND TORTILLA THEN TOP
WITH FRESH SPINACH LEAVES. PUT THE
2 TORTILLAS TOGETHER LIKE A SANDWICH. HEAT
OLIVE OIL ON MEDIUM-LOW IN LARGE FRYING PAN
AND BROWN TORTILLAS LIGHTLY ON BOTH SIDES
UNTIL CHEESE MELTS.

TO MAKE AIOLI: BLEND INGREDIENTS TOGETHER.

TO SERVE, CUT TORTILLAS INTO WEDGES AND
SERVE WARM WITH AIOLI DIP.

* AIOLI IS THE SALSA OF SOUTHERN FRANCE. IN
PROVENCE IT'S USED AS A SAUCE FOR
VEGETABLES, MEAT AND FISH.

# PASADENA PINWHEELS

FAST 'N' EASY!

| | |
|---|---|
| 8 OZ. CREAM CHEESE | 250 g |
| 2 TBSP. MAYONNAISE | 30 mL |
| 4 OZ. CAN DICED GREEN CHILIES, DRAINED | 114 mL |
| 1 LARGE TOMATO, SEEDED & CHOPPED | |
| ¼ CUP FINELY CHOPPED ONION | 60 mL |
| 1 LARGE GARLIC CLOVE, MINCED | |
| 1 TSP. CHILI POWDER | 5 mL |
| ½ TSP. SALT | 2 mL |
| FLOUR TORTILLAS | |

BLEND CREAM CHEESE AND MAYONNAISE. STIR IN REMAINING INGREDIENTS. COVER AND REFRIGERATE FOR 2 HOURS. SPREAD CHEESE MIXTURE OVER EACH TORTILLA AND ROLL UP TIGHTLY. TRIM ENDS. REFRIGERATE UNTIL FIRM. SLICE AND PLACE PINWHEELS FLAT ON COOKIE SHEET. BROIL UNTIL LIGHTLY GOLDEN.

THE CREAM CHEESE MIXTURE IS ALSO A TASTY DIP TO SERVE WITH TACO OR CORN CHIPS.

I GOLF IN THE LOW 80'S. IF IT'S ANY HOTTER THAN THAT, I WON'T PLAY.

# SMOKED SALMON QUESADILLAS

1 ANAHEIM PEPPER, CHARRED, PEELED
  & CUT INTO STRIPS
1 RED BELL PEPPER, CHARRED, PEELED
  & CUT INTO STRIPS
1/4 CUP CHÈVRE (GOAT CHEESE)                    60 mL
1/4 CUP CREAM CHEESE, ROOM                      60 mL
  TEMPERATURE
3-8" (20 cm) FLOUR TORTILLAS
1 AVOCADO, PEELED, PITTED & CUT INTO
  THIN SLICES
1/4 CUP MINCED SHALLOTS                         60 mL
2 OZ. SMOKED SALMON, CUT INTO STRIPS       60  g

TO CHAR PEPPERS: PLEASE REFER TO
"CHARRED PEPPER AND FETA DIP" ON PAGE 53.

IN A SMALL BOWL, MIX TOGETHER THE CHÈVRE
AND CREAM CHEESE UNTIL SMOOTH AND
CREAMY. SPREAD ONE-THIRD OF THE MIXTURE
OVER HALF OF EACH TORTILLA. DIVIDE THE
PEPPER STRIPS EVENLY OVER THE 3 HALVES OF
THE TORTILLAS. LAYER THE AVOCADO SLICES OVER
THE PEPPER STRIPS AND TOP WITH THE
CHOPPED SHALLOTS. DIVIDE THE SALMON EVENLY
ON THE TORTILLA HALVES. FOLD THE TORTILLAS
OVER, PRESSING TO SEAL. HEAT A NONSTICK PAN
OVER MEDIUM HEAT AND BROWN THE FOLDED
TORTILLAS UNTIL THE CHEESE MELTS. TURN OVER
AND BROWN ON THE OTHER SIDE. CUT EACH
QUESADILLA INTO 4 WEDGES AND SERVE
IMMEDIATELY.

# STACKED PIZZA

FOR ADULTS ONLY.

7 SHEETS PHYLLO PASTRY
½ CUP BUTTER, MELTED — 125 mL
½ CUP FRESHLY GRATED PARMESAN — 125 mL
    CHEESE
1½ CUPS GRATED MOZZARELLA CHEESE — 375 mL
1 ONION, THINLY SLICED
5-6 ROMA TOMATOES, THINLY SLICED
1 TSP. OREGANO — 5 mL
SALT & PEPPER TO TASTE
FRESH HERB SPRIGS: THYME, OREGANO,
    ROSEMARY

PREHEAT OVEN TO 375°F (190°C). THAW AND PREPARE PHYLLO FOLLOWING PACKAGE INSTRUCTIONS. BE SURE TO COVER EXTRA PHYLLO WITH A DAMP TOWEL WHILE BUILDING PIZZA. PLACE FIRST SHEET OF PHYLLO ON BAKING SHEET, BRUSH WITH BUTTER AND SPRINKLE WITH 1 TBSP. (15 ML) PARMESAN CHEESE. REPEAT UNTIL ALL SHEETS ARE USED. PRESS FIRMLY SO LAYERS WILL STICK TOGETHER. SPRINKLE TOP SHEET WITH MOZZARELLA AND ONIONS. ARRANGE TOMATO SLICES ON TOP. SEASON WITH OREGANO, SALT AND PEPPER. BAKE FOR 20-25 MINUTES, UNTIL EDGES ARE GOLDEN. DECORATE WITH HERBS AND CUT INTO SQUARES.

NOTE: OLIVES, ANCHOVIES, PEPPERS CAN ALSO BE USED - BUT DON'T OVERLOAD AS THIS IS A DELICATE CRUST!

# CURRIED CHICKEN TRIANGLES

| | |
|---|---|
| 2 TSP. BUTTER OR MARGARINE | 10 mL |
| 1/2 MEDIUM ONION, FINELY CHOPPED | |
| 1/2 CUP FINELY CHOPPED CELERY | 125 mL |
| 1 TBSP. FLOUR | 15 mL |
| 1 1/2 TSP. CURRY POWDER | 7 mL |
| 1/4 TSP. SALT | 1 mL |
| 1/2 CUP CHICKEN BROTH | 125 mL |
| 1 1/2 CUPS DICED COOKED CHICKEN | 375 mL |
| 1/4 CUP FAT-FREE SOUR CREAM | 60 mL |
| 1/4 CUP SKIM-MILK PLAIN YOGURT | 60 mL |
| PHYLLO PASTRY, THAWED (ABOUT 1/3 OF PKG.) | |
| 1/4 CUP MELTED BUTTER | 60 mL |

MELT BUTTER IN SAUCEPAN. ADD ONION AND CELERY; COOK UNTIL SOFT. ADD FLOUR, CURRY POWDER AND SALT. STIR FOR 1 MINUTE. ADD CHICKEN BROTH; SIMMER FOR 2 MINUTES. REMOVE FROM HEAT; ADD CHICKEN, SOUR CREAM AND YOGURT. TO MAKE TRIANGLES, UNROLL PHYLLO AND LAY FLAT. CUT A 2" (5 cm) WIDE STRIP. COVER REMAINING PHYLLO WITH A DAMP CLOTH. BRUSH THE STRIP WITH BUTTER. PLACE 1 TSP. (5 mL) OF FILLING IN BOTTOM CORNER OF STRIP AND FOLD CORNER TO CORNER (FLAG FASHION) USING ENTIRE STRIP. FILLING SHOULD BE SEALED IN. CONTINUE UNTIL ALL FILLING IS USED. BRUSH TRIANGLES WITH BUTTER; BAKE AT 350°F (180°C) FOR 20-25 MINUTES. MAKES ABOUT 50.

TO FREEZE: BEFORE BAKING, FREEZE ON BAKING SHEET THEN PLACE FROZEN TRIANGLES IN PLASTIC BAGS. NO NEED TO THAW BEFORE COOKING.

# SAMOSAS IN PHYLLO

THESE LOW-FAT APPETIZERS FREEZE WELL.
NOW YOU'RE READY FOR LAST-MINUTE GUESTS!

FILLING:

| | |
|---|---|
| 1 CUP PEELED & FINELY CHOPPED POTATOES | 250 mL |
| 1 TSP. VEGETABLE OIL | 5 mL |
| 1 ONION, FINELY CHOPPED | |
| 2 TSP. CURRY POWDER | 10 mL |
| 2 TSP. CUMIN | 10 mL |
| 1 TSP. TURMERIC | 5 mL |
| 1/4 TSP. SALT | 1 mL |
| PINCH CAYENNE PEPPER | |
| 1/2 LB. LEAN GROUND BEEF | 250 g |
| 1/2 CUP SMALL FROZEN PEAS | 125 mL |
| 3 TBSP. BEEF BROTH | 45 mL |
| 1 TBSP. CURRANTS | 15 mL |
| 1 TBSP. LEMON JUICE | 15 mL |
| 2 TSP. LIQUID HONEY | 10 mL |
| | |
| 9 SHEETS PHYLLO PASTRY | |
| 1/4 CUP BUTTER, MELTED | 60 mL |

TO MAKE FILLING: COOK POTATOES IN BOILING
WATER UNTIL TENDER BUT STILL FIRM; DRAIN
AND SET ASIDE. IN NONSTICK PAN, HEAT OIL
OVER MEDIUM HEAT AND COOK ONION, STIRRING,
UNTIL SOFTENED. STIR IN CURRY POWDER, CUMIN,
TURMERIC, SALT AND CAYENNE. STIR AND COOK
FOR 2 MINUTES. ADD BEEF, BREAKING UP INTO
SMALL PIECES; COOK UNTIL NO LONGER PINK.
STIR IN POTATOES, PEAS, BEEF BROTH,
CURRANTS, LEMON JUICE AND HONEY. COOK,

# SAMOSAS IN PHYLLO

CONTINUED FROM PAGE 66.

GENTLY STIRRING, UNTIL PEAS ARE THAWED. COOL. PLACE 1 SHEET OF PHYLLO ON WORK SURFACE (KEEP A SLIGHTLY DAMP CLEAN CLOTH OVER THE OTHER SHEETS SO THEY WILL NOT DRY OUT.) LIGHTLY BRUSH PHYLLO WITH SOME OF THE BUTTER. USING A SHARP KNIFE, CUT THE PHYLLO INTO 4, 3" (8 cm) WIDE STRIPS. SPOON 1 TBSP. (15 mL) FILLING ONTO PHYLLO ABOUT 1" (2.5 cm) FROM BOTTOM ON THE RIGHT SIDE. FOLD THE LEFT SIDE OVER FILLING AND CONTINUE FOLDING IN A TRIANGULAR SHAPE (FLAG-FASHION) TO THE END OF THE STRIP. PRESS EDGES TOGETHER AND PLACE ON BAKING SHEET. REPEAT WITH REMAINING STRIPS. BRUSH TOPS LIGHTLY WITH BUTTER. (THESE MAY BE FROZEN ON A COOKIE SHEET AND STORED IN A FREEZER BAG.) DO NOT THAW. BAKE AT 375°F (190°C) FOR 20 MINUTES, OR UNTIL SAMOSAS ARE GOLDEN. MAKES 36 APPETIZERS.

SERVE WITH CORIANDER CHUTNEY OR A HOT MANGO CHUTNEY OR GINGER PICKLE RELISH - ALL AVAILABLE AT LARGE GROCERIES OR EASTERN SPECIALTY STORES - EXPERIMENT! (PICTURED ON PAGE 49.)

NEVER LEND YOUR CAR TO ANYONE TO WHOM YOU HAVE GIVEN BIRTH - ERMA BOMBECK

# CHICKEN SATAY WITH SPICY PEANUT DIPPING SAUCE

2 WHOLE BONELESS SKINLESS CHICKEN BREASTS
12 SMALL WOODEN SKEWERS, SOAKED IN WATER

### GARLIC SOY MARINADE

| | |
|---|---|
| 2 GARLIC CLOVES, MINCED | |
| ¼ CUP SOY SAUCE | 60 mL |
| ¼ CUP LEMON JUICE | 60 mL |
| 2 TBSP. OIL | 30 mL |

### SPICY PEANUT DIPPING SAUCE

| | |
|---|---|
| ½ CUP CHUNKY PEANUT BUTTER | 125 mL |
| ½ CUP COCONUT MILK (LIGHT IS AVAILABLE) | 125 mL |
| 2 TBSP. SWEET HOT CHILE SAUCE | 30 mL |
| 2 TBSP. SOY SAUCE | 30 mL |
| 1 CLOVE GARLIC, MINCED | |
| ½ TSP. CUMIN | 2 mL |

CUT CHICKEN IN ½" (1.3 cm) CUBES AND THREAD 4-5 PIECES ONTO EACH SKEWER. COMBINE MARINADE INGREDIENTS; POUR OVER SKEWERED CHICKEN AND MARINATE FOR 1 HOUR. TO SERVE, GRILL OR BROIL UNTIL BROWN, TURN AS NEEDED.

TO PREPARE SAUCE: COMBINE ALL INGREDIENTS IN A SMALL SAUCEPAN. BRING TO A BOIL; SIMMER 10 MINUTES, STIRRING FREQUENTLY. IF SAUCE BECOMES TOO THICK, ADD MORE COCONUT MILK.

TO SERVE, ARRANGE SKEWERED CHICKEN ON A PLATTER AROUND A BOWL OF PEANUT SAUCE FOR DIPPING. SERVES 4-6.

# BUFFALO CHICKEN WINGS

HOT STUFF! PURISTS SAY YOU MUST SERVE WITH CELERY STICKS AND BLUE CHEESE DRESSING - SO DO IT!

CELERY STICKS, CUT IN STRIPS, STORE IN ICE WATER IN REFRIGERATOR

## BLUE CHEESE DRESSING

| | |
|---|---|
| 1 OZ. BLUE CHEESE, CRUMBLED | 30 g |
| 1/4 CUP MAYONNAISE (NOT MIRACLE WHIP) | 60 mL |
| 1/4 CUP SOUR CREAM OR YOGURT (FAT-FREE IS FINE) | 60 mL |

## WINGS

| | |
|---|---|
| 1/4 CUP BUTTER | 60 mL |
| 3-5 TBSP. HOT RED PEPPER SAUCE | 45-75 mL |
| 1 1/2 TBSP. RED WINE VINEGAR | 22 mL |
| OIL FOR DEEP-FRYING | |
| 2 1/2 LBS. CHICKEN WINGS, TIPS REMOVED, CUT IN 2 | 1.25 kg |

PREPARE CELERY STICKS.

TO PREPARE DRESSING: MIX INGREDIENTS IN FOOD PROCESSOR AND CHILL UNTIL SERVING TIME.

TO PREPARE WINGS: MELT BUTTER IN LARGE SAUCEPAN. STIR IN HOT SAUCE, 3 TBSP. (45 mL) IS RELATIVELY MILD, AND VINEGAR. SET ASIDE. HEAT OIL IN A LARGE HEAVY FRYING PAN OR WOK (HEAT UNTIL A PIECE OF POTATO CRISPS QUICKLY). ADD WINGS A FEW AT A TIME, COOK ABOUT 10 MINUTES, OR UNTIL BROWN AND CRISP. REMOVE TO A PAPER TOWEL TO DRAIN. WHEN ALL WINGS ARE COOKED, REHEAT HOT SAUCE AND TOSS WITH WINGS TO COAT. SERVES 6-8.

# HOT 'N' SPICY WINGS

GET OUT THE FINGER BOWLS FOR EVERYONE'S FAVORITE.

| | |
|---|---|
| 3 LBS. CHICKEN WINGS, CUT IN 2, TIPS REMOVED | 1.5 kg |
| 1/2 CUP KETCHUP (TRY "HOT" - IF YOU'RE NOT CHICKEN) | 125 mL |
| 1/4 CUP WATER | 60 mL |
| 1/4 CUP HONEY | 60 mL |
| 1/4 CUP RED WINE VINEGAR | 60 mL |
| 2 TBSP. BROWN SUGAR | 30 mL |
| 1 TBSP. DIJON MUSTARD | 15 mL |
| 1 TBSP. WORCESTERSHIRE SAUCE | 15 mL |
| 1 TBSP. SOY SAUCE | 15 mL |
| 2 TBSP. HOT PEPPER SAUCE | 30 mL |
| 2 GARLIC CLOVES, MINCED | |
| 2 TBSP. DRIED MINCED ONIONS | 30 mL |

COVER A BROILER PAN WITH FOIL. POKE HOLES IN FOIL. ARRANGE WINGS IN SINGLE LAYER. PLACE UNDER BROILER UNTIL LIGHTLY BROWNED. IN A SAUCEPAN, COMBINE ALL REMAINING INGREDIENTS AND BRING TO A BOIL; REDUCE HEAT AND SIMMER FOR 5-10 MINUTES. USING TONGS, DIP EACH WING IN HOT SAUCE AND PLACE ON BAKING SHEET; BAKE AT 375°F (190°C) FOR 35-40 MINUTES. BASTE WITH REMAINING SAUCE DURING BAKING. DURING THE LAST FEW MINUTES, TURN ON BROILER AND CRISP WINGS. SERVES 6-8.

WHY IS THERE AN EXPIRATION DATE ON SOUR CREAM?

# JELLY BALLS

RALLY 'ROUND THE CHAFING DISH!

| | |
|---|---|
| 1 LB. LEAN GROUND BEEF | 500 g |
| 1 EGG, BEATEN | |
| ½ CUP FINE BREAD CRUMBS | 125 mL |
| 3 TBSP. CHOPPED PARSLEY | 45 mL |
| ½ CUP CHOPPED ONION | 125 mL |
| 1 TSP. WORCESTERSHIRE SAUCE | 5 mL |
| SALT & PEPPER TO TASTE | |

CHILI GRAPE SAUCE:*

| | |
|---|---|
| 12 OZ. BOTTLE CHILI SAUCE | 341 mL |
| 10 OZ. JAR GRAPE JELLY | 284 mL |
| 1 TSP. LEMON JUICE | 5 mL |
| 2 TBSP. BROWN SUGAR | 30 mL |
| 1 TBSP. SOY SAUCE | 15 mL |

MIX GROUND BEEF WITH EGG, BREAD CRUMBS, PARSLEY, ONION, WORCESTERSHIRE SAUCE, SALT AND PEPPER. ROLL INTO BALLS 1" (2.5 cm) IN DIAMETER. HEAT CHILI SAUCE, JELLY, LEMON JUICE, BROWN SUGAR, AND SOY SAUCE IN A LARGE POT. BRING TO A BOIL AND ADD UNCOOKED MEATBALLS. SIMMER MEATBALLS IN SAUCE FOR 30 MINUTES. SERVE IN A CHAFING DISH. (AVEC TOOTHPICKS!) MAKES ABOUT 50 BALLS. FREEZES WELL.

* BELIEVE IT OR NOT - THIS SAUCE IS FANTASTIC. THE FLAVOR COMBINATION IS GREAT!

# SHRIMP 'N' BEER

## SHRIMP

| | |
|---|---|
| 3 LBS. SHRIMP IN THE SHELL | 1.5 kg |
| 4 GARLIC CLOVES, PEELED | |
| 6 ALLSPICE BERRIES | |
| 1 TBSP. RED PEPPER FLAKES | 15 mL |
| 1 BAY LEAF | |
| 6 SPRIGS FRESH PARSLEY | |
| 2 SPRIGS FRESH DILL | |
| 12 OZ. BEER | 341 mL |
| SALT & PEPPER TO TASTE | |

## LEMON BUTTER DIPPING SAUCE

| | |
|---|---|
| ½ CUP BUTTER | 250 mL |
| JUICE OF ½ LEMON | |
| 1 TSP. WORCESTERSHIRE SAUCE | 5 mL |
| SALT & PEPPER TO TASTE | |

TO COOK SHRIMP: COMBINE ALL INGREDIENTS IN LARGE POT AND COVER. BRING TO A BOIL. TURN DOWN HEAT AND LET THE SHRIMP SIMMER 2 MINUTES. (DON'T OVERCOOK!) THEN REMOVE FROM HEAT AND DRAIN.

TO PREPARE SAUCE: HEAT BUTTER IN A SAUCEPAN UNTIL ALMOST BUBBLING. STIR IN LEMON JUICE AND WORCESTERSHIRE, SALT AND PEPPER TO TASTE.

SERVE SHRIMP HOT, IN THE SHELL. SPREAD OUT THE NEWSPAPER ON YOUR PATIO TABLE AND LET YOUR GUESTS "PEEL 'N' EAT". SERVE SAUCE INDIVIDUALLY TO 8 HAPPY GUESTS. (PICTURED ON PAGE 50.)

# SALADS

Arizona Fruit Salad
Romaine with Oranges and Pecans
Papaya Avocado Salad
Committee Salad
Marinated Artichoke and Mushroom Salad
Caesar Salad
Strawberry and Chèvre Salad
Spinach and Strawberry Salad
Fresh Spinach Salad
Christmas Salad
Layered Southwest Salad
Santa Fe Salad
Beet, Red Onion & Orange Salad
Broccoli Mandarin Salad
Greek Salad
Regina Beach Coleslaw
Killer Coleslaw
Spicy Noodle Salad
Orzo with Veggies
Fresh Orange Pasta Salad
Fiesta Chicken Tortilla Salad
Korean Chicken Salad
Layered Chicken Salad

# DRESSINGS

Balsamic Vinaigrette
Roasted Garlic Caesar Dressing
Tarragon Mustard Dressing
Italian Dressing

# ARIZONA FRUIT SALAD

GREAT WITH MEXICAN FARE.

## SALAD

| | |
|---|---|
| 1 AVOCADO | |
| 2 TBSP. LIME JUICE | 30 mL |
| 1 PAPAYA | |
| 2 ORANGES | |
| 1 GRAPEFRUIT | |
| 1 SMALL RED ONION | |
| ½ POMEGRANATE (OPTIONAL) | |

## DRESSING

| | |
|---|---|
| 2 TBSP. ORANGE JUICE | 30 mL |
| 2 TBSP. LIME JUICE | 30 mL |
| 2 TSP. LIQUID HONEY | 10 mL |
| ¼ TSP. HOT PEPPER FLAKES | 1 mL |
| ½ CUP VEGETABLE OIL | 125 mL |

1 HEAD ROMAINE LETTUCE

TO MAKE SALAD: PEEL AND SLICE AVOCADO. SPRINKLE WITH 1 TBSP. (15 mL) LIME JUICE. PEEL, SEED AND SLICE PAPAYA THINLY. SPRINKLE WITH REMAINING LIME JUICE. PEEL ORANGES AND GRAPEFRUIT. CUT FRUIT INTO SEGMENTS. SLICE RED ONION. IN A LARGE BOWL, COMBINE AVOCADO, PAPAYA, ORANGE AND GRAPEFRUIT SEGMENTS AND ONION. SET ASIDE. IF USING POMEGRANATE, SCOOP OUT SEEDS AND SET ASIDE.

TO MAKE DRESSING: WHISK TOGETHER ORANGE JUICE, LIME JUICE, HONEY, PEPPER FLAKES AND OIL.

## ARIZONA FRUIT SALAD

THIS RECIPE CONTINUED FROM PAGE 74.

BEFORE SERVING, POUR DRESSING OVER FRUIT AND TOSS WELL. SPOON ONTO LETTUCE-LINED PLATTER. SPRINKLE POMEGRANATE SEEDS OVER ALL. DELICIOUS WITH OUR CHICKEN ENCHILADA CASSEROLE (PAGE 209).

## ROMAINE WITH ORANGES AND PECANS

A REAL FAVORITE!

| | |
|---|---|
| 2 HEADS ROMAINE LETTUCE (WASH AND TEAR INTO BITE-SIZED PIECES | |
| 1 CUP PECANS HALVES, TOASTED | 250 mL |
| 2 ORANGES, PEELED & SLICED | |

### DRESSING

| | |
|---|---|
| 1/4 CUP VINEGAR | 60 mL |
| 1/2 CUP VEGETABLE OIL | 125 mL |
| 1/4 CUP SUGAR | 60 mL |
| 1 TSP. SALT | 5 mL |
| 1/2 SMALL RED ONION, CHOPPED | |
| 1 TSP. DRY MUSTARD | 5 mL |
| 2 TBSP. WATER | 30 mL |

PLACE LETTUCE, PECANS AND ORANGES IN SALAD BOWL. COMBINE DRESSING INGREDIENTS IN BLENDER. BLEND UNTIL WELL MIXED. MAKE AHEAD AND REFRIGERATE UNTIL READY TO TOSS SALAD. USE EXTRA DRESSING AS A DIP FOR FRESH FRUIT! SERVES 6-8.

# PAPAYA AVOCADO SALAD

1 HEAD OF ROMAINE LETTUCE
1 RIPE PAPAYA (PAPAYAS ARE RIPE
    WHEN THEY HAVE TURNED YELLOW)
1 LARGE AVOCADO, PEELED & SLICED
RED ONION SLICES

## PAPAYA SEED DRESSING

| | |
|---|---:|
| ¼-½ CUP SUGAR | 60-125 mL |
| ½ TSP. DRY MUSTARD | 2 mL |
| 2 TSP. SALT | 10 mL |
| 2 TBSP. PAPAYA SEEDS | 30 mL |
| ½ CUP WHITE WINE VINEGAR OR | 125 mL |
|     TARRAGON VINEGAR | |
| ½ CUP SALAD OIL | 125 mL |
| 2 GREEN ONIONS, FINELY CHOPPED | |

WASH AND DRY LETTUCE. TEAR INTO BITE-SIZED
PIECES AND PLACE IN SALAD BOWL. HALVE AND
PEEL PAPAYA. SCOOP OUT SEEDS AND SAVE
2 TBSP. (30 mL). SLICE PAPAYA. COMBINE
DRESSING INGREDIENTS IN A BLENDER UNTIL
PAPAYA SEEDS HAVE THE APPEARANCE OF
GROUND PEPPER. STORE DRESSING IN
REFRIGERATOR. JUST BEFORE SERVING, ADD
PAPAYA, AVOCADO AND RED ONION SLICES TO
LETTUCE. POUR DRESSING OVER SALAD AND TOSS.
(YOU MIGHT HAVE SOME DRESSING LEFT OVER,
BUT YOU'RE GOING TO WANT TO MAKE THIS SALAD
AGAIN - SOON!) SERVES 6-8. (PICTURED ON
PAGE 84.)

# COMMITTEE SALAD

*WE ALL WORKED ON IT AND WE ALL LOVE IT.*

## DRESSING

| | |
|---|---|
| ½ CUP OIL | 125 mL |
| 3 TBSP. RED WINE VINEGAR | 45 mL |
| 1 TBSP. LEMON JUICE | 15 mL |
| 2 TSP. SUGAR | 10 mL |
| ½ TSP. SALT | 2 mL |
| ½ TSP. DRY MUSTARD | 2 mL |
| 1 GARLIC CLOVE, CRUSHED | |

## SALAD

| | |
|---|---|
| 2 TBSP. BUTTER | 30 mL |
| ½ CUP SUNFLOWER SEEDS, SHELLED | 125 mL |
| ½ CUP SLIVERED ALMONDS | 125 mL |
| 1 HEAD LEAF LETTUCE | |
| 2 GREEN ONIONS, FINELY CHOPPED | |
| 10 OZ. CAN MANDARIN ORANGES, DRAINED | 284 mL |
| 1 RIPE AVOCADO, PEELED & SLICED | |

COMBINE ALL DRESSING INGREDIENTS IN A JAR; SHAKE TO BLEND. HEAT BUTTER IN FRYING PAN AND SAUTÉ SUNFLOWER SEEDS AND ALMONDS UNTIL GOLDEN BROWN. PREPARE REMAINING INGREDIENTS. ADD COOLED SEEDS AND ALMONDS. TOSS WITH DRESSING JUST BEFORE SERVING. SERVES 6.

*THE TROUBLE WITH OPERA IS THERE'S TOO MUCH SINGING.*

# MARINATED ARTICHOKE AND MUSHROOM SALAD

## MARINADE

| | |
|---|---|
| ½ CUP TARRAGON VINEGAR | 12 mL |
| 2 TBSP. WATER | 30 mL |
| 1 TBSP. SUGAR | 15 mL |
| 1½ TSP. SALT | 7 mL |
| DASH OF PEPPER | |
| 1 GARLIC CLOVE, MINCED | |
| ½ CUP SALAD OIL | 125 mL |

## SALAD

| | |
|---|---|
| 14 OZ. CAN ARTICHOKE HEARTS, DRAINED | 398 mL |
| 1 CUP SLICED FRESH MUSHROOMS | 250 mL |
| 1 MEDIUM RED ONION, SLICED IN RINGS | |
| 1 HEAD ROMAINE LETTUCE, TORN INTO BITE-SIZED PIECES | |
| ½ CUP CHOPPED FRESH PARSLEY | 125 mL |
| PAPRIKA | |

COMBINE MARINADE INGREDIENTS AND MIX THOROUGHLY. TOSS ARTICHOKES, MUSHROOMS AND ONIONS WITH MARINADE. COVER AND REFRIGERATE AT LEAST 2 HOURS, STIRRING OCCASIONALLY. SERVE ON LETTUCE, USING MARINADE AS THE DRESSING. SPRINKLE WITH PARSLEY AND PAPRIKA. SERVES 6.

BEFORE THEY INVENTED DRAWING BOARDS, WHAT DID THEY GO BACK TO?

# CAESAR SALAD

YOU'LL DESERVE THE "HAILS" WHEN YOU SERVE THIS CLASSIC.

| | |
|---|---|
| 1 LARGE HEAD ROMAINE LETTUCE | |
| 1 GARLIC CLOVE, MINCED | |
| 1/3 CUP OIL | 75 mL |
| SALT & FRESH GROUND BLACK PEPPER TO TASTE | |
| 1/4 TSP. DRY MUSTARD | 1 mL |
| 1 1/2 TSP. WORCESTERSHIRE SAUCE | 7 mL |
| 3 (OR MORE) ANCHOVY FILETS, DRAINED | |
| 1 EGG | |
| 1-2 TBSP. FRESH LEMON JUICE | 15-30 mL |
| 2 TBSP. FRESHLY GRATED PARMESAN CHEESE | 30 mL |
| CROÛTONS | |

WASH AND TEAR ROMAINE INTO BITE-SIZED PIECES. BLENDERIZE REMAINING INGREDIENTS, EXCEPT PARMESAN AND CROÛTONS. TOSS LETTUCE AND DRESSING. SPRINKLE ON PARMESAN AND CROÛTONS. TOSS AGAIN.

WHERE DO THEY GET THE SEEDS TO GROW SEEDLESS ORANGES?

# STRAWBERRY AND CHÈVRE SALAD

WHEN NANNY (OR THE REST OF THE HERD) IS COMING FOR LUNCH. SERVE WITH BAGUETTE OR CROISSANTS AND A GLASS OF BUBBLY.

## BALSAMIC RASPBERRY VINAIGRETTE

| | |
|---|---:|
| 1 GARLIC CLOVE, MINCED | |
| ½ TSP. HONEY DIJON MUSTARD | 2 mL |
| 2 TBSP. RASPBERRY VINEGAR | 30 mL |
| 1 TBSP. BALSAMIC VINEGAR | 15 mL |
| 1 TBSP. BROWN SUGAR | 15 mL |
| ¼ CUP VEGETABLE OIL | 60 mL |

## SALAD

| | |
|---|---:|
| 6 CUPS MIXED GREENS | 1.5 L |
| ½ CUP CRUMBLED CHÈVRE (GOAT CHEESE) | 125 mL |
|    - BRIE IS GOOD TOO | |
| ¼ CUP SLIVERED ALMONDS, TOASTED | 60 mL |
| 2 CUPS HALVED STRAWBERRIES | 500 mL |
| SALT AND FRESHLY GROUND PEPPER TO TASTE | |

TO PREPARE VINAIGRETTE: IN A SMALL BOWL, COMBINE GARLIC, MUSTARD, VINEGARS AND BROWN SUGAR. WHISK IN OIL.

TO PREPARE SALAD: IN A LARGE BOWL, TOSS GREENS WITH VINAIGRETTE. PLACE AN EQUAL PORTION ON 4 SALAD PLATES. TOP WITH CHEESE, NUTS AND STRAWBERRIES. SPRINKLE WITH SALT AND PEPPER.

EVER STOP TO THINK AND FORGET TO START AGAIN?

# SPINACH AND STRAWBERRY SALAD

SPINACH - ENOUGH FOR YOUR CREW
STRAWBERRIES - SAME AS ABOVE!

## POPPYSEED WORCESTERSHIRE DRESSING

| | |
|---|---|
| 1/3 CUP WHITE SUGAR | 75 mL |
| 1/2 CUP OIL | 125 mL |
| 1/4 CUP WHITE VINEGAR | 60 mL |
| 2 TBSP. SESAME SEEDS | 30 mL |
| 2 TBSP. POPPY SEEDS | 30 mL |
| 1/4 TSP. PAPRIKA | 1 mL |
| 1/2 TSP. WORCESTERSHIRE SAUCE | 2 mL |
| 1 1/2 TSP. MINCED ONION | 7 mL |

TEAR SPINACH INTO BITE-SIZED PIECES. CUT
STRAWBERRIES IN HALF. COMBINE DRESSING
INGREDIENTS AND MIX WELL. TOSS WITH SPINACH
AND STRAWBERRIES.

CHILD'S OBSERVATIONS ON LOVE:

"NO ONE IS SURE WHY IT HAPPENS, BUT I HEARD IT
HAS SOMETHING TO DO WITH HOW YOU SMELL . . .
THAT'S WHY PERFUME AND DEODORANT ARE SO
POPULAR."

"I'M NOT RUSHING INTO BEING IN LOVE. I'M FINDING
FOURTH GRADE HARD ENOUGH."

# FRESH SPINACH SALAD

## DRESSING

| | |
|---|---:|
| 1 GARLIC CLOVE, MINCED | |
| 2 TBSP. CIDER OR RED WINE VINEGAR | 30 mL |
| 1 TSP. SUGAR | 5 mL |
| 1/2 TSP. SALT | 2 mL |
| 1 TSP. DRY MUSTARD | 5 mL |
| 1/2 TSP. FRESHLY GROUND PEPPER | 2 mL |
| 1/4 CUP SALAD OIL | 60 mL |

## SALAD

| | |
|---|---:|
| 8 CUPS CRISP YOUNG SPINACH, STEMS REMOVED | 2 L |
| 3 HARD-COOKED EGGS, GRATED | |
| 8 SLICES BACON, COOKED & CRUMBLED | |
| 4 GREEN ONIONS, FINELY CHOPPED | |
| FRESH MUSHROOMS, SLICED | |
| FRESH CAULIFLOWER, SLICED | |

TO MAKE DRESSING: BEAT ALL INGREDIENTS TOGETHER AND REFRIGERATE.

TO MAKE SALAD: PREPARE SALAD INGREDIENTS, TOSS WITH DRESSING JUST BEFORE SERVING. SERVES 4-6.

CHILD'S SUGGESTION FOR LOVE BALLAD:
"I'M IN LOVE WITH YOU MOST OF THE TIME, BUT DON'T BOTHER ME WHEN I'M WITH MY FRIENDS."

Orzo with Veggies, page 94

Papaya Avocado Salad, page 76

# CHRISTMAS SALAD

. . . OR THE FIRST DAY OF SPRING, OR GROUND HOG DAY, OR SECRETARIES' DAY OR . . .

## SALAD

| | |
|---|---|
| 8 CUPS SPINACH LEAVES | 2 L |
| 1 AVOCADO, THINLY SLICED | |
| ½ CUP THINLY SLICED RED ONION | 125 mL |
| ½ CUP DRIED CRANBERRIES | 125 mL |

OR 1 CUP (250 mL) POMEGRANATE SEEDS

## DRESSING

| | |
|---|---|
| ¼ CUP CRANBERRY JUICE CONCENTRATE | 60 mL |
| ¼ CUP WHITE WINE VINEGAR | 60 mL |
| 1½ TSP. DIJON MUSTARD | 7 mL |
| ¼ TSP. FRESHLY GROUND PEPPER | 1 mL |
| ½ CUP VEGETABLE OIL | 125 mL |

TO MAKE SALAD: STEM SPINACH, TEAR INTO BITE-SIZED PIECES AND PLACE IN A LARGE SALAD BOWL. PLACE AVOCADO AND ONION OVER SPINACH.

TO MAKE DRESSING: COMBINE CRANBERRY JUICE CONCENTRATE, VINEGAR, MUSTARD, PEPPER AND OIL IN A JAR WITH A TIGHT-FITTING LID. SHAKE UNTIL WELL BLENDED. DRIZZLE OVER SALAD. SPRINKLE DRIED CRANBERRIES OR POMEGRANATE SEEDS OVER SALAD, TOSS GENTLY AND SERVE 6 GUESTS.

FAVORITE OXYMORONS: ACT NATURALLY, AIRLINE FOOD, GOOD GRIEF.

# LAYERED SOUTHWEST SALAD

## CREAMY RANCH DRESSING

| | |
|---|---|
| 1 CUP COTTAGE CHEESE | 250 mL |
| 1 CUP BUTTERMILK | 250 mL |
| 2 TBSP. WHITE WINE VINEGAR | 30 mL |
| 1 LARGE GARLIC CLOVE, MINCED | |
| ½ TSP. SALT | 2 mL |
| ½ TSP. FRESHLY GROUND BLACK PEPPER | 2 mL |
| ½ TSP. CUMIN | 2 mL |
| 1 TSP. DRIED OREGANO LEAVES | 5 mL |

## SALAD

| | |
|---|---|
| 1 JICAMA, ¾ LB. (365 g) PEELED | |
| 14 OZ. CAN BLACK BEANS, DRAINED & RINSED | 398 mL |
| 1 CUP MILD SALSA | 250 mL |
| ½ CUP DICED RED ONION | 125 mL |
| 10 OZ. FRESH SPINACH, WASHED, STEMMED & CUT INTO PIECES | 300 g |
| 2 CUPS FROZEN WHOLE KERNEL CORN, COOKED, DRAINED & COOLED | 500 mL |
| 2 CUPS SHREDDED CHEDDAR CHEESE | 500 mL |

DRESSING: BLEND ALL INGREDIENTS IN BLENDER UNTIL SMOOTH. COVER AND REFRIGERATE 1 HOUR.

SALAD: CUT JICAMA INTO 6 WEDGES. SLICE CROSSWISE INTO ⅛" (3 mm) THICK SLICES. COMBINE BEANS, SALSA AND ONION IN MEDIUM BOWL. LAYER ½ OF SPINACH, JICAMA, BEAN MIXTURE, CORN AND 1 CUP (250 mL) OF DRESSING IN LARGE BOWL. REPEAT LAYERS. SPRINKLE WITH CHEESE; DRIZZLE WITH REMAINING DRESSING. COVER AND REFRIGERATE 1-2 HOURS. SERVE WITH JALAPEÑO CORN MUFFINS (PAGE 8). SERVES 6-8.

# SANTA FE SALAD

## CILANTRO LIME DRESSING

| | |
|---|---:|
| 1/4 CUP OLIVE OIL | 60 mL |
| JUICE OF 2 LIMES | |
| 1/4 CUP CHOPPED CILANTRO | 60 mL |
| 1 TSP. CUMIN | 5 mL |
| SALT & FRESHLY GROUND PEPPER | |
| TO TASTE | |

## SALAD

| | |
|---|---:|
| 19 OZ. CAN BLACK BEANS | 540 mL |
| (TURTLE BEANS), RINSED & DRAINED | |
| 1 RED BELL PEPPER, DICED | |
| 12 OZ. CAN KERNEL CORN, DRAINED | 341 mL |
| 1/3 CUP CHOPPED RED ONION | 75 mL |
| 1 JALAPEÑO PEPPER, SEEDED & MINCED | |

IN MEDIUM BOWL, WHISK TOGETHER OIL AND LIME JUICE. ADD CILANTRO, CUMIN, SALT AND PEPPER AND MIX WELL. STIR IN SALAD INGREDIENTS AND CORRECT SEASONING. SERVE AT ROOM TEMPERATURE. SERVES 6.

A MAN CELEBRATING HIS 50TH WEDDING ANNIVERSARY SAID TO HIS YOUNGER FRIEND: "I'M TAKING MY WIFE TO THE ORIENT."

"THAT'S INTERESTING." SAID THE YOUNGER MAN, "IT'S OUR 25TH AND I'M TAKING MY WIFE THERE TOO!"

"THAT'S A PRETTY BIG PRESENT - WHAT WILL YOU DO FOR YOUR 50TH?"

"GO AND GET HER."

# BEET, RED ONION AND ORANGE SALAD

## SALAD

| | |
|---|---|
| 1½ LBS. FRESH BEETS | 750 g |
| ½ RED ONION, THINLY SLICED | |
| 2 LARGE NAVAL ORANGES, PEELED & SECTIONED. | |

## VINAIGRETTE

| | |
|---|---|
| ¼ CUP RED WINE VINEGAR | 60 mL |
| ¼ CUP FRESH ORANGE JUICE | 60 mL |
| 2 TSP. DIJON MUSTARD | 10 mL |
| 2 TSP. ORANGE ZEST | 10 mL |
| ½ CUP OLIVE OIL | 125 mL |
| SALT & PEPPER TO TASTE | |

TO MAKE SALAD: COOK BEETS IN BOILING SALTED WATER 30-40 MINUTES, OR UNTIL TENDER. DRAIN, REMOVE SKINS AND COOL. CUT INTO ¼" (1 cm) SLICES. PLACE BEETS, ONIONS AND ORANGE SLICES IN A SALAD BOWL.

TO MAKE VINAIGRETTE: WHISK VINAIGRETTE INGREDIENTS TOGETHER IN BOWL. POUR OVER SALAD. COVER AND REFRIGERATE FOR SEVERAL HOURS. SERVES 8.

STUDENT: "IS IT TRUE THAT HISTORY REPEATS ITSELF?"

HISTORY PROFESSOR: "YES, PARTICULARLY IF YOU FLUNK IT."

# BROCCOLI MANDARIN SALAD

GREAT FOR BUFFETS OR PICNICS. EVERYONE WANTS THIS RECIPE.

## DRESSING

| | |
|---|---|
| 2 EGGS | |
| 1/2 CUP SUGAR | 125 mL |
| 1 TSP. CORNSTARCH | 5 mL |
| 1 TSP. DRY MUSTARD | 5 mL |
| 1/4 CUP WHITE WINE VINEGAR | 60 mL |
| 1/4 CUP WATER | 60 mL |
| 1/2 CUP MAYONNAISE | 125 mL |

## SALAD

| | |
|---|---|
| 4 CUPS FRESH BROCCOLI FLORETS | 1 L |
| 1/2 CUP RAISINS | 125 mL |
| 8 SLICES BACON, COOKED & CHOPPED | |
| 2 CUPS SLICED FRESH MUSHROOMS | 500 mL |
| 1/2 CUP SLIVERED TOASTED ALMONDS | 125 mL |
| 10 OZ. CAN MANDARIN ORANGES, DRAINED | 284 mL |
| 1/2 RED ONION, SLICED | |

TO MAKE DRESSING: IN A SAUCEPAN, WHISK TOGETHER EGGS, SUGAR, CORNSTARCH AND DRY MUSTARD. ADD VINEGAR AND WATER AND COOK SLOWLY UNTIL THICKENED. REMOVE FROM HEAT AND STIR IN MAYONNAISE. COOL.

TO MAKE SALAD: MARINATE BROCCOLI IN DRESSING FOR SEVERAL HOURS. ADD REMAINING INGREDIENTS AND TOSS WELL. SERVES 6.

CLONES ARE PEOPLE TWO.

# GREEK SALAD

ANY GREEK WHO BRINGS THIS IS BEARING A GIFT!

<u>SALAD</u>

| | |
|---|---|
| 1 HEAD ROMAINE LETTUCE, TORN | |
| 1 LARGE TOMATO, CUT IN WEDGES | |
| 1 GREEN PEPPER, CUT INTO STRIPS | |
| 1 SMALL RED ONION, SLICED & SEPARATED INTO RINGS | |
| 1 MEDIUM CUCUMBER, SEEDED & CHOPPED | |
| 1/4 CUP GREEK OLIVES (KALAMATA) | 60 mL |
| 1/2 CUP CRUMBLED FETA CHEESE | 125 mL |

<u>DRESSING</u>

| | |
|---|---|
| 6 TBSP. OLIVE OIL | 90 mL |
| 2 TBSP. FRESH LEMON JUICE | 30 mL |
| 1 TSP. OREGANO | 5 mL |
| SALT & COARSELY GROUND PEPPER TO TASTE | |

COMBINE ALL SALAD INGREDIENTS, EXCEPT FETA CHEESE, IN A LARGE SALAD BOWL. BEAT DRESSING INGREDIENTS UNTIL WELL BLENDED. POUR OVER SALAD, TOSS WELL AND SPRINKLE ON FETA CHEESE.

AS A VARIATION, SERVE IN A PITA POCKET!

MY HUSBAND THINKS THAT HEALTH FOOD IS ANYTHING HE EATS BEFORE THE EXPIRATION DATE.

# REGINA BEACH COLESLAW

A MUST WITH OUR BEST HOMEMADE FISH 'N' CHIPS (PAGE 191).

### SLAW

| | |
|---|---|
| 3 LBS. CABBAGE SHREDDED | 1.5 kg |
| 2 LARGE CARROTS, COARSELY GRATED | |
| 1 WHITE ONION, CHOPPED | |
| 1½ CUPS SUGAR | 375 mL |

### DRESSING

| | |
|---|---|
| 1 CUP SALAD OIL | 250 mL |
| 1 CUP VINEGAR | 250 mL |
| ½ CUP SUGAR | 125 mL |
| 2 TBSP. SALT | 30 mL |
| 1 TBSP. CELERY SEED | 15 mL |

PUT VEGETABLES IN A LARGE BOWL, SPRINKLE SUGAR OVER TOP. IN A SAUCEPAN, BOIL DRESSING INGREDIENTS UNTIL THE SUGAR HAS DISSOLVED. POUR OVER VEGETABLES AND MIX WELL. PACK INTO STERILIZED JARS. THIS SALAD WILL KEEP UP TO 2 WEEKS IN THE REFRIGERATOR. GREAT FOR A CROWD. MAKES 3 QUARTS (3 L). DRAIN BEFORE SERVING.

THESE DAYS, IF A LITTLE OLD LADY IS SITTING AT A SPINNING WHEEL CHANCES ARE SHE'S IN LAS VEGAS.

# KILLER COLESLAW

ANOTHER FOREVER FAVORITE!

## SALAD INGREDIENTS

½ CABBAGE, CHOPPED
5 GREEN ONIONS, CHOPPED
¼ CUP SLIVERED ALMONDS, TOASTED — 60 mL
¼ CUP SUNFLOWER SEEDS, TOASTED — 60 mL
    (OR SESAME SEEDS)
3 OZ. PKG. JAPANESE NOODLE SOUP MIX, — 85 g
    (SAVE SEASONING PACKAGE FOR
    DRESSING)

## DRESSING

¼ CUP RICE (OR WHITE) VINEGAR — 60 mL
¼ CUP SALAD OIL — 60 mL
SEASONING PACKAGE FROM NOODLES

COMBINE ALL SALAD INGREDIENTS EXCEPT NOODLES. BEFORE SERVING, CRUSH NOODLES, COMBINE WITH SALAD INGREDIENTS AND TOSS WITH DRESSING. SERVES 6. IF THERE'S ANY LEFT OVER - SAVE IT! KIDS LOVE IT THE NEXT DAY!

OUTSIDE OF A DOG, A MAN'S BEST FRIEND IS A BOOK; INSIDE OF A DOG, IT IS VERY DARK.

# SPICY NOODLE SALAD

THIS DRESSING CAN BE PREPARED UP TO 1 WEEK IN ADVANCE - IN FACT, THE FLAVOR IMPROVES.

### DRESSING

| | |
|---|---|
| ⅓ CUP SOY SAUCE | 75 mL |
| ¼ CUP WHITE WINE VINEGAR | 60 mL |
| 2 TBSP. CHILI SAUCE | 30 mL |
| 2 TBSP. SUGAR | 30 mL |
| 2 TBSP. SESAME OIL | 30 mL |
| 1" CHUNK FRESH GINGER, PEELED & FINELY CHOPPED | 2.5 cm |
| 4 GARLIC CLOVES, MINCED | |
| 2 TSP. CHILI FLAKES | 10 mL |
| FRESHLY GROUND BLACK PEPPER | |
| ¼ CUP VEGETABLE OIL | 60 mL |

SPAGHETTINI OR VERMICELLI
GRATED CARROTS
GREEN ONION, THINLY SLICED

IN A MEDIUM BOWL, WHISK SOY SAUCE WITH VINEGAR, CHILI SAUCE, SUGAR, SESAME OIL, GINGER, GARLIC, CHILI FLAKES AND PEPPER. GRADUALLY WHISK IN VEGETABLE OIL IN A THIN STREAM. REFRIGERATE UNTIL READY TO USE. WHISK AGAIN JUST BEFORE USING. MAKES ABOUT 1½ CUPS (375 mL).

TOSS WITH COOKED PASTA, CARROTS AND GREEN ONIONS.

I INTEND TO LIVE FOREVER - SO FAR, SO GOOD!

# ORZO WITH VEGGIES

A GREAT COMPLEMENT TO GRILLED MEATS.

## SALAD

| | |
|---|---:|
| 6 OZ. SNOW PEAS, TRIMMED | 170 g |
| 2 CUPS ORZO | 500 mL |
| 1½ CUPS CHERRY TOMATOES, CUT IN QUARTERS & SEEDED | 375 mL |
| 1 CUP SEEDED, CHOPPED CUCUMBER | 250 mL |
| ½ CUP CHOPPED GREEN ONIONS | 125 mL |
| ½ CUP CHOPPED FRESH PARSLEY | 125 mL |
| 2 TSP. GRATED LEMON RIND | 10 mL |
| SALT & PEPPER TO TASTE | |

## LEMON GARLIC DRESSING

| | |
|---|---:|
| ¼ CUP FRESH LEMON JUICE | 60 mL |
| 2 TBSP. WHITE WINE VINEGAR | 30 mL |
| 2 TSP. GRATED LEMON RIND | 10 mL |
| 1 TSP. MINCED GARLIC | 5 mL |
| ½ CUP OIL | 125 mL |
| SALT & PEPPER | |

LETTUCE

TO MAKE SALAD: BRING A LARGE POT OF SALTED WATER TO A BOIL. ADD SNOW PEAS AND COOK FOR 1 MINUTE. USING A SLOTTED SPOON, REMOVE PEAS TO A STRAINER; RINSE UNDER COLD WATER AND DRAIN ON PAPER TOWEL. ADD ORZO TO SAME POT AND BOIL UNTIL TENDER BUT STILL FIRM TO BITE, ABOUT 10 MINUTES. DRAIN; COOL AND PLACE IN A LARGE BOWL. ADD SNOW PEAS, TOMATOES, CUCUMBER, ONIONS, PARSLEY AND

## ORZO WITH VEGGIES

CONTINUED FROM PAGE 94.

LEMON RIND. SEASON WITH SALT AND PEPPER.

TO MAKE DRESSING: COMBINE LEMON JUICE, VINEGAR, LEMON RIND AND GARLIC IN MEDIUM BOWL. GRADUALLY BLEND IN OIL. SEASON TO TASTE WITH SALT AND PEPPER.

POUR HALF OF THE DRESSING OVER SALAD AND TOSS TO COAT. LET SIT AT LEAST 6 HOURS. COVER SALAD AND REMAINING DRESSING AND CHILL. BRING TO ROOM TEMPERATURE BEFORE CONTINUING. TO SERVE, TOSS SALAD WITH REMAINING DRESSING TO COAT GENEROUSLY. LINE SHALLOW SERVING BOWL WITH LETTUCE AND MOUND SALAD IN BOWL. SERVES 6-8. (PICTURED ON PAGE 83.)

IT'S BETTER TO BE NOUVEAU RICHE THAN NEVER TO HAVE BEEN RICHE AT ALL.

# FRESH ORANGE PASTA SALAD

*ATTRACTIVE, LIGHT AND ZESTY*

## ORANGE DILL DRESSING

| | |
|---|---|
| GRATED PEEL OF ½ ORANGE | |
| JUICE OF 1 ORANGE | |
| 3 TBSP. VEGETABLE OIL | 45 mL |
| ½ TSP. SEASONING SALT | 2 mL |
| ½ TSP. DRIED DILLWEED | 2 mL |
| | |
| 2 CUPS SPIRAL PASTA | 500 mL |
| 2 ORANGES - PEELED AND CUT INTO SEMICIRCULAR SLICES | |
| 2 CUPS BROCCOLI FLORETS, COOKED TENDER-CRISP | 500 mL |
| ½ CUP SLICED CELERY | 125 mL |
| ½ CUP SLICED GREEN ONIONS | 125 mL |
| PEPPER & SALT TO TASTE | |

IN A LARGE BOWL, COMBINE ORANGE PEEL, ORANGE JUICE, OIL, SEASONING SALT, AND DILL-WEED. COOK PASTA ACCORDING TO PACKAGE DIRECTIONS. DRAIN. TO DRESSING, ADD PASTA, ORANGE SLICES, BROCCOLI, CELERY, ONIONS, SALT AND PEPPER. GENTLY TOSS. COVER AND CHILL. SERVE WITH CHEESE BUNS. SERVES 6-8.

IF THE WORLD IS GETTING SMALLER, WHY DO THE POSTAL RATES KEEP GOING UP?

# FIESTA CHICKEN TORTILLA SALAD

A DELICIOUS DINNER SALAD FOR 2 - MUY SABROSO! - DON'T BE SHY, USE YOUR FINGERS FOR THE TORTILLA STRIPS.

| | |
|---|---|
| 1 WHOLE BONELESS, SKINLESS CHICKEN BREAST | |
| 1 TBSP. TABASCO | 15 mL |
| VEGETABLE OIL FOR FRYING | |
| 3 SOFT CORN TORTILLAS, IN 1/4" (1 cm) STRIPS | |
| SALT TO SPRINKLE | |
| 4 CUPS ROMAINE LETTUCE, SLICED IN STRIPS | 1 L |
| 1/2 RED PEPPER, CUT IN STRIPS | |

## DRESSING

| | |
|---|---|
| 4 TBSP. TOASTED SESAME SEEDS | 60 mL |
| 2 TBSP. WHITE WINE VINEGAR | 30 mL |
| 1 TBSP. DIJON MUSTARD | 15 mL |
| 1/2 CUP VEGETABLE OIL | 125 mL |
| SALT & PEPPER TO TASTE | |

TO PREPARE CHICKEN: CUT CHICKEN BREAST INTO 1/4" (1 cm) STRIPS AND TOSS WITH THE TABASCO. HEAT OIL, 1/4" (1 cm) DEEP, UNTIL HOT IN HEAVY FRYING PAN. FRY TORTILLA STRIPS QUICKLY UNTIL GOLDEN. SET ON PAPER TOWEL TO DRAIN. SEASON WITH SALT. POUR OFF ALL BUT A LITTLE OIL AND SAUTÉ CHICKEN FOR 2-3 MINUTES. SET ASIDE.

TO PREPARE DRESSING: COMBINE ALL INGREDIENTS IN BLENDER AND BLEND UNTIL SMOOTH.

TO PREPARE SALAD: PLACE LETTUCE, PEPPERS AND CHICKEN IN A BOWL AND TOSS WITH DRESSING. SERVE ON INDIVIDUAL PLATES AND ARRANGE TORTILLA STRIPS ON TOP.

# KOREAN CHICKEN SALAD

A PERFECT SUMMER MEAL. THE ONLY THING THAT'S DIFFICULT IS FINDING THE KOREAN CHICKENS!

| | |
|---|---|
| 3 LBS. BONELESS SKINLESS CHICKEN BREASTS | 1.5 kg |

## MARINADE

| | |
|---|---|
| 1/4 CUP SOY SAUCE | 60 mL |
| 2 TBSP. OIL | 30 mL |
| 2 TBSP. SHERRY OR WHITE WINE | 30 mL |
| 1/2 TSP. GROUND GINGER | 2 mL |
| 1/2 TSP. CINNAMON | 2 mL |
| 2 GARLIC CLOVES, FINELY CHOPPED | |

## SALAD VEGGIES

| | |
|---|---|
| 2 CUPS SHREDDED ICEBERG LETTUCE | 500 mL |
| 1 CUP THINLY SLICED CUCUMBER | 250 mL |
| 1 CUP THINLY SLICED CARROTS | 250 mL |
| 2/3 CUP CHOPPED GREEN ONION | 150 mL |
| 1 CUP BEAN SPROUTS | 250 mL |
| 3/4 CUP SLIVERED ALMONDS, TOASTED & SALTED | 175 mL |
| 2 TBSP. SESAME SEEDS, TOASTED | 30 mL |

## DRESSING

| | |
|---|---|
| 1/2 TSP. DRY MUSTARD | 2 mL |
| 1/2 TSP. SALT | 2 mL |
| 1/2 TSP. TABASCO SAUCE | 2 mL |
| 1 TBSP. SOY SAUCE | 15 mL |
| 1/4 CUP CORN OIL | 60 mL |
| 1/4 CUP SESAME OIL | 60 mL |
| 4 TSP. LEMON JUICE | 20 mL |

## KOREAN CHICKEN SALAD

CONTINUED FROM PAGE 98.

CUT CHICKEN BREASTS IN HALF. COMBINE MARINADE INGREDIENTS. THOROUGHLY COAT CHICKEN IN MARINADE. PLACE IN SHALLOW ROASTING PAN. POUR REMAINDER OF MARINADE OVER TOP AND COOK, UNCOVERED, AT 400°F (200°C) FOR 40 MINUTES, TURNING AT HALF TIME. (IF YOUR TEAM IS LOSING - HAVE ANOTHER BEER!) COOL COOKED CHICKEN AND CUT IN THIN STRIPS. PREPARE SALAD VEGGIES AND PLACE IN LARGE BOWL. WHISK TOGETHER ALL DRESSING INGREDIENTS. JUST BEFORE SERVING, TOSS THE CHICKEN AND VEGGIES WITH DRESSING, ALMONDS AND SESAME SEEDS. ENJOY! SERVES 6.

WHY DOES IT TAKE SO LITTLE TIME FOR A CHILD WHO IS AFRAID OF THE DARK TO BECOME A TEENAGER WHO WANTS TO STAY OUT ALL NIGHT?

# LAYERED CHICKEN SALAD

A REAL WINNER! PREPARE THIS SALAD THE NIGHT BEFORE AND SERVE FOR LUNCH TO 8-10 DELIGHTED GUESTS.

## SALAD

| | | |
|---|---|---|
| 4-5 CUPS SHREDDED ICEBERG LETTUCE | 1-1.25 | L |
| 1/4 LB. BEAN SPROUTS | 125 | g |
| 8 OZ. CAN WATER CHESTNUTS, SLICED | 227 | g |
| 1 MEDIUM-SIZED CUCUMBER, THINLY SLICED | | |
| 1/2 CUP THINLY SLICED GREEN ONIONS, | 125 mL | |
| 2 CUPS SNOW PEAS (OR FROZEN IS FINE) | 250 mL | |
| 4 CUPS COOKED CHICKEN, CUT INTO STRIPS | 1 | L |

## DRESSING

| | |
|---|---|
| 2 CUPS MAYONNAISE | 500 mL |
| 2 TSP. CURRY POWDER | 10 mL |
| 1/2 TSP. GROUND GINGER | 2 mL |
| 1 TBSP. SUGAR | 15 mL |
| 12 CHERRY TOMATOES, HALVED | |

SPREAD LETTUCE EVENLY IN A 4-QUART (4 L) GLASS BOWL. TOP WITH 1 LAYER EACH OF SPROUTS, WATER CHESTNUTS, CUCUMBER, ONIONS, PEA PODS AND CHICKEN. (MAKE SURE PEA PODS ARE DRY). STIR TOGETHER MAYONNAISE, CURRY, GINGER AND SUGAR. SPREAD EVENLY OVER THE SALAD. DECORATE WITH HALVED CHERRY TOMATOES. COVER AND REFRIGERATE UNTIL READY TO SERVE. (YOU MAY WANT TO MAKE EXTRA MAYONNAISE MIXTURE TO SERVE ON THE SIDE.)

## BALSAMIC VINAIGRETTE

DRIZZLE OVER A VARIETY OF GREENS: BIBB, LEAF, ENDIVE, RADICCHIO, ARUGULA (YOU CAN BUY THIS COMBO PACKAGED AT MOST STORES.)

| | |
|---|---|
| 1/3 CUP BALSAMIC VINEGAR | 75 mL |
| 1/4 CUP OLIVE OIL | 60 mL |
| 1/4 CUP DRY WHITE WINE | 60 mL |
| JUICE OF 1 LIME | |
| SALT & FRESHLY GROUND PEPPER TO TASTE | |

POUR VINEGAR INTO A SMALL BOWL AND GRADUALLY WHISK IN OIL. WHISK IN WINE AND LIME JUICE, SEASON AND STORE IN REFRIGERATOR. JUST BEFORE SERVING, SHAKE WELL AND DRIZZLE OVER GREENS.

## ROASTED GARLIC CAESAR DRESSING

| | |
|---|---|
| 1 GARLIC BULB, ROASTED | |
| 1-2 ANCHOVIES | |
| 1 TSP. DIJON MUSTARD | 5 mL |
| 1 TSP. WORCESTERSHIRE SAUCE | 5 mL |
| 2 TBSP. BALSAMIC VINEGAR | 30 mL |
| 2 TBSP. OLIVE OIL | 30 mL |
| 1/4 CUP GRATED PARMESAN CHEESE | 60 mL |
| 1/2 CUP YOGURT | 125 mL |
| SALT AND PEPPER TO TASTE | |

TO ROAST GARLIC: REMOVE LOOSE SKINS, RUB BULB WITH OIL AND WRAP IN FOIL. BAKE IN A 350°F (180°C) OVEN FOR ABOUT 1 HOUR.

TO MAKE DRESSING: CUT TOP OFF ROASTED GARLIC AND SQUEEZE INTO FOOD PROCESSOR. ADD REMAINING INGREDIENTS; BLEND UNTIL SMOOTH.

## TARRAGON MUSTARD DRESSING

MAHVALOUS!! ON SALMON OR SEAFOOD.

| | |
|---|---|
| 1 LARGE EGG | |
| 1 TBSP. DIJON MUSTARD | 15 mL |
| 2 TBSP. TARRAGON WINE VINEGAR | 30 mL |
| 1-2 TSP. TARRAGON | 5-10 mL |
| SALT & PEPPER TO TASTE | |
| 1¼ CUPS VEGETABLE OIL | 300 mL |

USING A FOOD PROCESSOR, BLEND TOGETHER EGG, MUSTARD, VINEGAR AND SEASONINGS. WITH MACHINE RUNNING, DRIZZLE IN OIL. MIXTURE WILL BE THICK AND SHINY.

I'M NOT GOING TO VACUUM UNTIL THEY MAKE A MODEL YOU CAN RIDE ON!

## ITALIAN DRESSING

| | |
|---|---|
| 1 CUP OLIVE OIL | 250 mL |
| ¼ CUP WHITE WINE VINEGAR | 60 mL |
| 1 TBSP. FRESH LEMON JUICE | 15 mL |
| ¾ TSP. OREGANO | 4 mL |
| ½ TSP. DRY MUSTARD | 2 mL |
| ¼ TSP. THYME | 1 mL |
| 1 GARLIC CLOVE, MINCED | |
| 1 TSP. MINCED ONION | 5 mL |
| 1 TSP. HONEY | 5 mL |
| SALT & PEPPER TO TASTE | |

COMBINE ALL INGREDIENTS. BLENDERIZE AND STORE IN REFRIGERATOR. MAKES ABOUT 1½ CUPS (375 mL).

# SOUPS

Cold Cucumber Soup
Gazpacho
Fresh Tomato Bisque
Red Pepper Soup
Champagne Squash Soup
Carrot Soup
Corn Chowder
French Onion Soup Au Gratin
Tortilla Soup
Moroccan Chicken-Vegetable Soup
Shooter's Soup
War Wonton Soup
Hamburger Soup
Best of Bridge Bean Soup

# COLD CUCUMBER SOUP

A DELICIOUS COLD SOUP. MAKE THE DAY BEFORE. (YOU'LL NEED A BLENDER.)

| | |
|---|---|
| 2-8" ENGLISH CUCUMBERS | 2-20 cm |
| 2 TBSP. BUTTER | 30 mL |
| 1/4 CUP CHOPPED GREEN ONIONS | 60 mL |
| 4 CUPS CHICKEN BROTH | 1 L |
| 1 TBSP. WHITE WINE VINEGAR | 15 mL |
| 1/2 TSP. DRIED TARRAGON (OR MORE) | 2 mL |
| 3 TBSP. CREAM OF WHEAT (QUICK COOKING) | 45 mL |
| SALT & WHITE PEPPER | |
| 1 CUP FAT-FREE SOUR CREAM | 250 mL |

CUT 12 PAPER-THIN SLICES OF CUCUMBER (SKIN ON) TO BE USED FOR GARNISH AND RESERVE. PEEL REMAINING CUCUMBERS AND CHOP INTO CHUNKS. IN A LARGE POT, MELT BUTTER; STIR IN ONIONS AND COOK 1 MINUTE OVER MODERATE HEAT. ADD CUCUMBER CHUNKS, CHICKEN BROTH, VINEGAR AND TARRAGON. BRING TO A BOIL. STIR IN CREAM OF WHEAT. SIMMER, UNCOVERED, FOR 20 MINUTES. BLENDERIZE (IF TOO THICK, ADD SMALL AMOUNT OF CHICKEN BROTH OR MILK). SEASON TO TASTE WITH SALT AND WHITE PEPPER. LET COOL AND ADD SOUR CREAM TO SOUP IN BLENDER. CHILL UNTIL READY TO SERVE. SERVE WITH 2 THIN SLICES OF RESERVED CUCUMBER ON TOP. SERVES 6.

ISN'T IT INCREDIBLE THAT THE NEWS FROM ALL OVER THE WORLD ALWAYS FITS EXACTLY INTO THE NEWSPAPER.

# GAZPACHO

A CHILLED TOMATO SOUP - PERFECT ON A HOT DAY!

| | |
|---|---|
| 3 LBS. FRESH TOMATOES, PEELED & CUT UP (6 CUPS/1.5 L) | 1.5 Kg |
| 1 ONION, CUT IN CHUNKS | |
| ½ CUP GREEN PEPPER CHUNKS | 125 mL |
| ½ CUP CUCUMBER CHUNKS | 125 mL |
| 2 CUPS TOMATO JUICE | 500 mL |
| 1 GARLIC CLOVE, MINCED | |
| ½ TSP. CUMIN | 2 mL |
| 1 TSP. SALT | 5 mL |
| 1 TSP. PEPPER | 5 mL |
| ¼ CUP OLIVE OIL | 60 mL |
| ¼ CUP WHITE WINE VINEGAR | 60 mL |

GARNISH:

| | |
|---|---|
| ½ CUP FINELY CHOPPED GREEN ONION | 125 mL |
| ½ CUP FINELY CHOPPED GREEN PEPPER | 125 mL |
| ½ CUP CROÛTONS | 125 mL |

IMMERSE TOMATOES IN BOILING WATER FOR 2 MINUTES. DRAIN AND SKIN. IN BLENDER OR FOOD PROCESSOR COMBINE TOMATOES, ONION, GREEN PEPPER AND CUCUMBER. WHIRL BUT LEAVE A LITTLE BIT CHUNKY. TRANSFER TO LARGE TUREEN. ADD JUICE, GARLIC, CUMIN, SALT AND PEPPER. COVER AND CHILL WELL. BEFORE SERVING, STIR IN OIL AND VINEGAR. GARNISH AND SERVE COLD.

# FRESH TOMATO BISQUE

| | |
|---|---|
| 3 LBS. FRESH RIPE TOMATOES (6 CUPS/1.5 L) | 1.5 kg |
| 1/3 CUP BUTTER | 75 mL |
| 2 CUPS DRY BREAD CRUMBS | 500 mL |
| 1½ TSP. SALT | 7 mL |
| GROUND PEPPER | |
| 3 GARLIC CLOVES, MINCED | |
| 6 CUPS WATER | 1.5 L |
| 1½ CUPS CREAM | 375 mL |
| 2 EGG YOLKS, BEATEN | |

PURÉE TOMATOES (SEEDS AND SKINS INCLUDED). STRAIN THROUGH SIEVE. HEAT BUTTER; ADD TOMATOES AND SIMMER FOR 5 MINUTES. ADD CRUMBS, SALT, PEPPER, GARLIC AND WATER; BRING TO A BOIL. BEAT CREAM INTO EGG YOLKS. ADD TO TOMATO PURÉE, STIRRING CONSTANTLY. HEAT TO SERVING TEMPERATURE. DO NOT BOIL. SERVES 8.

WHY IS A PACKAGE SENT BY LAND CARRIER CALLED A SHIPMENT, WHILE A PACKAGE SENT BY SHIP IS CALLED CARGO?

# RED PEPPER SOUP

WELL WORTH THE EFFORT! THE PERFECT LIGHT LUNCHEON STARTER SERVED HOT OR COLD. MAY BE PREPARED THE DAY BEFORE.

| | |
|---|---|
| 4 LARGE RED PEPPERS | |
| 2 TBSP. BUTTER OR MARGARINE | 30 mL |
| 1 LARGE RED ONION, CHOPPED | |
| 2 GARLIC CLOVES, MINCED | |
| 4 CUPS CHICKEN BROTH | 1 L |
| 1 TBSP. LEMON JUICE OR GIN | 15 mL |
| SALT TO TASTE | |
| 1/2 TSP. GROUND PEPPER | 2 mL |
| FRESH BASIL FOR GARNISH | |

CUT PEPPERS IN THIRDS; REMOVE SEEDS AND PLACE CUT SIDE DOWN ON A COOKIE SHEET. BROIL UNTIL SKINS ARE BLACKENED AND PUFFED. REMOVE FROM SHEET AND PLACE IN A PAPER BAG TO STEAM. MELT BUTTER AND SAUTÉ ONIONS AND GARLIC UNTIL SOFT. REMOVE COOLED PEPPERS FROM BAG AND PEEL OFF SKINS. CUT INTO CHUNKS AND ADD TO ONIONS AND GARLIC. COOK FOR 2-3 MINUTES. ADD BROTH, COVER AND SIMMER 20 MINUTES. ADD LEMON JUICE OR GIN. IN A BLENDER OR FOOD PROCESSOR, WHIRL 1/3 OF THE MIXTURE AT A TIME UNTIL SMOOTH. (STRAIN IF YOU WISH.) SEASON WITH SALT AND PEPPER. GARNISH WITH BASIL. SERVES 4-6.

WHAT'S ANOTHER WORD FOR SYNONYM?

# CHAMPAGNE SQUASH SOUP

WHEN YOU WANT TO FUSS . . .

| | |
|---|---|
| 4 LBS. SQUASH, ACORN OR BUTTERNUT | 2 kg |
| 2 MEDIUM ONIONS, HALVED & THINLY SLICED | |
| 2 TBSP. BUTTER | 30 mL |
| 1/4 CUP CHAMPAGNE (YOU'LL FIND SOME WAY | 60 mL |
| TO USE THE REMAINDER OF THE BOTTLE) | |
| 4-5 CUPS CHICKEN BROTH | 1-1.25 L |
| 2 TBSP. BUTTER | 30 mL |
| 1/2 TSP. NUTMEG | 2 mL |
| SALT & PEPPER TO TASTE | |
| 1/4 CUP SOUR CREAM | 60 mL |

PREHEAT OVEN TO 350°F (180°C). LINE A COOKIE
SHEET WITH FOIL. QUARTER SQUASH. SCOOP OUT
SEEDS. PLACE SKIN-SIDE UP ON COOKIE SHEET
AND BAKE 1-1½ HOURS, UNTIL SQUASH IS TENDER.
(YOU MAY MICROWAVE, USING THE SAME METHOD,
COVERED WITH PLASTIC WRAP, ON HIGH UNTIL A
SKEWER CAN PENETRATE THE SKIN, ABOUT
10 MINUTES.) COOL. SCOOP OUT PULP AND PURÉE
IN BATCHES IN FOOD PROCESSOR. SAUTÉ ONIONS
IN 2 TBSP. (30 mL) BUTTER. ADD CHAMPAGNE.
COOK UNTIL LIQUID IS ABSORBED AND ONIONS ARE
GOLDEN BROWN, STIRRING OFTEN. PURÉE ONIONS
IN FOOD PROCESSOR WITH A LITTLE OF THE
SQUASH PURÉE. IN LARGE SAUCEPAN, COMBINE
ONION AND SQUASH PURÉES. WHISK IN BROTH TO
DESIRED CONSISTENCY. COVER AND HEAT
THROUGH OVER MEDIUM HEAT, STIRRING
OCCASIONALLY. WHISK IN 2 TBSP. (30 mL) BUTTER.

## CHAMPAGNE SQUASH SOUP

CONTINUED FROM PAGE 108.

SEASON WITH NUTMEG, SALT AND PEPPER. TO DECORATE, DROP A SMALL SPOONFUL OF SOUR CREAM IN EACH BOWL OF SOUP AND SWIRL WITH A KNIFE. SERVES 6-8. (PICTURED ON PAGE 117.)

## CARROT SOUP

SOMETHING ELSE TO DO WITH YOUR CARROTS!

| | |
|---|---|
| ¼ CUP BUTTER | 60 mL |
| 2 CUPS FINELY CHOPPED ONION | 500 mL |
| 12 LARGE CARROTS, PEELED & SLICED | |
| 4 CUPS CHICKEN BROTH | 1 L |
| 1 CUP FRESH ORANGE JUICE | 250 mL |
| SALT & PEPPER TO TASTE | |
| GRATED ORANGE ZEST | |

MELT BUTTER IN POT AND ADD ONIONS, COOKING OVER LOW HEAT UNTIL LIGHTLY BROWNED. ADD CARROTS AND BROTH AND BRING TO A BOIL. REDUCE HEAT. COVER AND COOK UNTIL CARROTS ARE VERY TENDER, ABOUT 30 MINUTES. POUR THROUGH A STRAINER, RESERVING BROTH. ADD STRAINED VEGETABLES IN BATCHES TO FOOD PROCESSOR OR BLENDER AND PURÉE UNTIL SMOOTH. RETURN PURÉE TO POT, ADD ORANGE JUICE AND RESERVED BROTH. SEASON TO TASTE. ADD ORANGE ZEST. SIMMER UNTIL HEATED THROUGH. SERVES 6-8.

# CORN CHOWDER

RICH AND CREAMY - AND HEALTHY TOO!

| | |
|---|---|
| 10 OZ. PKG. FROZEN KERNEL CORN | 300 g |
| 1 LARGE PEELED POTATO, CHOPPED | |
| 1 MEDIUM ONION, CHOPPED | |
| 1 SMALL RED OR ORANGE PEPPER, CHOPPED | |
| 10 OZ. CAN CHICKEN BROTH | 284 mL |
| 6 OZ. CAN EVAPORATED SKIM MILK | 160 mL |
| 1/4 CUP APPLE JUICE | 60 mL |
| 1/2 TSP. CUMIN | 2 mL |
| SALT & FRESHLY GROUND PEPPER TO TASTE | |
| FRESH CILANTRO LEAVES (OPTIONAL) | |

COMBINE ALL INGREDIENTS IN A LARGE SAUCEPAN. BRING TO A BOIL; REDUCE HEAT AND SIMMER, COVERED, FOR 10 MINUTES, UNTIL POTATO IS TENDER. PUT 2 CUPS (500 mL) OF THE CHOWDER INTO A BLENDER AND PURÉE UNTIL SMOOTH. RETURN TO SAUCEPAN, COOK AND STIR UNTIL HEATED THROUGH. SERVES 4.

I USED TO WISH MY COMPUTER WERE AS EASY TO USE AS MY TELEPHONE. THAT WISH HAS COME TRUE SINCE I NO LONGER KNOW HOW TO USE MY TELEPHONE.

# FRENCH ONION SOUP AU GRATIN

THIS IS THE BEST!

| | |
|---|---|
| 4 LARGE ONIONS, THINLY SLICED | |
| 1/4 CUP BUTTER | 60 mL |
| 4-10 OZ. CANS BEEF BROTH | 4-284 mL |
| 1/2 CUP DRY SHERRY | 125 mL |
| 2 TSP. WORCESTERSHIRE SAUCE | 10 mL |
| DASH OF PEPPER | |
| 6 SLICES FRENCH BREAD, 1/2" (1.3 cm) THICK, TOASTED | |
| 3/4 CUP GRATED PARMESAN CHEESE | 175 mL |
| 1-2 CUPS GRATED MOZZARELLA CHEESE | 250-500 mL |

IN A LARGE SAUCEPAN, COOK ONIONS IN BUTTER UNTIL TENDER BUT NOT BROWN. ADD BEEF BROTH, SHERRY, WORCESTERSHIRE SAUCE AND PEPPER AND BRING TO A BOIL. POUR INTO INDIVIDUAL OVENPROOF BOWLS. FLOAT A SLICE OF TOASTED FRENCH BREAD IN EACH. SPRINKLE WITH PARMESAN AND TOP WITH MOZZARELLA. PLACE UNDER BROILER AND HEAT UNTIL CHEESE BUBBLES. SERVE WITH A SALAD AND GARLIC BREAD. SCRUMPTIOUS! SERVES 6.

ISN'T IT A BIT UNNERVING THAT DOCTORS CALL WHAT THEY DO "PRACTICE"?

# TORTILLA SOUP

## SOUP

| | |
|---|---|
| 2 TBSP. OIL | 30 mL |
| 3 CORN TORTILLAS, CUT INTO 1" (2.5 cm) PIECES | |
| ½ CUP FINELY CHOPPED ONION | 125 mL |
| 3 GARLIC CLOVES, MINCED | |
| 1 JALAPEÑO PEPPER, SEEDED & MINCED | |
| 2 ANAHEIM CHILIES, ROASTED, PEELED, SEEDED & FINELY CHOPPED | |
| 8 ROMA TOMATOES, SEEDED & DICED | |
| 2 TBSP. TOMATO PASTE | 30 mL |
| 2 TSP. CUMIN | 10 mL |
| ¼ TSP. CAYENNE PEPPER | 1 mL |
| 5 CUPS CHICKEN BROTH | 1.2 L |
| 1 CUP PICANTE SAUCE (MEDIUM) | 250 mL |
| 2 WHOLE COOKED CHICKEN BREASTS, SHREDDED | |
| 1 RIPE AVOCADO, PITTED, PEELED & DICED | |

## GARNISH

| | |
|---|---|
| ½ CUP GRATED MONTEREY JACK CHEESE | 125 mL |
| ⅓ CUP CHOPPED FRESH CILANTRO (OPTIONAL) | 75 mL |
| 2 CORN TORTILLAS | |

TO MAKE SOUP: HEAT THE OIL IN A LARGE POT. ADD THE TORTILLAS, REDUCE HEAT AND COOK UNTIL THEY ARE GOLDEN BROWN AND SLIGHTLY CRISP. ADD THE ONION AND COOK 3 MINUTES LONGER; ADD GARLIC AND JALAPEÑO CHILI AND COOK ANOTHER 2 MINUTES. ADD THE ANAHEIM CHILIES, TOMATOES AND TOMATO PASTE; COOK

# TORTILLA SOUP

CONTINUED FROM PAGE 112.

FOR 10 MINUTES. STIR IN THE CUMIN AND CAYENNE. SLOWLY WHISK IN THE CHICKEN BROTH AND PICANTE SAUCE. SIMMER THE SOUP FOR ABOUT 20 MINUTES, OR UNTIL SLIGHTLY REDUCED. ADD THE SHREDDED CHICKEN AND AVOCADO AND HEAT UNTIL WARMED THROUGH.

TO MAKE GARNISH: PREHEAT OVEN TO 350°F (180°C). CUT TORTILLAS INTO STRIPS. PLACE THE STRIPS ON A BAKING SHEET AND BAKE FOR 10-15 MINUTES, OR UNTIL CRISP.

TO SERVE, LADLE SOUP INTO 6 BOWLS AND GARNISH WITH THE GRATED CHEESE, CILANTRO AND BAKED TORTILLA STRIPS. SERVES 6. (PICTURED ON PAGE 118.)

THE DIFFERENCE BETWEEN A PESSIMIST AND AN OPTIMIST: THE PESSIMIST SAYS, "THINGS ARE SO BAD, THEY CAN'T GET ANY WORSE." AND THE OPTIMIST SAYS, "OH YES THEY CAN!"

# MOROCCAN CHICKEN-VEGETABLE SOUP

SEEMS LIKE A LONG WAY TO GO FOR A GOOD BOWL OF SOUP.

|  | |
|---|---|
| 3 LBS. CUT-UP CHICKEN, SKIN & FAT REMOVED | 1.5 kg |
| 2 LARGE RED ONIONS, CHOPPED | |
| 6 CARROTS, PEELED & SLICED | |
| 6 GARLIC CLOVES, MINCED (YES - ALL OF IT!) | |
| 2 BAY LEAVES | |
| ½ TSP. SALT | 2 mL |
| ½ TSP. TURMERIC | 2 mL |
| ½ TSP. CINNAMON | 2 mL |
| 1 TSP. CUMIN | 5 mL |
| 8 CUPS CHICKEN BROTH | 2 L |
| ⅓ CUP COUSCOUS | 75 mL |
| ½ CUP SLICED GREEN ONIONS | 125 mL |

PLACE CHICKEN PIECES IN DUTCH OVEN WITH ONIONS, CARROTS, GARLIC, BAY LEAVES, SEASONINGS AND CHICKEN BROTH. BRING TO A BOIL AND REDUCE HEAT TO LOW. SIMMER FOR 1 HOUR, STIRRING OCCASIONALLY. REMOVE CHICKEN PIECES FROM SOUP AND REMOVE BONES. CUT CHICKEN INTO BITE-SIZED PIECES AND RETURN TO POT. ADD COUSCOUS AND GREEN ONIONS. SIMMER UNTIL HEATED THROUGH. SERVES 6.

FAVORITE OXYMORONS: NEW CLASSIC, CHILDPROOF, TAPED LIVE, PLASTIC GLASSES.

# SHOOTER'S SOUP

LISA, OUR PHOTOGRAPHER, CREATED THIS TERRIFIC THAI RECIPE. A GREAT LUNCH FOR THE LADIES.

| | |
|---|---|
| 2 SKINLESS, BONELESS CHICKEN BREASTS | |
| 1 TSP. GRATED GINGER ROOT | 5 mL |
| 2 GARLIC CLOVES, MINCED | |
| 1/4 CUP FRESH LIME JUICE | 60 mL |
| 2-10 OZ. CANS CHICKEN BROTH | 2-284 mL |
| 1 1/2 CANS WATER | 425 mL |
| 1 RIPE PAPAYA, PEELED & CUBED | |
| 4 GREEN ONIONS, SLICED | |
| 2 TBSP. CHOPPED CILANTRO | 30 mL |
| 1-2 TBSP. FRESH LIME JUICE | 15-30 mL |
| 1 TSP. CHILI OIL OR CAYENNE, TO TASTE | 5 mL |

CUT CHICKEN IN BITE-SIZED PIECES. MARINATE IN GINGER, GARLIC AND LIME JUICE FOR 1/2 HOUR. ADD CHICKEN AND MARINADE TO BROTH AND WATER. BRING TO BOIL; REDUCE TO SIMMER FOR ABOUT 5 MINUTES. ADD PAPAYA. SIMMER 3 MINUTES. ADD GREEN ONIONS, CILANTRO, LIME JUICE AND CHILI OIL. SERVE WITH BREAD STICKS. SERVES 4.

BOY'S COMMENT TO HIS MOM - "DADDY TOOK ME TO THE ZOO AND ONE OF THE ANIMALS PAID $46.20 ACROSS THE BOARD."

# WAR WONTON SOUP

CELEBRATE CHINESE NEW YEAR WITH THIS SAVORY SOUP.

| | |
|---|---|
| 3 - 10 OZ. CANS CHICKEN BROTH | 3 - 284 mL |
| 3 CUPS WATER | 750 mL |
| 1 TSP. SESAME OIL | 5 mL |
| 3 THIN SLICES FRESH GINGER | |
| 1 CUP LEFTOVER RARE ROAST BEEF | 250 mL |
| (OR COOKED SLICED CHICKEN), CUT IN STRIPS | |
| ½ LB. RAW SHRIMP, PEELED & DEVEINED | 250 g |
| 1-2 CUPS FRESH PEAPODS | 250-500 mL |
| 1 CUP THINLY CHOPPED CARROTS | 250 mL |
| 8 OZ. CAN SLICED WATER CHESTNUTS, DRAINED | 236 mL |
| 14 OZ. CAN BABY CORN COBS, DRAINED | 398 mL |
| 3 STALKS BOK CHOY, CHOPPED | |
| 4 OZ. PKG. FROZEN WONTONS | 115 g |
| 1 CUP THINLY SLICED GREEN ONIONS | 250 mL |

IN LARGE POT COMBINE BROTH, WATER, OIL AND GINGER. BRING TO BOIL. ADD REMAINING INGREDIENTS, EXCEPT WONTONS & GREEN ONIONS. REDUCE HEAT AND SIMMER 12 MINUTES. MEANWHILE, COOK WONTONS ACCORDING TO PACKAGE DIRECTIONS. DRAIN, ADD WONTONS TO BROTH MIXTURE AND SPRINKLE WITH GREEN ONIONS. MAKES ENOUGH FOR 8 LARGE SERVINGS.

IF A PARSLEY FARMER IS SUED, CAN THEY GARNISH HIS WAGES?

Champagne Squash Soup, page 108

Tortilla Soup, page 112

# HAMBURGER SOUP

DON'T BE DECEIVED BY THE NAME, THIS IS A FAMILY FAVORITE. FREEZES VERY WELL.

| | |
|---|---|
| 1½ LBS. LEAN GROUND BEEF | 750 g |
| 1 MEDIUM ONION, FINELY CHOPPED | |
| 28 OZ. CAN TOMATOES | 796 mL |
| 2 CUPS WATER | 500 mL |
| 3-10 OZ. CANS CONSOMMÉ | 3-284 mL |
| 10 OZ. CAN TOMATO SOUP | 284 mL |
| 4 CARROTS, FINELY CHOPPED | |
| 1 BAY LEAF | |
| 3 CELERY STALKS, FINELY CHOPPED | |
| PARSLEY | |
| ½ TSP. THYME | 2 mL |
| PEPPER TO TASTE | |
| ½ CUP BARLEY | 125 mL |

BROWN MEAT AND ONIONS. DRAIN WELL. COMBINE ALL INGREDIENTS IN LARGE POT. SIMMER, COVERED, A MINIMUM OF 2 HOURS. SERVES 10.

THEY SAY THAT A DOG IS A MAN'S BEST FRIEND. I DON'T THINK SO. HOW MANY FRIENDS HAVE YOU HAD NEUTERED?

# BEST OF BRIDGE BEAN SOUP

YOUR NEXT FAMILY FAVORITE! THE VERY THING FOR A COLD WINTER'S NIGHT.

| | |
|---|---|
| 1 LB. HOT ITALIAN SAUSAGE | 500 g |
| 2 SMOKED PORK HOCKS OR 2-3 CUPS (500-750 mL) CUBED HAM | |
| 3 MEDIUM POTATOES, PEELED & CUBED | |
| 2 MEDIUM ONIONS, DICED | |
| 3 CELERY STALKS WITH LEAVES, CHOPPED | |
| 5 CARROTS, PEELED & DICED | |
| 1 GREEN PEPPER, SEEDED & CHOPPED | |
| 1 CUP CHOPPED FRESH PARSLEY OR 2 TBSP. (30 mL) DRIED | 250 mL |
| 3-14 OZ. CANS KIDNEY BEANS | 3-398 mL |
| 14 OZ. CAN TOMATO SAUCE | 398 mL |
| 28 OZ. CAN TOMATOES, CHOPPED | 796 mL |
| 1-2 TSP. SALT | 5-10 mL |
| 1 TSP. PEPPER | 5 mL |
| 1 TSP. HOT PEPPER SAUCE | 5 mL |
| 2 BAY LEAVES | |
| 1 TSP. WORCESTERSHIRE SAUCE | 5 mL |
| 2 GARLIC CLOVES, CRUSHED | |

BOIL SAUSAGE TO REMOVE EXCESS FAT; CUT INTO BITE-SIZED PIECES. SKIN PORK HOCKS AND REMOVE EXCESS FAT. BROWN SAUSAGE AND PORK HOCKS IN A LARGE, HEAVY POT. DRAIN. ADD ALL OTHER INGREDIENTS AND ADD JUST ENOUGH WATER TO COVER. BRING TO A BOIL THEN REDUCE TO SIMMER. COVER AND COOK FOR 2-3 HOURS. REMOVE PORK HOCKS AND CUT MEAT INTO BITE-SIZED PIECES. RETURN MEAT TO POT. SERVE WITH CRUSTY BREAD. SERVES 8-10.

HINDSIGHT: SITTING ON YOUR GLASSES!

# PIZZA

Fast and Easy Pizza Crust
Pear and Cambozola Pizza
Mexican Pizza
Pizza Primavera

# POCKETS & WRAPS

Tuna Terrific
Turkey, Apple and Spinach Pockets
Turkey, Blue Cheese 'N' Pear Wrap
Zucchini, Peppers & Feta Cheese Wrap
Teriyaki Ginger Steak Wrap
Tex-Mex Fajitas

# FAST AND EASY PIZZA CRUST

PUT THIS TOGETHER WHEN YOU COME HOME FROM WORK - TAKES ABOUT 20 MINUTES.

| | |
|---|---|
| 3/4 CUP WARM WATER | 175 mL |
| 1 TBSP. ACTIVE DRY YEAST (1 PKG.) | 15 mL |
| 1 TSP. SUGAR | 5 mL |
| 1½ CUPS FLOUR | 375 mL |
| ¼ TSP. SALT | 1 mL |
| 1 TBSP. YELLOW CORNMEAL | 15 mL |
| 1 TBSP. OLIVE OIL | 15 mL |
| CORNMEAL TO SPRINKLE | |

PREHEAT OVEN TO 450°F (230°C). LIGHTLY OIL A 12" (30 cm) PIZZA PAN. IN A SMALL BOWL, MIX WARM WATER, YEAST AND SUGAR TOGETHER. LET SIT UNTIL YEAST ACTIVATES, ABOUT 5 MINUTES. IN A LARGE BOWL, STIR TOGETHER FLOUR, SALT AND CORNMEAL. ADD YEAST MIXTURE AND OLIVE OIL AND KNEAD TO A SMOOTH DOUGH, ABOUT 10 MINUTES. SPRINKLE A WORK SURFACE WITH CORNMEAL AND ROLL DOUGH INTO A 13" (33 cm) CIRCLE AND PLACE ON PIZZA PAN. CRIMP EDGES AND ADD YOUR FAVORITE TOPPINGS. BAKE FOR 10-15 MINUTES. MAKES 1, 12" (30 cm) PIZZA.

IF YOU CAN'T SWIM, IS IT REALLY NECESSARY TO WAIT A HALF AN HOUR AFTER EATING BEFORE YOU GO IN THE WATER?

# PEAR AND CAMBOZOLA PIZZA

THIS IS SOOO GOOD!

| | |
|---|---|
| 12" PIZZA CRUST (PAGE 122) OR PURCHASED PIZZA CRUST | 30 cm |
| OLIVE OIL TO BRUSH ON CRUST | |
| 14 OZ. CAN PEARS, DRAINED AND SLICED IN THIN STRIPS | 398 mL |
| 2 TBSP. TOASTED PINE NUTS | 30 mL |
| 3 OZ. CAMBOZOLA CHEESE, SLICED OR CRUMBLED | 85 g |
| FRESHLY GROUND PEPPER | |

PREHEAT OVEN TO 450°F (230°C). BRUSH CRUST WITH OLIVE OIL, ARRANGE PEARS ON CRUST IN PINWHEEL PATTERN, SPRINKLE WITH PINE NUTS, TOP WITH CHEESE AND A SPRINKLE OF PEPPER. BAKE 10-15 MINUTES, UNTIL CRUST IS GOLDEN.

ANOTHER GOOD IDEA: FOR APPLE AND BRIE PIZZA, SAUTÉ SLICED APPLES IN BUTTER AND BROWN SUGAR. SPRINKLE WITH CINNAMON. DOT PIZZA CRUST WITH BROKEN PIECES OF BRIE CHEESE, ARRANGE APPLES ON TOP AND SPRINKLE WITH CHOPPED WALNUTS AND FRESH ROSEMARY. BAKE AS ABOVE.

FAVORITE OXYMORONS: TEMPORARY TAX INCREASE, TIGHT SLACKS, TWELVE-OUNCE POUND CAKE, EXACT ESTIMATE.

## RANCHERO SAUCE

| | |
|---|---|
| 2 TBSP. VEGETABLE OIL | 30 mL |
| 1 CUP FINELY CHOPPED ONION | 250 mL |
| 1 GARLIC CLOVE, MINCED | |
| 4 CUPS FINELY CHOPPED FRESH OR CANNED TOMATOES | 1 L |
| 2 ANAHEIM OR OTHER MILD CHILIES, CORED, SEEDED & CHOPPED | |
| 1 TSP. SUGAR | 5 mL |
| SALT & FRESHLY GROUND PEPPER TO TASTE | |
| 2 TBSP. MINCED CILANTRO | 30 mL |
| 12" PIZZA CRUST (PAGE 122) OR PURCHASED PIZZA CRUST | 30 cm |

## TOPPING

| | |
|---|---|
| 1 CUP RANCHERO SAUCE | 250 mL |
| ½ LB. HOT SAUSAGE, COOKED, CRUMBLED & DRAINED | 250 g |
| 1½ CUPS GRATED MONTEREY JACK CHEESE | 375 mL |
| ½ CUP THINLY SLICED RED ONION | 125 mL |
| 1 RED, YELLOW OR GREEN BELL PEPPER, SLICED IN STRIPS | |
| 1 PICKLED JALAPEÑO PEPPER, SEEDED & DICED | |

TO PREPARE SAUCE: IN LARGE SKILLET, HEAT OIL OVER MEDIUM HEAT AND ADD ONION. COOK 2 MINUTES, STIRRING CONSTANTLY. ADD GARLIC AND COOK 2 MINUTES MORE, OR UNTIL ONION IS TRANSLUCENT. ADD TOMATOES, CHILIES, SUGAR, SALT AND PEPPER. SIMMER UNTIL SLIGHTLY THICKENED, ABOUT 15 MINUTES, STIRRING

# MEXICAN PIZZA

CONTINUED FROM PAGE 124.

OCCASIONALLY. STIR IN CILANTRO. THIS RECIPE MAKES 4 CUPS (1 L) AND WILL KEEP REFRIGERATED FOR UP TO 1 WEEK. ALSO DELICIOUS USED AS A PASTA SAUCE.

TO PREPARE PIZZA: PREHEAT OVEN TO 500°F (260°C). SPREAD RANCHERO SAUCE EVENLY OVER ROLLED PIZZA DOUGH. COVER WITH COOKED SAUSAGE AND SPRINKLE CHEESE OVER ALL. EVENLY DISTRIBUTE ONION, PEPPER AND PICKLED JALAPEÑO OVER CHEESE. BAKE PIZZA IN THE LOWER THIRD OF OVEN UNTIL CRUST IS BROWNED AND CHEESE IS MELTED, ABOUT 15-20 MINUTES.

IF MEN CAN RUN THE WORLD, WHY CAN'T THEY STOP WEARING NECKTIES? HOW INTELLIGENT IS IT TO START THE DAY BY TYING A LITTLE NOOSE AROUND YOUR NECK?

# PIZZA PRIMAVERA

12" PIZZA CRUST (PAGE 122) OR          30 CM
       PURCHASED PIZZA CRUST

## VEGETABLE TOPPINGS

MARINATED ARTICHOKE HEARTS, RESERVE
     MARINADE
ASPARAGUS TIPS OR BROCCOLI FLORETS
RED PEPPER CUT IN THIN STRIPS
MARINATED SUN-DRIED TOMATOES, CUT IN
     THIN SLIVERS
ROMA TOMATOES, THINLY SLICED
FETA CHEESE, CRUMBLED
BASIL, DRIED OR FRESH
PITTED OLIVES, SLICED
GRATED MOZZARELLA CHEESE TO SPRINKLE

PREHEAT OVEN TO 450°F (230°C). BRUSH CRUST
WITH SOME OF RESERVED ARTICHOKE MARINADE.
SPRINKLE WITH ANY OR ALL OF THE TOPPINGS
LISTED. TOP WITH MOZZARELLA CHEESE AND
BAKE 10-15 MINUTES, OR UNTIL CRUST IS GOLDEN.

I CAN REMEMBER WHEN YOU USED TO KISS YOUR
MONEY GOOD-BYE. NOW YOU DON'T EVEN GET A CHANCE
TO BLOW IN ITS EAR.

# TUNA TERRIFIC

A PERFECTLY POPULAR PITA POCKET.

## CURRY TUNA FILLING

| | | |
|---|---|---|
| 7 OZ. CAN TUNA | 170 | g |
| 1 CELERY STALK, FINELY CHOPPED | | |
| 2 GREEN ONIONS, FINELY CHOPPED | | |
| 1 GRANNY SMITH APPLE, CORED & CHOPPED | | |
| 2 TSP. FRESH LEMON JUICE | 10 | mL |
| 1 TSP. CURRY POWDER | 5 | mL |
| 3 TBSP. MAYONNAISE (FAT-FREE - ALL THE BETTER FOR YOU!) | 45 | mL |

2 PITA ROUNDS, CUT IN HALF
LETTUCE

DRAIN TUNA AND PUT IN BOWL. ADD REMAINING FILLING INGREDIENTS, MIX WELL. CHILL TO LET FLAVORS GET TO KNOW EACH OTHER. TO SERVE, PLACE ONE HALF OF A PITA INTO THE OTHER HALF. THIS MAKES A STURDIER POCKET. LINE EACH POCKET WITH LETTUCE AND SPOON HALF THE TUNA MIXTURE INTO EACH POCKET. SERVES 2.

IF A MAN IS STANDING IN THE MIDDLE OF THE FOREST SPEAKING AND THERE IS NO WOMAN AROUND TO HEAR HIM - IS HE STILL WRONG?

# TURKEY, APPLE AND SPINACH POCKETS

FAST 'N' HEALTHY.

## DIJON HONEY DRESSING

| | |
|---|---|
| ⅓ CUP FAT-FREE SOUR CREAM | 75 mL |
| 1 TBSP. HONEY | 15 mL |
| 1 TSP. DIJON MUSTARD | 5 mL |

| | |
|---|---|
| 2 LARGE PITA BREAD ROUNDS | |
| 1 CUP TORN FRESH SPINACH OR ROMAINE LEAVES | 250 mL |
| THINLY SLICED RED ONION, TO TASTE | |
| 6 OZ. THINLY SLICED, COOKED TURKEY OR CHICKEN BREAST | 170 g |
| 1 SMALL APPLE, CORED & THINLY SLICED | |

TO MAKE DRESSING: IN A SMALL BOWL, STIR TOGETHER SOUR CREAM, HONEY AND MUSTARD. SET ASIDE.

CUT EACH PITA BREAD ROUND IN HALF CROSSWISE. OPEN EACH PITA HALF TO FORM A POCKET. LAYER SPINACH, ONION, TURKEY AND APPLE. DRIZZLE WITH MUSTARD DRESSING. SERVES 4.

HELP STAMP OUT AND ERADICATE SUPERFLUOUS REDUNDANCY.

# TURKEY, BLUE CHEESE 'N' PEAR WRAP

SANDWICH BORED? TRY THIS!

| | |
|---|---|
| 1 TBSP. OLIVE OIL | 15 mL |
| ½ CUP COARSELY CHOPPED PECANS | 125 mL |
| ¼ TSP. SALT | 1 mL |
| ½ LB. SLICED, SMOKED OR COOKED TURKEY, CUT IN THIN STRIPS | 250 g |
| 1 LARGE PEAR, CORED & DICED | |
| 3 CUPS ROMAINE LETTUCE CUT IN STRIPS | 750 mL |
| ⅓ CUP RAISINS | 75 mL |
| ¼-⅓ CUP CRUMBLED BLUE CHEESE | 60-75 mL |
| 1 TBSP. FRESH LEMON JUICE | 15 mL |
| 4-10" (25 cm) FLOUR TORTILLAS | |

HEAT OIL IN FRYING PAN. ADD NUTS AND SALT. SAUTÉ ABOUT 2 MINUTES. IN LARGE BOWL, ADD NUTS TO TURKEY, PEAR, LETTUCE, RAISINS, BLUE CHEESE, AND LEMON JUICE. TOSS TO COAT WELL.

WRAP & ROLL: PLACE EACH FLOUR TORTILLA ON A PIECE OF WAXED PAPER. PILE ¼ OF THE FILLING IN A STRIP ABOUT ⅓ OF THE WAY FROM THE BOTTOM OF TORTILLA. FOLD BOTTOM OVER FILLING AND ROLL ONCE. THEN FOLD 1 SIDE OVER AND CONTINUE TO ROLL TORTILLA, LEAVING THE SIDE OPEN. BE CAREFUL NOT TO ROLL IN THE WAXED PAPER. WHEN FINISHED, ROLL FILLED TORTILLAS IN THEIR WAXED PAPER WITH THE TOP OPEN SO PAPER CAN BE PEELED DOWN AS THEY ARE EATEN. (PICTURED ON PAGE 135.)

# ZUCCHINI, PEPPERS AND FETA CHEESE WRAP

## BALSAMIC VINAIGRETTE

| | |
|---|---|
| 2 TBSP. BALSAMIC VINEGAR | 30 mL |
| 1/4 CUP OLIVE OIL | 60 mL |
| SALT & FRESHLY GROUND PEPPER TO TASTE | |

| | |
|---|---|
| 1 SMALL RED ONION, SLICED | |
| 1 TBSP. OIL | 15 mL |
| 1 MEDIUM ZUCCHINI, HALVED & SLICED IN STRIPS | |
| 1 SMALL GREEN PEPPER, SLICED IN STRIPS | |
| 1 SMALL RED PEPPER, SLICED IN STRIPS | |
| 1/2 CUP BEAN SPROUTS | 125 mL |
| 1/2 CUP COOKED COUSCOUS (OPTIONAL) | 125 mL |

| | |
|---|---|
| 2-3 FLOUR TORTILLAS | |
| 2 OZ. FETA CHEESE (GOAT CHEESE IS GOOD TOO!) | 60 g |

COMBINE ALL VINAIGRETTE INGREDIENTS. IN A FRYING PAN, SAUTÉ ONION IN OIL. ADD ZUCCHINI AND PEPPERS AND STIR BRIEFLY. ADD BEAN SPROUTS; STIR, THEN ADD COUSCOUS AND MIX WELL. COOK FOR 30 SECONDS; ADD VINAIGRETTE AND MIX WELL. TO SERVE, DISTRIBUTE MIXTURE EVENLY ON TORTILLAS, CRUMBLE CHEESE OVER VEGETABLE MIXTURE AND ROLL UP. MMMMMM! MMMMMMM! SERVES 2-3.
(PICTURED ON PAGE 135.)

# — TERIYAKI GINGER STEAK WRAP —

| | |
|---|---|
| ½ LB. SIRLOIN STEAK, THINLY SLICED | 250 g |
| 4 TSP. MINCED FRESH GINGER | 20 mL |
| 2 TBSP. OIL | 30 mL |
| 1 MEDIUM RED ONION, THINLY SLICED | |
| 2 CUPS SLICED FRESH MUSHROOMS | 500 mL |
| ½ RED PEPPER, SLICED | |
| ½ GREEN PEPPER, SLICED | |
| 1½ CUPS COOKED BASMATI RICE | 375 mL |
| ¼ CUP TERIYAKI SAUCE | 60 mL |
| 1 TBSP. HOT & SPICY SZECHUAN SAUCE | 15 mL |
| 1 TSP. SESAME OIL | 5 mL |
| 1 CUP BEAN SPROUTS | 250 mL |
| 4-10" (25 cm) FLOUR TORTILLAS | |

TOSS STEAK SLICES WITH GINGER AND LET STAND FOR AT LEAST ½ HOUR. HEAT OIL IN LARGE FRYING PAN AND SAUTÉ ONION, STEAK AND GINGER UNTIL STEAK IS BROWN. ADD MUSHROOMS AND STIR-FRY. ADD PEPPERS AND RICE. STIR IN SAUCES AND SESAME OIL. ADD BEAN SPROUTS JUST BEFORE YOU'RE READY TO WRAP AND ROLL, DIVIDE MIXTURE EVENLY BETWEEN TORTILLAS. ROLL 1 END OVER FILLING, THEN BOTH SIDES OVER. ROLL AGAIN UNTIL YOU HAVE A CLOSED PACKAGE. CUT WRAP IN HALF DIAGONALLY. ADJUST YOUR OBI! (PICTURED ON PAGE 135.)

THE REPAIRMAN WILL NEVER HAVE SEEN A MODEL LIKE YOURS.

# TEX-MEX FAJITAS

OLÉ YOUSE GRINGOS!!

2 LBS. FLANK STEAK (1 LB. SERVES 3 PEOPLE) OR 3 CHICKEN BREASTS, SKINNED, BONED & HALVED — 1 kg

## FAJITA MARINADE

| | |
|---|---|
| ½ CUP VEGETABLE OIL | 125 mL |
| ⅓ CUP FRESH LIME JUICE | 75 mL |
| ⅓ CUP RED WINE VINEGAR (ELIMINATE FOR CHICKEN) | 75 mL |
| ⅓ CUP CHOPPED ONION | 75 mL |
| 1 TSP. SUGAR | 5 mL |
| 1 TSP. OREGANO | 5 mL |
| SALT & PEPPER TO TASTE | |
| ¼ TSP. CUMIN | 1 mL |
| 2 GARLIC CLOVES, MINCED | |
| 6 LARGE FLOUR TORTILLAS | |

## TOPPINGS

ONION SLICES, SAUTÉED
GREEN & RED PEPPER STRIPS, SAUTÉED
SHREDDED LETTUCE
GUACAMOLE, SOUR CREAM & SALSA

COMBINE MARINADE INGREDIENTS IN SHALLOW CASSEROLE. SCORE BOTH SIDES OF STEAK. ADD MEAT. COVER AND REFRIGERATE SEVERAL HOURS. REMOVE FROM MARINADE AND BAR-B-QUE. SLICE IN THIN STRIPS ACROSS THE GRAIN. WRAP IN WARM TORTILLAS WITH ONIONS AND PEPPERS AND ANY OR ALL OF THE OTHER TOPPINGS.
SERVES 6 GRINGOS.

# PASTA

Fettuccine with Sambuca and Cranberries
Fresh Pear and Curry Pasta
Spicy Penne
Pasta with Peppers
Pasta Fasta
Gnocchi with Red Pepper Sauce
Red and White Tortellini
Alfredo Sauce
Gourmet Macaroni and Cheese
Bow Ties with Lemon Chicken
Lemon Fettuccine with Chicken
Chicken with Spaghettini
Traditional Lasagne
"Death to Dieters" Chicken Lasagna
Broccoli Lasagne Au Gratin
Pesto Lasagne
Linguine with Red Clam Sauce
Linguine with White Clam Sauce
Fettuccine with Asparagus and Shrimp

# FETTUCCINE WITH SAMBUCA AND CRANBERRIES

PASTA FOR COMPANY - ESTUPENDO!

| | |
|---|---|
| ¼ CUP BUTTER | 60 mL |
| 2 WHOLE BONELESS, SKINLESS CHICKEN BREASTS, CUBED | |
| 2 GARLIC CLOVES, MINCED | |
| 3 CUPS WHIPPING CREAM | 750 mL |
| ¼ CUP SAMBUCA LIQUEUR | 60 mL |
| ¼ CUP ORANGE JUICE CONCENTRATE | 60 mL |
| ½ CUP FRESHLY GRATED PARMESAN CHEESE | 125 mL |
| ¼ TSP. NUTMEG | 1 mL |
| SALT & PEPPER TO TASTE | |
| 14 OZ. CAN ARTICHOKES (10-12 COUNT), DRAINED & CHOPPED | 398 mL |
| 3 OZ. PKG. DRIED CRANBERRIES | 85 g |
| 1 LB. FETTUCCINE | 500 g |
| CHOPPED FRESH PARSLEY & ORANGE ZEST FOR GARNISH | |

IN A LARGE FRYING PAN, HEAT BUTTER AND SAUTÉ CUBED CHICKEN AND GARLIC UNTIL BARELY COOKED (DO NOT OVER COOK!). REMOVE CHICKEN FROM PAN AND SET ASIDE. ADD WHIPPING CREAM, SAMBUCA AND ORANGE JUICE TO PAN AND STIR WELL. ADD PARMESAN, NUTMEG, SALT AND PEPPER, STIRRING UNTIL SMOOTH. SIMMER FOR 5 MINUTES. ADD CHOPPED ARTICHOKES, CRANBERRIES AND CHICKEN; SIMMER AND STIR FOR 10 MINUTES. THAT'S IT FOR THE SAUCE! NOW, COOK THE FETTUCCINE ACCORDING TO PACKAGE DIRECTIONS. CAREFULLY FOLD SAUCE INTO PASTA AND GARNISH WITH PARSLEY AND ORANGE ZEST. SERVE WITH GARLIC TOAST. SERVES 6-8.

Wraps — Turkey / Teriyaki Steak / Vegetarian, page 129-131

Vegetable Frittata, page 34

# FRESH PEAR AND CURRY PASTA

VEGETARIAN DINNER FOR 2.

| | |
|---|---|
| ½ SMALL ONION, CHOPPED | |
| 2 TBSP. OIL | 30 mL |
| 2 GARLIC CLOVES, MINCED | |
| 1 TBSP. MEDIUM CURRY PASTE | 15 mL |
| 1 TSP. TOMATO PASTE | 5 mL |
| 2 TBSP. HONEY | 30 mL |
| 2 CUPS VEGETABLE OR CHICKEN BROTH | 500 mL |
| 1 UNPEELED RIPE PEAR, SLICED IN THIN WEDGES | |
| 2 ROMA TOMATOES, CHOPPED | |
| 2 TBSP. CREAM OR MILK | 30 mL |
| 3 TBSP. CHOPPED CILANTRO | 45 mL |
| PASTA FOR 2: ROTINI, BOW TIES OR SHELLS | |

IN A FRYING PAN OVER MEDIUM HEAT, SAUTÉ
ONION IN OIL UNTIL SOFT. ADD GARLIC AND CURRY
PASTE AND STIR 2-3 MINUTES. ADD TOMATO
PASTE AND HONEY AND STIR ANOTHER
2 MINUTES. ADD BROTH, INCREASE HEAT TO
MEDIUM HIGH AND BOIL GENTLY, REDUCING LIQUID
TO LESS THAN 1 CUP (250 mL). (THIS TAKES
ABOUT 15 MINUTES; NOW IS A GOOD TIME TO
START COOKING THE PASTA.) ADD PEAR SLICES
AND COOK FOR 1 MINUTE. ADD TOMATOES AND
CREAM AND STIR ANOTHER 2 MINUTES. STIR IN
CHOPPED CILANTRO. POUR OVER PASTA AND TOSS
GENTLY. IF YOUR DINNER COMPANION INSISTS ON
MEAT, SERVE WITH GRILLED CHICKEN BREAST OR
PORK TENDERLOIN. MIXED GREENS AND
BALSAMIC VINAIGRETTE (PAGE 101) IS A PERFECT
COMPLEMENT.

# SPICY PENNE

*EASY AND GOOD!*

| | |
|---|---|
| 2 TBSP. OLIVE OIL | 30 mL |
| 4 GARLIC CLOVES, MINCED | |
| ½ TSP. HOT RED PEPPER FLAKES | 2 mL |
| 28 OZ. CAN CRUSHED ITALIAN TOMATOES | 796 mL |
| 1 TSP. SALT | 5 mL |
| ½ TSP. FRESHLY GROUND PEPPER | 2 mL |
| ¼ CUP CHOPPED FRESH PARSLEY | 60 mL |
| 1 LB. PENNE NOODLES | 500 g |
| ½ CUP FRESHLY GRATED PARMESAN CHEESE | 125 mL |

IN A LARGE HEAVY FRYING PAN, HEAT OIL, ADD GARLIC AND PEPPER FLAKES. DO NOT BROWN. STIR IN TOMATOES, SALT AND PEPPER. COOK FOR 10-15 MINUTES, OR UNTIL THICKENED. STIR IN HALF OF THE PARSLEY. SET ASIDE. IN A LARGE POT OF BOILING, SALTED WATER, COOK PENNE FOR 10-15 MINUTES. DRAIN WELL. REHEAT SAUCE AND POUR OVER PENNE. SPRINKLE WITH PARMESAN AND REMAINING PARSLEY. TOSS WELL. SERVE IN INDIVIDUAL PASTA BOWLS. SERVES 6.

CANDY IS DANDY BUT ASPARTAME IS PHENYLKETONURIC.

## PASTA WITH PEPPERS

*AFTER FIVE AND STILL ALIVE!*

4 PEPPERS, USE MIXTURE OF RED,
    GREEN & YELLOW

⅓ CUP OLIVE OIL          75 mL

3 GARLIC CLOVES, MINCED

½ LB. SPAGHETTINI         250 g

2 CUPS GRATED ASIAGO OR FRESHLY   500 mL
    GRATED PARMESAN CHEESE

CUT PEPPERS INTO STRIPS. SAUTÉ IN OIL WITH GARLIC. COOK PASTA ACCORDING TO PACKAGE DIRECTIONS. DRAIN. POUR PEPPER-OIL MIXTURE OVER HOT PASTA AND TOSS WITH GRATED CHEESE. SERVES 4 AS A SIDE DISH.

IF THE DOCTOR TELLS YOU TO TAKE AN ASPIRIN A DAY FOR YOUR HEART, HOW DO YOU KNOW WHEN YOU'VE GOT A HEADACHE?

# PASTA FASTA

*After a busy day - you've got it made!*

| | |
|---|---|
| 2 cups halved cherry tomatoes | 500 mL |
| 1/2 cup chopped fresh basil | 125 mL |
| 2 garlic cloves, minced | |
| 3 tbsp. olive oil | 45 mL |
| Salt & pepper to taste | |
| Enough rotini or penne for 2 | |
| 1 cup grated mozzarella cheese | 250 mL |

In the morning: Combine tomatoes, basil, garlic, olive oil, salt and pepper. Cover and refrigerate.

Dinnertime: Cook the pasta according to package directions. Drain and return to pot. Add marinated veggies (don't drain) and cheese. Toss, cover. Set aside for 5 minutes, until cheeses melt. Place in your favorite pasta bowl and serve immediately. Good with baguette sticks (page 20). (Pictured on page 153.) Serves 2.

I couldn't repair your brakes, so I made your horn louder.

# GNOCCHI WITH RED PEPPER SAUCE

| | |
|---|---|
| 3 TBSP. OLIVE OIL | 45 mL |
| 3 RED PEPPERS, CUT INTO ¼" (1 cm) PIECES | |
| 1 LARGE ONION, FINELY CHOPPED | |
| 4 GARLIC CLOVES, MINCED | |
| 1½ TSP. DRIED BASIL | 7 mL |
| ½ TSP. PEPPER | 2 mL |
| ¼ TSP. SALT | 1 mL |
| 28 OZ. CAN PLUM TOMATOES, DRAINED & CHOPPED | 796 mL |
| 1 CUP CHICKEN BROTH | 250 mL |
| 1 TBSP. BALSAMIC VINEGAR | 15 mL |
| ½ TSP. SUGAR | 2 mL |
| 1½ LBS. FRESH OR FROZEN GNOCCHI | 750 g |
| FRESHLY GRATED PARMESAN CHEESE | |

IN A LARGE FRYING PAN, HEAT OIL OVER MEDIUM-HIGH HEAT. COOK RED PEPPERS, ONION, GARLIC, BASIL, PEPPER AND SALT, STIRRING OFTEN, FOR ABOUT 10 MINUTES, OR UNTIL ONIONS ARE SOFTENED. ADD TOMATOES, BROTH, VINEGAR AND SUGAR; BRING TO BOIL. REDUCE HEAT AND SIMMER FOR 10 MINUTES.

IN LARGE POT OF BOILING SALTED WATER, COOK GNOCCHI ACCORDING TO PACKAGE DIRECTIONS OR UNTIL THEY FLOAT TO SURFACE. DRAIN; RETURN TO POT AND TOSS GENTLY WITH THE SAUCE. SERVES 4.

DON'T FORGET TO PASS THE PARMESAN!

# RED AND WHITE TORTELLINI

TORTELLINI IN TWO SAUCES.

## TOMATO SAUCE

| | |
|---|---|
| 1 TBSP. BUTTER | 15 mL |
| 2 GARLIC CLOVES, MINCED | |
| ¼ CUP CHOPPED ONION | 60 mL |
| 14 OZ. CAN TOMATO SAUCE | 398 mL |
| 12 OZ. TORTELLINI, FRESH OR FROZEN | 340 g |

## MUSHROOM PARMESAN SAUCE

| | |
|---|---|
| 2 TBSP. BUTTER | 30 mL |
| 2 CUPS SLICED FRESH MUSHROOMS | 500 mL |
| ¼ CUP CHOPPED GREEN ONION | 60 mL |
| 2 TBSP. FLOUR | 30 mL |
| 2 CUPS MILK | 500 mL |
| ⅔ CUP GRATED PARMESAN CHEESE | 150 mL |
| SALT & PEPPER | |
| 1½ CUPS GRATED MOZZARELLA CHEESE | 375 mL |
| GRATED PARMESAN CHEESE | |

TO MAKE TOMATO SAUCE: MELT BUTTER AND SAUTÉ GARLIC AND ONION UNTIL TENDER. ADD TOMATO SAUCE AND BRING TO BOIL. REDUCE HEAT, COVER AND SIMMER 10 MINUTES.

COOK TORTELLINI ACCORDING TO PACKAGE DIRECTIONS.

TO MAKE MUSHROOM SAUCE: MELT BUTTER AND SAUTÉ MUSHROOMS AND GREEN ONION UNTIL TENDER. SPRINKLE WITH FLOUR AND GRADUALLY

## RED AND WHITE TORTELLINI

### CONTINUED FROM PAGE 142.

STIR IN MILK. COOK AND STIR OVER MEDIUM HEAT UNTIL MIXTURE THICKENS TO CONSISTENCY OF MUSHROOM SOUP. REMOVE FROM HEAT. STIR IN PARMESAN CHEESE, SALT AND PEPPER TO TASTE. ADD MUSHROOM PARMESAN SAUCE TO COOKED, DRAINED TORTELLINI.

TO SERVE: SPREAD TOMATO SAUCE OVER BOTTOM OF A LARGE SHALLOW CASSEROLE. SPOON TORTELLINI MUSHROOM MIXTURE ON TOP LEAVING A RED BORDER OF TOMATO SAUCE. SPRINKLE WITH MOZZARELLA CHEESE AND ADDITIONAL PARMESAN CHEESE. PLACE UNDER BROILER UNTIL CHEESE IS MELTED AND GOLDEN. SERVE IMMEDIATELY. SERVES 4-6.

POSTED NEXT TO A TRAY OF PENNIES AT CASHIER'S COUNTER: "NEED A PENNY, TAKE A PENNY; NEED TWO PENNIES, GET A JOB!"

# ALFREDO SAUCE

BASIC AND A BREEZE TO MAKE. SERVE WITH ANY PASTA. OUR FAVORITE IS FETTUCCINE OR TORTELLINI.

| | |
|---|---|
| 1/3 CUP BUTTER | 75 mL |
| 1½ CUPS WHIPPING CREAM | 375 mL |
| 3-4 CUPS COOKED PASTA | 750 mL-1 L |
| 1 CUP FRESHLY GRATED PARMESAN | 250 mL |
| ¼ CUP MILK | 60 mL |
| 1 TSP. SALT | 5 mL |
| ½ TSP. PEPPER | 2 mL |
| DASH OF NUTMEG | |

IN A LARGE FRYING PAN, MELT BUTTER OVER HIGH HEAT UNTIL IT TURNS LIGHT BROWN. ADD ½ CUP (125 mL) OF CREAM AND BOIL, STIRRING CONSTANTLY, UNTIL MIXTURE BECOMES SHINY AND LARGE BUBBLES FORM. SET ASIDE IF MAKING AHEAD.

COOK PASTA ACCORDING TO PACKAGE DIRECTIONS. OVER MEDIUM HEAT ADD PASTA TO SAUCE, MIXING WITH 2 FORKS TO COAT WELL. ADD PARMESAN CHEESE, REMAINING CREAM AND MILK, A LITTLE OF EACH AT A TIME UNTIL ALL ARE COMBINED. SEASON WITH SALT, PEPPER AND NUTMEG, ADDING MORE OF EACH IF DESIRED. SERVES 4-6.

BAROQUE: WHEN YOU ARE OUT OF MONET.

# GOURMET MACARONI AND CHEESE

COMFORT FOOD.

| | |
|---|---|
| 2½ CUPS MACARONI | 625 mL |
| ¼ CUP BUTTER | 60 mL |
| ¼ CUP FLOUR | 60 mL |
| 2 CUPS MILK | 500 mL |
| 1 TSP. SALT | 5 mL |
| 1 TSP. SUGAR | 5 mL |
| ½ LB. PROCESSED CHEESE, CUBED (VELVEETA) | 250 g |
| ⅔ CUP SOUR CREAM (FAT-FREE IS FINE) | 150 mL |
| 1⅓ CUPS COTTAGE CHEESE | 325 mL |
| 2 CUPS GRATED OLD CHEDDAR CHEESE | 500 mL |
| 1½ CUPS SOFT BREADCRUMBS | 375 mL |
| 2 TBSP. BUTTER | 30 mL |
| PAPRIKA | |

COOK AND DRAIN MACARONI AND PLACE IN A 2½-QUART (2.5 L). GREASED CASSEROLE. MELT BUTTER OVER MEDIUM HEAT; STIR IN FLOUR; MIX WELL. ADD MILK AND COOK OVER MEDIUM HEAT, STIRRING CONSTANTLY UNTIL SAUCE THICKENS. ADD SALT, SUGAR AND CHEESE. MIX WELL. MIX SOUR CREAM AND COTTAGE CHEESE INTO SAUCE. POUR OVER MACARONI. MIX WELL. SPRINKLE CHEDDAR CHEESE AND CRUMBS OVER TOP. DOT WITH BUTTER AND SPRINKLE WITH PAPRIKA. MAY BE FROZEN AT THIS POINT. BAKE AT 350°F (180°C) FOR 45-50 MINUTES. SERVES 6.

THE FACE OF A CHILD CAN SAY IT ALL - ESPECIALLY THE MOUTH PART OF THE FACE.

# BOW TIES WITH LEMON CHICKEN

| | | |
|---|---|---|
| 2 BONELESS, SKINLESS CHICKEN BREAST HALVES | | |
| 3/4 LB. BOW-TIE PASTA | 365 | g |
| 10 OZ. BAG PREWASHED SPINACH, TRIMMED, TORN INTO BITE-SIZED PIECES | 300 | g |
| 1 MEDIUM ONION, HALVED LENGTHWISE & THINLY SLICED CROSSWISE | | |
| 1 1/2 CUPS CHICKEN BROTH | 375 mL | |
| 1/4 CUP WHITE WINE | 60 mL | |
| 1 TSP. GRATED LEMON ZEST | 5 mL | |
| 3 TBSP. FRESH LEMON JUICE | 45 mL | |
| 2 TSP. MINCED GARLIC | 10 mL | |
| SALT & PEPPER TO TASTE | | |
| 1/4 CUP CHICKEN BROTH | 60 mL | |
| 1 TBSP. FLOUR | 15 mL | |
| 2 TSP. CHOPPED FRESH THYME | 10 mL | |
| 2 TSP. BUTTER | 10 mL | |

POACH CHICKEN IN WATER TO COVER FOR
5 MINUTES, OR UNTIL NO LONGER PINK IN THE
MIDDLE. CUT INTO BITE-SIZED PIECES. IN LARGE
POT, COOK PASTA ACCORDING TO PACKAGE
DIRECTIONS. WHEN COOKED, ADD SPINACH TO
PASTA AND BOIL UNTIL WILTED, ABOUT
10-20 SECONDS. DRAIN AND RETURN TO POT. COAT
FRYING PAN WITH COOKING SPRAY. SAUTÉ ONION
OVER MEDIUM-LOW HEAT, STIRRING OCCASIONALLY,
UNTIL WELL BROWNED AND CARAMELIZED,
ABOUT 7 MINUTES. STIR IN BROTH, WHITE WINE,

## BOW TIES WITH LEMON CHICKEN

CONTINUED FROM PAGE 146.

LEMON ZEST, JUICE, GARLIC, SALT AND PEPPER.
SIMMER 2 MINUTES. WHISK TOGETHER BROTH AND
FLOUR. STIR INTO MIXTURE. SIMMER AND STIR,
UNTIL SLIGHTLY THICKENED. ADD THYME AND
BUTTER AND STIR IN CHICKEN. REMOVE FROM
HEAT AND POUR OVER PASTA AND SPINACH IN
POT. TOSS TO MIX. SERVES 4.

## LEMON FETTUCCINE WITH CHICKEN

DEE-LICIOUS AND INCREDIBLY EASY.

| | |
|---|---|
| ¾ LB. FETTUCCINE | 365 g |
| ¼ CUP MELTED BUTTER | 60 mL |
| 1 CUP HALF & HALF CREAM | 250 mL |
| 1 LEMON, JUICE & GRATED RIND | |
| 1 SKINLESS, BONELESS CHICKEN BREAST, COOKED & CUBED | |
| ½ CUP PINE NUTS | 125 mL |

COOK PASTA ACCORDING TO PACKAGE
DIRECTIONS. COMBINE BUTTER, CREAM, LEMON
JUICE AND GRATED RIND. TOSS WITH PASTA,
CHICKEN AND PINE NUTS.

# CHICKEN WITH SPAGHETTINI

A NIFTY NOODLE DISH WITH A WONDERFUL TARRAGON FLAVOR.

| | |
|---|---|
| 2 CHICKEN BREASTS, SKINNED & BONED | |
| 1/4 CUP BUTTER OR MARGARINE | 60 mL |
| 3 GARLIC CLOVES, MINCED | |
| 1 ONION, FINELY CHOPPED | |
| 3 MEDIUM TOMATOES, CHOPPED | |
| 1 TBSP. DRIED TARRAGON OR BASIL | 15 mL |
| 3/4 LB. SPAGHETTINI OR LINGUINE | 365 g |
| 3 TBSP. DRY WHITE WINE OR VERMOUTH | 45 mL |
| 1/4 CUP CHICKEN BROTH | 60 mL |
| 1 CUP MILK | 250 mL |
| 1/4 TSP. EACH SALT & PEPPER | 1 mL |
| 1/2 CUP CHOPPED FRESH PARSLEY | 125 mL |
| FRESHLY GRATED PARMESAN CHEESE | |

CUT CHICKEN INTO CUBES AND SAUTÉ IN BUTTER, STIRRING UNTIL OPAQUE. TRANSFER TO A PLATE. ADD GARLIC AND ONION TO FRYING PAN. SAUTÉ UNTIL SOFTENED. ADD TOMATOES AND TARRAGON AND COOK 3 MINUTES. COOK SPAGHETTINI ACCORDING TO PACKAGE DIRECTIONS. DRAIN. MEANWHILE, POUR WINE AND BROTH INTO FRYING PAN AND COOK UNTIL REDUCED BY TWO-THIRDS. STIR IN MILK, SALT AND PEPPER AND COOK UNTIL SLIGHTLY THICKENED. ADD COOKED CHICKEN AND ACCUMULATED JUICES; SIMMER UNTIL HEATED THROUGH. STIR IN 1/3 CUP (75 mL) PARSLEY AND TOSS WITH HOT PASTA IN LARGE SERVING BOWL. TOP WITH REMAINING PARSLEY. PASS THE PARMESAN. SERVES 4.

## MEAT SAUCE

| | |
|---|---|
| 1½ LBS. LEAN GROUND BEEF | 750 g |
| 1 CUP DICED ONIONS | 250 mL |
| 1 GARLIC CLOVE, MINCED | |
| 19 OZ. CAN ITALIAN TOMATOES | 540 mL |
| 14 OZ. CAN TOMATO SAUCE | 398 mL |
| 5½ OZ. CAN TOMATO PASTE | 156 mL |
| ½ CUP RED WINE | 125 mL |
| 2 TBSP. WORCESTERSHIRE SAUCE | 30 mL |
| 1 TSP. SUGAR | 5 mL |
| SALT & PEPPER TO TASTE | |
| 1 TSP. BASIL | 5 mL |
| 1 TSP. OREGANO | 5 mL |

| | |
|---|---|
| 8 LASAGNE NOODLES, COOKED ACCORDING TO PACKAGE DIRECTIONS | |
| 2 CUPS RICOTTA OR COTTAGE CHEESE | 500 mL |
| 1 LB. SLICED MOZZARELLA CHEESE | 500 g |
| ½ CUP GRATED PARMESAN CHEESE | 125 mL |

BROWN BEEF, ONIONS AND GARLIC. DRAIN OFF FAT. ADD TOMATOES, TOMATO SAUCE, PASTE, WINE, WORCESTERSHIRE SAUCE, SUGAR AND SEASONINGS. COVER AND SIMMER FOR 1 HOUR. IN A 9 X 13" (23 X 33 cm) PAN, LAYER ½ OF THE MEAT SAUCE, ½ OF THE NOODLES, ½ OF THE RICOTTA CHEESE AND ½ OF THE MOZZARELLA CHEESE. REPEAT LAYERS. SPRINKLE WITH PARMESAN AND BAKE AT 350°F (180°C) FOR 40 MINUTES. LET SIT FOR 10 MINUTES BEFORE SERVING. SERVE WITH CAESAR SALAD (PAGE 79). THE MEAT SAUCE MAY BE SERVED OVER ANY COOKED PASTA.

# "DEATH TO DIETERS"
## CHICKEN LASAGNE

| | |
|---|---|
| 3 CUPS FRESH MUSHROOMS, SLICED | 750 mL |
| 2 CUPS CHOPPED ONION | 500 mL |
| 2 PKGS. KNORRS HOLLANDAISE SAUCE, | 750 mL |
| (PREPARED ACCORDING TO PACKAGE | |
| DIRECTIONS) YIELD 3 CUPS (750 mL) | |
| 8 LASAGNE NOODLES, COOKED | |
| 2 LBS. CHICKEN OR TURKEY BREAST, | 1 kg |
| COOKED & THINLY SLICED | |
| SALT & PEPPER TO TASTE | |
| 1 TSP. DRIED BASIL | 5 mL |
| 1 TSP. DRIED OREGANO | 5 mL |
| 3 CUPS SHREDDED MOZZARELLA CHEESE | 750 mL |
| 1 CUP GRATED PARMESAN CHEESE | 250 mL |
| 1 LB. FRESH ASPARAGUS, COOKED | 500 kg |
| TENDER-CRISP | |

SPRAY A NON-STICK FRYING PAN WITH COOKING
SPRAY. SAUTÉ MUSHROOMS AND ONIONS UNTIL
SOFT. SPREAD A SMALL AMOUNT OF
HOLLANDAISE ON THE BOTTOM OF A 9 x 13"
(23 x 33 cm) PAN. PLACE A LAYER OF NOODLES
ON TOP, THEN COVER WITH HALF OF THE
CHICKEN AND SPRINKLE WITH SALT AND PEPPER
TO TASTE. TOP WITH HALF OF THE MUSHROOM
AND ONION MIXTURE, THEN HALF OF THE
REMAINING HOLLANDAISE AND SPRINKLE WITH
HALF OF THE BASIL AND OREGANO. TOP THIS
WITH HALF OF THE MOZZARELLA AND PARMESAN
CHEESES. PLACE ALL OF THE ASPARAGUS
NEATLY IN A LAYER OVER CHEESE. REPEAT THE

## "DEATH TO DIETERS" CHICKEN LASAGNE

### CONTINUED FROM PAGE 150.

LAYERS, ENDING WITH THE CHEESES. COOK, UNCOVERED, AT 350°F (180°C) OVEN FOR 35 MINUTES, OR UNTIL HOT AND BUBBLY. LET STAND FOR 10 MINUTES BEFORE CUTTING. SERVE A SALAD WITH A TART DRESSING TO OFFSET THE RICHNESS. SERVES 10-12.

## BROCCOLI LASAGNE AU GRATIN

| | |
|---|---|
| 5 CUPS FRESH BROCCOLI FLORETS | 1.25 L |
| 24 oz. JAR SPICY SPAGHETTI SAUCE | 750 mL |
| 8 LASAGNE NOODLES, COOKED | |
| 2 CUPS RICOTTA CHEESE | 500 mL |
| 2 EGGS, SLIGHTLY BEATEN | |
| 2 CUPS SHREDDED MOZZARELLA CHEESE | 500 mL |
| ½ CUP GRATED PARMESAN CHEESE | 125 mL |

PARBOIL BROCCOLI FOR 1 MINUTE. SPREAD A THIN LAYER OF SPAGHETTI SAUCE IN A 9 X 13" (23 X 33 cm). COVER WITH 4 LASAGNE NOODLES. MIX TOGETHER BROCCOLI, RICOTTA CHEESE AND EGGS. SPREAD ½ OF MIXTURE OVER NOODLES. TOP WITH ½ OF REMAINING SPAGHETTI SAUCE, ½ MOZZARELLA AND ½ PARMESAN. REPEAT LAYERS. BAKE AT 350°F (180°C) FOR 30-35 MINUTES. SERVES 8-10. (PICTURED ON PAGE 153.)

# PESTO LASAGNE

GOOD AS A SIDE DISH WITH BAR-B-QUED CHICKEN OR STEAK.

## TOMATO SAUCE

| | |
|---|---|
| 4 GARLIC CLOVES, MINCED | |
| 2 ONIONS, CHOPPED | |
| 1/3 CUP OLIVE OIL | 75 mL |
| 28-OZ. CAN CRUSHED TOMATOES | 796 mL |
| SALT TO TASTE | |

## PESTO

| | |
|---|---|
| 1 CUP FRESH BASIL | 250 mL |
| 1/2 CUP PINE NUTS | 125 mL |
| 1/3 CUP GRATED PARMESAN | 75 mL |
| 1/3 CUP OLIVE OIL | 75 mL |

## BÉCHAMEL SAUCE

| | |
|---|---|
| 3 TBSP. BUTTER | 45 mL |
| 1/4 CUP FLOUR | 60 mL |
| 1/4 TSP. NUTMEG | 1 mL |
| SALT & PEPPER TO TASTE | |
| 2 CUPS MILK | 500 mL |

| | |
|---|---|
| 8-10 LASAGNA NOODLES | |
| 1 LB. BOCCONCINI OR MOZZARELLA CHEESE, SLICED | 500 g |
| 1/2 CUP GRATED PARMESAN CHEESE | 125 mL |

TO MAKE TOMATO SAUCE: SAUTÉ GARLIC AND ONION IN OIL UNTIL SOFTENED. ADD TOMATOES AND SALT. COOK UNTIL THICKENED. SET ASIDE.

CONTINUED ON PAGE 155.

Pasta Fasta, page 140
Baguette Sticks, page 20

Broccoli Lasagne, page 151

# PESTO LASAGNE

CONTINUED FROM PAGE 152.

TO MAKE THE PESTO: PURÉE ALL INGREDIENTS IN FOOD PROCESSOR. SET ASIDE.

TO MAKE THE BÉCHAMEL SAUCE: MELT BUTTER, ADD FLOUR AND SEASONINGS AND STIR FOR A FEW MINUTES. ADD MILK, STIRRING CONSTANTLY. COOK SLOWLY UNTIL THICKENED.

TO MAKE LASAGNE: COOK PASTA ACCORDING TO PACKAGE DIRECTIONS. DRAIN, PLUNGE INTO COLD WATER AND SET ASIDE. LADLE 1/3 OF BÉCHAMEL SAUCE INTO BOTTOM OF 9 X 13" (23 X 33 cm) PAN. THEN LAYER PASTA, TOMATO SAUCE, CHEESE AND PESTO. REPEAT LAYERS AND FINISH WITH GRATED PARMESAN. BAKE AT 350°F (180°C) OR 40 MINUTES. SERVES 12.

HEAVY MEDDLE: WHAT YOU GET WHEN YOUR MOTHER-IN-LAW SHOWS UP TO HELP WITH THE BABY.

# LINGUINE WITH RED CLAM SAUCE

| | |
|---|---:|
| 1 MEDIUM ONION, CHOPPED | |
| 3-4 GARLIC CLOVES, MINCED | |
| 3 CELERY STALKS, SLICED | |
| 3 TBSP. OLIVE OIL | 45 mL |
| 28 OZ. CAN ITALIAN TOMATOES | 796 mL |
| 1 TSP. SALT | 5 mL |
| 2-7 OZ. CANS BABY CLAMS, WITH LIQUID | 2-189 mL |
| 1 BAY LEAF | |
| 1 TSP. DRIED OREGANO | 5 mL |
| 8 SLICES BACON, COOKED & CRUMBLED | |
| COARSELY GROUND BLACK PEPPER TO TASTE | |
| LINGUINE FOR 4 PEOPLE | |

IN MEDIUM FRYING PAN SAUTÉ ONION, GARLIC AND CELERY IN OIL UNTIL LIGHTLY GOLDEN. ADD NEXT 7 INGREDIENTS AND SIMMER, COVERED, FOR 1 HOUR OR MORE. JUST BEFORE SERVING, COOK LINGUINE. DRAIN WELL. MIX WITH HALF THE CLAM SAUCE AND TOSS. SERVE IN BOWLS AND PASS THE REMAINING SAUCE.

IF LOVE IS BLIND, WHY IS LINGERIE SO POPULAR?

# LINGUINE WITH WHITE CLAM SAUCE

THIS IS A SMOOTH WHITE CLAM SAUCE - THE ULTIMATE!

| | |
|---|---|
| 1 GARLIC CLOVE, MASHED | |
| 1 MEDIUM ONION, FINELY CHOPPED | |
| 2 TSP. OLIVE OIL | 10 mL |
| ½ CUP DRY WHITE WINE | 125 mL |
| 2 CUPS CHICKEN BROTH | 500 mL |
| 2-5 OZ. CANS BABY CLAMS, RESERVE LIQUID | 2-142 g |
| 4 OZ. CAN SHRIMP, DRAINED (OPTIONAL) | 113 g |
| 4 OZ. CAN CRABMEAT, DRAINED (OPTIONAL) | 113 g |
| DASH OF FRESH GROUND PEPPER | |
| 3 DASHES TABASCO | |
| 1 TSP. OREGANO | 5 mL |
| 8 OZ. LIGHT CREAM CHEESE (CUT INTO SMALL PIECES) | 250 g |
| 1 LB. LINGUINE NOODLES | 500 g |
| GRATED PARMESAN CHEESE | |
| CHOPPED FRESH PARSLEY | |

IN A 4-QUART (1 L). SAUCEPAN, SAUTÉ GARLIC AND ONION IN OIL UNTIL SOFT. DO NOT BROWN. ADD WINE, CHICKEN BROTH AND CLAM LIQUID. ADD PEPPER, TABASCO AND OREGANO. SIMMER FOR 15 MINUTES. ADD CREAM CHEESE; STIR INTO SAUCE UNTIL WELL BLENDED. ADD CLAMS AND, IF DESIRED, OTHER SEAFOOD. COOK LINGUINE ACCORDING TO PACKAGE DIRECTIONS. DRAIN WELL AND ADD TO SAUCE. LET PASTA REST IN SAUCE FOR 5 MINUTES TO ABSORB FLAVORS. SERVE IN A PASTA BOWL AND SPRINKLE WITH PARMESAN AND PARSLEY. SERVE IMMEDIATELY TO 6 LINGUINE LOVERS!

# FETTUCCINE WITH ASPARAGUS AND SHRIMP

| | | |
|---|---|---|
| 1 LB. LARGE SHRIMP, SHELLED & DEVEINED | 500 | g |
| 1 LEMON, JUICE & GRATED RIND | | |
| 1/4-1/2 TSP. HOT RED PEPPER FLAKES | 1-2 | mL |
| 1/2 TSP. SALT | 2 | mL |
| 16 OZ. PKG. FETTUCCINE OR LINGUINE | 500 | g |
| 1 TBSP. VEGETABLE OIL | 15 | mL |
| 1 MEDIUM ONION, DICED | | |
| 2 RED PEPPERS, SLICED IN STRIPS | | |
| 1/2 TSP. SALT | 2 | mL |
| 1 TBSP. VEGETABLE OIL | 15 | mL |
| 1 LB. FRESH ASPARAGUS, CUT IN 3" (8 cm) PIECES | 500 | g |
| 1/2 CUP WATER | 125 | mL |
| 1 TBSP. SOY SAUCE | 15 | mL |

IN A BOWL, MIX SHRIMP WITH LEMON JUICE, PEPPER FLAKES AND SALT. COOK FETTUCCINE ACCORDING TO PACKAGE DIRECTIONS. KEEP WARM IN POT. HEAT OIL AND STIR-FRY ONION, PEPPER STRIPS AND SALT UNTIL PEPPERS ARE TENDER-CRISP; REMOVE TO BOWL. IN SAME PAN HEAT OIL AND ADD ASPARAGUS AND SHRIMP MIXTURE. STIR-FRY UNTIL ASPARAGUS ARE TENDER-CRISP AND SHRIMP TURN OPAQUE, ABOUT 3 MINUTES. STIR IN PEPPER MIXTURE AND WATER; HEAT THROUGH. TO SERVE, TOSS FETTUCCINE WITH SHRIMP MIXTURE AND SOY SAUCE. SPRINKLE WITH GRATED LEMON RIND. SERVES 4.

# VEGGIES

Grilled Veggies with Oil and Balsamic Vinegar
Asparagus Vinaigrette
Tolerable Brussels Sprouts
Tomatoes Florentine
Sesame Broccoli
Green Beans Guido
Teriyaki Portobello Mushrooms
Parmesan Portobellos
Spaghetti Squash Primavera
Nifty Carrots
Gingered Carrot Purée
Holiday Parsnips
Turnip Puff
Sweet Potato Supreme
Roasted New Potatoes with Rosemary
Elsie's Potatoes
Gruyère Scalloped Potatoes
Butter-Baked Taters
Schwarties Hash Browns
Wild Rice Broccoli Casserole
Wild Rice and Artichoke Hearts
Wild Rice, Orzo and Mushroom Casserole
Orzo with Parmesan & Basil
Risotto
Curried Apple and Sweet Potato Pilaf
Barber's Best Chili
Calico Bean Pot
Vegetable Couscous

# GRILLED VEGGIES WITH OIL AND BALSAMIC VINEGAR

A LICENSE TO GRILL! TRY SERVING AS A SANDWICH ON TOASTED FOCACCIA.

1 SMALL EGGPLANT
1 SMALL ZUCCHINI
1 RED PEPPER
1 YELLOW PEPPER
1 RED ONION
3 TBSP. OLIVE OIL                                45 mL
3 TBSP. BALSAMIC VINEGAR                         45 mL
FRESHLY GROUND PEPPER

FIRE UP THE GRILL! CUT EGGPLANT AND ZUCCHINI INTO THICK DIAGONAL SLICES (LEAVE THE SKINS ON). QUARTER AND SEED PEPPERS. CUT ONION INTO 4 THICK SLICES (A WOODEN TOOTHPICK INSERTED INTO EACH SLICE WILL KEEP IT TOGETHER ON THE GRILL). IN A SMALL BOWL, COMBINE OLIVE OIL AND BALSAMIC VINEGAR; BRUSH ON ALL SIDES OF VEGGIES. SPRINKLE WITH FRESHLY GROUND PEPPER. SPRAY GRILL WITH COOKING SPRAY AND GRILL VEGGIES UNTIL TENDER, TURNING ONCE. SERVES 4.

WHERE ARE WE GOING? AND WHAT'S WITH THIS HANDBASKET?

# ASPARAGUS VINAIGRETTE

AN ELEGANT SPRING VEGETABLE.

| | | |
|---|---|---|
| 1 LB. FRESH ASPARAGUS | 500 | g |

### DRESSING

| | | |
|---|---|---|
| 1 TBSP. DIJON MUSTARD | 15 mL | |
| 2 TBSP. WHITE WINE VINEGAR | 30 mL | |
| 3 TBSP. FRESH LEMON JUICE | 45 mL | |
| 1 TSP. SUGAR | 5 mL | |
| SALT & PEPPER TO TASTE | | |
| 1/3 CUP VEGETABLE OIL | 75 mL | |
| LEMON ZEST | | |

TO PREPARE ASPARAGUS: PLACE ASPARAGUS IN SMALL AMOUNT OF BOILING WATER AND COOK FOR 2 MINUTES. (ASPARAGUS WILL TURN BRIGHT GREEN AND SHOULD STILL BE CRUNCHY.) REMOVE ASPARAGUS AND PLUNGE INTO ICE WATER. WHEN COOL, DRY AND PLACE ON SERVING PLATTER.

TO PREPARE DRESSING: PLACE ALL INGREDIENTS IN A BOWL AND WHISK TOGETHER. POUR OVER ASPARAGUS AND GARNISH WITH LEMON ZEST. SERVE WITH SWISS APPLE QUICHE (PAGE 22) OR POTLATCH SALMON (PAGE 188). SERVES 4-6. (PICTURED ON FRONT COVER AND PAGE 172.)

BEFORE CREDIT CARDS, WE ALWAYS KNEW EXACTLY HOW MUCH WE WERE BROKE.

# TOLERABLE BRUSSELS SPROUTS

IF YOU HAVE TO HAVE THEM - TRY THESE - THEY'RE DELICIOUS!

| | |
|---|---|
| 4 CUPS (2 LBS./1 kg) FRESH BRUSSELS SPROUTS | 1 L |
| ½ CUP CHOPPED ONION | 125 mL |
| 2 TBSP. BUTTER | 30 mL |
| 1 TBSP. FLOUR | 15 mL |
| 1 TBSP. PACKED BROWN SUGAR | 15 mL |
| ½ TSP. SALT | 2 mL |
| ½ TSP. DRY MUSTARD | 2 mL |
| ½ CUP MILK | 125 mL |
| 1 CUP FAT-FREE SOUR CREAM | 250 mL |
| 1 TBSP. PARSLEY | 15 mL |

WASH AND TRIM SPROUTS; COOK UNTIL TENDER. SAUTÉ ONION IN BUTTER UNTIL TRANSLUCENT. STIR IN FLOUR, SUGAR, SALT AND MUSTARD. ADD MILK AND COOK SLOWLY UNTIL THICKENED. BLEND IN SOUR CREAM. ADD SPROUTS AND HEAT THROUGH. SPRINKLE WITH PARSLEY BEFORE SERVING. SERVES 6.

WHY IS THE ALPHABET IN THAT ORDER? IS IT BECAUSE OF THAT SONG?

## TOMATOES FLORENTINE

6 FAIRLY FIRM TOMATOES (NOT A CHORUS LINE!)
10 OZ. PKG. FROZEN, CHOPPED SPINACH — 283 g
1 TBSP. INSTANT MINCED ONION — 15 mL
1 GARLIC CLOVE, MINCED
1 TSP. OREGANO — 5 mL
DASH OF NUTMEG
1 CUP GRATED CHEDDAR CHEESE — 250 mL
FRESHLY GRATED PARMESAN CHEESE

SLICE OFF TOP OF TOMATOES AND SCOOP OUT PULP. CHOP AND DRAIN THE PULP. THAW SPINACH AND DRAIN WELL. COMBINE SPINACH, PULP, ONION, SPICES AND GRATED CHEESE. FILL TOMATOES AND TOP WITH PARMESAN. BAKE AT 350°F (180°C). FOR 20-30 MINUTES. SERVES 6. WONDERFUL WITH BEEF EXTRAORDINAIRE. (PAGE 228).

## SESAME BROCCOLI

2 LBS. FRESH BROCCOLI — 1 kg
2 TBSP. SALAD OIL — 30 mL
2 TBSP. VINEGAR — 30 mL
2 TBSP. SOY SAUCE — 30 mL
4 TBSP. SUGAR — 60 mL
2 TBSP. TOASTED SESAME SEEDS — 30 mL

POUR BOILING WATER OVER BROCCOLI AND LET STAND 5 MINUTES. DRAIN. HEAT REMAINING INGREDIENTS AND POUR OVER BROCCOLI IN A CASSEROLE. HEAT IN OVEN BEFORE SERVING. SERVES 8.

# GREEN BEANS GUIDO

| | |
|---|---|
| 2 TBSP. VEGETABLE OIL | 30 mL |
| 4 CUPS SLICED FRESH MUSHROOMS | 1 L |
| 2 TBSP. CHOPPED ONION | 30 mL |
| 1 GARLIC CLOVE, MINCED | |
| 1 RED PEPPER, CUT IN STRIPS | |
| 10 OZ. PKG. FROZEN WHOLE GREEN BEANS | 285 g |
| 1 TBSP. CHOPPED FRESH BASIL | 15 mL |
|     OR 1½ TSP. (7 mL) DRIED | |
| ½ CUP GRATED PARMESAN CHEESE | 125 mL |

HEAT OIL IN LARGE SKILLET OVER MEDIUM HEAT. ADD MUSHROOMS, ONION, GARLIC AND RED PEPPER. COOK UNTIL ONION IS SOFT, ABOUT 5 MINUTES. ADD BEANS AND BASIL. CONTINUE TO COOK, STIRRING FREQUENTLY, UNTIL BEANS ARE TENDER-CRISP, ABOUT 10 MINUTES. ADD SEVERAL SPOONFULS OF CHEESE AND MIX WELL. PLACE IN SHALLOW CASSEROLE AND SPRINKLE REMAINING CHEESE ON TOP. SERVES 4.

WHY DOES AN INSPIRING SIGHT LIKE A SUNRISE ALWAYS HAVE TO TAKE PLACE AT SUCH AN INCONVENIENT TIME?

## TERIYAKI PORTOBELLO MUSHROOMS

ONE BIG STEAK PLUS ONE BIG MUSHROOM EQUALS DINNER FOR TWO!

| | |
|---|---|
| 1 TBSP. BUTTER | 15 mL |
| 2 TBSP. OIL | 30 mL |
| 1 GARLIC CLOVE, MINCED | |
| 1 PORTOBELLO MUSHROOM, THICKLY SLICED | |
| 2 TBSP. THICK TERIYAKI SAUCE | 30 mL |
| 1 TBSP. LEMON JUICE | 15 mL |
| 1 TBSP. WHITE WINE (VERMOUTH IS FINE) | 15 mL |
| SALT & PEPPER TO TASTE | |

HEAT BUTTER AND OIL. SAUTÉ GARLIC AND MUSHROOM SLICES FOR 5 MINUTES. ADD TERIYAKI SAUCE, LEMON JUICE AND WINE. CONTINUE TO COOK, STIRRING UNTIL MUSHROOMS SOAK UP THE LIQUID. SPRINKLE WITH SALT AND PEPPER. SERVES 2.

## PARMESAN PORTOBELLOS

| | |
|---|---|
| 2 TBSP. SLICED SHALLOTS | 30 mL |
| 2 GARLIC CLOVES, CHOPPED | |
| 2 TBSP. OLIVE OIL | 30 mL |
| 1/4 CUP BUTTER | 60 mL |
| 1 LB. SLICED PORTOBELLO MUSHROOMS | 500 g |
| 1/4 CUP BALSAMIC VINEGAR | 60 mL |
| 1/3 CUP GRATED PARMESAN CHEESE | 75 mL |
| PEPPER TO TASTE | |

CLEAN TOPS OF MUSHROOMS WITH BRUSH OR MOIST PAPER TOWEL. DON'T PEEL THEM - YOU'LL LOSE THE FLAVOR! SAUTÉ SHALLOTS AND GARLIC IN OIL AND BUTTER FOR 2-3 MINUTES. ADD MUSHROOMS, STIRRING UNTIL GOLDEN. ADD VINEGAR AND STIR WELL TO DEGLAZE PAN. ADD THE CHEESE AND STIR UNTIL MELTED. SEASON WITH PEPPER AND SERVE IMMEDIATELY. SERVES 4.

# — SPAGHETTI SQUASH PRIMAVERA —

A WONDERFUL VEGETARIAN DINNER - OR - IF YOU'RE NOT INTO THAT, SERVE WITH BEEF, BOOZE AND A GOOD STOGIE!

| | |
|---|---|
| 1 MEDIUM SPAGHETTI SQUASH | |
| 1/3 CUP BUTTER | 75 mL |
| 2 MEDIUM ONIONS, DICED | |
| 1/2 LB. MUSHROOMS, SLICED | 250 g |
| 1 GARLIC CLOVE, MINCED | |
| 1 1/2 CUPS BROCCOLI FLORETS | 375 mL |
| 1 CUP PEAS | 250 mL |
| 1 MEDIUM ZUCCHINI, SLICED | |
| 4 CARROTS, CUT DIAGONALLY | |
| 1 CUP MILK OR HALF & HALF CREAM | 250 mL |
| 1/2 CUP CHICKEN BROTH | 125 mL |
| 1/4 CUP FRESH BASIL LEAVES OR | 60 mL |
|     1 TBSP. (15 mL) DRIED BASIL | |
| 1 RED BELL PEPPER, SLICED | |
| 6 GREEN ONIONS, CHOPPED | |
| 12 SMALL CHERRY TOMATOES | |
| 1 1/2 CUPS GRATED PARMESAN CHEESE | 375 mL |

CUT SQUASH IN HALF LENGTHWISE AND REMOVE SEEDS. PLACE CUT-SIDE DOWN IN A BAKING DISH, ADD 1" (2.5 cm) OF WATER AND BAKE AT 375°F (190°C) FOR 1 HOUR. (OR MICROWAVE USING THE SAME METHOD, COVERED, ON HIGH UNTIL A SKEWER CAN PENETRATE THE SKIN, ABOUT 20 MINUTES.) MELT BUTTER IN A LARGE FRYING PAN AND SAUTÉ ONIONS, MUSHROOMS AND GARLIC UNTIL SOFT. ADD BROCCOLI, PEAS, ZUCCHINI AND CARROTS. STIR. ADD MILK, CHICKEN BROTH AND BASIL. BOIL BRISKLY TO REDUCE SAUCE A LITTLE,

# SPAGHETTI SQUASH PRIMAVERA

CONTINUED FROM PAGE 166.

ABOUT 2 MINUTES. ADD RED PEPPER, GREEN ONIONS, CHERRY TOMATOES AND CHEESE. HEAT THOROUGHLY. USING A FORK, SCRAPE STRANDS OF SQUASH INTO A LARGE, HEATED, SHALLOW CASSEROLE. TOP IMMEDIATELY WITH HOT VEGETABLE MIXTURE. SERVE WITH EXTRA PARMESAN CHEESE. SERVES 8-10.

# NIFTY CARROTS

EVEN GOOD FOR YOUR HEARING!

| | |
|---|---|
| 5-6 LARGE CARROTS PEELED, SLICED & COOKED UNTIL TENDER-CRISP (RESERVE COOKING WATER) | |
| 1/4 CUP RESERVED CARROT WATER | 60 mL |
| 1/4 CUP MAYONNAISE | 60 mL |
| 1/4 CUP SOUR CREAM (FAT-FREE IS FINE) | 60 mL |
| 2 TBSP. FINELY CHOPPED ONION | 30 mL |
| 1 TBSP. HORSERADISH | 15 mL |
| SALT AND PEPPER TO TASTE | |
| 1 TBSP. BUTTER, MELTED | 15 mL |
| 1/2 CUP BREAD CRUMBS | 125 mL |

PLACE COOKED CARROTS IN A SHALLOW CASSEROLE. COMBINE CARROT WATER, MAYONNAISE, SOUR CREAM, ONION, HORSERADISH, SALT AND PEPPER AND POUR OVER CARROTS. COMBINE BUTTER AND BREAD CRUMBS AND SPRINKLE OVER TOP. BAKE AT 375°F (190°C) FOR 30 MINUTES. SERVES 6.

## GINGERED CARROT PURÉE

SPICY YET SWEET!

| | |
|---|---|
| 3 LBS. CARROTS, CUT INTO 1" (2.5 cm) PIECES | 1.5 kg |
| 3 TBSP. BUTTER | 45 mL |
| 1 TBSP. GRATED FRESH GINGER OR ½ TSP. (2 mL) GROUND GINGER | 15 mL |
| ¼ TSP. SALT | 1 mL |
| ¼ TSP. PEPPER | 1 mL |
| ¼ CUP HALF & HALF CREAM | 60 mL |

BOIL CARROTS UNTIL VERY TENDER, 25-30 MINUTES. DRAIN AND TRANSFER TO A FOOD PROCESSOR. ADD REMAINING INGREDIENTS. WHIRL, SCRAPING SIDES OCCASIONALLY, UNTIL FAIRLY SMOOTH. PLACE "SIDE-BY-SIDE" IN SERVING DISH WITH HOLIDAY PARSNIPS.

## HOLIDAY PARSNIPS

ENHANCED BY A LITTLE TASTE OF NUTMEG.

| | |
|---|---|
| 3 LBS. PARSNIPS, PEELED & SLICED | 1.5 kg |
| 3 TBSP. BUTTER | 45 mL |
| ¼ TSP. NUTMEG | 1 mL |
| ¼ TSP. SALT | 1 mL |
| ¼ TSP. WHITE PEPPER | 1 mL |
| ¼ CUP HALF & HALF CREAM | 60 mL |

BOIL PARSNIPS UNTIL VERY TENDER (15-20 MINUTES). DRAIN. IN A FOOD PROCESSOR, WHIRL UNTIL FAIRLY SMOOTH. ADD BUTTER, NUTMEG, SALT AND PEPPER. GIVE IT A WHIRL. ADD CREAM AND WHIRL AGAIN. THIS MAY BE MADE A DAY AHEAD. ARE YOU DIZZY YET? SERVE WITH GINGERED CARROT PURÉE.

# TURNIP PUFF

IDEAL FOR THANKSGIVING AND CHRISTMAS DINNERS.

| | |
|---|---|
| 6 CUPS CUBED TURNIPS | 1.5 L |
| 2 TBSP. BUTTER | 30 mL |
| 2 EGGS, BEATEN | |
| 3 TBSP. FLOUR | 45 mL |
| 1 TBSP. BROWN SUGAR | 15 mL |
| 1 TSP. BAKING POWDER | 5 mL |
| SALT & PEPPER TO TASTE | |
| PINCH NUTMEG | |
| 1/2 CUP FINE BREAD CRUMBS | 125 mL |
| 2 TBSP. BUTTER, MELTED | 30 mL |

COOK TURNIPS UNTIL TENDER. DRAIN AND MASH. ADD BUTTER AND EGGS. BEAT WELL. (THIS MUCH CAN BE DONE THE DAY AHEAD.) COMBINE FLOUR, SUGAR, BAKING POWDER, SALT, PEPPER AND NUTMEG. STIR INTO TURNIPS. BUTTER A CASSEROLE AND PUT IN TURNIP MIXTURE. COMBINE CRUMBS AND BUTTER. SPRINKLE ON TOP. BAKE AT 375°F (190°C) FOR 25 MINUTES, OR UNTIL LIGHT BROWN ON TOP. SERVES 6.

BRIDE TO NEW HUSBAND: "THERE YOU ARE DARLING - MY FIRST MEAL COOKED JUST THE WAY YOU BETTER LIKE IT!"

# SWEET POTATO SUPREME

GREAT WITH HAM OR TURKEY.

| | |
|---|---|
| 4 CUPS COOKED, MASHED SWEET POTATOES | 1 L |
| 2 TBSP. CREAM OR MILK | 30 mL |
| 1 TSP. SALT | 5 mL |
| 1/4 TSP. PAPRIKA | 1 mL |
| 1/2 CUP BROWN SUGAR, PACKED | 125 mL |
| 1/3 CUP BUTTER | 75 mL |
| 1 CUP PECAN HALVES, TO COVER CASSEROLE | 250 mL |

THOROUGHLY MIX POTATOES, CREAM, SALT AND PAPRIKA. SPREAD IN GREASED CASSEROLE. MAKE THE TOPPING BY HEATING BROWN SUGAR AND BUTTER OVER LOW HEAT, STIRRING CONSTANTLY, UNTIL BUTTER IS BARELY MELTED. (IT IS IMPORTANT NOT TO COOK AFTER BUTTER IS MELTED, OR THE TOPPING WILL HARDEN WHEN CASSEROLE IS HEATED.) SPREAD TOPPING OVER POTATOES AND COVER WITH PECAN HALVES. REFRIGERATE UNTIL READY TO HEAT. THIS CASSEROLE MAY BE WARMED IN AN OVEN OF ANY TEMPERATURE. SHOULD BE BUBBLING HOT BEFORE SERVING. SERVES 6-8.

CLASSICAL RADIO STATION MORNING PROGRAM:
"BAROQUE AND EGGS".

Curried Apple and Sweet Potato Pilaf, page 181

Asparagus Vinaigrette, page 161

## ROASTED NEW POTATOES WITH ROSEMARY

| | |
|---|---|
| 8 MEDIUM NEW RED POTATOES | |
| 1/4 CUP OLIVE OIL | 60 mL |
| 2-3 GARLIC CLOVES, MINCED | |
| 2 TBSP. CHOPPED FRESH ROSEMARY | 30 mL |

WASH POTATOES AND CUT INTO QUARTERS. ARRANGE IN SHALLOW BAKING DISH AND TOSS WITH OIL, GARLIC AND ROSEMARY. BAKE AT 375°F (190°C). FOR 1 HOUR, TURNING OCCASIONALLY. SERVES 4-6. IF THE TINY RED POTATOES ARE AVAILABLE USE THEM. THEY'RE THE BEST.

## ELSIE'S POTATOES

A MUST WITH TURKEY DINNER . . . CAN BE MADE AHEAD AND FROZEN.

| | |
|---|---|
| 5 LBS. POTATOES OR 9 LARGE | 2.5 kg |
| 8 OZ. LOW-FAT CREAM CHEESE | 250 g |
| 1 CUP FAT-FREE SOUR CREAM | 250 mL |
| 2 TSP. ONION SALT | 10 mL |
| 1 TSP. SALT | 5 mL |
| PINCH OF PEPPER | |
| 2 TBSP. BUTTER | 30 mL |

COOK AND MASH POTATOES. ADD ALL INGREDIENTS, EXCEPT BUTTER, AND COMBINE. PUT INTO LARGE GREASED CASSEROLE. DOT WITH BUTTER. BAKE, COVERED, AT 350°F (180°C). FOR 30 MINUTES. IF MAKING AHEAD, COVER AND REFRIGERATE OR FREEZE. THAW BEFORE BAKING. SERVES 10-12.

# GRUYÈRE SCALLOPED POTATOES

2 GARLIC CLOVES, MINCED
2½ CUPS HALF & HALF CREAM          625 mL
6 BAKING POTATOES, PEELED
2 TBSP. FLOUR                      30 mL
3 CUPS GRATED GRUYÈRE CHEESE       750 mL
SALT AND PEPPER TO TASTE

STIR GARLIC INTO CREAM AND SET ASIDE. SLICE
POTATOES INTO PAPER-THIN ROUNDS AND TOSS
WITH FLOUR. ARRANGE HALF THE POTATOES IN A
9 X 13" (23 X 33 cm) GLASS BAKING DISH.
SPRINKLE WITH HALF OF THE CHEESE; POUR
HALF OF THE CREAM MIXTURE OVER TOP.
SPRINKLE WITH SALT AND PEPPER. REPEAT
LAYERS. COVER AND BAKE AT 325°F (160°C) FOR
1 HOUR. REMOVE COVER AND CONTINUE BAKING
FOR ½ HOUR, OR UNTIL POTATOES ARE TENDER.

SIGN ON DOOR: "DOORBELL BROKEN. PLEASE KNOCK
LOUDLY TO ACTIVATE DOG."

# BUTTER-BAKED TATERS

| | |
|---|---|
| ¼ CUP BUTTER | 60 mL |
| 3 TBSP. GREEN ONIONS, FINELY CHOPPED | 45 mL |
| 3 LARGE POTATOES, PEELED | |
| SALT AND PEPPER TO TASTE | |
| 2 TBSP. GRATED PARMESAN CHEESE | 30 mL |

PREHEAT OVEN TO 500°F (290°C). MELT BUTTER IN A FRYING PAN, ADD ONION AND SAUTÉ UNTIL TENDER. HALVE POTATOES LENGTHWISE, THEN SLICE CROSSWISE INTO ⅛" (3 mm) THICK SLICES. IMMEDIATELY LINE UP IN BUTTERED 9 X 13" (23 X 33 cm) BAKING PAN WITH SLICES OVERLAPPING. POUR BUTTER MIXTURE OVER POTATOES. SEASON WITH SALT AND PEPPER. BAKE 20 MINUTES. REMOVE FROM OVEN AND SPRINKLE WITH PARMESAN CHEESE. BAKE AN ADDITIONAL 5-7 MINUTES, OR UNTIL CHEESE IS SLIGHTLY BROWNED AND MELTED. SERVES 4.

## VARIATIONS: SOME LIKE 'EM HOT!

| | |
|---|---|
| 1 CUP GRATED CHEDDAR CHEESE | 250 mL |
| 1 CUP CORNFLAKES, CRUSHED | 250 mL |
| 1 TSP. CAYENNE PEPPER | 5 mL |

COMBINE CHEESE, CORNFLAKES AND CAYENNE. SPRINKLE OVER BUTTERED POTATOES AND BAKE AT 400°F (200°C) FOR 30 MINUTES, OMITTING THE PARMESAN CHEESE.

COUNTING CALORIES HAS BEEN FOR MANY PEOPLE, A WEIGH OF LIFE.

# SCHWARTIES HASH BROWNS

GREAT FOR BUFFETS! FREEZES WELL.

| | |
|---|---|
| 2 LBS. FROZEN HASH BROWNS | 1 kg |
| 2 CUPS FAT-FREE SOUR CREAM | 500 mL |
| 2-10 OZ. CANS MUSHROOM SOUP | 2-284 mL |
| 1/4 CUP MELTED BUTTER | 60 mL |
| GRATED ONION & SALT TO TASTE | |
| 2 CUPS GRATED LIGHT CHEDDAR CHEESE | 500 mL |
| 2 TBSP. PARMESAN CHEESE | 30 mL |

THAW POTATOES SLIGHTLY. MIX FIRST 6 INGREDIENTS IN A 9 X 13" (23 X 33 cm) BAKING DISH. SPRINKLE PARMESAN ON TOP. BAKE AT 350°F (180°C) FOR 1 HOUR. SERVES 8-10.

# WILD RICE BROCCOLI CASSEROLE

THIS COMPLEMENTS ANY MEAT OR FOWL.

| | |
|---|---|
| 6 OZ. PKG. UNCLE BEN'S WILD RICE MIXTURE | 170 g |
| 2 HEADS BROCCOLI, CUT INTO FLORETS | |
| 2-10 OZ. CANS MUSHROOM SOUP | 2-284 mL |
| 2 CUPS GRATED CHEDDAR CHEESE | 500 mL |

COOK RICE MIXTURE AS DIRECTED. COOK BROCCOLI UNTIL CRUNCHY. MIX SOUP AND 1½ CUPS (375 mL) CHEESE. BUTTER A CASSEROLE. ALTERNATE SOUP MIXTURE, BROCCOLI AND RICE IN LAYERS. SPRINKLE WITH REMAINING ½ CUP (125 mL) CHEESE. COOK AT 350°F (180°C). FOR 1 HOUR. SERVES 6.

# WILD RICE AND ARTICHOKE HEARTS

| | |
|---|---|
| 1 CUP UNCOOKED WILD RICE | 250 mL |
| 10 OZ. CAN CONSOMMÉ | 284 mL |
| 1¾ CUPS WATER | 425 mL |
| ½ TSP. SALT | 2 mL |
| 3 TBSP. BUTTER | 45 mL |
| ⅓ CUP CHOPPED ONION | 75 mL |
| 2 GARLIC CLOVES, MINCED | |
| 2-6 OZ. JARS MARINATED ARTICHOKE HEARTS | 2-175 mL |
| 1 TBSP. FRESH, CHOPPED PARSLEY | 15 mL |
| ¼ TSP. OREGANO | 1 mL |

WASH AND DRAIN WILD RICE. PLACE RICE, CONSOMMÉ, WATER AND SALT IN SAUCEPAN. HEAT TO BOILING; REDUCE HEAT AND SIMMER, COVERED, UNTIL TENDER, ABOUT 45 MINUTES.

IN A LARGE FRYING PAN, MELT BUTTER AND SAUTÉ ONION AND GARLIC UNTIL SOFT. DRAIN AND CUT ARTICHOKES INTO QUARTERS. ADD TO FRYING PAN WITH COOKED RICE, PARSLEY AND OREGANO. STIR UNTIL HEATED THROUGH. SERVES 4-6.

MEN WAKE UP AS GOOD-LOOKING AS THEY WENT TO BED. WOMEN SOMEHOW DETERIORATE DURING THE NIGHT.

# WILD RICE, ORZO AND MUSHROOM CASSEROLE

A GREAT MAKE-AHEAD.

| | |
|---|---|
| 1 CUP ORZO | 250 mL |
| 1 CUP WILD RICE | 250 mL |
| 2½ CUPS BEEF BROTH | 625 mL |
| 8 CUPS SLICED MUSHROOMS | 2 L |
| 1 TBSP. OIL | 15 mL |
| 2 TBSP. BUTTER | 30 mL |
| ¼ CUP FRESH PARSLEY | 60 mL |

COOK ORZO ACCORDING TO PACKAGE DIRECTIONS. COOK THE WILD RICE IN THE BROTH ACCORDING TO PACKAGE DIRECTIONS. SAUTÉ MUSHROOMS IN OIL AND BUTTER AND COOK UNTIL LIQUID HAS ALMOST EVAPORATED. ADD MUSHROOMS AND PARSLEY TO RICE AND ORZO. MIX WELL. THIS MAY BE PREPARED AHEAD AND REFRIGERATED. BRING TO ROOM TEMPERATURE AND BAKE AT 350°F (180°C) FOR 30 MINUTES, UNTIL HEATED THROUGH. SERVES 6-8.

THERE ARE TWO TIMES WHEN A MAN DOESN'T UNDERSTAND A WOMAN - BEFORE MARRIAGE AND AFTER MARRIAGE.

# ORZO WITH PARMESAN AND BASIL

THE PASTA THAT LOOKS LIKE RICE - GREAT WITH CHICKEN OR FISH.

| | |
|---|---|
| 3 TBSP. BUTTER | 45 mL |
| 1½ CUPS ORZO | 375 mL |
| 3 CUPS CHICKEN BROTH | 750 mL |
| ½ CUP GRATED PARMESAN CHEESE | 125 mL |
| 6 TBSP. CHOPPED FRESH BASIL OR | 90 mL |
|      1½ TSP. (7 mL) DRIED | |
| SALT & PEPPER TO TASTE | |

MELT BUTTER IN SKILLET OVER MEDIUM-HIGH HEAT. ADD ORZO AND SAUTÉ 2 MINUTES, UNTIL SLIGHTLY BROWN. ADD BROTH AND BRING TO A BOIL. REDUCE HEAT, COVER AND SIMMER UNTIL ORZO IS TENDER AND LIQUID IS ABSORBED, ABOUT 20 MINUTES. MIX IN PARMESAN AND BASIL. SEASON WITH SALT AND PEPPER. TRANSFER TO SHALLOW BOWL. SERVES 6.

VARIATION: FOR A CREAMIER PASTA DISH, TRY STIRRING IN 2 TBSP. (30 mL) PLAIN YOGURT THINNED WITH A LITTLE MILK.

POLITICALLY CORRECT SEMANTICS: SNOW W.A.S.P. AND THE SEVEN VERTICALLY IMPAIRED MINERS.

# RISOTTO

THE CLASSIC COMPLEMENT TO OSSO BUCO (PAGE 226).

| | |
|---|---:|
| ½ CUP BUTTER OR MARGARINE | 125 mL |
| ½ CUP FINELY CHOPPED ONION | 125 mL |
| 1½ CUPS UNCOOKED RICE | 375 mL |
| 3½ CUPS CHICKEN BROTH | 875 mL |
| ½ CUP DRY WHITE WINE | 125 mL |
| 1 TSP. CRUSHED SAFFRON | 5 mL |
| 2 TBSP. CHICKEN BROTH | 30 mL |
| 2 TBSP. FRESHLY GRATED PARMESAN CHEESE | 30 mL |

MELT ¼ CUP (60 mL) BUTTER IN MEDIUM SAUCEPAN AND SAUTÉ ONION UNTIL TRANSLUCENT. ADD THE RICE AND STIR TO MIX. ADD BROTH AND WINE AND BRING TO BOIL. COVER AND COOK OVER LOW HEAT FOR 25 MINUTES, STIRRING OCCASIONALLY. STIR IN ¼ CUP (60 mL) OF BUTTER. SOFTEN SAFFRON IN 2 TBSP. (30 mL) OF CHICKEN BROTH; ADD TO RICE AND COOK, UNCOVERED, OVER LOW HEAT FOR 4 MORE MINUTES. TO SERVE, SPRINKLE WITH PARMESAN CHEESE. SERVES 6-8.

THE EARLY BIRD GETS THE WORM, BUT THE SECOND MOUSE GETS THE CHEESE.

# CURRIED APPLE AND SWEET POTATO PILAF

| | |
|---|---|
| 1 TBSP. OLIVE OIL | 15 mL |
| ½ CUP CHOPPED GREEN ONIONS | 125 mL |
| 2 GARLIC CLOVES, MINCED | |
| 1 CUP UNCOOKED LONG-GRAIN RICE | 250 mL |
| 2 CUPS WATER | 500 mL |
| 1½ CUPS PEELED & DICED SWEET POTATO | 375 mL |
| 2 CUPS PEELED & CUBED GRANNY SMITH APPLES | 500 mL |
| ½ CUP FROZEN GREEN PEAS | 125 mL |
| ¼ CUP CURRANTS | 60 mL |
| ½ TSP. CURRY POWDER | 2 mL |
| ½ TSP. CUMIN | 2 mL |
| ¼ TSP. SALT | 1 mL |
| PEPPER TO TASTE | |

HEAT OIL IN A MEDIUM SAUCEPAN OVER MEDIUM-HIGH HEAT. ADD ONIONS AND GARLIC; SAUTÉ 1 MINUTE. STIR IN RICE AND SAUTÉ 1 MINUTE. ADD WATER AND SWEET POTATO; BRING TO A BOIL. COVER, REDUCE HEAT, AND SIMMER 15 MINUTES, OR UNTIL LIQUID IS ALMOST ABSORBED. STIR IN APPLE, PEAS, CURRANTS AND SEASONINGS. COVER AND SIMMER 3 MINUTES, OR UNTIL THOROUGHLY HEATED. A GREAT ACCOMPANIMENT FOR HAM. SERVES 4-6. (PICTURED ON PAGE 171.)

HAPPINESS IS WHEN YOUR PLANE AND LUGGAGE ARRIVE AT THE SAME TIME.

# BARBER'S BEST CHILI

*A VEGETARIAN VERSION.*

| | |
|---|---:|
| 1½ CUPS CHOPPED ONION | 375 mL |
| 2 GREEN PEPPERS, CHOPPED | |
| 3 CELERY STALKS, CHOPPED | |
| 4 GARLIC CLOVES, MINCED | |
| 2 TBSP. OIL | 30 mL |
| 2-28 OZ. CANS TOMATOES | 2-796 mL |
| 14 OZ. CAN KIDNEY BEANS | 398 mL |
| 14 OZ. CAN BROWN BEANS | 398 mL |
| 2 CUPS SLICED FRESH MUSHROOMS | 500 mL |
| 1½ CUPS WATER | 375 mL |
| ½ CUP RAISINS | 125 mL |
| ¼ CUP VINEGAR | 60 mL |
| 1 BAY LEAF | |
| 1 TBSP. CHILI POWDER | 15 mL |
| 1 TBSP. PARSLEY | 15 mL |
| 1½ TSP. BASIL | 7 mL |
| 1½ TSP. OREGANO | 7 mL |
| ½ TSP. PEPPER | 2 mL |
| ¼ TSP. TABASCO | 1 mL |
| 1 CUP CASHEWS (OPTIONAL) | 250 mL |
| GRATED CHEDDAR CHEESE | |
| SOUR CREAM | |

SAUTÉ ONION, GREEN PEPPER, CELERY AND GARLIC IN OIL UNTIL TENDER. ADD TOMATOES AND BEANS WITH LIQUID, ALONG WITH REMAINING INGREDIENTS, EXCEPT CASHEWS, CHEESE AND SOUR CREAM. COVER AND SIMMER FOR 1 HOUR. UNCOVER AND SIMMER ANOTHER HOUR. REMOVE BAY LEAF (IF YOU CAN FIND IT). IF USING

# BARBER'S BEST CHILI

## CONTINUED FROM PAGE 182.

CASHEWS, ADD AT THE END. SERVE WITH GRATED CHEDDAR CHEESE AND A DOLLOP OF SOUR CREAM. SERVES 8-10 - DEPENDING ON WHAT SIZE YOUR BARBERS ARE!

# CALICO BEAN POT

### THE WORLD'S BEST BEAN CASSEROLE!

| | |
|---|---|
| 8 SLICES BACON | |
| 1 CUP CHOPPED ONION | 250 mL |
| 14 OZ. CAN GREEN BEANS, DRAINED | 398 mL |
| 14 OZ. CAN LIMA BEANS, DRAINED | 398 mL |
| 14 OZ. CAN PORK & BEANS | 398 mL |
| 14 OZ. CAN KIDNEY BEANS, DRAINED | 398 mL |
| 3/4 CUP BROWN SUGAR, FIRMLY PACKED | 175 mL |
| 1/2 CUP VINEGAR | 125 mL |
| 1/2 TSP. GARLIC SALT | 2 mL |
| 1/2 TSP. DRY MUSTARD | 2 mL |
| PEPPER TO TASTE | |

CUT BACON INTO SMALL PIECES AND COOK UNTIL CRISP. COOK ONION UNTIL SOFT. ADD REMAINING INGREDIENTS IN A 2½-QUART (2.5 L) CASSEROLE. BAKE AT 350°F (180°C) FOR 1 HOUR, UNCOVERED. PERFECT WITH HAMBURGERS OR BAR-B-QUED BEEF. SERVES 12.

# VEGETABLE COUSCOUS

| | |
|---|---|
| 1 ONION, CHOPPED | |
| 1 RED PEPPER, CHOPPED | |
| 1 GREEN PEPPER, CHOPPED | |
| 2 TBSP. OLIVE OIL | 30 mL |
| 1-2 GARLIC CLOVES, MINCED | |
| 1½ TSP. PAPRIKA | 7 mL |
| ¼ TSP. CAYENNE PEPPER | 1 mL |
| 2 CUPS CHICKEN OR VEGETABLE BROTH | 500 mL |
| 3-4 ROMA TOMATOES, CHOPPED | |
| 1 CUP FROZEN PEAS | 250 mL |
| 1 CUP GARBANZO BEANS, DRAINED | 250 mL |
|    (CHICK-PEAS) | |
| 2 CARROTS, PEELED & CHOPPED | |
| 1 CUP COUSCOUS | 250 mL |
| 14 OZ. CAN ARTICHOKE HEARTS, DRAINED | 398 mL |
|    & QUARTERED | |
| 1 LEMON, CUT IN WEDGES | |
| FRESH PARSLEY, CHOPPED | |

SAUTÉ ONION AND PEPPERS IN OIL UNTIL THEY BEGIN TO SOFTEN. STIR IN GARLIC, PAPRIKA AND CAYENNE PEPPER. ADD BROTH, TOMATOES, PEAS, GARBANZO BEANS AND CARROTS. COVER AND SIMMER FOR 5 MINUTES. ADD COUSCOUS TO VEGETABLE MIXTURE. COVER AND SIMMER 1 MINUTE MORE. REMOVE FROM HEAT AND LET STAND 5 MINUTES. WHEN SERVING, FLUFF COUSCOUS WITH FORK. GARNISH WITH ARTICHOKE HEARTS, LEMON WEDGES AND PARSLEY. SERVES 6-8. SERVE WITH CHICKEN IN PHYLLO (PAGE 210) (PICTURED ON PAGE 205.)

# FISH

Poached Salmon with Piquant Sauce and Veggies
Potlatch Salmon
Grilled Halibut and Peppers Julienne
Red Snapper Parmesan
O-Sole-O-Mio
Fish 'N' Chips

# SEAFOOD

Orange Stir-Fried Shrimp
Shrimp and Scallop Supreme

# CHICKEN

Lime-Grilled Chicken
Orange-Rosemary Chicken
Honey-Mustard Chicken
Bare-Naked Chicken
Ginger Chicken Stir-Fry
Sweet and Spicy Cashew Chicken
Crunchy Garlic Chicken
Oven-Fried Chicken
Layered Chicken Tortilla
El Grando Chicken Quesadillas
Southwestern Chicken Chili
Chicken Enchilada Casserole
Chicken in Phyllo
Chicken Breasts Zelda
Chicken Breasts Stuffed with Asparagus
Chicken Pot Pie
Chicken in Wine
Classy Chicken
Japanese Chicken Wings

# POACHED SALMON WITH PIQUANT SAUCE AND VEGGIES

A DELICIOUS DINNER FOR 4. SERVE WITH STEAMED RICE.

## PIQUANT SAUCE

| | |
|---|---|
| 3 TBSP. LOW-FAT MAYONNAISE | 45 mL |
| 1 TBSP. CHOPPED FRESH DILL, | 15 mL |
| OR 1 TSP. (5 mL) DRY DILL | |
| 1 TBSP. SKIM MILK | 15 mL |
| 1 TBSP. CAPERS | 15 mL |
| 2 TSP. JUICE FROM CAPERS | 10 mL |
| 1½ TSP. DIJON MUSTARD | 7 mL |
| ¼ TSP. GRATED LEMON RIND | 1 mL |

## SALMON

| | |
|---|---|
| 1 LB. SALMON FILLET | 500 g |
| 3 CUPS WATER | 750 mL |
| 1 SMALL LEMON, THINLY SLICED | |
| 2 TSP. INSTANT CHICKEN BOUILLON POWDER | 10 mL |

## VEGETABLES

| | |
|---|---|
| 1½ CUPS WATER | 375 mL |
| 1 TSP. INSTANT CHICKEN BOUILLON POWDER | 5 mL |
| 3 MEDIUM CARROTS, SLICED INTO MATCHSTICKS | |
| 1 MEDIUM ZUCCHINI (UNPEELED), SLICED INTO MATCHSTICKS | |
| CHOPPED FRESH DILL FOR GARNISH | |

TO PREPARE PIQUANT SAUCE: COMBINE ALL INGREDIENTS IN SMALL BOWL AND SET ASIDE.

# POACHED SALMON WITH PIQUANT SAUCE AND VEGGIES

CONTINUED FROM PAGE 186.

TO POACH SALMON: REMOVE ANY SMALL BONES WITH TWEEZERS AND CUT SALMON INTO 4 PIECES. IN LARGE FRYING PAN, BRING 3 CUPS (750 mL) WATER TO A BOIL. ADD LEMON SLICES AND CHICKEN BOUILLON POWDER. COVER AND SIMMER FOR 5 MINUTES. ADD SALMON AND HEAT TO BOILING. REDUCE HEAT TO LOW; COVER AND SIMMER 8-10 MINUTES, UNTIL FISH FLAKES EASILY WHEN TESTED WITH FORK.

TO PREPARE VEGGIES: WHILE FISH IS POACHING, HEAT WATER AND BOUILLON TO BOILING. ADD CARROTS; REDUCE HEAT TO LOW; COVER AND SIMMER 2 MINUTES. ADD ZUCCHINI; HEAT TO BOILING; COVER AND SIMMER 2 MINUTES LONGER, OR UNTIL VEGETABLES ARE TENDER-CRISP. DRAIN. ARRANGE SALMON, STEAMED RICE, AND VEGETABLES ON A WARM PLATTER. GARNISH WITH DILL.

REMEMBER WHEN A HARD DRIVE WAS A LONG TRIP AND NOT A COMPUTER PART?

# POTLATCH SALMON

A WONDERFUL WAY TO BAR-B-QUE A WHOLE SALMON.

| | |
|---|---|
| 1 WHOLE SALMON, BUTTERFLIED | |
| 2 TBSP. BUTTER, SOFTENED | 30 mL |
| JUICE OF 1 LEMON | |
| 2 TSP. DRY MUSTARD | 10 mL |
| 2/3 -1 CUP BROWN SUGAR | 150-250 mL |

TO BUTTERFLY SALMON: REMOVE HEAD, TAIL AND FINS. RUN SHARP KNIFE DOWN BACKBONE UNTIL SALMON OPENS FLAT. PLACE SKIN-SIDE DOWN ON A GREASED SHEET OF FOIL. SPREAD BUTTER OVER FISH. SPRINKLE LIBERALLY WITH LEMON JUICE AND MUSTARD. COVER WITH 1/4-1/2" (1-1.3 cm) BROWN SUGAR.

TO COOK: PLACE SALMON ON BAR-B-QUE, LOWER LID AND COOK OVER LOW HEAT FOR 20-30 MINUTES. SALMON IS COOKED WHEN FLESH FLAKES. DON'T OVERCOOK! NOW IS THE TIME TO REMOVE THE BONES. LIFT BACKBONE AT ONE END AND GENTLY REMOVE IN ONE PIECE.

THE BOTTOM LINE: DEE-LISHUS!! SERVES 6-8.

START OFF EVERY DAY WITH A SMILE AND GET IT OVER WITH.

# GRILLED HALIBUT AND PEPPERS JULIENNE

A POTPOURRI OF PEPPERS - THE PERFECT PARTNER FOR YOUR FAVORITE FISH. SERVE WITH ORZO WITH PARMESAN AND BASIL (PAGE 179).

| | |
|---|---|
| 1 RED PEPPER | |
| 1 GREEN PEPPER | |
| 1 YELLOW PEPPER | |
| 1 ONION | |
| 2 CELERY STALKS | |
| 1 TOMATO | |
| 2 TBSP. BUTTER OR MARGARINE | 30 mL |
| 1 TSP. CHOPPED FRESH PARSLEY | 5 mL |
| A GENEROUS SPRINKLE OF: PAPRIKA, CURRY POWDER & CAYENNE | |
| SALT & PEPPER TO TASTE | |
| 2/3 CUP WHITE WINE | 150 mL |
| 4 HALIBUT STEAKS | |
| SPRINKLING OF PAPRIKA & PEPPER | |

CUT PEPPERS (REMOVE SEEDS), ONION AND CELERY INTO THIN STRIPS. COARSELY CHOP THE TOMATO. MELT BUTTER IN SKILLET. ADD PREPARED VEGGIES AND ALL REMAINING INGREDIENTS, EXCEPT THE FISH. SIMMER 5 MINUTES. WHILE VEGGIES ARE COOKING, PREPARE AND COOK FISH. BRUSH WITH OIL AND SPRINKLE WITH PAPRIKA AND PEPPER. GRILL UNTIL FISH IS OPAQUE AND FLAKES EASILY, ABOUT 4 MINUTES EACH SIDE. SPOON SIMMERED VEGGIES AND PAN JUICES OVER FISH. GOOD FOR YOUR BOD AND GREAT FOR YOUR CULINARY REPUTATION!! SERVES 4.

## RED SNAPPER PARMESAN

| | | |
|---|---|---|
| ¾ LB. RED SNAPPER | 365 | g |
| 1 TBSP. LEMON JUICE | 15 | mL |
| 2 TBSP. GRATED PARMESAN CHEESE | 30 | mL |
| 2 TBSP. SKIM MILK YOGURT | 30 | mL |
| 2 TBSP. LOW-FAT MAYONNAISE | 30 | mL |
| 2 TBSP. FINELY CHOPPED GREEN ONION | 30 | mL |
| 2 TBSP. CHOPPED PIMIENTO OR RED PEPPER | 30 | mL |
| ½ TSP. DRIED DILL | 2 | mL |

PLACE FILLETS IN BAKING DISH AND BRUSH WITH LEMON JUICE. LET STAND 20 MINUTES. PREHEAT BROILER. COMBINE REMAINING INGREDIENTS. BROIL FILLETS 6-8 MINUTES, UNTIL FLAKY. SPOON PARMESAN MIXTURE OVER FILLETS AND BROIL ANOTHER 3 MINUTES. SERVE WITH RICE. SERVES 2.

## O-SOLE-O-MIO

OR SOLE FOR FOUR!

| | | |
|---|---|---|
| 4 FRESH SOLE FILLETS | | |
| 4 TSP. BUTTER | 20 | mL |
| 4 TBSP. FROZEN ORANGE JUICE CONCENTRATE | 60 | mL |
| 4 GREEN ONIONS, CHOPPED | | |
| SALT & PEPPER TO TASTE | | |

PREHEAT OVEN TO 450°F (230°C). USING 4, 10" (25 cm) PIECES OF FOIL, PLACE 1 FILLET IN CENTER OF EACH. PLACE 1 TSP. (5 mL) BUTTER, 1 TBSP. (15 mL) ORANGE CONCENTRATE AND CHOPPED GREEN ONION ON EACH FILLET. WRAP AND SEAL. PLACE ON BAKING SHEET; BAKE FOR 15 MINUTES. SERVE WITH RICE AND A GREEN VEGETABLE.

# FISH 'N' CHIPS

DUST, DIP & ROLL. VERY HEALTHY. VERY DELICIOUS!

| | |
|---|---|
| 3 LBS. BAKER POTATOES, UNPEELED | 1.5 kg |
| 1 TBSP. VEGETABLE OIL | 15 mL |
| ½ TSP. SALT | 2 mL |
| ½ TSP. PEPPER | 2 mL |
| 1½ LBS. ATLANTIC COD | 750 g |
| ½ CUP FLOUR | 125 mL |
| 2 TSP. DRY MUSTARD | 10 mL |
| 1 EGG, BEATEN | |
| ¼ CUP BREAD CRUMBS | 60 mL |
| ¾ CUP CORNFLAKE CRUMBS | 175 mL |
| 1 TBSP. VEGETABLE OIL | 15 mL |

SCRUB POTATOES AND CUT INTO THICK FRENCH FRIES. PAT DRY AND TOSS WITH OIL, SALT AND PEPPER. ARRANGE IN A SINGLE LAYER ON A NON-STICK COOKIE SHEET; BAKE AT 425°F (220°C) FOR 40 MINUTES TURNING TWICE. CUT FISH INTO SERVING-SIZED PIECES. PAT DRY. PLACE FLOUR AND MUSTARD IN A SHALLOW DISH. BEAT EGG IN ANOTHER SHALLOW DISH. COMBINE CRUMBS AND CORNFLAKES IN YET ANOTHER DISH! DUST EACH PIECE OF FISH WITH FLOUR. DIP INTO EGG AND ROLL IN CRUMB MIXTURE. BRUSH ANOTHER BAKING SHEET WITH OIL AND ARRANGE FISH IN A SINGLE LAYER. WHEN POTATOES HAVE COOKED FOR 40 MINUTES, PLACE FISH IN OVEN AND BAKE BOTH FOR 5 MINUTES. TURN AND BAKE ANOTHER 5 MINUTES, UNTIL FISH IS COOKED THROUGH (SHOULD BE FLAKY). SERVE WITH REGINA BEACH COLESLAW (PAGE 91). SERVES 6.

# ORANGE STIR-FRIED SHRIMP

## ZIPPY GARLIC ORANGE MARINADE

| | | |
|---|---|---|
| 1 GARLIC CLOVE, MINCED | | |
| 1 TSP. GRATED ORANGE RIND | 5 | mL |
| 1/4 TSP. HOT RED PEPPER FLAKES | 1 | mL |
| 1 TSP. SOY SAUCE | 5 | mL |
| 1 TSP. SESAME OIL | 5 | mL |
| | | |
| 1 LB. SHRIMP, SHELLED & DEVEINED | 500 | g |

## ORANGE SOY SAUCE

| | | |
|---|---|---|
| 1/2 CUP ORANGE JUICE | 125 | mL |
| 2 TBSP. SOY SAUCE | 30 | mL |
| 1 TBSP. HONEY OR SUGAR | 15 | mL |
| 2 TSP. CORNSTARCH | 10 | mL |
| 1 TSP. SESAME OIL | 5 | mL |

## STIR-FRY

| | | |
|---|---|---|
| 1 TBSP. OIL | 15 | mL |
| 1 TBSP. FINELY CHOPPED FRESH GINGER | 15 | mL |
| 1 GARLIC CLOVE, MINCED | | |
| 1/2 LB. GREEN BEANS, SLICED | 250 | g |
| 1 1/2 CUPS MUSHROOMS, SLICED | 375 | mL |
| 1 RED PEPPER, CUT IN STRIPS | | |
| 3 SCALLIONS OR GREEN ONIONS, SLICED DIAGONALLY | | |

TO PREPARE MARINADE: IN A LARGE BOWL, BLEND ALL MARINADE INGREDIENTS. ADD SHRIMP; COVER AND REFRIGERATE 1 HOUR.

# ORANGE STIR-FRIED SHRIMP

CONTINUED FROM PAGE 192.

TO MAKE SAUCE: IN A SMALL BOWL, MIX ALL INGREDIENTS UNTIL SMOOTH AND SET ASIDE.

TO STIR-FRY: HEAT WOK OR LARGE FRYING PAN UNTIL HOT. ADD OIL, GINGER AND GARLIC AND STIR-FRY 20 SECONDS. ADD GREEN BEANS, STIR-FRY 3 MINUTES. ADD MUSHROOMS AND RED PEPPER AND STIR-FRY 3 MINUTES MORE. ADD SHRIMP AND MARINADE; STIR-FRY 4 MINUTES, OR JUST UNTIL SHRIMP TURNS PINK. STIR SAUCE. ADD SCALLIONS; STIR INTO SHRIMP UNTIL MIXTURE IS COATED AND SAUCE THICKENS. (AREN'T YOU JUST EXHAUSTED??) SERVES 4.

IF MOST CAR ACCIDENTS OCCUR WITHIN 5 MILES OF HOME, WHY DOESN'T EVERYONE JUST MOVE 10 MILES AWAY?

# SHRIMP AND SCALLOP SUPREME

| | |
|---|---|
| 2 TBSP. OLIVE OIL | 30 mL |
| 1 ONION, CHOPPED | |
| 3 GARLIC CLOVES, MINCED | |
| 2-28 OZ. CANS TOMATOES, PURÉED WITH JUICE | 2-796 mL |
| 1 LB. SHRIMP, DEVEINED & BUTTERFLIED | 500 g |
| ¾ LB. SCALLOPS, HALVED IF LARGE | 365 g |
| 1 CUP FROZEN PEAS, THAWED | 250 mL |
| ¼ CUP CHOPPED FRESH PARSLEY | 60 mL |
| 1 TSP. SALT | 5 mL |
| ½ TSP. PEPPER | 2 mL |
| 3 CUPS COOKED LONG-GRAIN RICE | 750 mL |

## TOPPING

| | |
|---|---|
| ⅓ CUP BUTTER | 75 mL |
| 2 GARLIC CLOVES, MINCED | |
| 2 CUPS FRESH BREAD CRUMBS | 500 mL |
| SALT & PEPPER TO TASTE | |

IN DUTCH OVEN HEAT OIL OVER MEDIUM HEAT. COOK ONION AND GARLIC FOR 5 MINUTES. ADD TOMATOES; COOK 15 MINUTES. ADD SEAFOOD; COOK 5 MINUTES. STIR IN PEAS, PARSLEY, SALT AND PEPPER. SEASON RICE WITH SALT AND PEPPER TO TASTE AND SPREAD IN GREASED GLASS 9 X 13" (23 X 33 cm) PAN. SPREAD SEAFOOD MIXTURE OVER RICE.

TO MAKE TOPPING: MELT BUTTER AND SAUTÉ GARLIC. ADD BREAD CRUMBS AND SEASON WITH SALT AND PEPPER. SPRINKLE OVER CASSEROLE. MAY BE REFRIGERATED AT THIS POINT FOR UP

## SHRIMP AND SCALLOP SUPREME

CONTINUED FROM PAGE 194.

TO 24 HOURS. REMOVE FROM REFRIGERATOR ½ HOUR BEFORE BAKING. BAKE AT 350°F (180°C) FOR 30-40 MINUTES, OR UNTIL BUBBLING AND TOP IS BROWNED AND CRISP. DO NOT OVERCOOK. SERVE WITH ASPARAGUS AND WARM ROLLS. SERVES 8-10.

## LIME-GRILLED CHICKEN

A LOW-CAL. CREATION TO BROIL OR GRILL. RUB HERBS BETWEEN YOUR HANDS TO RELEASE FLAVORS.

| | |
|---|---|
| ½ CUP FRESH LIME JUICE (2 LARGE LIMES) | 125 mL |
| ¼ CUP VEGETABLE OIL | 60 mL |
| 2 TBSP. HONEY | 30 mL |
| 1 TSP. THYME | 5 mL |
| 1 TSP. ROSEMARY | 5 mL |
| 1 GARLIC CLOVE, CRUSHED | |
| 2 WHOLE CHICKEN BREASTS, SKINNED, BONED & HALVED | |

IN A BOWL COMBINE ALL INGREDIENTS, EXCEPT CHICKEN, WHISKING UNTIL WELL BLENDED. MARINATE CHICKEN BREASTS IN LIME MIXTURE 1-2 HOURS. BROIL OR GRILL APPROXIMATELY 4 MINUTES PER SIDE, UNTIL CHICKEN IS COOKED THROUGH. BASTE DURING COOKING. SERVES 4.

# ORANGE-ROSEMARY CHICKEN

SPLENDIFEROUS!

2 GARLIC CLOVES
1 ROASTING CHICKEN
1 ORANGE, QUARTERED
4 SPRIGS FRESH ROSEMARY OR
    1 TBSP. (15 mL) DRY
1 TBSP. OIL                          15 mL
2 TBSP. ORANGE MARMALADE       30 mL
1 TBSP. CHOPPED FRESH ROSEMARY OR   15 mL
    1½ TSP. ( 7 mL) DRY

PREHEAT OVEN TO 325°F (160°C). PEEL GARLIC
AND PLACE IN CHICKEN CAVITY. STUFF
UNPEELED ORANGE WEDGES INTO CAVITY WITH
ROSEMARY. CLOSE THE CAVITY AND LOOSELY TIE
LEGS TOGETHER. PLACE CHICKEN ON RACK IN
ROASTING PAN. BRUSH WITH OIL. ROAST CHICKEN,
UNCOVERED, FOR 2 HOURS. BASTE FREQUENTLY
WITH PAN JUICES. MIX MARMALADE WITH
ROSEMARY. BRUSH OVER CHICKEN AND ROAST,
BASTING WITH MIXTURE, ABOUT 10 MORE MINUTES.
MAKE GRAVY WITH PAN DRIPPINGS. SERVE WITH
MASHED POTATOES.

CLASSIFIED AD: "KITTENS, $1 EACH. CALL ASHLEY."
                "KITTENS FREE. CALL ASHLEY'S
                MOM."

# HONEY-MUSTARD CHICKEN

MAKES LOTS OF SAUCE; GREAT WITH RICE.

| | |
|---|---:|
| 3 LBS. CHICKEN PIECES | 1.5 kg |
| ½ CUP LIQUID HONEY | 125 mL |
| ¼ CUP BUTTER OR MARGARINE | 60 mL |
| ¼ CUP DIJON MUSTARD | 60 mL |
| 2-4 TSP. CURRY POWDER | 10-20 mL |
| PINCH CAYENNE PEPPER | |

PLACE CHICKEN IN SINGLE LAYER IN LARGE OVENPROOF DISH. COMBINE HONEY, BUTTER, MUSTARD, CURRY POWDER AND CAYENNE. POUR OVER CHICKEN. BAKE, UNCOVERED, AT 350°F (180°C) FOR 20 MINUTES, BASTING ONCE. TURN PIECES OVER, BASTE AGAIN AND BAKE ANOTHER 20 MINUTES, OR UNTIL PIECES ARE NO LONGER PINK INSIDE. SERVES 4-6.

THE ONE NICE THING ABOUT STARTING TO FORGET THINGS IS THAT YOU CAN HIDE YOUR OWN EASTER EGGS.

# BARE-NAKED CHICKEN

FAST AND EASY!

| | | |
|---|---|---|
| 4 BONELESS, SKINLESS CHICKEN BREAST HALVES | | |
| SALT & PEPPER TO TASTE | | |
| 1 TBSP. BUTTER | 15 | mL |
| ½ CUP FINELY CHOPPED SHALLOTS | 125 | mL |
| ¼ CUP BALSAMIC VINEGAR | 60 | mL |
| 1½ CUPS CHICKEN BROTH | 375 | mL |

SEASON CHICKEN AND BROWN IN BUTTER OVER MEDIUM-HIGH HEAT. REDUCE HEAT AND COOK UNTIL CHICKEN IS NO LONGER PINK IN MIDDLE. DO NOT OVERCOOK! REMOVE TO HEATED DISH AND SET IN WARM OVEN. ADD SHALLOTS TO PAN AND COOK UNTIL TRANSLUCENT. ADD VINEGAR, BOIL AND REDUCE TO GLAZE, STIRRING CONSTANTLY. ADD CHICKEN BROTH AND BOIL UNTIL REDUCED TO ¾ CUP (175 mL). SPOON OVER CHICKEN AND RETURN DISH TO OVEN UNTIL SERVING TIME. EXCELLENT WITH RICE OR FETTUCCINE. SERVES 4.

TACT IS THE ABILITY TO NOT SAY WHAT YOU REALLY THINK.

# GINGER CHICKEN STIR-FRY

DINNER'S READY IN 20 MINUTES.

| | |
|---|---|
| 3 TBSP. LEMON JUICE, FRESH IS BEST | 45 mL |
| 3 TBSP. SOY SAUCE | 45 mL |
| 1 TBSP. GRATED FRESH GINGER | 15 mL |
| 2 GARLIC CLOVES, MINCED | |
| 1 CHICKEN BREAST, SKINNED & BONED, CUT INTO 1/2" (1.3 cm) STRIPS | |
| 2 TSP. CORNSTARCH | 10 mL |
| 1/3 CUP CHICKEN BROTH | 75 mL |
| 1 TBSP. COOKING OIL | 15 mL |
| 1 CUP SLICED MUSHROOMS | 250 mL |
| 1 1/2 CUPS ASPARAGUS OR GREEN BEANS CUT IN 1 1/2" (4 cm) PIECES | 375 mL |
| 3 GREEN ONIONS, SLICED DIAGONALLY INTO 1" (2.5 cm) PIECES | |
| TOASTED SESAME SEEDS | |

IN A BOWL COMBINE LEMON JUICE, SOY SAUCE, GINGER AND GARLIC. SPRINKLE 3 TBSP. (45 mL) OF MIXTURE OVER CHICKEN, TOSSING TO COAT. RESERVE REMAINING LIQUID. DISSOLVE CORN-STARCH IN BROTH. HEAT OIL IN FRYING PAN OR WOK. ADD MUSHROOMS AND CHICKEN. STIR OVER HIGH HEAT UNTIL CHICKEN LOSES PINK COLOR. ADD ASPARAGUS AND ONIONS; CONTINUE TO STIR OVER HIGH HEAT UNTIL VEGETABLES ARE TENDER-CRISP. ADD BROTH MIXTURE AND RESERVED LIQUID AND STIR UNTIL THICKENED. SPRINKLE WITH SESAME SEEDS. SERVE HOT OVER RICE OR PASTA. SERVES 4.

# SWEET AND SPICY CASHEW CHICKEN

A DELICIOUS AND COLORFUL STIR-FRY. SERVE OVER RICE ON A LARGE PLATTER OR TAKE THE WOK RIGHT TO THE TABLE.

### SAUCE

| | |
|---|---|
| ½ CUP KETCHUP | 125 mL |
| 4 TSP. SOY SAUCE | 20 mL |
| ½ TSP. SALT | 2 mL |
| 2 TBSP. WORCESTERSHIRE SAUCE | 30 mL |
| 3 TBSP. SUGAR | 45 mL |
| 1½ TSP. SESAME OIL | 7 mL |
| ¼ TSP. CAYENNE PEPPER | 1 mL |
| ½ CUP CHICKEN BROTH | 125 mL |

### THE REST

| | |
|---|---|
| 2 TBSP. CORNSTARCH | 30 mL |
| ½ TSP. SUGAR | 2 mL |
| ¼ TSP. SALT | 1 mL |
| 3 WHOLE BONELESS, SKINLESS CHICKEN BREASTS, CUT INTO CUBES | |
| ¼ CUP OIL | 60 mL |
| 2-3 TBSP. MINCED FRESH GINGER | 30-45 mL |
| 1 TBSP. MINCED GARLIC | 15 mL |
| 1 SMALL ONION, CHOPPED | |
| 2 RED PEPPERS, CUT IN STRIPS | |
| 2 CARROTS, THINLY SLICED ON DIAGONAL | |
| 2 CUPS SNOW PEAS | 500 mL |
| 1½ CUPS CASHEWS | 375 mL |
| SPRINKLING OF SESAME SEEDS, TOASTED | |

# SWEET AND SPICY CASHEW CHICKEN

CONTINUED FROM PAGE 200.

ARE YOU READY? COMBINE SAUCE INGREDIENTS* AND SET ASIDE. IN A BOWL, COMBINE CORNSTARCH, SUGAR AND SALT. ADD CHICKEN AND TOSS. HEAT WOK OR FRYING PAN TO HIGHEST HEAT. ADD OIL. HEAT TO HOT, NOT SMOKING. ADD CHICKEN, GINGER, GARLIC AND ONION. STIR UNTIL CHICKEN IS OPAQUE (ABOUT 1 MINUTE). ADD PEPPERS AND CARROTS. STIR 2-3 MINUTES. ADD PEAS AND SAUCE. COOK UNTIL SAUCE COMES TO A BOIL. ADD CASHEWS AND SPRINKLE WITH SESAME SEEDS. SERVE IMMEDIATELY. SERVES 6.

(PICTURED ON PAGE 224.)

I HAVE AN AGREEMENT WITH MY WIFE. SHE DOESN'T COMPARE THE MEN IN PLAYGIRL MAGAZINE TO ME - AND I DON'T COMPARE THE MEALS IN GOURMET MAGAZINE TO HERS.

# CRUNCHY GARLIC CHICKEN

| | |
|---|---|
| 2 TBSP. BUTTER, MELTED | 30 mL |
| 2 TBSP. MILK | 30 mL |
| 1 TSP. CHOPPED FRESH CHIVES | 5 mL |
| ½ TSP. SALT | 2 mL |
| 1 LARGE GARLIC CLOVE, MINCED | |
| 2 CUPS CORNFLAKES, CRUSHED | 500 mL |
| 3 TBSP. CHOPPED FRESH PARSLEY | 45 mL |
| ½ TSP. PAPRIKA | 2 mL |
| 6 CHICKEN BREAST HALVES, BONELESS, SKINLESS | |

HEAT OVEN TO 425°F (220°C). USE NONSTICK SPRAY OR PARCHMENT PAPER ON A BAKING SHEET. IN A DISH, MIX BUTTER, MILK, CHIVES, SALT AND GARLIC TOGETHER. MIX CORNFLAKES, PARSLEY AND PAPRIKA TOGETHER. DIP CHICKEN IN BUTTER MIXTURE, THEN COAT EVENLY IN CORNFLAKE MIXTURE. PLACE ON BAKING SHEET AND SPRAY LIGHTLY WITH COOKING SPRAY. BAKE, UNCOVERED, 20-25 MINUTES. SERVES 4-6.

WHY DO NEWLY MARRIED MEN TWIRL THEIR WEDDING RINGS? THEY'RE LOOKING FOR THE COMBINATION.

# OVEN-FRIED CHICKEN

A PERFECT PICNIC "PACK ALONG".

<u>SEASONED FLOUR</u>

| | |
|---|---|
| 1½ CUPS FLOUR | 375 mL |
| 4 TSP. DRY MUSTARD | 20 mL |
| 1 TBSP. PAPRIKA | 15 mL |
| SALT & PEPPER TO TASTE | |
| CHICKEN PIECES, AS NEEDED | |
| ¼ CUP BUTTER OR MARGARINE | 60 mL |

COMBINE SEASONED FLOUR INGREDIENTS AND STORE IN A JAR. PREHEAT OVEN TO 400°F (200°C). PLACE REQUIRED AMOUNT OF DRY MIXTURE IN A PAPER BAG; ADD CHICKEN AND SHAKE DEM BONES. MELT MARGARINE IN BAKING PAN. PLACE CHICKEN IN PAN AND BAKE 20 MINUTES. TURN AND BAKE ANOTHER 20 MINUTES, OR UNTIL GOLDEN BROWN.

AEROBIC WORKOUTS AREN'T A NEW INVENTION. BACK ON THE FARM, WE CALLED THEM CHORES.

# LAYERED CHICKEN TORTILLA

FAST, EASY AND DELICIOUS. GARNISH WITH SLICES OF CANTALOUPE AND HONEYDEW - ADD A GREEN SALAD AND OLE! DINNER FOR 6.

| | |
|---|---|
| 3 CUPS COOKED SHREDDED CHICKEN | 750 mL |
| 1 CUP GRATED CHEDDAR CHEESE | 250 mL |
| ½ CUP SLICED GREEN ONIONS | 125 mL |
| 2 CUPS FAT-FREE SOUR CREAM | 500 mL |
| 4 OZ. CAN DICED GREEN CHILIES, DRAINED | 113 mL |
| ¾ TSP. CUMIN | 4 mL |
| 12 OZ. JAR SALSA, MEDIUM HEAT | 341 mL |
| 8, 8" (20 cm) FLOUR TORTILLAS | |
| ½ CUP GRATED CHEDDAR CHEESE | 125 mL |

PREHEAT OVEN TO 400°F (200°C). IN LARGE BOWL STIR TOGETHER CHICKEN, CHEESE, GREEN ONIONS, SOUR CREAM, CHILIES AND CUMIN. POUR 1 CUP (250 mL) SALSA INTO A 10" (25 cm) PIE PLATE. LAY 1 TORTILLA IN SALSA, COATING 1 SIDE. PLACE TORTILLA, SALSA SIDE DOWN, IN A 9" (23 cm) SPRING FORM PAN OR 2-QUART (2 L) ROUND CASSEROLE. SPREAD ½ CUP (125 mL) CHICKEN MIXTURE ON TOP OF TORTILLA. REPEAT WITH 3 MORE LAYERS OF TORTILLAS AND CHICKEN. SPREAD WITH ½ CUP (125 mL) SALSA. CONTINUE LAYERING TORTILLAS AND CHICKEN MIXTURE, ENDING WITH TORTILLA. TOP WITH THE SALSA LEFT OVER FROM DIPPING THE TORTILLAS. SPRINKLE ON THE CHEESE. BAKE FOR 35-40 MINUTES. LET STAND 10 MINUTES AND CUT INTO WEDGES. SERVE WITH ADDITIONAL SALSA.

Chicken in Phyllo, page 210
Vegetable Couscous, page 184

Chicken Pot Pie, page 213

# EL GRANDO CHICKEN QUESADILLAS

NOT YOUR ORDINARY QUESADILLA, IT'S A KNIFE AND FORKER!

| | |
|---|---|
| 1 MILD GREEN CHILI | |
| 1/2 RED PEPPER | |
| 1/2 YELLOW PEPPER | |
| 1 WHOLE CHICKEN BREAST, BONED & SKINNED | |
| 1/2 TSP. CHILI POWDER | 2 mL |
| 1/2 TSP. CUMIN | 2 mL |
| SALT & FRESHLY GROUND PEPPER TO TASTE | |
| 2-10" (25 cm) FLOUR TORTILLAS | |
| 1/3 CUP GRATED MONTEREY JACK CHEESE | 75 mL |
| 1/3 CUP GRATED JALAPEÑO JACK CHEESE | 75 mL |
| 1/4 CUP DICED RIPE PAPAYA | 60 mL |

## FOR GARNISH

| | |
|---|---|
| 1/4 CUP GUACAMOLE | 60 mL |
| 1/4 CUP SOUR CREAM | 60 mL |
| 1/4 CUP CHUNKY SALSA | 60 mL |

ROAST THE CHILI AND PEPPERS UNDER THE BROILER UNTIL CHARRED. PUT IN A PLASTIC BAG AND LET STAND 10 MINUTES TO STEAM. COOL, PEEL AND DICE. SEASON CHICKEN WITH CHILI POWDER, CUMIN, SALT AND PEPPER. GRILL CHICKEN UNTIL JUST OPAQUE THROUGHOUT. CUT INTO THIN STRIPS. PLACE TORTILLA ON MEDIUM HOT GRILL OR IN FRYING PAN OVER MEDIUM-HIGH HEAT. SPRINKLE WITH HALF OF THE CHEESES, DICED CHILI PEPPERS, PAPAYAS AND WARM CHICKEN. WHEN CHEESE IS MELTED AND TORTILLA IS LIGHTLY BROWNED, FOLD TORTILLA IN HALF AND PLACE IN OVEN TO KEEP WARM. REPEAT WITH SECOND TORTILLA. CUT EACH QUESADILLA INTO 4 WEDGES. GARNISH WITH GUACAMOLE, SOUR CREAM AND SALSA. SERVE IMMEDIATELY.

# SOUTHWESTERN CHICKEN CHILI

CHILI, LIKE MEN, IMPROVES WITH AGE!

| | |
|---|---|
| 2½ LBS. SKINLESS, BONELESS CHICKEN BREASTS | 1.25 kg |
| 2 TBSP. VEGETABLE OIL | 30 mL |
| 2 ONIONS, CHOPPED | |
| 2 GARLIC CLOVES, MINCED | |
| 3 TBSP. CHILI POWDER (USE ALL OF IT!) | 45 mL |
| 2 TSP. CUMIN | 10 mL |
| 1 TSP. OREGANO | 5 mL |
| 3 TBSP. CORIANDER | 45 mL |
| SALT & PEPPER TO TASTE | |
| 4 CARROTS, SLICED | |
| 3 STALKS CELERY, CHOPPED | |
| 28 OZ. CAN TOMATOES | 796 mL |
| 3 TBSP. TOMATO PASTE | 45 mL |
| 2 TBSP. LIME JUICE | 30 mL |
| 1 TSP. SUGAR | 5 mL |
| 12 OZ. CAN KERNEL CORN | 341 mL |
| 14 OZ. CAN KIDNEY BEANS | 398 mL |
| 14 OZ. CAN GARBANZO BEANS | 398 mL |
| 1 GREEN PEPPER, SEEDED & CHOPPED | |

CUT CHICKEN INTO BITE-SIZED PIECES. IN A DUTCH OVEN, BROWN CHICKEN IN OIL. ADD ONIONS AND GARLIC AND SAUTÉ UNTIL ONIONS ARE SOFT. ADD CHILI, CUMIN, OREGANO, CORIANDER, SALT AND PEPPER. COOK AND STIR FOR 3 MINUTES. ADD CARROTS, CELERY, TOMATOES, TOMATO PASTE, LIME JUICE AND SUGAR TO CHICKEN MIXTURE. BRING TO BOIL, REDUCE TO SIMMER, COVER AND COOK FOR 1 HOUR. ADD CORN, KIDNEY BEANS, GARBANZO BEANS AND GREEN PEPPER.

## SOUTHWESTERN CHICKEN CHILI

CONTINUED FROM PAGE 208.

SIMMER 30 MINUTES MORE. SERVES MORE THAN 8 GOOD FRIENDS (OR 9 RELATIVES AND 1 AMAZED MOTHER-IN-LAW!). SERVE WITH A SALAD AND CRUSTY ROLLS.

## CHICKEN ENCHILADA CASSEROLE

*THIS IS A MUST!*

| | |
|---|---|
| 6 SMALL CORN OR 3 LARGE FLOUR TORTILLAS | |
| 1 LARGE ONION, DICED | |
| 2 TBSP. OIL | 30 mL |
| 4 OZ. CAN GREEN CHILIES, SEEDED & FINELY CHOPPED | 114 mL |
| 10 OZ. CAN CREAM OF MUSHROOM SOUP | 284 mL |
| 2 CUPS GRATED CHEDDAR CHEESE | 500 mL |
| 2 CUPS GRATED MOZZARELLA CHEESE | 500 mL |
| 1 CUP SALSA | 250 mL |
| 3-4 CUPS COOKED CHICKEN, CUT INTO LARGE BITE-SIZED PIECES | 750 mL-1 L |

CUT EACH TORTILLA INTO 6 PIECES. SAUTÉ ONION IN OIL. ADD CHILIES, SOUP AND HALF THE GRATED CHEESES. COOK SLOWLY UNTIL CHEESE MELTS. LINE A BUTTERED 1½-QUART (1.5 L) CASSEROLE WITH HALF THE TORTILLA PIECES. COVER WITH ½ CUP (125 mL) SALSA. LAYER WITH HALF THE CHICKEN, THEN HALF THE CHEESE SAUCE. REPEAT LAYERS. TOP WITH THE REMAINING GRATED CHEESES. BAKE AT 325°F (160°C) FOR 50-60 MINUTES. LET STAND (OR SIT IF YOUR PREFER!) FOR 10 MINUTES. SERVES 6.

# CHICKEN IN PHYLLO

CHICKEN FOR COMPANY!

| | |
|---|---|
| 8 PHYLLO PASTRY SHEETS | |
| 1/4 CUP BUTTER, MELTED | 60 mL |
| 4 BONELESS, SKINLESS CHICKEN BREASTS, HALVED | |
| 1 BUNCH OF FRESH SPINACH LEAVES, STEMS REMOVED | |
| 1 BUNCH FRESH BASIL LEAVES, CHOPPED | |
| 1 LARGE RED PEPPER, CUT IN STRIPS | |
| 3/4 CUP FETA CHEESE, CRUMBLED | 175 mL |

LAY 1 SHEET OF PHYLLO ON COUNTER AND FOLD IN HALF (NOT LENGTH-WISE). BRUSH MELTED BUTTER ON EDGES. PLACE ONE-HALF CHICKEN BREAST IN THE MIDDLE, NEAR THE BOTTOM OF PHYLLO. LAYER SPINACH LEAVES, A SPRINKLING OF BASIL, A FEW PEPPER STRIPS AND SOME FETA CHEESE ON TOP OF CHICKEN. ROLL CHICKEN AND PHYLLO OVER ONCE. FOLD EDGES TOWARD THE MIDDLE AND CONTINUE ROLLING TO FORM A SMALL RECTANGULAR PACKAGE. BRUSH WITH A LITTLE BUTTER. PLACE ON A COOKIE SHEET AND COVER WITH A SLIGHTLY DAMP CLOTH WHILE MAKING THE OTHERS. THESE CAN BE WRAPPED IN PLASTIC WRAP AND REFRIGERATED OVERNIGHT. PREHEAT OVEN TO 375°F (190°C) AND PLACE RACK IN MIDDLE OF OVEN. BAKE FOR 25-30 MINUTES. SERVE WITH VEGETABLE COUSCOUS (PAGE 184). (PICTURED ON PAGE 205.)

# CHICKEN BREASTS ZELDA

WHY DOES DIANE ALWAYS GET THE CREDIT?

| | |
|---|---|
| 4 BONELESS, SKINLESS CHICKEN BREAST HALVES | |
| ½ TSP. SALT | 2 mL |
| ½ TSP. FRESHLY GROUND PEPPER | 2 mL |
| 1 TBSP. BUTTER OR VEGETABLE OIL | 15 mL |
| 1 TBSP. BUTTER OR MARGARINE | 15 mL |
| 3 TBSP. CHOPPED GREEN ONION | 45 mL |
| JUICE OF ½ LIME OR LEMON | |
| 2 TBSP. BRANDY, OPTIONAL (ZELDA LOVES THIS) | 30 mL |
| 3 TBSP. CHOPPED FRESH PARSLEY | 45 mL |
| 2 TSP. DIJON MUSTARD | 10 mL |
| ¼ CUP CHICKEN BROTH | 60 mL |

PLACE CHICKEN BREAST HALVES BETWEEN SHEETS OF WAXED PAPER AND POUND SLIGHTLY WITH FLAT SIDE OF MALLET. SPRINKLE WITH SALT AND PEPPER. HEAT OIL AND BUTTER TOGETHER IN LARGE FRYING PAN. COOK CHICKEN OVER MEDIUM-HIGH HEAT 4 MINUTES EACH SIDE. PLACE IN SERVING DISH AND SET IN WARM OVEN. ADD ONIONS, LIME JUICE, BRANDY, PARSLEY AND MUSTARD TO PAN. COOK 15 SECONDS, WHISKING CONSTANTLY. WHISK IN BROTH, STIRRING UNTIL SAUCE IS SMOOTH. POUR OVER WARM CHICKEN AND SERVE WITH NOODLES OR NEW POTATOES AND A SALAD. SERVES 4.

# CHICKEN BREASTS STUFFED WITH ASPARAGUS

CELEBRATE THE RITES OF SPRING!

| | |
|---|---|
| 4 WHOLE CHICKEN BREASTS, HALVED, BONED & POUNDED | |
| 24 MEDIUM ASPARAGUS SPEARS, LIGHTLY BLANCHED | |
| 1/4 CUP BUTTER, MELTED | 60 mL |
| 1/4 CUP DIJON MUSTARD | 60 mL |
| 2 GARLIC CLOVES, FINELY CHOPPED | |
| 1/4 CUP WHITE WINE | 60 mL |
| 1 1/2 CUPS BREAD CRUMBS | 375 mL |
| 1 TBSP. GRATED PARMESAN CHEESE | 15 mL |
| 2 TBSP. FINELY CHOPPED PARSLEY | 30 mL |

PREPARE CHICKEN AND ASPARAGUS. COMBINE THE BUTTER, MUSTARD, GARLIC AND WINE. DIP THE CHICKEN BREASTS IN THIS MIXTURE TO COAT THEM. PLACE 3 ASPARAGUS SPEARS ON EACH BREAST AND ROLL, SECURING WITH A TOOTHPICK. MIX BREAD CRUMBS, PARMESAN AND PARSLEY TOGETHER AND ROLL THE BREASTS IN THIS MIXTURE. BAKE 30 MINUTES AT 350°F (180°C). SERVES 4-6. PASS THE BLENDER HOLLANDAISE SAUCE (PAGE 38) AND HEAR THE RAVES.

A MAN GETTING A DIVORCE: GOING THROUGH THE CHANGE OF WIFE.

# CHICKEN POT PIE

THANKS FOR THE MEMORIES!

| | |
|---|---|
| 1/4 CUP BUTTER | 60 mL |
| 1/4 CUP FLOUR | 60 mL |
| SALT & PEPPER TO TASTE | |
| 2 TBSP. FINELY CHOPPED ONION | 30 mL |
| 3 CUPS CHICKEN BROTH | 750 mL |
| 2 CARROTS, CHOPPED IN SMALL PIECES | |
| 2 CELERY STALKS, CHOPPED IN SMALL PIECES | |
| 2 POTATOES, CUBED IN SMALL PIECES | |
| 3 CUPS SLICED MUSHROOMS | 750 mL |
| 2 TBSP. BUTTER | 30 mL |
| 1/2 CUP PEAS | 125 mL |
| 3 CUPS COOKED & DICED CHICKEN | 750 mL |
| PASTRY TO COVER 3-QT. (3 L) CASSEROLE | |
|     OR FROZEN PUFF PASTRY DOUGH | |

MELT BUTTER IN LARGE SAUCEPAN OVER MEDIUM HEAT. BLEND IN FLOUR, SALT, PEPPER AND ONION. GRADUALLY STIR IN CHICKEN BROTH. COOK, STIRRING CONSTANTLY, UNTIL SMOOTH AND THICKENED. ADD CARROTS, CELERY AND POTATOES. COOK UNTIL FORK TENDER. IN A SMALL FRYING PAN, COOK THE MUSHROOMS IN BUTTER. ADD MUSHROOMS, PEAS AND CHICKEN TO VEGETABLE MIXTURE. MIX WELL AND POUR INTO LARGE CASSEROLE. COVER WITH ROLLED PASTRY AND SLASH (WATCH IT!) TO ALLOW STEAM TO ESCAPE. BAKE IN PREHEATED 400°F (200°C) OVEN FOR ABOUT 45 MINUTES, OR UNTIL PASTRY IS GOLDEN. IF PASTRY BECOMES TOO BROWN, COVER LOOSELY WITH FOIL. (PICTURED ON PAGE 206.)

# CHICKEN IN WINE

VERY QUICK - AND VERY GOOD!

| | |
|---|---|
| 3 LBS. CUT-UP CHICKEN PIECES | 1.5 kg |
| 1/2 CUP SEASONED FLOUR | 125 mL |
| 6 TBSP. OIL | 90 mL |
| 2 CUPS SLICED FRESH MUSHROOMS | 500 mL |
| 1 TBSP. BUTTER | 15 mL |
| 10 OZ. CAN MUSHROOM SOUP | 284 mL |
| 1/2 CUP CHICKEN BROTH | 125 mL |
| 1/2 CUP ORANGE JUICE | 125 mL |
| 1/2 CUP DRY WHITE WINE (VERMOUTH IS FINE) | 125 mL |
| 1 TBSP. BROWN SUGAR | 15 mL |
| 1/2 TSP. SALT | 2 mL |
| 4 CARROTS, SLICED | |

WASH AND PAT DRY CHICKEN PIECES. PUT FLOUR IN PLASTIC BAG AND SHAKE CHICKEN IN IT. IN FRYING PAN, HEAT OIL AND BROWN CHICKEN. REMOVE CHICKEN TO LARGE CASSEROLE. COOK MUSHROOMS IN BUTTER AND ADD TO CASSEROLE. COMBINE REMAINING INGREDIENTS; POUR OVER CHICKEN AND MUSHROOMS AND BAKE AT 350°F (180°C) FOR 1 HOUR. SERVE OVER RICE WITH A FRESH GREEN SALAD.

THERE'S A NEW RESTAURANT THAT FEATURES HOMESTYLE BREAKFAST. THE WAITER WEARS A BATHROBE AND ASKS YOU TO LET THE DOG IN.

# CLASSY CHICKEN

THIS IS REALLY EASY AND YOUR COMPANY WILL LOVE IT.

| | |
|---|---|
| 3 CHICKEN BREASTS, SKINNED & BONED | |
| 1/4 TSP. PEPPER | 1 mL |
| 3 TBSP. OIL | 45 mL |
| 10 OZ. PKG. FROZEN ASPARAGUS OR BROCCOLI (FRESH IS EVEN BETTER) | 280 g |
| 10 OZ. CAN CREAM OF CHICKEN SOUP | 284 mL |
| 1/2 CUP MAYONNAISE | 125 mL |
| 1 TSP. CURRY POWDER | 5 mL |
| 1 TSP. LEMON JUICE | 5 mL |
| 1 CUP GRATED CHEDDAR CHEESE | 250 mL |

CUT CHICKEN INTO BITE-SIZED PIECES AND SPRINKLE WITH PEPPER. SAUTÉ IN OIL OVER MEDIUM HEAT UNTIL OPAQUE, ABOUT 6 MINUTES. DRAIN. COOK ASPARAGUS OR BROCCOLI UNTIL TENDER CRISP; DRAIN AND ARRANGE IN BOTTOM OF BUTTERED CASSEROLE. PLACE CHICKEN ON TOP. MIX TOGETHER SOUP, MAYONNAISE, CURRY AND LEMON JUICE AND POUR OVER CHICKEN. SPRINKLE WITH CHEDDAR CHEESE AND BAKE, UNCOVERED, AT 350°F (180°C) FOR 30-35 MINUTES. SERVES 6.

IT MAKES NO SENSE TO WALK TO THE CARWASH!

# JAPANESE CHICKEN WINGS

GREAT FOR CROWDS AND KIDS! TASTES GOOD WARMED UP IF THERE'S ANY LEFT.

| | |
|---|---|
| 3 LBS. CHICKEN WINGS, TIPS REMOVED | 1.5 kg |
| 1 EGG | |
| 1/3 CUP FLOUR | 75 mL |
| 1 CUP BUTTER | 250 mL |

### SAUCE

| | |
|---|---|
| 3 TBSP. SOY SAUCE | 45 mL |
| 3 TBSP. WATER | 45 mL |
| 1 CUP WHITE SUGAR | 250 mL |
| 1/2 CUP VINEGAR | 125 mL |

CUT WINGS IN HALF. DIP IN SLIGHTLY BEATEN EGG AND THEN IN FLOUR. FRY IN BUTTER UNTIL DEEP BROWN AND CRISP. PLACE IN SHALLOW ROASTING PAN. MIX ALL SAUCE INGREDIENTS TOGETHER AND POUR OVER CHICKEN WINGS. BAKE AT 350°F (180°C) FOR 1/2 HOUR. BASTE WINGS WITH SAUCE DURING COOKING.

THE RACE TRACK IS WHERE ONE FILLY CAN BE ANOTHER MAN'S FOLLY.

# LAMB
Marinated Bar-B-Qued Lamb
Greek Lamb Stew

# PORK
Greek Ribs
Pork Loin Roast
Satay

# VEAL
Veal Scallopini and Mushrooms
Osso Buco Milanese

# BEEF
Beef Extraordinaire with Sauce Diane
Baked Steak with Mustard Sauce
Marinated Flank Steak
Cabbage Roll Casserole
Ginger-Fried Beef
Burritos
Shepherd's Pie
Family Favorite Meatloaf
Stroganoff Meatballs
Casserole for a Cold Night
Spaghetti Skillet Dinner
Bean Stuff

# MARINATED BAR-B-QUED LAMB

USE THIS MARINADE ON LAMB CHOPS OR A BUTTERFLIED LEG OF LAMB (ONLY YOUR BUTCHER KNOWS FOR SURE).

## GARLIC AND HERB MARINADE

| | |
|---|---|
| 1 CUP DRY RED WINE | 250 mL |
| ½ CUP OLIVE OIL | 125 mL |
| 2-3 GARLIC CLOVES, MINCED | |
| 1 TSP. DRIED OREGANO | 5 mL |
| 1 TSP. DRIED THYME | 5 mL |
| 1 TSP. DRIED PARSLEY | 5 mL |
| SALT & PEPPER TO TASTE | |
| JUICE OF 1 LEMON | |

BONED LEG OF LAMB

MIX ALL MARINADE INGREDIENTS TOGETHER. POUR OVER LAMB, COVER AND MARINATE FOR 24 HOURS IN REFRIGERATOR. TURN OCCASIONALLY.

PREHEAT BAR-B-QUE TO HIGH. SEAR LAMB OVER HIGH HEAT FOR 5 MINUTES ON EACH SIDE. REDUCE TO MEDIUM HEAT AND FINISH COOKING UNTIL DESIRED DONENESS, BASTING FREQUENTLY WITH REMAINING MARINADE. LAMB CAN BE SLIGHTLY PINK.

A SMITH AND WESSON BEATS 4 ACES.

# GREEK LAMB STEW

MOUTH-WATERING AROMAS FROM YOUR KITCHEN AND KUDOS FROM YOUR COMPANY.

| | |
|---|---|
| 3 LBS. BONELESS LAMB (LEG OR SHOULDER) | 1.5 kg |
| 3 TBSP. OLIVE OIL | 45 mL |
| 4 MEDIUM ONIONS, CHOPPED | |
| 4 GARLIC CLOVES, MINCED | |
| 28 OZ. CAN TOMATOES | 796 mL |
| 5½ OZ. CAN TOMATO PASTE | 156 mL |
| 1 CUP DRY RED WINE | 250 mL |
| ½ CUP CURRANTS, RINSED IN WARM WATER | 125 mL |
| 2 TBSP. BROWN SUGAR | 30 mL |
| 1½ TSP. CUMIN | 7 mL |
| 1 TSP. GRATED ORANGE RIND | 5 mL |
| 2 BAY LEAVES | |
| 1 CINNAMON STICK | |
| ½ CUP CHOPPED FRESH PARSLEY | 125 mL |
| 1-2 TSP. SALT | 5-10 mL |
| 1 TSP. FRESHLY GROUND PEPPER | 5 mL |

TRIM LAMB AND CUT INTO BITE-SIZED PIECES. IN DUTCH OVEN, BROWN LAMB IN 3 BATCHES USING 1 TBSP. (15 mL) OIL WITH EACH BATCH. RETURN LAMB (AND ALL THOSE ACCUMULATED JUICES) TO THE POT. ADD ONIONS AND GARLIC AND COOK, COVERED, UNTIL ONIONS ARE SOFTENED. PURÉE TOMATOES AND ADD TO POT. ADD REMAINING INGREDIENTS AND BRING TO BOIL. REDUCE HEAT AND SIMMER, COVERED, AT LEAST 1 HOUR. DISCARD BAY LEAVES AND CINNAMON. SERVES 8. SERVE OVER RICE. THE FLAVOR IMPROVES IF YOU MAKE THIS DELICIOUS STEW THE DAY BEFORE.

# GREEK RIBS

DON'T ASK! JUST MAKE THEM.

SPARERIBS
FRESH LEMON JUICE
SEASONING SALT
GARLIC SALT
DRIED TARRAGON OR OREGANO

COVER RIBS WITH WATER; BRING TO A BOIL. REDUCE HEAT AND SIMMER FOR 20 MINUTES. DRAIN RIBS AND PLACE ON BROILER PAN. SQUEEZE LEMON JUICE LIBERALLY OVER RIBS AND THEN SPRINKLE THE SEASONINGS TO YOUR HEART'S CONTENT. BAKE AT 350°F (180°C) FOR 30-40 MINUTES. SERVE WITH RICE AND PAPAYA AVOCADO SALAD (PAGE 76). YOUR COMPANY WILL BE THRILLED.

BEFORE I GOT MARRIED, I HAD THREE THEORIES ABOUT RAISING CHILDREN. NOW I HAVE THREE CHILDREN AND NO THEORIES.

# PORK LOIN ROAST

YOU NEED A ZINGER - THIS IS IT!! SURE TO BECOME A FAVORITE.

| | |
|---|---:|
| 4-6 LB. BONELESS PORK LOIN ROAST | 2-2.5 kg |

PLUM SAUCE:

| | |
|---|---:|
| 1 CUP PLUM JAM | 250 mL |
| 1/3 CUP ORANGE JUICE CONCENTRATE | 75 mL |
| 1/3 CUP PINEAPPLE JUICE | 75 mL |
| 1/4 CUP SOY SAUCE | 60 mL |
| 1 TSP. ONION POWDER | 5 mL |
| 1/4 TSP. GARLIC POWDER | 1 mL |

PREHEAT OVEN TO 350°F (180°C). LINE ROASTING PAN WITH FOIL. COOK ROAST UNTIL TEMPERATURE ON MEAT THERMOMETER REACHES 170°F (77°C) (30 MINUTES PER POUND). COMBINE SAUCE INGREDIENTS IN A SMALL SAUCEPAN AND SIMMER FOR 5 MINUTES. AFTER ROAST REACHES 170°F (77°C), BRUSH FREQUENTLY WITH SAUCE WHILE CONTINUING TO ROAST FOR A FURTHER 30 MINUTES. PASS REMAINING SAUCE WITH ROAST. SERVE WITH ROASTED NEW POTATOES WITH ROSEMARY (PAGE 173) AND A VEGETABLE. SERVES 6.

NOWADAYS TWO CAN LIVE AS CHEAPLY AS ONE - IF BOTH ARE WORKING.

# SATAY

RAVE NOTICES: A BAR-B-QUED INDONESIAN DISH WE HIGHLY RECOMMEND FOR YOUR NEXT DINNER PARTY OR SUMMER COOKOUT. THERE WON'T BE A SPECK LEFT OVER.

| | |
|---|---|
| 1½ LBS. PORK TENDERLOIN (OR CHICKEN BREAST), IN 1" (2.5 cm) CUBES | 750 g |
| 2 TBSP. BUTTER | 30 mL |
| 1 TBSP. LEMON JUICE | 15 mL |
| GRATED RIND OF 1 LEMON | |
| ½ TSP. TABASCO | 2 mL |
| 3 TBSP. GRATED ONION | 45 mL |
| 1 TBSP. BROWN SUGAR | 15 mL |
| 1 TSP. CORIANDER | 5 mL |
| ½ TSP. GROUND CUMIN | 2 mL |
| ¼ TSP. GINGER | 1 mL |
| 1 GARLIC CLOVE, CRUSHED | |
| ½ CUP INDONESIAN SOY SAUCE OR TERIYAKI SAUCE | 125 mL |
| SALT & PEPPER TO TASTE | |
| WOODEN SKEWERS | |

PLACE PORK TENDERLOIN IN SHALLOW DISH. MELT BUTTER IN SAUCEPAN AND ADD REMAINING INGREDIENTS. BRING TO A BOIL AND SIMMER 5 MINUTES. POUR OVER MEAT, COVER AND REFRIGERATE OVERNIGHT. TURN MEAT PERIODICALLY (BUTTER WILL CONGEAL BUT DON'T WORRY). REMOVE MEAT FROM MARINADE (RESERVE) AND PUT 5-6 PIECES ON EACH SKEWER. GRILL ON BAR-B-QUE, TURNING FREQUENTLY, FOR 15 MINUTES (DON'T OVERCOOK).

CONTINUED ON PAGE 225.

Satay, page 222

Sweet & Spicy Cashew Chicken, page 200

CONTINUED FROM PAGE 222.

REHEAT MARINADE AND DRIZZLE OVER MEAT. SET ON A PLATTER ON A BED OF RICE. SERVE WITH FRESH SPINACH SALAD (PAGE 82). SERVES 6-8. (PICTURED ON PAGE 223.)

## VEAL SCALLOPINI AND MUSHROOMS

| | |
|---|---|
| 1½ LBS. VEAL SCALLOPINI | 750 g |
| ¼ CUP FLOUR | 60 mL |
| ½ TSP. SALT | 2 mL |
| ¼ CUP BUTTER | 60 mL |
| 1 GARLIC CLOVE, MINCED | |
| 3 CUPS SLICED MUSHROOMS | 750 mL |
| 3 TBSP. LEMON JUICE | 45 mL |
| ¼ CUP CHICKEN BROTH | 60 mL |
| ¼ CUP DRY WHITE WINE (VERMOUTH IS FINE) | 60 mL |

CUT VEAL INTO SERVING-SIZE PIECES. MIX FLOUR AND SALT TOGETHER IN A BAG AND SHAKE WITH VEAL TO COAT. SAUTÉ IN BUTTER. REMOVE MEAT AND SET ASIDE. SAUTÉ GARLIC AND MUSHROOMS; ADD LEMON JUICE, CHICKEN BROTH AND WINE. ADD VEAL, COVER AND SIMMER OVER MEDIUM HEAT FOR 20 MINUTES. SERVE WITH BUTTERED NOODLES AND PAPAYA AVOCADO SALAD (PAGE 76). SERVES 4-6.

# OSSO BUCO MILANESE

*CLASSIC ITALIAN FARE - A FLAVORFUL STEW MADE WITH VEAL SHANKS.*

| | |
|---|---|
| ¼ CUP FLOUR | 60 mL |
| SALT & FRESHLY GROUND PEPPER | |
| 6 PIECES VEAL SHANK, ½ LB. (250 g) EACH | |
| ⅓ CUP OLIVE OIL | 75 mL |
| 3 TBSP. BUTTER | 45 mL |
| 2 LARGE CARROTS, PEELED & SLICED | |
| 1 LARGE ONION, DICED | |
| 2 CELERY STALKS, SLICED | |
| 1 TBSP. CHOPPED GARLIC | 15 mL |
| 2 BAY LEAVES, CRUSHED | |
| 3 TBSP. CHOPPED FRESH MARJORAM OR 1 TBSP. (15 mL) DRIED | 45 mL |
| 3 TBSP. CHOPPED FRESH BASIL OR 1 TBSP. (15 mL) DRIED | 45 mL |
| 1 CUP CHOPPED FRESH PARSLEY | 250 mL |
| GRATED RIND OF 1 LEMON | |
| 1½ CUPS DRY WHITE WINE | 375 mL |
| 19 OZ. CAN ITALIAN PLUM TOMATOES, DRAINED & COARSELY CHOPPED | 540 mL |
| 1½ CUPS CHICKEN BROTH | 375 mL |

## GREMOLATA*

| | |
|---|---|
| 4 TSP. CHOPPED FRESH PARSLEY | 20 mL |
| 2 TSP. GRATED LEMON RIND | 10 mL |
| 1 GARLIC CLOVE, FINELY CHOPPED | |

COMBINE FLOUR, SALT AND PEPPER IN A PLASTIC BAG. ADD VEAL SHANKS AND COAT WITH FLOUR MIXTURE. HEAT OIL IN A LARGE FRYING PAN AND

# OSSO BUCO MILANESE

CONTINUED FROM PAGE 226.

BROWN VEAL ON BOTH SIDES. REMOVE VEAL AND REDUCE HEAT. ADD BUTTER, CARROTS, ONION, CELERY, GARLIC, BAY LEAVES, MARJORAM, BASIL, PARSLEY AND LEMON RIND. SAUTÉ FOR 5 MINUTES. ADD WINE AND CONTINUE COOKING FOR 5 MINUTES MORE. STIR IN TOMATOES AND BROTH. PLACE VEAL IN A CASSEROLE WITH THE SAUCE AND BAKE, COVERED, AT 325°F (160°C) FOR 2 HOURS. SERVE WITH RISOTTO, (PAGE 180.) AND GARNISH WITH GREMOLATA. SERVES 6.

✳ GREMOLATA, ADDS A FRESH INTENSE FLAVOR TO OSSO BUCO AND OTHER DISHES. FOR MINT GREMOLATA, MINT CAN BE SUBSTITUTED FOR PARSLEY AND FOR ORANGE GREMOLATA, SUBSTITUTE ORANGE RIND FOR LEMON. ALL 3 VERSIONS ARE DELICIOUS WITH OSSO BUCO.

NEVER TRUST A MAN WHO SAYS HE'S THE BOSS AT HOME - HE PROBABLY LIES ABOUT OTHER THINGS TOO.

# BEEF EXTRAORDINAIRE
## WITH SAUCE DIANE

WHEN THE BOSS COMES TO DINNER . . .

| | |
|---|---|
| 4 LBS. BEEF TENDERLOIN | 2 kg |
| 3/4 LB. MUSHROOMS, SLICED | 365 g |
| 1 1/2 CUPS SLICED GREEN ONIONS | 375 mL |
| 1/2 CUP BUTTER, MELTED | 125 mL |
| 2 TSPS. DRY MUSTARD | 10 mL |
| 1 TBSP. LEMON JUICE | 15 mL |
| 1 TBSP. WORCESTERSHIRE SAUCE | 15 mL |
| 1 TSP. SALT | 5 mL |

PREHEAT OVEN TO 500°F (260°C). PLACE TENDERLOIN ON RACK IN PAN AND ROAST FOR 30 MINUTES. ADD 1/4 CUP (60 mL) WATER TO PAN TO STOP ANY SMOKING.) USE MEAT THERMOMETER - 30 MINUTES WILL COOK BEEF TO MEDIUM-RARE STAGE. WHILE MEAT IS COOKING, SAUTÉ THE MUSHROOMS AND GREEN ONIONS IN THE MELTED BUTTER WITH MUSTARD FOR 5 MINUTES. ADD REMAINING INGREDIENTS AND COOK AN ADDITIONAL 5 MINUTES. KEEP WARM. PLACE MEAT ON PLATTER. SERVE WITH SAUCE, ROASTED NEW POTATOES WITH ROSEMARY (PAGE 173) AND ASPARAGUS VINAIGRETTE (PAGE 161). SERVES 8. SO, DID YOU GET THE RAISE?

BACHELOR PAD: A PLACE WHERE ALL THE HOUSEPLANTS ARE DEAD, BUT SOMETHING'S GROWING IN THE FRIDGE.

# BAKED STEAK WITH MUSTARD SAUCE

| | |
|---|---|
| 2½" THICK SIRLOIN STEAK | 6 cm |
| FRESHLY GROUND PEPPER, TO TASTE | |
| 1 MEDIUM ONION, FINELY CHOPPED | |
| 1 CUP KETCHUP | 250 mL |
| 3 TBSP. BUTTER, MELTED | 45 mL |
| 1 TBSP. LEMON JUICE | 15 mL |
| 1 SMALL GREEN PEPPER, SEEDED & SLICED | |
| FEW DROPS WORCESTERSHIRE SAUCE | |
| CHOPPED FRESH PARSLEY (1 SMALL BUNCH) | |

## MUSTARD SAUCE

| | |
|---|---|
| 2 TBSP. BUTTER | 30 mL |
| 2 TBSP. BAR-B-QUE SAUCE | 30 mL |
| 2 TSP. WORCESTERSHIRE SAUCE | 10 mL |
| 2 TSP. DRY MUSTARD | 10 mL |
| 2 TBSP. CREAM | 30 mL |

PREHEAT BROILER. PLACE STEAK IN BROILER PAN 4" (10 cm) BELOW HEAT. SEAR BOTH SIDES. REMOVE MEAT AND DRAIN OFF FAT. SEASON WITH PEPPER. MIX ALL INGREDIENTS AND POUR OVER STEAK IN PAN. BAKE AT 425°F (220°C) FOR 30 MINUTES. REMOVE TO A WARM PLATTER.

TO MAKE MUSTARD SAUCE: MELT BUTTER AND MIX ALL INGREDIENTS EXCEPT CREAM. HEAT OVER MEDIUM HEAT. REMOVE FROM HEAT; STIR IN CREAM. HEAT AGAIN. POUR OVER COOKED STEAK AND SPRINKLE WITH PARSLEY. SERVE WITH BAKED POTATOES AND CAESAR SALAD (PAGE 79).

# MARINATED FLANK STEAK

THIS TENDER, TASTY STEAK MAY BE SERVED HOT ON FRENCH BREAD OR COLD THE NEXT DAY FOR SANDWICHES. EXCELLENT BAR-B-QUE FARE.

| | |
|---|---|
| 2 LB. FLANK STEAK | 1 kg |

## DIJON MARINADE

| | |
|---|---|
| 3 TBSP. DIJON MUSTARD | 45 mL |
| 1 TBSP. SOY SAUCE | 15 mL |
| 1 TBSP. GRATED FRESH GINGER OR | 15 mL |
|     1 TSP. (5 mL) GROUND GINGER | |
| ½ TSP. DRIED THYME | 2 mL |
| ½ TSP. FRESHLY GROUND PEPPER | 2 mL |

OR

## SUPER TENDER MARINADE

| | |
|---|---|
| ⅓ CUP VEGETABLE OIL | 75 mL |
| ⅓ CUP RED WINE VINEGAR | 75 mL |
| ⅓ CUP DARK SOY SAUCE | 75 mL |

COMBINE MARINADE INGREDIENTS. SLASH EDGES OF STEAK SO THEY WON'T CURL UP DURING COOKING. PLACE STEAK IN MARINADE, COVER AND REFRIGERATE SEVERAL HOURS OR OVERNIGHT, TURNING ONCE OR TWICE. REMOVE FROM MARINADE AND BAR-B-QUE OR BROIL 4 MINUTES EACH SIDE - MEAT MUST BE PINK ON INSIDE. SLICE THINLY ACROSS THE GRAIN. DON'T DISCARD THE DELICIOUS DRIPPINGS - SPOON OVER BEEF. SERVES 4.

# CABBAGE ROLL CASSEROLE

### A FAST ALTERNATIVE FOR CABBAGE ROLLS!

| | |
|---|---|
| 1½ LBS. GROUND BEEF | 750 g |
| 2 MEDIUM ONIONS, CHOPPED | |
| 1 GARLIC CLOVE, MINCED | |
| 1 TSP. SALT | 5 mL |
| ¼ TSP. PEPPER | 1 mL |
| 14 OZ. CAN TOMATO SAUCE | 398 mL |
| 14 OZ. CAN WATER | 398 mL |
| ½ CUP UNCOOKED LONG-GRAIN RICE | 125 mL |
| 4 CUPS SHREDDED CABBAGE | 1 L |
| SOUR CREAM | |

BROWN BEEF WITH ONIONS. ADD GARLIC, SALT, PEPPER, TOMATO SAUCE AND WATER. BRING TO A BOIL AND STIR IN RICE. COVER AND SIMMER FOR 20 MINUTES. PLACE ½ OF THE CABBAGE IN A GREASED BAKING DISH; COVER WITH ½ THE RICE MIXTURE. REPEAT LAYERS. COVER AND BAKE IN 350°F (180°C) OVEN FOR 1 HOUR. SERVE WITH SOUR CREAM. MAY BE REFRIGERATED BEFORE BAKING. SERVES 6.

EVERYBODY SHOULD PAY HIS INCOME TAX WITH A SMILE. I TRIED - BUT THEY WANTED CASH.

# GINGER-FRIED BEEF

| | |
|---|---|
| 1 LB. FLANK OR SIRLOIN STEAK | 500 g |
| 2 EGGS, BEATEN | |
| ¾ CUP CORNSTARCH | 175 mL |
| ½ CUP WATER | 125 mL |
| VEGETABLE OIL | |
| ⅔ CUP SHREDDED CARROTS | 150 mL |
| 2 TBSP. CHOPPED GREEN ONIONS | 30 mL |
| ¼ CUP FINELY CHOPPED FRESH GINGER | 60 mL |
| 4 GARLIC CLOVES, CHOPPED | |
| 3 TBSP. SOY SAUCE | 45 mL |
| 2 TBSP. WINE, RED OR WHITE | 30 mL |
| 2 TBSP. WHITE VINEGAR | 30 mL |
| 1 TBSP. SESAME OIL | 15 mL |
| ½ CUP SUGAR | 125 mL |
| DASH CRUSHED CHILI FLAKES | |

SLICE PARTIALLY FROZEN STEAK ACROSS THE GRAIN INTO NARROW STRIPS. MIX BEEF AND EGGS. DISSOLVE CORNSTARCH IN WATER AND MIX WITH BEEF-EGG MIXTURE. POUR 1" (2.5 cm) OF OIL INTO WOK, HEAT TO BOILING HOT, BUT NOT SMOKING. ADD BEEF TO OIL, ¼ AT A TIME. SEPARATE WITH A FORK (OR CHOPSTICKS IF YOU'RE TALENTED) AND COOK, STIRRING FREQUENTLY UNTIL CRISPY. REMOVE, DRAIN AND SET ASIDE. (THIS MUCH CAN BE DONE IN ADVANCE.) PUT 1 TBSP. (15 mL) OIL IN WOK. ADD CARROTS, ONION, GINGER AND GARLIC AND STIR BRIEFLY OVER HIGH HEAT. ADD REMAINING INGREDIENTS AND BRING TO A BOIL. ADD BEEF; MIX WELL. SERVE WITH STEAMED RICE OF COURSE. SERVES 4.

# BURRITOS

GREAT FOR HUNGRY KIDS! NUKE 'EM WHEN YOU NEED 'EM. MAKES 20.

| | |
|---|---:|
| 2 LBS. LEAN GROUND BEEF | 1 kg |
| 1 MEDIUM ONION, CHOPPED | |
| 2 TBSP. TACO SEASONING (1 PKG.) | 30 mL |
| 1/4 TSP. PEPPER | 1 mL |
| 1/4 TSP. OREGANO | 1 mL |
| 2 TBSP. CHOPPED FRESH PARSLEY | 30 mL |
| 1 CUP SOUR CREAM (FAT-FREE IS FINE) | 250 mL |
| 2 LBS. MONTEREY JACK CHEESE, GRATED | 1 kg |
| 1 CUP MEDIUM TACO SAUCE | 250 mL |
| 20 FLOUR TORTILLA SHELLS | |

IN A LARGE FRYING PAN, BROWN GROUND BEEF AND ONIONS. ADD TACO SEASONING, PEPPER, OREGANO, PARSLEY AND SOUR CREAM. ADD 1/2 THE CHEESE AND 1/2 THE TACO SAUCE, MIXING WELL. PLACE 2 TBSP. (30 ML) OR MORE OF BEEF MIXTURE ON EACH TORTILLA SHELL AND ROLL UP. PLACE SEAM SIDE DOWN IN 9 X 13" (23 X 33 cm) CASSEROLE. TOP WITH REMAINING CHEESE AND TACO SAUCE. BAKE AT 350°F. (180°C) FOR 15 MINUTES, OR UNTIL CHEESE MELTS AND IS HEATED THROUGH. IF YOU WANT TO MAKE INDIVIDUAL BURRITOS, USE ALL THE CHEESE AND TACO SAUCE, THEN WRAP EACH BURRITO IN PLASTIC AND FREEZE.

THE TROUBLE WITH JOGGING IS THAT BY THE TIME YOU REALIZE YOU'RE NOT IN SHAPE FOR IT, IT'S TOO FAR TO WALK BACK!

# SHEPHERD'S PIE

THIS COMFORT-FOOD FAVORITE TASTES EVEN
BETTER TOPPED WITH GARLIC MASHED POTATOES.

| | |
|---|---|
| 1½ LBS. LEAN GROUND BEEF OR GROUND LEFT-OVER ROAST | 750 g |
| 1 CUP CHOPPED ONIONS | 250 mL |
| 2 GARLIC CLOVES, MINCED | |
| ¼ CUP FLOUR | 60 mL |
| SALT & PEPPER TO TASTE | |
| ¼ TSP. DRIED THYME | 1 mL |
| ¼ TSP. DRIED SAVORY | 1 mL |
| 10 OZ. CAN BEEF BROTH | 284 mL |
| ½ CAN WATER | 142 mL |
| 2 TSP. WORCESTERSHIRE SAUCE | 10 mL |
| 1 BAY LEAF | |
| ½ CUP FINELY DICED CARROTS | 125 mL |
| ½ CUP FROZEN CORN | 125 mL |

## GARLIC MASHED POTATOES

| | |
|---|---|
| 2 LBS. POTATOES (5-6 MEDIUM), PEELED AND CUBED | 1 kg |
| 6 GARLIC CLOVES, PEELED & LIGHTLY CRUSHED | |
| ¾ CUP BUTTERMILK OR 2% MILK | 175 mL |
| SALT & PEPPER TO TASTE | |
| 1 EGG, LIGHTLY BEATEN | |

USING A LARGE NONSTICK FRYING PAN, COOK
GROUND BEEF OVER MEDIUM HEAT UNTIL NO
LONGER PINK. BREAK MEAT UP AS IT COOKS.
ADD ONIONS AND GARLIC; COOK UNTIL SOFTENED.
STIR IN FLOUR, SALT, PEPPER, THYME AND
SAVORY. ADD BROTH, WATER, WORCESTERSHIRE,

# SHEPHERD'S PIE

CONTINUED FROM PAGE 234.

BAY LEAF AND CARROTS. SIMMER, STIRRING OCCASIONALLY, FOR ABOUT 20 MINUTES, OR UNTIL QUITE THICK AND CARROTS ARE TENDER. STIR IN CORN. REMOVE BAY LEAF. SPREAD MIXTURE IN A DEEP CASSEROLE. LET COOL SLIGHTLY.

TO MAKE GARLIC MASHED POTATOES: PLACE POTATOES IN A SAUCEPAN WITH GARLIC AND COVER WITH WATER. ADD SALT, BRING TO BOIL AND SIMMER GENTLY UNTIL TENDER. DRAIN WELL AND MASH. BEAT IN BUTTERMILK, SALT AND PEPPER. RESERVE 1 TBSP. (15 mL) OF BEATEN EGG AND ADD REMAINDER TO MIXTURE. SPREAD POTATO MIXTURE OVER MEAT AND BRUSH WITH RESERVED EGG. BAKE AT 350°F (180°C) FOR 40-45 MINUTES. SERVES 6.

A WOMAN'S WORK THAT IS NEVER DONE IS THE STUFF SHE ASKED HER HUSBAND TO DO.

# FAMILY FAVORITE MEATLOAF

WE ARE AMAZED AT HOW OFTEN WE ARE ASKED FOR GOOD OLD MEAT LOAF - HERE'S OUR FAVORITE.

| | |
|---|---|
| 1 LB. LEAN GROUND BEEF | 500 g |
| 1 MEDIUM ONION, CHOPPED | |
| ½ CUP MILK | 125 mL |
| 1 EGG, BEATEN | |
| 8 CRUSHED SODA CRACKERS | |
| SALT & PEPPER TO TASTE | |

## SAUCE

| | |
|---|---|
| ¼ CUP KETCHUP | 60 mL |
| ¼ CUP WATER | 60 mL |
| 1 TSP. DRY MUSTARD | 5 mL |
| ½ CUP BROWN SUGAR | 125 mL |

COMBINE GROUND BEEF, ONION, MILK, EGG, CRACKERS, SALT AND PEPPER AND MIX WELL. PLACE IN A LARGE LOAF PAN AND MAKE A GROOVE DOWN THE CENTER OF LOAF. IN A BOWL COMBINE KETCHUP, WATER, MUSTARD AND BROWN SUGAR. POUR OVER MEAT AND BAKE AT 350°F (180°C) FOR 1 HOUR; DRAIN. SERVE WITH BAKED POTATOES AND A GREEN VEGETABLE.
SERVES 4-6.

IF A BOOK ABOUT FAILURES DOESN'T SELL, IS IT A SUCCESS?

# STROGANOFF MEATBALLS

*A GUARANTEED FAMILY HIT!*

## MEATBALLS

| | |
|---|---|
| 2 LBS. LEAN GROUND BEEF | 1 kg |
| 1½ CUPS BREAD CRUMBS | 375 mL |
| ¼ CUP MILK | 60 mL |
| ¼ CUP FINELY CHOPPED ONION | 60 mL |
| 2 EGGS, BEATEN | |
| SALT & PEPPER TO TASTE | |

## SOUR-CREAM SAUCE

| | |
|---|---|
| 1 CUP CHOPPED ONION | 250 mL |
| ¼ CUP BUTTER | 60 mL |
| ¼ CUP FLOUR | 60 mL |
| ¼ CUP KETCHUP | 60 mL |
| 2-10 OZ. CANS CONSOMMÉ (UNDILUTED) | 2-284 mL |
| 2 CUPS FAT-FREE SOUR CREAM | 500 mL |

TO MAKE MEATBALLS: COMBINE ALL INGREDIENTS IN LARGE BOWL. MIX WELL AND ROLL IN BALLS OF DESIRED SIZE. PLACE ON EDGED COOKIE SHEET AND BAKE AT 375°F (190°C) FOR 25-30 MINUTES. REMOVE FROM OVEN, DRAIN AND SET ASIDE.

TO MAKE SAUCE: BROWN ONION IN BUTTER. ADD FLOUR AND MIX WELL. ADD KETCHUP AND CONSOMMÉ, COOKING SLOWLY UNTIL THICKENED. ADD SOUR CREAM, THEN MEATBALLS. PLACE IN CASSEROLE AND KEEP WARM IN 250°F (120°C) UNTIL SERVING TIME. SERVE OVER BROAD EGG NOODLES. SERVES 6.

# CASSEROLE FOR A COLD NIGHT

| | | |
|---|---|---|
| 1 LB. LEAN GROUND BEEF | 500 | g |
| 7½ OZ. CAN TOMATO SAUCE | 213 | g |
| 1 GARLIC CLOVE, MINCED | | |
| SALT AND PEPPER TO TASTE | | |
| 2 TSP. SUGAR | 10 | mL |
| 14-OZ. CAN TOMATOES | 398 | mL |
| 3 CUPS BROAD EGG NOODLES, COOKED | 750 | mL |
|     AND DRAINED | | |
| 4 OZ. LIGHT CREAM CHEESE, CUBED | 115 | g |
| 1 CUP SOUR CREAM (FAT-FREE IS FINE) | 250 | mL |
| 6 GREEN ONIONS, CHOPPED | | |
| 1½ CUPS GRATED LIGHT CHEDDAR | 375 | mL |
|     CHEESE | | |

BROWN MEAT AND DRAIN. ADD TOMATO SAUCE, GARLIC, SALT, PEPPER, SUGAR AND TOMATOES. COVER AND SIMMER OVER LOW HEAT FOR 45 MINUTES. PREHEAT OVEN TO 350°F (180°C). COMBINE HOT NOODLES WITH CUBED CREAM CHEESE. STIR TO MELT CHEESE. ADD SOUR CREAM AND GREEN ONIONS. IN A GREASED 3-QUART (3 L) BAKING DISH, LAYER MEAT SAUCE, NOODLE MIXTURE AND CHEDDAR CHEESE ALTERNATELY. BAKE, UNCOVERED, FOR 30 MINUTES. SERVES 6.

WHY ISN'T PHONETICS SPELLED THE WAY IT SOUNDS?

# SPAGHETTI SKILLET DINNER

FIXIN'S FOR YOUR FAMILY IN ONE PAN.

| | | |
|---|---|---|
| 1 LB. LEAN HAMBURGER | 500 | g |
| 1 CUP CHOPPED ONION | 250 | mL |
| ½ CUP CHOPPED GREEN PEPPER | 125 | mL |
| 1 CUP SLICED MUSHROOMS | 250 | mL |
| 28 OZ. CAN TOMATOES | 796 | mL |
| 1 HANDFUL SPAGHETTI, BROKEN | | |
| 1 CUP WATER | 250 | mL |
| 1½ TSP. ITALIAN SEASONING | 7 | mL |
| SALT & PEPPER TO TASTE | | |
| 1 CUP GRATED MOZZARELLA CHEESE | 250 | mL |

BROWN HAMBURGER AND ONIONS. MIX IN GREEN
PEPPER AND MUSHROOMS AND COOK FOR A FEW
MINUTES. ADD TOMATOES WITH JUICE, BROKEN
SPAGHETTI AND WATER. STIR. ADD SPICES.
COVER AND COOK ABOUT 15 MINUTES, OR UNTIL
SPAGHETTI IS TENDER, STIRRING OCCASIONALLY.
ADD CHEESE AND STIR UNTIL MELTED.
SERVES 4-6.

EAGLES MAY SOAR, BUT WEASELS DON'T GET
SUCKED INTO JET ENGINES.

# BEAN STUFF

*A TASTY VARIATION OF CHILI!*

| | |
|---|---|
| 6 SLICES BACON | |
| 1 LB. LEAN GROUND BEEF | 500 g |
| 1 ONION, CHOPPED | |
| 1 GREEN PEPPER, CHOPPED | |
| 1 GARLIC CLOVE, MINCED | |
| 2 TBSP. MOLASSES | 30 mL |
| 2 TBSP. BROWN SUGAR | 30 mL |
| 1 TSP. DRY MUSTARD | 5 mL |
| 1/3 CUP VINEGAR | 75 mL |
| 19 OZ. CAN TOMATOES | 540 mL |
| 14 OZ. CAN KIDNEY BEANS | 398 mL |
| 14 OZ. CAN LIMA BEANS, DRAINED | 398 mL |
| 14 OZ. CAN PORK & BEANS | 398 mL |
| 1 TSP. WORCESTERSHIRE SAUCE | 5 mL |
| SALT, PEPPER & TABASCO SAUCE, TO TASTE | |

FRY BACON UNTIL CRISP. CRUMBLE. BROWN BEEF AND ONION. COMBINE WITH REMAINING INGREDIENTS IN A LARGE CASSEROLE. BAKE AT 300°F (150°C). OVEN FOR 2 HOURS. SERVE WITH CAESAR SALAD (PAGE 79) AND BAGUETTE STICKS (PAGE 20). SERVES 4-6.

IF BARBIE IS SO POPULAR, WHY DO YOU HAVE TO BUY HER FRIENDS.

# COOKIES

Whipped Shortbread
Jewish Shortbread
Ginger Snaps
Fresh Apple Cookies
Tutti-Frutti Cookies
B.L.'s Cookies
Mona's Mother's Mother's Best Friend's Favorite
Cookie of the Month
After Angel Food Cookies
Peanut Butter Cookies
Chocolate Whammy Cookies
Chocolate-Chocolate Chip Cookies
Chocolate Rum Cookies
Chocolate Espresso Cookies

# SQUARES

Fantastic Fudge Brownies
Decadent Caramel-Pecan Brownies
Apple Brownies
Pecan Shortbread Squares
Butter Tart Slice
Cranberry Squares
Nanaimo Bars
Matrimonial Bars
Lemon Bars
Puffed Wheat Squares

# CANDIES & NUTS

Cranberry Pistachio Bark
Shortcut Almond Roca
Turtles
Xmas Toffee
Nutchos
Spiced Pecans
Magic Mixed Nuts

## WHIPPED SHORTBREAD

THESE MELT IN YOUR MOUTH. THE SECRET IS IN THE BEATING.

| | |
|---|---|
| 1 CUP BUTTER (DO NOT USE MARGARINE) | 250 mL |
| ½ CUP ICING SUGAR | 125 mL |
| 1½ CUPS FLOUR | 375 mL |

CREAM BUTTER AND SUGAR; ADD FLOUR AND BEAT FOR 10 MINUTES. DROP FROM SMALL SPOON ONTO COOKIE SHEET. DECORATE WITH MARASCHINO CHERRY PIECES, IF YOU WISH. BAKE AT 350°F (180°C) FOR ABOUT 10-12 MINUTES, UNTIL BOTTOMS ARE LIGHTLY BROWNED. MAKES ABOUT 3 DOZEN SMALL COOKIES. THIS RECIPE DOUBLES WELL.

## JEWISH SHORTBREAD

| | |
|---|---|
| 1 CUP BUTTER, ROOM TEMPERATURE | 250 mL |
| (NEVER USE MARGARINE) | |
| ⅓ CUP WHITE SUGAR | 75 mL |
| 1 TSP. VANILLA | 5 mL |
| ½ CUP FINELY GROUND WALNUTS OR PECANS | 125 mL |
| 1⅔ CUPS FLOUR | 400 mL |
| PINCH OF SALT | |
| ½ CUP WHITE SUGAR | 125 mL |
| 4 TSP. CINNAMON | 20 mL |

CREAM TOGETHER BUTTER AND SUGAR. ADD VANILLA, NUTS, FLOUR AND SALT AND BEAT WELL. SHAPE INTO CRESCENTS AND PLACE 1" (2.5 cm) APART ON AN UNGREASED COOKIE SHEET. BAKE AT 325°F (160°C) FOR 15-20 MINUTES. WHILE STILL WARM, COAT WITH SUGAR AND CINNAMON OR FOR VARIETY COAT WITH ICING SUGAR. MAKES 2-3 DOZEN COOKIES.

# GINGER SNAPS

ALSO PERFECT FOR GINGERBREAD MEN.

| | |
|---|---|
| 3/4 CUP BUTTER OR MARGARINE | 175 mL |
| 1 CUP SUGAR | 250 mL |
| 1/4 CUP MOLASSES | 60 mL |
| 1 EGG, BEATEN | |
| 2 CUPS FLOUR | 500 mL |
| 1/4 TSP. SALT | 1 mL |
| 2 TSP. BAKING SODA | 10 mL |
| 1-2 TSP. CINNAMON | 5-10 mL |
| 1-2 TSP. GROUND CLOVES | 5-10 mL |
| 1-2 TSP. GROUND GINGER | 5-10 mL |
| WHITE SUGAR | |

CREAM TOGETHER BUTTER AND SUGAR. ADD MOLASSES AND EGG. BEAT TOGETHER. COMBINE FLOUR, SALT, BAKING SODA AND SPICES. ADD TO CREAMED MIXTURE AND MIX WELL. ROLL INTO BALLS, THEN IN SUGAR. PRESS FLAT WITH A FORK. BAKE AT 375°F (190°C) FOR 15 MINUTES. MAKES 4 DOZEN COOKIES. (DEPENDING ON THE SIZE OF YOUR BALLS)

THERE ARE THREE KINDS OF PEOPLE: THOSE WHO CAN COUNT AND THOSE WHO CAN'T.

# FRESH APPLE COOKIES

TEACHER'S CHOICE.

| | |
|---|---|
| 2 CUPS FLOUR | 500 mL |
| 1 TSP. BAKING SODA | 5 mL |
| 1/2 CUP BUTTER, SOFTENED | 125 mL |
| 1 1/3 CUPS PACKED BROWN SUGAR | 325 mL |
| 1/2 TSP. SALT | 2 mL |
| 1 TSP. CINNAMON | 5 mL |
| 1 TSP. GROUND CLOVES | 5 mL |
| 1/2 TSP. NUTMEG | 2 mL |
| 1 EGG, BEATEN | |
| 1/4 CUP APPLE JUICE OR MILK | 60 mL |
| 1 CUP CHOPPED PEELED APPLES | 250 mL |
| 1/2 CUP CHOPPED NUTS | 125 mL |
| 1 CUP RAISINS | 250 mL |

## VANILLA GLAZE

| | |
|---|---|
| 1 CUP ICING SUGAR | 250 mL |
| 1 TBSP. BUTTER, SOFTENED | 15 mL |
| 1/4 TSP. VANILLA | 1 mL |
| 1/4 TSP. SALT | 1 mL |
| 1 1/2 TBSP. MILK | 22 mL |

TO MAKE COOKIES: PREHEAT OVEN TO 375°F (190°C). COMBINE FLOUR AND BAKING SODA IN MEDIUM BOWL. IN A LARGE BOWL, CREAM TOGETHER BUTTER, BROWN SUGAR, SALT, CINNAMON, CLOVES, NUTMEG AND EGG. ADD HALF THE FLOUR TO THE BUTTER MIXTURE AND BLEND WELL. MIX IN JUICE OR MILK. ADD THE APPLES, NUTS AND RAISINS TO THE REMAINING FLOUR. ADD THIS APPLE MIXTURE TO THE BUTTER MIXTURE. DROP BY SPOONFULS ON GREASED COOKIE SHEETS AND BAKE FOR 10 MINUTES OR UNTIL COOKIES ARE FIRM.

TO MAKE GLAZE: BLEND ALL INGREDIENTS TOGETHER UNTIL SMOOTH. WHILE COOKIES ARE HOT, SPREAD WITH VANILLA GLAZE. MAKES 3 DOZEN.

# TUTTI-FRUTTI COOKIES

A BOP BOPPA LOOMA A BOP, BAM BOOM!

| | |
|---|---:|
| 1½ CUPS FLOUR | 375 mL |
| 2 TSP. BAKING POWDER | 10 mL |
| ½ TSP. SALT | 2 mL |
| ½ CUP BUTTER, SOFTENED | 125 mL |
| 1 CUP SUGAR | 250 mL |
| ¼ CUP SOUR CREAM (FAT-FREE IS FINE) | 60 mL |
| 1 LARGE EGG | |
| 2 CUPS SWEETENED FLAKED COCONUT, TOASTED GOLDEN, COOLED | 500 mL |
| 1 CUP PACKED DRIED APRICOTS, QUARTERED | 250 mL |
| 1 CUP DRIED CRANBERRIES | 250 mL |

IN A BOWL, MIX TOGETHER FLOUR, BAKING POWDER AND SALT. IN ANOTHER BOWL BEAT TOGETHER BUTTER AND SUGAR UNTIL LIGHT AND FLUFFY. ADD FLOUR MIXTURE, SOUR CREAM AND EGG AND MIX WELL. STIR IN COCONUT, APRICOTS AND CRANBERRIES. HALVE DOUGH. ON A SHEET OF WAXED PAPER, FORM EACH HALF INTO A 10" (25 cm) LOG. WRAP IN WAXED PAPER AND CHILL FOR 4 HOURS, OR UNTIL FIRM. PREHEAT OVEN TO 350°F (180°C). SPRAY BAKING SHEETS. CUT LOGS INTO ⅓" (1 cm) THICK SLICES AND ARRANGE ON BAKING SHEETS. BAKE IN MIDDLE OF OVEN UNTIL GOLDEN, ABOUT 10 MINUTES. TRANSFER TO RACKS TO COOL. MAKES ABOUT 4 DOZEN COOKIES.

TO TOAST COCONUT: SPREAD ON BAKING SHEET, PLACE ON TOP OVEN RACK, TURN ON BROILER AND WATCH CAREFULLY. STIR FREQUENTLY.

# B.L.'S COOKIES

GUESS WHAT! - YOU'RE ABOUT TO MAKE DAD'S COOKIES!

|  |  |
|---|---|
| 1 CUP BUTTER OR MARGARINE | 250 mL |
| 1 CUP WHITE SUGAR | 250 mL |
| ½ CUP BROWN SUGAR | 125 mL |
| 1 EGG | |
| 1 TSP. VANILLA | 5 mL |
| 1½ CUPS ROLLED OATS | 375 mL |
| 1½ CUPS FLOUR | 375 mL |
| 1 CUP COCONUT | 250 mL |
| 1 TSP. BAKING SODA | 5 mL |
| 1 TSP. BAKING POWDER | 5 mL |
| 2 TBSP. MOLASSES | 30 mL |
| 1½ TSP. CINNAMON | 7 mL |
| 1 TSP. ALLSPICE | 5 mL |
| 1 TSP. NUTMEG | 5 mL |

CREAM TOGETHER BUTTER AND SUGARS. ADD EGG AND VANILLA. STIR IN REMAINING INGREDIENTS. MIX WELL. ROLL IN SMALL BALLS AND PLACE ON COOKIE SHEET. DO NOT PRESS DOWN. BAKE AT 350°F (180°C) FOR 10-12 MINUTES. MAKES 4 DOZEN.

A CONCLUSION IS THE PLACE WHERE YOU GOT TIRED OF THINKING.

# MONA'S MOTHER'S MOTHER'S BEST FRIEND'S FAVORITE

THIS IS A VERRRY OLD RECIPE!

| | |
|---|---|
| 1 CUP BUTTER | 250 mL |
| 1 CUP WHITE SUGAR | 250 mL |
| ½ CUP BROWN SUGAR | 125 mL |
| 1 EGG | |
| 1½ CUPS FLOUR | 375 mL |
| 1 TSP. BAKING POWDER | 5 mL |
| 1 TSP. BAKING SODA | 5 mL |
| 1¼ CUPS ROLLED OATS | 300 mL |
| ¾ CUP COCONUT | 175 mL |

CREAM BUTTER AND SUGARS. ADD EGG AND BEAT WELL. MIX IN FLOUR, BAKING POWDER AND SODA UNTIL JUST BLENDED. STIR IN OATS AND COCONUT. ROLL INTO 1" (2.5 cm) BALLS AND PRESS WITH A FORK DIPPED IN WATER. BAKE AT 350°F (180°C) FOR 12-15 MINUTES. MAKES 3 DOZEN COOKIES.

WHAT HAPPENS IF YOU GET SCARED HALF TO DEATH TWICE?

# COOKIE OF THE MONTH

THESE WILL FILL UP EVERY COOKIE JAR YOU OWN - THEY FREEZE WELL!

| | |
|---|---|
| 1 CUP BUTTER | 250 mL |
| 1 CUP SUGAR | 250 mL |
| 1 CUP BROWN SUGAR | 250 mL |
| 1 EGG | |
| 1 CUP VEGETABLE OIL | 250 mL |
| 1 TSP. VANILLA | 5 mL |
| 1 CUP ROLLED OATS | 250 mL |
| 1 CUP CRUSHED CORNFLAKES | 250 mL |
| ½ CUP SHREDDED COCONUT | 125 mL |
| ½ CUP CHOPPED WALNUTS OR PECANS | 125 mL |
| 3½ CUPS FLOUR | 825 mL |
| 1 TSP. BAKING SODA | 5 mL |
| 1 TSP. SALT | 5 mL |

PREHEAT OVEN TO 325°F (160°C). CREAM TOGETHER BUTTER AND SUGARS UNTIL LIGHT AND FLUFFY. ADD EGG, OIL AND VANILLA. MIX WELL. ADD OATS, CORNFLAKES, COCONUT AND NUTS. STIR WELL. ADD FLOUR, SODA AND SALT. STIR UNTIL WELL BLENDED. DROP BY TEASPOONFULS ON GREASED COOKIE SHEETS AND FLATTEN WITH FORK DIPPED IN WATER. BAKE 15 MINUTES. MAKES 8 DOZEN.

HOW DO YOU GET RID OF A GARBAGE CAN?

# AFTER ANGEL FOOD COOKIES

THE VERY THING FOR LEFTOVER EGG YOLKS. SOFT AND CHEWY; ALSO KNOWN AS AFTER MERINGUE COOKIES.

| | |
|---|---|
| 2/3 CUP BUTTER | 150 mL |
| 1/2 CUP BROWN SUGAR | 125 mL |
| 1/2 CUP WHITE SUGAR | 125 mL |
| 1/2 TSP. VANILLA | 2 mL |
| 5 EGG YOLKS | |
| 1 1/2 CUPS FLOUR | 375 mL |
| 1/2 TSP. BAKING SODA | 2 mL |
| 1 TSP. BAKING POWDER | 5 mL |
| 1/4 TSP. SALT | 1 mL |
| 1/2 TSP. CINNAMON | 2 mL |
| 1/2 CUP CHOPPED WALNUTS | 125 mL |
| 1/2 CUP CHOPPED DATES | 125 mL |
| 1/2 CUP RAISINS | 125 mL |

CREAM BUTTER AND SUGARS. ADD VANILLA AND EGG YOLKS. MIX FLOUR, BAKING SODA, BAKING POWDER, SALT AND CINNAMON. ADD TO CREAMED MIXTURE AND MIX UNTIL SMOOTH. ADD WALNUTS, DATES AND RAISINS AND BLEND WELL. PLACE MEDIUM SPOONFULS OF DOUGH ON A GREASED COOKIE SHEET. BAKE AT 350°F (180°C) FOR 15 MINUTES. MAKES 4 DOZEN COOKIES.

I DRIVE WAY TOO FAST TO WORRY
ABOUT CHOLESTEROL

# PEANUT BUTTER COOKIES

YOU ASKED FOR IT! YOU GOT IT!

| | |
|---|---|
| 1/3 CUP BUTTER OR MARGARINE | 75 mL |
| 1/2 CUP BROWN SUGAR | 125 mL |
| 1/2 CUP WHITE SUGAR | 125 mL |
| 1/2 CUP PEANUT BUTTER | 125 mL |
| 1 EGG, LIGHTLY BEATEN | |
| 1 CUP FLOUR | 250 mL |
| 1 TSP. BAKING SODA | 5 mL |
| 1/2 TSP. SALT | 2 mL |
| SUGAR FOR COATING | |

CREAM TOGETHER BUTTER AND SUGARS. ADD
PEANUT BUTTER AND MIX WELL. ADD EGG AND
THEN THE DRY INGREDIENTS. ROLL INTO BALLS
AND THEN IN SUGAR. PLACE ON GREASED COOKIE
SHEET. PRESS FLAT WITH A FORK. BAKE AT
350°F (180°C) FOR 10 MINUTES. MAKES 3 DOZEN
COOKIES.

I CAN ONLY PLEASE ONE PERSON EACH DAY. TODAY
ISN'T YOUR DAY. TOMORROW ISN'T LOOKING TOO GOOD
EITHER.

# CHOCOLATE WHAMMY COOKIES

THESE ARE A KNOCK-OUT!

| | |
|---|---|
| 2½ CUPS OATMEAL | 625 mL |
| 1 CUP BUTTER | 250 mL |
| 1 CUP WHITE SUGAR | 250 mL |
| 1 CUP BROWN SUGAR | 250 mL |
| 2 EGGS | |
| 1 TSP. VANILLA | 5 mL |
| 2 CUPS FLOUR | 500 mL |
| ½ TSP. SALT | 2 mL |
| 1 TSP. BAKING POWDER | 5 mL |
| 1 TSP. BAKING SODA | 5 mL |
| 2 CUPS CHOCOLATE CHIPS | 500 mL |
| 4 OZ. HERSHEY BAR, GRATED | 115 g |
| 1½ CUPS CHOPPED NUTS (YOUR CHOICE) | 375 mL |

PLACE OATMEAL IN A FOOD PROCESSOR AND BLEND TO A FINE POWDER. CREAM TOGETHER BUTTER AND SUGARS. ADD EGGS AND VANILLA. ADD FLOUR, OATMEAL, SALT, BAKING POWDER AND BAKING SODA. MIX WELL. ADD CHOCOLATE CHIPS, HERSHEY BAR AND NUTS. (YOU MAY HAVE TO USE YOUR HANDS TO GET THIS WELL COMBINED). ROLL INTO BALLS AND PLACE 2" (5 cm) APART ON A COOKIE SHEET. DON'T PRESS DOWN. BAKE FOR 10-12 MINUTES AT 375°F (190°C). MAKES 4-5 DOZEN COOKIES.

LAUGHING STOCK: CATTLE WITH A SENSE OF HUMOR.

# CHOCOLATE-CHOCOLATE CHIP COOKIES

*YUMMY - TASTES LIKE A BROWNIE!*

| | |
|---|---|
| 1¾ CUPS FLOUR | 425 mL |
| ¾ TSP. BAKING SODA | 3 mL |
| 1 CUP BUTTER OR MARGARINE | 250 mL |
| 1 TSP. VANILLA | 5 mL |
| 1 CUP SUGAR | 250 mL |
| ½ CUP PACKED BROWN SUGAR | 125 mL |
| 1 EGG | |
| ⅓ CUP COCOA POWDER | 75 mL |
| 2 TBSP. MILK | 30 mL |
| 1 CUP CHOPPED PECANS OR WALNUTS | 250 mL |
| ¾ CUP SEMISWEET CHOCOLATE CHIPS | 175 mL |

PREHEAT OVEN TO 350°F (180°C). STIR TOGETHER FLOUR AND BAKING SODA. SET ASIDE. IN A LARGE BOWL, CREAM TOGETHER BUTTER, VANILLA AND SUGARS. BEAT UNTIL FLUFFY. BEAT IN EGG, THEN COCOA, THEN MILK. MIX IN FLOUR UNTIL JUST BLENDED. STIR IN NUTS AND CHOCOLATE CHIPS. DROP BY SPOONFULS ON GREASED COOKIE SHEETS AND BAKE FOR 12 MINUTES. COOL SLIGHTLY BEFORE REMOVING FROM COOKIE SHEET. MAKES 3 DOZEN COOKIES.

WHEN IT RAINS, WHY DON'T SHEEP SHRINK?

# CHOCOLATE RUM COOKIES

NO SUGAR IN THESE COOKIES! CHOCOLATEY AND SLIGHTLY BITTER - VERY ADDICTIVE!

| | |
|---|---:|
| 1¼ CUPS FLOUR | 300 mL |
| 1½ TSP. BAKING POWDER | 7 mL |
| ½ TSP. SALT | 2 mL |
| ½ CUP GROUND HAZELNUTS | 125 mL |
| 12 OZ. BITTERSWEET CHOCOLATE | 340 g |
| ¼ CUP BUTTER | 60 mL |
| ¼ CUP DARK RUM | 60 mL |
| 2 LARGE EGGS | |
| ¼ CUP ICING SUGAR (FOR SPRINKLING) | 60 mL |

IN A BOWL, MIX FLOUR, BAKING POWDER, SALT AND HAZELNUTS TOGETHER. IN A DOUBLE-BOILER WITH BARELY SIMMERING WATER, MELT CHOCOLATE AND BUTTER, STIRRING OCCASIONALLY. STIR IN RUM AND COOL. WHISK IN EGGS AND STIR IN FLOUR MIXTURE. COVER AND CHILL DOUGH ABOUT 1 HOUR, OR UNTIL FIRM ENOUGH TO HANDLE.

HALVE DOUGH AND FORM INTO TWO 10" (25 cm) LOGS ON WAXED PAPER. WRAP IN PAPER AND CHILL 4 HOURS, OR UNTIL FIRM. PREHEAT OVEN TO 350°F (180°C). SPRAY 2 BAKING SHEETS. CUT LOGS INTO ½" (1.3 cm) ROUNDS AND ARRANGE ABOUT 1" (2.5 cm) APART ON BAKING SHEETS. BAKE COOKIES IN BATCHES FOR 8 MINUTES AND TRANSFER TO RACK. COOKIES SHOULD BE THICK AND CAKE-LIKE. COOL COOKIES COMPLETELY AND SPRINKLE WITH ICING SUGAR. MAKES ABOUT 3 DOZEN COOKIES.

# CHOCOLATE ESPRESSO COOKIES

SPECIAL ENOUGH TO SERVE AT A DINNER PARTY WITH A DISH OF FRESH STRAWBERRIES.

| | |
|---|---:|
| 1 CUP FLOUR | 250 mL |
| ½ CUP COCOA POWDER | 125 mL |
| ½ TSP. SALT | 2 mL |
| ¼ TSP. BAKING SODA | 1 mL |
| 3 TBSP. BUTTER | 45 mL |
| 3 TBSP. MARGARINE | 45 mL |
| ½ CUP PLUS 2 TBSP. SUGAR | 155 mL |
| ½ CUP BROWN SUGAR | 125 mL |
| 1½ TBSP. INSTANT ESPRESSO POWDER | 22 mL |
|     OR INSTANT COFFEE POWDER | |
| 1 TSP. VANILLA | 5 mL |
| 1 EGG WHITE | |

SIFT FLOUR, COCOA POWDER, SALT AND BAKING SODA IN A SMALL BOWL. IN ANOTHER BOWL, BEAT BUTTER AND MARGARINE UNTIL CREAMY. ADD SUGARS, ESPRESSO POWDER AND VANILLA AND BEAT UNTIL BLENDED. MIX IN EGG WHITE. ADD DRY INGREDIENTS AND BEAT JUST UNTIL BLENDED. KNEAD UNTIL DOUGH IS SMOOTH. WRAP DOUGH IN WAXED PAPER AND REFRIGERATE FOR 1 HOUR. PREHEAT OVEN TO 350°F (180°C). ROLL DOUGH TO ¼" (1 cm) THICKNESS ON BOARD SPRINKLED WITH ICING SUGAR AND CUT WITH COOKIE CUTTER. TRANSFER TO COOKIE SHEET AND BAKE 10-12 MINUTES. MAKES 3-4 DOZEN CRISP COOKIES.

NEVER EAT PRUNES WHEN YOU'RE FAMISHED.

# FANTASTIC FUDGE BROWNIES

MEN LOVE THEM - SO DO CHILDREN, (AND MOMS NOT ON DIETS.!).

## BROWNIES

| | |
|---|---|
| 1 CUP BUTTER | 250 mL |
| 2 CUPS SUGAR | 500 mL |
| 1/4 CUP COCOA POWDER | 60 mL |
| 4 EGGS, BEATEN | |
| 1 TSP. VANILLA | 5 mL |
| 1 CUP FLOUR | 250 mL |
| 1 CUP CHOPPED WALNUTS OR PECANS | 250 mL |

## ICING

| | |
|---|---|
| 2 CUPS ICING SUGAR | 500 mL |
| 2 TBSP. BUTTER | 30 mL |
| 2 TBSP. COCOA POWDER | 30 mL |
| 2 TBSP. BOILING WATER | 30 mL |
| 2 TSP. VANILLA | 10 mL |

TO MAKE BROWNIES: CREAM TOGETHER BUTTER, SUGAR AND COCOA POWDER. MIX IN BEATEN EGGS AND VANILLA. ADD FLOUR AND STIR. FOLD IN NUTS. BAKE IN A GREASED 9 x 13" (23 x 33 cm) PAN AT 350°F (180°C) FOR 40-45 MINUTES. TOP WILL APPEAR TO BE UNDERDONE (FALLS IN MIDDLE) BUT DON'T OVERCOOK. SHOULD BE MOIST AND CHEWY.

TO MAKE ICING: BEAT ALL INGREDIENTS TOGETHER WHILE BROWNIES ARE BAKING. POUR ON TOP AS SOON AS BROWNIES COME OUT OF THE OVEN. IT WILL MELT INTO A SHINY GLAZE.

# DECADENT CARAMEL-PECAN BROWNIES

*BROWNIES WITH A CARAMEL SURPRISE!*

| | |
|---|---|
| 1 CUP PECANS | 250 mL |
| 4 OZ. UNSWEETENED CHOCOLATE (4 SQUARES) | 115 g |
| 2/3 CUP BUTTER | 150 mL |
| 1 1/4 CUPS SUGAR | 300 mL |
| 3 EGGS, BEATEN | |
| 1 TSP. VANILLA | 5 mL |
| 1 CUP FLOUR | 250 mL |
| 4-1 3/4 OZ. CARAMILK BARS | 4-52 g |

## ICING

| | |
|---|---|
| 2 CUPS SEMISWEET CHOCOLATE CHIPS | 500 mL |
| 1/2 CUP HALF & HALF CREAM | 125 mL |

PREHEAT OVEN TO 325°F (160°C). ON A COOKIE SHEET, TOAST WHOLE PECANS FOR 10 MINUTES. COOL AND COARSELY CHOP. GREASE A 9 X 13" (23 X 33 cm) GLASS PAN. COARSELY CHOP CHOCOLATE AND COMBINE WITH BUTTER IN SAUCEPAN. STIR OVER LOW HEAT UNTIL MELTED. (DON'T BURN THE CHOCOLATE!) COOL UNTIL LUKEWARM. STIR IN SUGAR, EGGS AND VANILLA. GRADUALLY ADD FLOUR TO MIXTURE. ADD PECANS AND CARAMILK SECTIONS. SPREAD INTO PAN AND BAKE IN CENTER OF OVEN 20-25 MINUTES. DO NOT OVER BAKE.

TO MAKE THE ICING, MELT CHOCOLATE CHIPS AND CREAM OVER LOW HEAT, STIRRING UNTIL MIXTURE IS SMOOTH. SPREAD OVER WARM BROWNIE. "ON-REAL"!

A "Grand" Cake, page 306

Shortcut Almond Roca, page 268
Cranberry Pistachio Bark, page 267

# APPLE BROWNIES

THIS IS IT - EVERYONE'S NEXT FAVORITE.

| | |
|---|---|
| 1 CUP BUTTER OR MARGARINE | 250 mL |
| ½ TSP. SALT | 2 mL |
| 2 CUPS SUGAR | 500 mL |
| 2 EGGS, BEATEN | |
| 2 CUPS FLOUR | 500 mL |
| 1 TSP. BAKING POWDER | 5 mL |
| 1 TSP. BAKING SODA | 5 mL |
| 1 TSP. CINNAMON | 5 mL |
| 2 CUPS PEELED, SLICED GRANNY SMITH APPLES | 500 mL |
| ½ CUP CHOPPED PECANS OR WALNUTS | 125 mL |

PREHEAT OVEN TO 325°F (160°C). GREASE A
9 X 13" (23 X 33 cm) PAN. CREAM TOGETHER
BUTTER, SALT AND SUGAR. BEAT IN EGGS. ADD
FLOUR, BAKING POWDER, BAKING SODA AND
CINNAMON; MIX WELL. ADD APPLE SLICES AND
NUTS. MIXTURE IS QUITE THICK - DON'T BE
SNITCHING ANY DOUGH! SPREAD EVENLY IN PAN
AND BAKE FOR 35-40 MINUTES. SERVE WARM
WITH VANILLA ICE CREAM OR FROZEN YOGURT.

DID YOU HEAR ABOUT THE NEW DOLL, DIVORCE
BARBIE!? IT COMES WITH ALL OF KEN'S STUFF.

# PECAN SHORTBREAD SQUARES

## CRUST

| | |
|---|---:|
| 1 CUP BUTTER | 250 mL |
| 1/3 CUP FIRMLY PACKED BROWN SUGAR | 75 mL |
| 1 EGG | |
| 1 TSP. LEMON JUICE | 5 mL |
| 3 CUPS FLOUR | 750 mL |
| 2 1/2 CUPS PECAN HALVES | 625 mL |

## HONEY BUTTER FILLING

| | |
|---|---:|
| 3/4 CUP BUTTER | 175 mL |
| 1/2 CUP HONEY | 125 mL |
| 3/4 CUP BROWN SUGAR | 175 mL |
| 3 TBSP. CREAM | 45 mL |

TO MAKE CRUST: PREHEAT OVEN TO 350°F (180°C). THOROUGHLY MIX BUTTER, SUGAR, EGG, LEMON JUICE AND FLOUR AND PRESS INTO A 10 x 15" (25 x 38 cm) EDGED COOKIE SHEET. PRICK WITH A FORK AND BAKE FOR 20 MINUTES. COVER CRUST WITH PECAN HALVES.

TO MAKE FILLING: IN A HEAVY SAUCEPAN, MELT BUTTER AND HONEY. ADD BROWN SUGAR AND BRING TO A BOIL, WHISKING CONTINUOUSLY, UNTIL DARK BROWN, 5-7 MINUTES. REMOVE FROM HEAT AND ADD CREAM. MIX AND POUR OVER CRUST. RETURN TO OVEN FOR 20 MINUTES. COOL BEFORE CUTTING.

A KNIFE THAT CUTS FOUR LOAVES OF BREAD SIMULTANEOUSLY - A FOUR LOAF CLEAVER.

# BUTTER TART SLICE

A SLICE OF LIFE - ALL TARTS SHOULD TASTE SO GOOD!

## CRUST

| | |
|---|---|
| 1 CUP BUTTER | 250 mL |
| 2 CUPS FLOUR | 500 mL |
| 1/4 CUP SUGAR | 60 mL |
| PINCH SALT | |

## BUTTER TART FILLING

| | |
|---|---|
| 1/4 CUP BUTTER | 60 mL |
| 3 EGGS, BEATEN | |
| 2 CUPS BROWN SUGAR | 500 mL |
| 1 TBSP. BAKING POWDER | 15 mL |
| PINCH SALT | |
| 3/4 CUP COCONUT | 175 mL |
| 1 TSP. VANILLA | 5 mL |
| 1 CUP RAISINS | 250 mL |
| 1 TBSP. FLOUR | 15 mL |
| 1 CUP CHOPPED PECANS (OPTIONAL) | 250 mL |

TO MAKE CRUST: CUT BUTTER INTO DRY INGREDIENTS WITH PASTRY BLENDER UNTIL CRUMBLY. PRESS INTO AN UNGREASED 9 X 13" (23 X 33 cm) PAN.

TO MAKE FILLING: MELT BUTTER; ADD EGGS AND REMAINING INGREDIENTS. MIX AND POUR OVER CRUST. BAKE AT 350°F (180°C) FOR 35 MINUTES. CUT WHEN COOL.

# CRANBERRY SQUARES

ADD THIS GOODIE TO YOUR HOLIDAY BAKING LIST.

## CRUST

| | |
|---|---|
| ½ CUP COLD BUTTER | 125 mL |
| ¼ CUP SUGAR | 60 mL |
| 1 CUP FLOUR | 250 mL |

## CRANBERRY FILLING

| | |
|---|---|
| 1½ CUPS FRESH OR FROZEN CRANBERRIES | 375 mL |
| ¼ CUP PACKED BROWN SUGAR | 60 mL |
| 2 EGGS | |
| 1 CUP FIRMLY PACKED BROWN SUGAR | 250 mL |
| 1 TSP. VANILLA | 5 mL |
| ⅓ CUP FLOUR | 75 mL |
| ½ TSP. BAKING POWDER | 2 mL |
| ¼ TSP. SALT | 1 mL |

TO MAKE CRUST: CUT BUTTER INTO SUGAR AND FLOUR UNTIL CRUMBLY. PAT INTO AN 8" (20 cm) SQUARE PAN. BAKE AT 350°F (180°C) FOR 15-20 MINUTES, OR UNTIL GOLDEN.

TO MAKE FILLING: IN A SAUCEPAN, COOK CRANBERRIES AND ¼ CUP (60 mL) BROWN SUGAR OVER MEDIUM-LOW HEAT UNTIL BERRIES ARE SOFTENED AND THE SKINS POP (ABOUT 10 MINUTES). COOL. IN A LARGE BOWL, BEAT EGGS AND GRADUALLY ADD 1 CUP (250 mL) OF BROWN SUGAR. BEAT UNTIL THICKENED. BEAT IN VANILLA. COMBINE DRY INGREDIENTS AND ADD TO EGG MIXTURE. STIR IN COOLED CRANBERRIES AND SPREAD MIXTURE OVER CRUST. BAKE AT 350°F (180°C) FOR 35-40 MINUTES. DON'T OVERBAKE.

# NANAIMO BARS

THIS RECIPE IS OLDER THAN WE ARE!
A.K.A. "GEORGE.!"

### FIRST LAYER

| | |
|---|---|
| ½ CUP BUTTER, MELTED | 125 mL |
| ¼ CUP BROWN SUGAR | 60 mL |
| 3 TBSP. COCOA POWDER | 45 mL |
| 1 EGG, BEATEN | |
| 2 CUPS GRAHAM WAFER CRUMBS | 500 mL |
| 1 CUP FLAKED COCONUT | 250 mL |
| ½ CUP CHOPPED WALNUTS | 125 mL |

### SECOND LAYER

| | |
|---|---|
| 2 CUPS ICING SUGAR | 500 mL |
| ¼ CUP BUTTER, SOFTENED | 60 mL |
| ¼ CUP CREAM OR MILK | 60 mL |
| 2 TBSP. CUSTARD POWDER | 30 mL |

### THIRD LAYER

| | |
|---|---|
| 3-1 OZ. CHOCOLATE SQUARES (SWEET OR SEMISWEET) | 3-30 g |
| ¼ CUP BUTTER | 60 mL |

TO MAKE FIRST LAYER: COMBINE INGREDIENTS AND PAT INTO A 9" (23 cm) SQUARE UNGREASED PAN. CHILL FOR ½ HOUR.

TO MAKE SECOND LAYER: BEAT ALL INGREDIENTS UNTIL SMOOTH AND FLUFFY. SPREAD CAREFULLY ON TOP OF FIRST LAYER.

TO MAKE THIRD LAYER: MELT CHOCOLATE AND BUTTER TOGETHER. SPREAD OVER SECOND LAYER AND CHILL. CUT IN SMALL BARS - VERY RICH AND VERY DELICIOUS!

# MATRIMONIAL BARS

AT LAST - THE VERY THING FOR ALL THAT RHUBARB YOU FROZE LAST FALL, OR USE THE TRADITIONAL DATE FILLING.

## RHUBARB FILLING

| | |
|---|---|
| 3 CUPS CHOPPED RHUBARB | 750 mL |
| 1½ CUPS SUGAR | 375 mL |
| 2 TBSP. CORNSTARCH | 30 mL |
| 1 TSP. VANILLA | 5 mL |

## OR

## DATE FILLING

| | |
|---|---|
| ½ LB. CHOPPED DATES | 250 g |
| ½ CUP WATER | 125 mL |
| 2 TBSP. BROWN SUGAR | 30 mL |
| 1 TSP. GRATED ORANGE RIND | 5 mL |
| 2 TBSP. ORANGE JUICE | 30 mL |
| 1 TSP. LEMON JUICE | 5 mL |

## CRUST

| | |
|---|---|
| 1½ CUPS ROLLED OATS | 375 mL |
| 1½ CUPS FLOUR | 375 mL |
| ½ TSP. BAKING SODA | 2 mL |
| 1 TSP. BAKING POWDER | 5 mL |
| ¼ TSP. SALT | 1 mL |
| 1 CUP BROWN SUGAR | 250 mL |
| 1 CUP BUTTER | 250 mL |

TO MAKE FILLING: COMBINE FILLING INGREDIENTS AND COOK UNTIL THICK. IF MAKING DATE FILLING, ADD FRUIT JUICES AFTER COOKING. COOL COMPLETELY.

## MATRIMONIAL BARS

CONTINUED FROM PAGE 264.

TO MAKE CRUST: PREHEAT OVEN TO 350°F (180°C). COMBINE INGREDIENTS AND PAT 2/3 OF MIXTURE INTO A GREASED 9" (23 cm) SQUARE PAN. SPREAD FILLING AND SPRINKLE WITH REMAINING CRUMBS. BAKE FOR 30-35 MINUTES. CHILL BEFORE CUTTING.

## LEMON BARS

ANOTHER CLASSIC!

### CRUST

| | |
|---|---|
| 1 CUP FLOUR | 250 mL |
| 1/2 CUP BUTTER | 125 mL |
| 1/4 CUP SUGAR | 60 mL |
| PINCH OF SALT | |

### LEMON CUSTARD

| | |
|---|---|
| 1 CUP SUGAR | 250 mL |
| 2 TBSP. FLOUR | 30 mL |
| 1/4 TSP. BAKING POWDER | 1 mL |
| RIND OF 1 LEMON, FINELY GRATED | |
| JUICE OF 1 LEMON, 3 TBSP. (45 mL) | |
| 2 EGGS, BEATEN | |

SPRINKLING OF ICING SUGAR

TO MAKE CRUST: CUT BUTTER INTO DRY INGREDIENTS AND PRESS INTO UNGREASED 9" (23 cm) SQUARE PAN. BAKE AT 350°F (180°C) FOR 20 MINUTES.

TO MAKE CUSTARD: BEAT ALL INGREDIENTS TOGETHER AND POUR OVER CRUST. BAKE AT 350°F (180°C) FOR 25 MINUTES. COOL AND SPRINKLE WITH ICING SUGAR. CUT INTO SQUARES.

# PUFFED WHEAT SQUARES

AUNT EDITH'S PUFFED WHEAT SQUARES
HELPED PUT LONGVIEW ON THE MAP!

| | |
|---|---|
| ½ CUP BUTTER OR MARGARINE | 125 mL |
| 1 CUP CORN SYRUP | 250 mL |
| 1 CUP WHITE SUGAR | 250 mL |
| ¼ CUP BROWN SUGAR | 60 mL |
| 6 HEAPING TBSP. COCOA POWDER | 90 mL |
| 1 TSP. VANILLA | 5 mL |
| 10 CUPS PUFFED WHEAT | 2.5 L |

COMBINE BUTTER, CORN SYRUP, SUGARS AND
COCOA POWDER IN A HEAVY SAUCEPAN. BRING TO
BOIL. REMOVE FROM HEAT AND ADD VANILLA.
POUR OVER PUFFED WHEAT. MIX WELL AND
PRESS INTO A GREASED 9 X 13" (23 X 33 cm)
PAN. MAKES 24 SQUARES.

AN APPLE A DAY WILL KEEP THE DOCTOR AWAY –
ASSUMING OF COURSE THAT IT HASN'T BEEN GROWN IN
CHEMICAL SOIL, SPRAYED WITH PESTICIDES AND THEN
COVERED WITH WAX.

# CRANBERRY PISTACHIO BARK

A FOOLPROOF CANDY FOR CHRISTMAS GIFT-GIVING.

| | |
|---|---|
| 1 LB. GOOD QUALITY WHITE CHOCOLATE | 500 g |
| 1 CUP DRIED CRANBERRIES | 250 mL |
| 1 CUP SHELLED PISTACHIOS | 250 mL |

BE SURE AND BUY EXTRA – YOU'LL HAVE TO BRIBE THE PISTACHIO SHELLER!

MELT CHOCOLATE IN THE TOP OF A DOUBLE BOILER. LET COOL TO ROOM TEMPERATURE. ROAST PISTACHIOS AT 350°F (180°C) FOR 5-7 MINUTES. SET ASIDE TO COOL.

STIR CRANBERRIES AND PISTACHIOS INTO MELTED CHOCOLATE. POUR ONTO FOIL-LINED 10 x 15" (25 x 38 cm) EDGED COOKIE SHEET. REFRIGERATE FOR AT LEAST 1 HOUR, THEN BREAK INTO PIECES. MAKES ABOUT 1½ POUNDS (750 g). (PICTURED ON PAGE 257.)

SANTA'S ELVES ARE JUST A BUNCH OF SUBORDINATE CLAUSES.

# SHORTCUT ALMOND ROCA

THE SECRET TO THIS POPULAR TREAT IS OWNING A CANDY THERMOMETER.

| | |
|---|---|
| 1 TBSP. CORN SYRUP | 15 mL |
| 1¼ CUPS WHITE SUGAR | 300 mL |
| 1 CUP BUTTER | 250 mL |
| ¼ CUP WATER | 60 mL |
| 1¼ CUPS TOASTED SLIVERED ALMONDS | 300 mL |
| ¾ CUP CHOCOLATE CHIPS | 175 mL |

IN A LARGE HEAVY SAUCEPAN, GENTLY BOIL SYRUP, SUGAR, BUTTER AND WATER UNTIL "HARD CRACK" APPEARS ON CANDY THERMOMETER, 300°F (150°C). DO NOT STIR. THIS STEP TAKES AT LEAST 20 MINUTES. REMOVE FROM HEAT, ADD ALMONDS AND STIR WELL. SPREAD ON AN UNGREASED COOKIE SHEET AND, BEFORE CANDY IS ALLOWED TO COOL, SPRINKLE WITH CHOCOLATE CHIPS. AS THEY MELT, SPREAD THE CHOCOLATE CHIPS EVENLY OVER THE CANDY. COOL IN REFRIGERATOR OR FREEZER. BREAK INTO BITE-SIZED PIECES AND HIDE SOME. WHATEVER YOU LEAVE OUT DISAPPEARS! (THIS DOES NOT DOUBLE WELL.) (PICTURED ON PAGE 257.)

ESCHEW OBFUSCATION

# TURTLES

*THESE ARE BETTER THAN STORE BOUGHT!*

| | | |
|---|---|---|
| 50 CARAMELS, UNWRAPPED | | |
| 2 TBSP. HALF & HALF CREAM | 30 | mL |
| 1½ LBS. GOOD-QUALITY MILK CHOCOLATE | 750 | g |
| ¾ LB. PECAN HALVES | 365 | g |

PLACE CARAMELS IN FREEZER FOR ½ HOUR - WRAPPERS COME OFF IN A FLASH! MELT CARAMELS OVER LOW HEAT AND ADD CREAM. IN A DOUBLE BOILER, MELT CHOCOLATE TO A SMOOTH CONSISTENCY. TO MAKE EACH TURTLE PLACE 3 PECANS ON THE COOKIE SHEET, LAYING 2 PECANS BESIDE EACH OTHER AND THE OTHER ON TOP. TURTLES SHOULD BE 1" (2.5 cm) APART. DIP A SPOON INTO MELTED CARAMEL AND DIP THE BOTTOM OF THE TOP PECAN INTO IT. PLACE IT ON TOP OF THE OTHER 2. (THIS HOLDS THEM TOGETHER). SPOON MORE CARAMEL OVER THE NUTS. WHEN COOKIE SHEET IS FULL, PLACE IN FREEZER UNTIL CARAMEL IS SET. WHEN READY TO "DIP", PUT A TURTLE ON A FORK AND POUR CHOCOLATE FROM A LARGE SPOON OVER THE NUTS AND CARAMEL. IT SHOULD COVER THE TURTLE COMPLETELY. PLACE TURTLE ON COOKIE SHEET AND CONTINUE UNTIL ALL TURTLES ARE DIPPED. REFRIGERATE UNTIL COMPLETELY SET. STORE IN AN AIRTIGHT CONTAINER AND KEEP IN A COOL PLACE. MAKES 50 TURTLES.

## XMAS TOFFEE

YOUR KIDS WILL LOVE HELPING YOU - FOR THE FIRST 3 MINUTES! SOFT CHEWY CANDIES.

| | | |
|---|---|---|
| 1 LB. BUTTER | 500 | g |
| 4 CUPS WHITE SUGAR | 1 | L |
| 10 OZ. CAN SWEETENED CONDENSED MILK | 300 | mL |
| 2 CUPS GOLDEN CORN SYRUP | 500 | mL |

MIX ALL INGREDIENTS IN LARGE SAUCEPAN. GRADUALLY BRING TO BOIL. REDUCE HEAT AND COOK GENTLY 20-30 MINUTES, UNTIL MIXTURE REACHES THE SOFT BALL STAGE, 250°F (120°C) (USE CANDY THERMOMETER). POUR ONTO 2 WELL-BUTTERED COOKIE SHEETS. WHEN SET, CUT INTO SMALL PIECES AND WRAP IN WAXED PAPER, TWISTING BOTH ENDS CLOSED. MAKES 20 DOZEN.

FAVORITE OXYMORONS:
PRETTY UGLY, WORKING VACATION, RAP MUSIC.

## NUTCHOS

CALL THEM COOKIES - CALL THEM CANDIES - CALL THEM DELICIOUS!

| | | |
|---|---|---|
| 2-10 OZ. PKGS. SEMISWEET CHOCOLATE CHIPS | 2-300 | g |
| 10 OZ. PKG. PEANUT BUTTER CHIPS | 300 | g |
| 2 CUPS SALTED PEANUTS | 500 | mL |
| 7 OZ. BOX RIPPLE POTATO CHIPS, COARSELY CRUMBLED | 200 | g |

# Nutchos

CONTINUED FROM PAGE 270.

IN A DOUBLE BOILER, MELT CHOCOLATE AND PEANUT BUTTER CHIPS. STIR IN PEANUTS AND CRUMBLED CHIPS. DROP ON COOKIE SHEET AND LEAVE TO COOL. STORE IN REFRIGERATOR. YOU CAN ALSO FREEZE THESE AND EAT THEM WHEN YOU'RE DOING THE LAUNDRY! MAKES ABOUT 48.

HOW DO THEY GET THE DEER TO CROSS AT THE YELLOW ROAD SIGN?

# SPICED PECANS

A GREAT GIFTABLE.

| | |
|---|---|
| 2 CUPS PECAN HALVES | 500 mL |
| 1½ TBSP. BUTTER | 22 mL |
| 1 TSP. SALT | 5 mL |
| 2 TSP. SOY SAUCE | 10 mL |
| ¼ TSP. TABASCO SAUCE | 1 mL |

PREHEAT OVEN TO 300°F (150°C). PLACE PECANS ON A BAKING SHEET. MELT BUTTER AND ADD REMAINING INGREDIENTS. POUR OVER PECANS. BAKE 15 MINUTES. STIR AND TOSS DURING COOKING TIME. COOL AND DIG IN - YUMMY!

# MAGIC MIXED NUTS

THESE SWEET AND SPICY NUTS JUST PLAIN DISAPPEAR!

| | |
|---|---|
| 2 EGG WHITES | |
| 4 CUPS UNSALTED NUTS: CASHEWS, ALMONDS, PECANS & HAZELNUTS | 1 L |
| 1/2 CUP SUGAR | 125 mL |
| 1 TSP. CINNAMON | 5 mL |
| 1 TSP. CAYENNE PEPPER | 5 mL |
| 1/2 TSP. SALT | 2 mL |

PREHEAT OVEN TO 325°F (160°C). PLACE EGG WHITES IN A LARGE BOWL. WHISK JUST UNTIL FOAMY. STIR IN NUTS UNTIL COATED. COMBINE SUGAR WITH CINNAMON, CAYENNE PEPPER AND SALT. POUR OVER NUTS AND TOSS UNTIL COATED. SPREAD EVENLY ON GREASED COOKIE SHEETS AND BAKE 20-25 MINUTES, STIRRING FREQUENTLY. COOL AND STORE IN SEALED CONTAINERS. MAKES 4 CUPS (1 L).

THREE RABBITS IN A ROW HOPPING BACKWARDS SIMULTANEOUSLY - A RECEDING HARELINE.

# DESSERTS

Chilled Lemon Soufflé
Frozen Lemon Puff
Fruit 'N' Booze
Brandy Mint Cream
Crème Brûlée
Shortbread Tarts with Cheese 'N' Fruit
Shortbread Tarts with Lemon Filling
Pavlova
Rhubarb & Strawberry Crumble
Social Apple Betty
Apple Pecan Phyllo Crisps
Tiramisu
Grand Slam Finale
Blueberry Bonanza
Chocolate Mocha Cheesecake
Best of Bridge Classic Cheesecake
Pumpkin Cheesecake
Aces
Upside-Down Chocolate Fudge Pudding
Country Spice Pudding Cake
Fruit Cocktail Cake
Good Old-Fashioned Gingerbread
Lemon Sauce
Victorian Orange 'Peel' Cake
Poppy Seed Cake
Sensational Lemon Roll
Chocolate Roll
A "Grand" Cake
Chocolate Raspberry Torte
Super Chocolate Cake
Chocolate Zucchini Cake
Chocolate Angel Food Cake
Karrot's Cake

# CHILLED LEMON SOUFFLÉ

THIS SIMPLE CITRUS SOUFFLÉ HITS THE SPOT AFTER A SPICY MEAL. SERVES 6-8.

| | |
|---|---:|
| 1 TBSP. UNFLAVORED GELATIN (1 PKG.) | 15 mL |
| 1/4 CUP COLD WATER | 60 mL |
| 4 EGGS, SEPARATED | |
| 1 CUP SUGAR | 250 mL |
| 1/2 CUP FRESH LEMON JUICE | 125 mL |
| 1 1/2 TBSP. GRATED LEMON ZEST | 22 mL |
| 1 CUP WHIPPING CREAM | 250 mL |

PLACE GELATIN IN WATER AND SET ASIDE TO SOFTEN. IN A HEAVY SAUCEPAN, OVER LOW HEAT, WHISK THE EGG YOLKS UNTIL SMOOTH. WHISK IN THE SUGAR, LEMON JUICE AND ZEST. COOK, STIRRING, UNTIL SLIGHTLY THICKENED, ABOUT 10 MINUTES. STIR IN SOFTENED GELATIN AND COOK UNTIL DISSOLVED, 1-2 MINUTES. POUR INTO LARGE MIXING BOWL AND ALLOW TO COOL. WHIP CREAM UNTIL SOFT PEAKS FORM, DO NOT OVERBEAT. FOLD WHIPPED CREAM INTO CHILLED LEMON MIXTURE UNTIL BLENDED. BEAT EGG WHITES UNTIL STIFF BUT NOT DRY. FOLD INTO LEMON-CREAM MIXTURE. SPOON MIXTURE INTO A GLASS DISH AND REFRIGERATE UNTIL SET - ABOUT 2 HOURS.

CHANGE IS INEVITABLE - EXCEPT FROM A VENDING MACHINE.

# FROZEN LEMON PUFF

GUARANTEED RAVES AND A GREAT MAKE AHEAD.

| | |
|---|---|
| 5 EGGS (SEPARATE 3 AND RESERVE WHITES) | |
| 3/4 CUP FRESH LEMON JUICE | 175 mL |
| 1 CUP SUGAR | 250 mL |
| 2 CUPS WHIPPING CREAM | 500 mL |
| VANILLA WAFERS TO COVER BOTTOM AND SIDES OF PAN | |
| DASH CREAM OF TARTAR | |
| 1/4 CUP ICING SUGAR | 60 mL |

WHISK 2 EGGS AND 3 EGG YOLKS, LEMON JUICE AND SUGAR TOGETHER IN THE TOP OF A DOUBLE BOILER AND COOK UNTIL THICK, STIRRING CONSTANTLY. COOL. WHIP THE CREAM AND FOLD INTO LEMON MIXTURE. LINE SIDES AND BOTTOM OF A 9" (23 cm) SPRINGFORM PAN WITH VANILLA WAFERS. POUR LEMON MIXTURE INTO THE PAN. BEAT THE 3 EGG WHITES UNTIL FOAMY. ADD CREAM OF TARTAR AND ICING SUGAR AND BEAT UNTIL PEAKS ARE STIFF. SPREAD ON THE LEMON MIXTURE AND BROWN UNDER THE BROILER. (WATCH CAREFULLY!) COVER WITH FOIL MAKING SURE IT DOESN'T TOUCH THE MERINGUE. FREEZE 8 HOURS OR MORE. REMOVE FROM FREEZER (TAKING FOIL OFF IMMEDIATELY) AT LEAST 1½ HOURS BEFORE SERVING. SERVES 10-12.

THE PEOPLE WHO ASSURE YOU THAT MONEY ISN'T EVERYTHING USUALLY HAVE EVERYTHING.

## FRUIT 'N' BOOZE

CAP'N MORGAN WAS NO FUN TIL HE HAD HIS FRUIT WITH RUM.

### FRUIT

| | |
|---|---|
| 1 CANTALOUPE | |
| 1 HONEY DEW MELON | |
| 1/4 OF A SMALL WATERMELON | |
| 1 CUP FRESH OR FROZEN BLUEBERRIES | 250 mL |

### SAUCE

| | |
|---|---|
| 2/3 CUP SUGAR | 150 mL |
| 1/3 CUP WATER | 75 mL |
| 1 TSP. LIME RIND | 5 mL |
| 6 TBSP. LIME JUICE | 90 mL |
| 1/2 CUP LIGHT RUM | 125 mL |

FRUIT: SCOOP MELON INTO BALLS AND ADD BERRIES. CHILL.

SAUCE: MIX SUGAR WITH WATER IN SAUCEPAN, BRING TO BOIL, REDUCE HEAT AND SIMMER FOR 5 MINUTES. ADD LIME RIND AND LET COOL TO ROOM TEMPERATURE. STIR IN LIME JUICE AND RUM. POUR OVER FRUIT AND CHILL SEVERAL HOURS. SERVES 6-8.

## BRANDY MINT CREAM

THIS IS A TERRIFIC DRINK TO SERVE AS A DESSERT.

| | |
|---|---|
| 2 QTS. FRENCH VANILLA ICE CREAM | 2 L |
| 1/2 CUP CRÈME DE MENTHE | 125 mL |
| 1 CUP BRANDY | 250 mL |

LET ICE CREAM SIT AT ROOM TEMPERATURE TO SOFTEN. WHIRL ALL INGREDIENTS TOGETHER IN A BLENDER. POUR INTO STEM GLASSES. SERVES 6.

# CRÈME BRÛLÉE

AN OLDE ENGLISH TRADITION . . . PIP PIP STIFF UPPER CRUST AND ALL THAT.

| | |
|---|---|
| 2 CUPS WHIPPING CREAM | 500 mL |
| 1/3 CUP WHITE SUGAR | 75 mL |
| 5 EGG YOLKS | |
| BROWN SUGAR | |

SCALD CREAM (BRING IT JUST TO A BOIL). ADD SUGAR AND STIR TO DISSOLVE. REMOVE FROM HEAT. IN A LARGE BOWL, BEAT EGG YOLKS. WHISK CREAM VERY SLOWLY INTO YOLKS. POUR MIXTURE INTO AN 8" (20 cm) SHALLOW BOWL OR 6-8 RAMEKINS. BAKE IN A LARGE PAN WITH 1" (2.5 cm) OF WATER AT 325°F (160°C) FOR 30-40 MINUTES. AT THE END OF 30 MINUTES GIVE A "SHAKE" TEST AND CONTINUE TO COOK IF THE CUSTARD DOESN'T LOOK FIRM. COOL. REFRIGERATE 12 HOURS. SPRINKLE 1/4" (1 cm) BROWN SUGAR ON TOP. BROIL UNTIL IT MELTS AND IS GOLDEN BROWN.

NOTE: EGG WHITES MAY BE FROZEN IN SEALED CONTAINERS FOR USE LATER.

KINDRED: FEAR OF RELATIVES

# SHORTBREAD TARTS WITH CHEESE 'N' FRUIT OR LEMON FILLING

*SO PRETTY TO LOOK AT - MORE FUN TO EAT!*

## SHORTBREAD TARTS

| | |
|---|---|
| 1 CUP BUTTER | 250 mL |
| ½ CUP ICING SUGAR | 125 mL |
| 1½ CUPS FLOUR | 375 mL |
| 1 TBSP. CORNSTARCH | 15 mL |

MIX INGREDIENTS IN MIXMASTER. DON'T ROLL BUT PAT INTO TINY TART TINS, 1½" (4 cm), WITH YOUR FINGERS TO FORM SHELLS. PRICK THE BOTTOMS WITH A FORK AND BAKE 20 MINUTES AT 300°F-325°F (150-160°C). AFTER 10 MINUTES, PRICK BOTTOMS AGAIN AS SHELLS PUFF UP. THIS RECIPE DOUBLES WELL AND THEY FREEZE BEAUTIFULLY.

## CHEESE 'N' FRUIT FILLING

| | |
|---|---|
| 8 OZ. CREAM CHEESE, SOFTENED | 250 g |
| 10 OZ. CAN SWEETENED CONDENSED MILK (EAGLE BRAND) | 300 mL |
| ⅓ CUP LEMON JUICE | 75 mL |
| 1 TSP. VANILLA | 5 mL |

IN A LARGE BOWL BEAT CHEESE UNTIL FLUFFY. GRADUALLY BEAT IN MILK. STIR IN LEMON JUICE AND VANILLA. CHILL SEVERAL HOURS. KEEPS WELL IN REFRIGERATOR. FILL TARTS AND DECORATE WITH SMALL PIECES OF KIWI AND STRAWBERRIES.

# SHORTBREAD TARTS

CONTINUED FROM PAGE 278.

## LEMON FILLING

| | |
|---|---|
| ½ CUP FRESH LEMON JUICE | 125 mL |
| 1 TBSP. GRATED LEMON RIND | 15 mL |
| 1 CUP SUGAR | 250 mL |
| 3 EGGS, WELL BEATEN | |
| ½ CUP BUTTER, ROOM TEMPERATURE | 125 mL |

PUT JUICE AND RIND IN DOUBLE-BOILER. WHISK IN SUGAR, EGGS AND BUTTER AND BLEND WELL. PLACE OVER GENTLY BOILING WATER AND WHISK CONSTANTLY UNTIL MIXTURE BECOMES CLEAR AND THICKENS. COOL. KEEPS WELL IN THE REFRIGERATOR.

FAVORITE OXYMORONS: FOUND MISSING, ALONE TOGETHER, LIVING DEAD

# PAVLOVA

NEW ZEALAND'S NATIONAL DESSERT.

| | |
|---|---|
| 4 EGG WHITES | |
| 1 CUP WHITE SUGAR | 250 mL |
| ½ TSP. VANILLA | 2 mL |
| 1 TSP. VINEGAR | 5 mL |
| 2 CUPS WHIPPING CREAM | 500 mL |
| FRESH FRUIT: KIWI, BLUEBERRIES & STRAWBERRIES ARE PERFECT | |
| ½ CUP TOASTED SLIVERED ALMONDS | 125 mL |

BEAT EGG WHITES UNTIL SOFT PEAKS FORM. CONTINUE BEATING WHILE ADDING SUGAR SLOWLY, 1 TBSP. (15 mL) AT A TIME. ADD VANILLA AND VINEGAR. BEAT UNTIL VERY STIFF. PLACE WAXED OR BROWN PAPER ON A COOKIE SHEET AND SPREAD MIXTURE IN A CIRCLE, SLIGHTLY SMALLER THAN DESIRED SIZE. BAKE 1 HOUR AT 275°F (140°C). TURN OVEN OFF AND LEAVE MERINGUE IN OVEN OVERNIGHT TO DRY. PEEL OFF PAPER. TOP WITH WHIPPED CREAM, FRESH FRUIT, AND TOASTED ALMONDS.

HOW DO YOU KEEP A DUMMY IN SUSPENSE? . . . I'LL LET YOU KNOW TOMORROW.

# RHUBARB AND STRAWBERRY CRUMBLE

*A CLASSIC PAIR IN A CLASSIC DESSERT.*

## TOPPING

| | |
|---|---|
| 3/4 CUP PECAN HALVES, TOASTED | 175 mL |
| 1 1/2 CUPS FLOUR | 375 mL |
| 1/2 CUP FIRMLY PACKED BROWN SUGAR | 125 mL |
| 1 1/2 TSP. GRATED ORANGE ZEST | 7 mL |
| 1/4 TSP. NUTMEG | 1 mL |
| 1/2 CUP BUTTER, SOFTENED | 125 mL |

## FILLING

| | |
|---|---|
| 4 CUPS 1" (2.5 cm) PIECES OF RHUBARB | 1 L |
| 2 CUPS SLICED STRAWBERRIES | 500 mL |
| 3 TBSP. FLOUR | 45 mL |
| 1/2 CUP SUGAR | 125 mL |

TO MAKE TOPPING: PREHEAT OVEN TO 350°F (180°C). SPREAD PECANS ON A BAKING SHEET AND PLACE IN OVEN FOR 5-7 MINUTES, OR UNTIL LIGHTLY TOASTED. REMOVE AND LET COOL. COARSELY CHOP NUTS AND SET ASIDE. STIR TOGETHER FLOUR, BROWN SUGAR, ORANGE ZEST AND NUTMEG. ADD THE FLOUR MIXTURE TO THE SOFTENED BUTTER AND MIX WITH A FORK TO FORM A CRUMBLY MIXTURE; ADD PECANS AND STIR INTO MIXTURE UNTIL EVENLY DISTRIBUTED.

TO MAKE FILLING: PLACE CUT FRUIT IN AN 8 X 11" (20 X 28 cm) CASSEROLE OR SHALLOW BAKING DISH, ADD FLOUR AND SUGAR AND TOSS UNTIL WELL MIXED. SPRINKLE WITH TOPPING AND BAKE AT 375°F (180°C) FOR 35-40 MINUTES, UNTIL TOP IS GOLDEN. COOL FOR 10 MINUTES AND SERVE WITH VANILLA ICE CREAM. SERVES 8. (PICTURED ON PAGE 292.)

# SOCIAL APPLE BETTY

EVERYONE LOVES THIS OLD ENGLISH RECIPE. BE SURE TO SERVE IT WARM WITH WHIPPING CREAM OR ICE CREAM.

6 APPLES, PEELED, SLICED
CINNAMON - TO TASTE

### CRUST

| | |
|---|---|
| ½ CUP BUTTER, ROOM TEMPERATURE | 125 mL |
| 1 CUP BROWN SUGAR | 250 mL |
| ¾ CUP FLOUR | 175 mL |

FILL A SMALL CASSEROLE ⅔ FULL WITH SLICED APPLES, ADDING THE CINNAMON TO TASTE. IF THE APPLES ARE TART, YOU MAY WANT TO ADD SOME SUGAR.

TO MAKE CRUST: CREAM BUTTER AND BROWN SUGAR. ADD FLOUR AND MIX TO A CRUMBLY MIXTURE. SPRINKLE MIXTURE OVER APPLES AND PAT FIRMLY INTO A CRUST. BAKE AT 350°F (180°C) FOR 40 MINUTES. SERVES 6.

OK - SO WHAT'S THE SPEED OF DARK?

# APPLE PECAN PHYLLO CRISPS

YES! - A YUMMY SKINNY DESSERT!

## SHELLS

| | |
|---|---|
| 2 SHEETS PHYLLO PASTRY | |
| 2 TSP. BUTTER, MELTED | 10 mL |

## FILLING

| | |
|---|---|
| 1/3 CUP BROWN SUGAR | 75 mL |
| 1 TSP. GRATED LEMON RIND | 5 mL |
| 1 TBSP. LEMON JUICE | 15 mL |
| 1/2 TSP. CINNAMON | 2 mL |
| 3 CUPS PEELED, SLICED APPLES | 750 mL |
| 2 TBSP. CHOPPED TOASTED PECANS | 30 mL |
| ICING SUGAR TO SPRINKLE | |

TO PREPARE SHELLS: PREHEAT OVEN TO 400°F (200°C). LAY PHYLLO SHEET ON WORK SURFACE AND BRUSH WITH HALF THE BUTTER. USING SCISSORS, CUT INTO 3, 5" (13 cm) WIDE STRIPS. FOLD ENDS IN TO MAKE A RECTANGLE OF 3 LAYERS AND GENTLY MOLD INTO MUFFIN CUPS. REPEAT WITH REMAINING PHYLLO AND BUTTER - MAKES 6 SHELLS. BAKE 5 MINUTES, OR UNTIL GOLDEN. THESE CAN BE STORED IN AN AIRTIGHT CONTAINER FOR UP TO 3 DAYS.

TO PREPARE FILLING: IN A HEAVY SKILLET, HEAT SUGAR, LEMON RIND, LEMON JUICE AND CINNAMON UNTIL BUBBLY. ADD APPLES AND COOK, STIRRING FREQUENTLY, FOR 5 MINUTES, OR UNTIL TENDER. LET COOL SLIGHTLY. SPOON INTO PREPARED SHELLS. SPRINKLE WITH TOASTED PECANS, THEN ICING SUGAR. SERVES 6.

## TIRAMISU

THIS MEANS "IT LIFTS ME UP".

| | | |
|---|---|---|
| 4 EGGS, SEPARATED | | |
| 3/4 CUP SUGAR | 175 | mL |
| 2-8 OZ. PKGS. CREAM CHEESE, ROOM TEMPERATURE | 2-250 | g |
| 1/2 CUP STRONG COFFEE | 125 | mL |
| 1/4 CUP KAHLÚA OR RUM | 60 | mL |
| 8 OZ. PKG. LADY FINGERS OR VANILLA WAFERS | 250 | g |
| 2-1 OZ. SQUARES SEMI-SWEET CHOCOLATE, FINELY GRATED | 2-30 | g |

BEAT EGG YOLKS IN MEDIUM-SIZED BOWL. ADD SUGAR GRADUALLY UNTIL WELL MIXED. ADD CREAM CHEESE AND MIX WELL. IN A DEEP BOWL, BEAT EGG WHITES UNTIL SOFT PEAKS FORM. FOLD INTO CHEESE MIXTURE. SPREAD 1/4 OF CHEESE MIXTURE INTO A LARGE GLASS SERVING BOWL. DIP LADY FINGERS IN MIXTURE OF KAHLÚA AND COFFEE AND COVER CHEESE LAYER. REPEAT 3 TIMES, SPRINKLING CHOCOLATE ON EACH AND ENDING WITH CHEESE AND CHOCOLATE. REFRIGERATE 6 HOURS OR OVERNIGHT. SERVE CHILLED TO 8-10 UPLIFTED GUESTS.

HOW IS IT POSSIBLE TO HAVE A CIVIL WAR?

# GRAND SLAM FINALE

*A BEST OF BRIDGE TRADITION!*

| | |
|---|---|
| 1 CUP VANILLA WAFER COOKIE CRUMBS (24 WAFERS) | 250 mL |
| ½ CUP TOASTED ALMONDS, FINELY CHOPPED | 125 mL |
| ¼ CUP BUTTER, MELTED | 60 mL |
| 4 CUPS FRESH STRAWBERRIES | 1 L |
| 12 OZ. GOOD QUALITY WHITE CHOCOLATE | 340 g |
| 4 OZ. CREAM CHEESE | 115 g |
| ¼ CUP SUGAR | 60 mL |
| ¼ CUP ORANGE LIQUEUR OR FROZEN ORANGE JUICE CONCENTRATE | 60 mL |
| 1 TSP. VANILLA | 5 mL |
| 2 CUPS WHIPPING CREAM | 500 mL |
| COCOA POWDER | |

COMBINE WAFER CRUMBS, ALMONDS AND BUTTER. PRESS INTO BOTTOM OF A 9" (23 cm) SPRINGFORM PAN. WASH, DRY AND HULL BERRIES. RESERVE A COUPLE FOR GARNISH. CUT A FEW STRAWBERRIES IN HALF, LENGTHWISE, AND PRESS FLAT SIDES ALL AROUND SIDE OF SPRINGFORM PAN. ARRANGE WHOLE BERRIES, POINTS UP, ON CRUST. CHOP CHOCOLATE AND MELT IN DOUBLE BOILER OR MICROWAVE. COOL SLIGHTLY. BEAT CHEESE UNTIL SMOOTH, THEN BEAT IN SUGAR. MIX IN LIQUEUR (OR JUICE) AND VANILLA. SLOWLY BEAT IN CHOCOLATE. WHIP THE CREAM. STIR ABOUT ⅓ OF CREAM INTO CHOCOLATE MIXTURE AND FOLD IN THE REMAINDER. POUR OVER BERRIES, SHAKING PAN GENTLY TO FILL IN BETWEEN BERRIES. REFRIGERATE AT LEAST 3 HOURS (OVERNIGHT IS FINE). REMOVE SIDES AND BOTTOM OF SPRINGFORM PAN. DUST WITH COCOA AND GARNISH WITH RESERVED STRAWBERRIES. (PICTURED ON PAGE 291.)

# BLUEBERRY BONANZA

YOU'VE GOT IT - ANOTHER EASY DESSERT GUARANTEED TO PLEASE.

### CRUST

| | |
|---|---|
| 3 CUPS DIGESTIVE BISCUIT CRUMBS (27 BISCUITS) | 750 mL |
| 1 TSP. SUGAR | 5 mL |
| 1/4 TSP. CINNAMON | 1 mL |
| 1/2 CUP BUTTER, MELTED | 125 mL |

### CHEESE LAYER

| | |
|---|---|
| 8 OZ. PKG. CREAM CHEESE | 250 g |
| 1/2 CUP SUGAR | 125 mL |
| 2 EGGS | |
| 1 TSP. VANILLA | 5 mL |

### BLUEBERRY LAYER

| | |
|---|---|
| 3 CUPS FROZEN BLUEBERRIES | 750 mL |
| 1/2 CUP SUGAR | 125 mL |
| 1/2 CUP WATER | 125 mL |
| 1 TBSP. LEMON JUICE | 15 mL |
| 4 TSP. CORNSTARCH | 20 mL |
| 1/2 CUP COLD WATER | 125 mL |

### TOPPING

| | |
|---|---|
| 2 CUPS WHIPPING CREAM | 500 mL |
| 2 TBSP. SUGAR | 30 mL |
| 3 DIGESTIVE BISCUITS, CRUSHED | |

THE REASON ADULTS ARE ALWAYS ASKING LITTLE KIDS WHAT THEY WANT TO BE WHEN THEY GROW UP IS BECAUSE THEY'RE LOOKING FOR IDEAS.

# BLUEBERRY BONANZA

CONTINUED FROM PAGE 286.

TO MAKE CRUST: MIX INGREDIENTS TOGETHER AND PAT LIGHTLY INTO A 9 X 13" (23 X 33 cm) PAN AND BAKE AT 325°F (160°C) FOR 10 MINUTES.

TO MAKE CHEESE LAYER: MIX INGREDIENTS TOGETHER AND SPREAD OVER CRUST. BAKE AT 325°F (160°C) FOR 20 MINUTES.

TO MAKE BLUEBERRY LAYER: COMBINE BLUEBERRIES, SUGAR, WATER AND LEMON JUICE IN A SAUCEPAN AND BRING TO A BOIL. DISSOLVE CORNSTARCH IN THE COLD WATER AND ADD TO THE BLUEBERRY MIXTURE. STIR UNTIL THICKENED AND POUR OVER BAKED CHEESE LAYER. COOL COMPLETELY.

TO MAKE TOPPING: WHIP CREAM WITH SUGAR AND SPREAD ON TOP OF BLUEBERRY LAYER. SPRINKLE WITH DIGESTIVE BISCUIT CRUMBS AND REFRIGERATE UNTIL SERVING TIME. IF YOU MAKE THIS THE NIGHT BEFORE, DON'T WHIP THE CREAM UNTIL JUST BEFORE SERVING. SERVES 10-12.

IF THE NUMBER 2 PENCIL IS THE MOST POPULAR, WHY IS IT STILL NUMBER 2?

# CHOCOLATE-MOCHA CHEESECAKE

*WHO'D BELIEVE THIS IS LOW FAT?*

| | | |
|---|---:|---|
| 16 OZ. LOW-FAT SMALL-CURD COTTAGE CHEESE | 500 | g |
| 8 OZ. FAT-REDUCED CREAM CHEESE, ROOM TEMPERATURE | 250 | g |
| 1 CUP SUGAR | 250 | mL |
| 1 TBSP. VANILLA | 15 | mL |
| 2 TSP. INSTANT ESPRESSO POWDER OR INSTANT COFFEE POWDER | 10 | mL |
| 1/4 TSP SALT | 1 | mL |
| 3 LARGE EGGS, ROOM TEMPERATURE | | |
| 5-6 TBSP. UNSWEETENED COCOA POWDER | 75-90 | mL |
| 1/4 CUP SUGAR | 60 | mL |

PREHEAT OVEN TO 350°F (180°C). LINE BOTTOM OF 8" (20 cm) CIRCULAR CAKE PAN OR PIE PLATE AND BUILD SIDES UP TO 2" (5 cm) WITH PARCHMENT OR BROWN PAPER. SPRAY SIDES WITH VEGETABLE OIL SPRAY.

BLEND COTTAGE CHEESE IN PROCESSOR UNTIL SMOOTH. ADD CHEESE AND MIX WELL. ADD 1 CUP (250 mL) SUGAR, VANILLA, ESPRESSO POWDER AND SALT; BLEND. ADD EGGS AND PROCESS JUST UNTIL SMOOTH. POUR 2 CUPS (500 mL) OF BATTER INTO MEASURING CUP. ADD COCOA POWDER AND 1/4 CUP (60 mL) SUGAR TO BATTER IN PROCESSOR AND BLEND WELL. POUR COCOA BATTER INTO PREPARED PAN. POUR COFFEE BATTER DIRECTLY INTO CENTER OF COCOA

# CHOCOLATE-MOCHA CHEESECAKE

CONTINUED FROM PAGE 288.

BATTER (COFFEE BATTER WILL PUSH COCOA BATTER TO EDGE). RUN A SMALL KNIFE THROUGH BATTERS TO CREATE A MARBLED PATTERN. SET CAKE PAN INTO 9 X 13" (23 X 33 cm) PAN. POUR ENOUGH BOILING WATER INTO BAKING PAN TO COME HALFWAY UP SIDES OF CAKE PAN. SET PAN IN OVEN. BAKE CAKE UNTIL EDGES JUST BEGIN TO PUFF AND CRACK AND CENTER IS JUST SET, ABOUT 50 MINUTES. REMOVE CAKE PAN FROM WATER AND SET ON RACK TO COOL. COVER CAKE IN PAN WITH PLASTIC WRAP AND REFRIGERATE FOR ABOUT 6 HOURS. REMOVE WRAP; PUT PLATE ON TOP OF CAKE PAN AND INVERT. TAP BOTTOM LIGHTLY TO LOOSEN CAKE FROM PAN. COVER AND REFRIGERATE. THIS CAN BE MADE AHEAD. SERVES 10-12.

WHATEVER A MAN SEWS, HE RIPS.

# BEST OF BRIDGE CLASSIC CHEESECAKE

## CRUST

| | |
|---|---|
| 1¾ CUPS GRAHAM WAFER CRUMBS | 425 mL |
| ¼ CUP FINELY CHOPPED WALNUTS | 60 mL |
| ½ TSP. CINNAMON | 2 mL |
| ½ CUP BUTTER, MELTED | 125 mL |

## FILLING

| | |
|---|---|
| 2-8 OZ. PKGS. CREAM CHEESE | 2-250 g |
| 1 CUP SUGAR | 250 mL |
| 3 EGGS | |
| 3 CUPS SOUR CREAM | 750 mL |
| 2 TSP. VANILLA | 10 mL |

## TOPPING

| | |
|---|---|
| 15 OZ. PKG. FROZEN SLICED STRAWBERRIES WITH JUICE, THAWED | 425 g |

TO MAKE CRUST: COMBINE INGREDIENTS AND PRESS INTO A LIGHTLY GREASED 10" (25 cm) SPRINGFORM PAN.

TO MAKE FILLING: PREHEAT OVEN TO 375°F (190°C). BLEND CHEESE, SUGAR AND EGGS. ADD SOUR CREAM AND VANILLA. MIX WELL AND POUR ONTO CRUST. BAKE FOR 50-60 MINUTES.

SERVE WEDGES WITH STRAWBERRY TOPPING.

BUFFET: A FRENCH WORD THAT MEANS "GET UP AND GET IT YOURSELF".

Grand Slam Finale, page 285

Rhubarb and Strawberry Crumble, page 281

# PUMPKIN CHEESECAKE

*A GRAND FINALE FOR THANKSGIVING DINNER.*

## GINGER SNAP CRUST

| | |
|---|---|
| 1 CUP CRUSHED GINGER SNAPS | 250 mL |
| 3 TBSP. BUTTER, MELTED | 45 mL |
| 1 TSP. CINNAMON | 5 mL |
| 2 TBSP. BROWN SUGAR | 30 mL |

## FILLING

| | |
|---|---|
| 4-8 OZ. PKGS. CREAM CHEESE, SOFTENED | 4-250 g |
| 1½ CUPS SUGAR | 375 mL |
| 5 EGGS | |
| ¼ CUP FLOUR | 60 mL |
| 2 TSP. PUMPKIN PIE SPICE OR EQUAL PARTS GINGER, CINNAMON & NUTMEG | 10 mL |
| 14 OZ. CAN PUMPKIN | 398 mL |
| 2 TBSP. RUM | 30 mL |
| 1 CUP WHIPPING CREAM, WHIPPED | 250 mL |

CRUST: COMBINE INGREDIENTS. LIGHTLY GREASE A 10" (25 cm) SPRINGFORM PAN AND LINE BOTTOM WITH CRUMB MIXTURE. PAT FIRM AND CHILL.

FILLING: PREHEAT OVEN TO 325°F (160°C). BEAT SOFTENED CREAM CHEESE TILL FLUFFY. SLOWLY BEAT IN SUGAR. ADD EGGS, 1 AT A TIME, BEATING WELL AFTER EACH ADDITION. GRADUALLY BEAT IN FLOUR, SPICES, PUMPKIN AND RUM. POUR BATTER OVER CRUST. BAKE FOR 1½ TO 1¾ HOURS, OR TILL FILLING IS SET. COOL FOR AN HOUR. REFRIGERATE SEVERAL HOURS. GARNISH WITH WHIPPED CREAM AND A SPRINKLE OF CINNAMON. SERVES 10-12.

MAKE IT AHEAD. YOU'LL WANT TO STEAL SPOONFULS BEFORE SERVING TIME.

### CHOCOLATE NUT CRUST

| | |
|---|---|
| 1½ CUPS CRUSHED CHOCOLATE WAFERS | 375 mL |
| ¼ CUP BUTTER | 60 mL |
| ¾ CUP CRUSHED PECANS OR ALMONDS | 175 mL |

### CHOCOLATE MOUSSE

| | |
|---|---|
| ¾ CUP CHOCOLATE CHIPS | 175 mL |
| 8 OZ. CREAM CHEESE | 250 g |
| ¼ CUP SUGAR | 60 mL |
| 1 TSP. VANILLA | 5 mL |
| 2 EGGS, SEPARATED | |
| ¼ CUP SUGAR | 60 mL |
| 1 CUP WHIPPING CREAM | 250 mL |
| CHOCOLATE CURLS | |

TO MAKE CRUST: PREHEAT OVEN TO 325°F (160°C). COMBINE CHOCOLATE CRUMBS AND BUTTER AND PRESS INTO A 9" (23 cm) SPRINGFORM PAN. SPRINKLE NUTS OVER CRUST. BAKE FOR 10 MINUTES.

TO MAKE MOUSSE: MELT CHOCOLATE CHIPS AND SET ASIDE TO COOL. BLEND CREAM CHEESE, SUGAR AND VANILLA. BEAT EGG YOLKS, ADD AND STIR. MIX IN COOLED CHOCOLATE.

BEAT EGG WHITES UNTIL SOFT PEAKS FORM. ADD SUGAR SLOWLY AND BEAT UNTIL STIFF. FOLD INTO CHOCOLATE MIXTURE. WHIP CREAM AND FOLD INTO THE CHOCOLATE MOUSSE. POUR INTO

CONTINUED FROM PAGE 294.

SPRINGFORM PAN. COVER AND PLACE IN FREEZER OVERNIGHT. REMOVE FROM FREEZER AND REFRIGERATE 5 HOURS BEFORE SERVING. REMOVE FROM PAN AND GARNISH WITH CHOCOLATE CURLS. SERVES 8-10.

## UPSIDE-DOWN CHOCOLATE FUDGE PUDDING

A GREAT WINTER DESSERT - THE SAUCE ENDS UP ON THE BOTTOM AND THE CAKE ON TOP!

| | |
|---|---|
| 1 CUP FLOUR | 250 mL |
| 2 TSP. BAKING POWDER | 10 mL |
| 3/4 CUP SUGAR | 175 mL |
| 1/2 TSP. SALT | 2 mL |
| 3 TBSP. COCOA POWDER | 45 mL |
| 1/2 CUP MILK | 125 mL |
| 2 TBSP. BUTTER OR MARGARINE, MELTED | 30 mL |
| 1/4 CUP CHOPPED PECANS (OPTIONAL) | 60 mL |
| 3/4 CUP BROWN SUGAR | 175 mL |
| 1/2 CUP COCOA POWDER | 125 mL |
| 2 CUPS BOILING WATER | 500 mL |

PREHEAT OVEN TO 350°F (180°C). MIX FLOUR, BAKING POWDER, SUGAR, SALT AND COCOA TOGETHER. COMBINE MILK AND MELTED BUTTER. ADD TO DRY INGREDIENTS TO FORM A STIFF MIXTURE. ADD NUTS IF DESIRED. PUT INTO A GREASED 8" (20 cm) SQUARE BAKING PAN. COMBINE BROWN SUGAR, COCOA AND BOILING WATER. POUR OVER BATTER AND BAKE FOR 40 MINUTES. SERVE WARM WITH A BIG SCOOP OF VANILLA ICE CREAM. SERVES 4-6.

# COUNTRY SPICE PUDDING CAKE

ANOTHER ONE OF THOSE CAKES WITH BUILT-IN SAUCE - DEELISH!!

## PUDDING

| | |
|---|---|
| 1 CUP FLOUR | 250 mL |
| 2 TSP. BAKING POWDER | 10 mL |
| ½ CUP BROWN SUGAR | 125 mL |
| ¼ TSP CINNAMON | 1 mL |
| ¼ TSP. SALT | 1 mL |
| ¾ CUP RAISINS | 175 mL |
| ½ CUP MILK | 125 mL |
| 1 TSP. VANILLA | 5 mL |

## SAUCE

| | |
|---|---|
| 1 CUP BROWN SUGAR | 250 mL |
| ½ TSP. NUTMEG | 2 mL |
| 1 TSP. CINNAMON | 5 mL |
| ⅓ CUP BUTTER | 75 mL |
| 2 CUPS BOILING WATER | 500 mL |
| 1 TSP. VANILLA OR 1 TBSP. RUM (15 mL) | 5 mL |

TO MAKE PUDDING: PREHEAT OVEN TO 375°F (190°C). GREASE AN 8" (20 cm) SQUARE BAKING PAN. COMBINE FLOUR, BAKING POWDER, SUGAR, CINNAMON, SALT AND RAISINS. STIR IN MILK AND VANILLA. SPOON INTO DISH.

TO MAKE SAUCE: COMBINE ALL INGREDIENTS, EXCEPT VANILLA, AND STIR UNTIL BUTTER IS MELTED. NOW, STIR IN THE VANILLA. POUR SAUCE OVER PUDDING AND BAKE, UNCOVERED, FOR 30-35 MINUTES. CAKE IS DONE WHEN A TOOTHPICK INSERTED IN THE CENTER COMES OUT CLEAN. SERVE WARM WITH ICE CREAM OR FROZEN YOGURT. SERVES 6.

# FRUIT COCKTAIL CAKE

A GREAT LAST MINUTE DESSERT. ONE FAMILY ALWAYS TAKES THIS SAILING - NOW IT'S CALLED "FRUIT COCKPIT CAKE".

## CAKE

| | |
|---|---|
| 2 EGGS | |
| 1½ CUPS SUGAR | 375 mL |
| 2 TSP. BAKING SODA | 10 mL |
| ½ TSP. SALT | 2 mL |
| 14 OZ. CAN FRUIT COCKTAIL WITH JUICE OR CRUSHED PINEAPPLE | 398 mL |
| 2 CUPS FLOUR | 500 mL |

## SAUCE

| | |
|---|---|
| ¾ CUP SUGAR | 175 mL |
| ½ CUP MILK | 125 mL |
| ½ CUP BUTTER | 125 mL |
| 1 TSP. VANILLA OR 2 TBSP. (30 mL) | 5 mL |

RUM IS A SUPERB SUBSTITUTE!

TO MAKE CAKE: BEAT EGGS. ADD ALL INGREDIENTS, EXCEPT FLOUR, AND MIX. ADD FLOUR AND MIX AGAIN. GREASE A 9 X 13" (23 X 33 cm) PAN OR A BUNDT PAN AND POUR IN MIXTURE. BAKE AT 350°F (180°C) FOR 45 MINUTES.

TO MAKE SAUCE: HEAT SUGAR, MILK AND BUTTER IN SAUCEPAN AND BRING TO A BOIL. REMOVE FROM HEAT AND ADD VANILLA. POUR OVER HOT CAKE. (MAKES A LOT, BUT USE ALL OF IT! THE CAKE WILL ABSORB IT.)

SERVE WARM WITH WHIPPED CREAM OR FROZEN VANILLA YOGURT. KEEPS FOR SEVERAL DAYS REFRIGERATED (IF NO ONE KNOWS IT'S THERE).

# GOOD OLD-FASHIONED GINGERBREAD

FOUR GENERATIONS CAN'T BE WRONG - IT'S DELICIOUS. SERVE WARM WITH WHIPPED CREAM OR WITH THE FOLLOWING LEMON SAUCE.

| | |
|---|---|
| 1/4 CUP BUTTER | 60 mL |
| 1/4 CUP SUGAR | 60 mL |
| 1 TSP. CINNAMON | 5 mL |
| 1 TSP. GINGER | 5 mL |
| 1 TSP. CLOVES | 5 mL |
| 1 TSP. SALT | 5 mL |
| 1 TSP. BAKING POWDER | 5 mL |
| 1 1/4 CUPS FLOUR | 300 mL |
| 1/2 TSP. BAKING SODA | 2 mL |
| 1/2 CUP MOLASSES | 125 mL |
| 1/4 TSP. BAKING SODA | 1 mL |
| 3/4 CUP BOILING WATER | 175 mL |
| 1 EGG, BEATEN | |

CREAM TOGETHER BUTTER AND SUGAR. IN A SEPARATE BOWL MIX CINNAMON, GINGER, CLOVES, SALT, BAKING POWDER AND FLOUR. BEAT BAKING SODA INTO MOLASSES UNTIL FOAMY. ADD TO BUTTER MIXTURE. ADD THE 1/4 TSP. (1 mL) OF BAKING SODA TO THE BOILING WATER. ADD THIS ALTERNATELY WITH THE DRY INGREDIENTS TO THE BUTTER-MOLASSES MIXTURE. FOLD IN BEATEN EGG. (THE BATTER WILL BE THIN). POUR INTO GREASED LOAF PAN AND BAKE 30 MINUTES AT 400°F (200°C).

PMS: PARDON MY SCREAMING.

# LEMON SAUCE

EXCELLENT ON GINGERBREAD AND CAKES.

| | |
|---|---|
| 1 LEMON, GRATED RIND AND JUICE | |
| 1¼ CUPS BOILING WATER | 300 mL |
| 2 TBSP. CORNSTARCH | 30 mL |
| ½ CUP SUGAR | 125 mL |
| PINCH SALT | |
| 2 TBSP. BUTTER | 30 mL |

ADD LEMON RIND TO BOILING WATER, REDUCE HEAT AND SIMMER FOR 5 MINUTES. IN A SMALL BOWL, MIX CORNSTARCH, SUGAR AND SALT. ADD WATER GRADUALLY, STIRRING CONSTANTLY. RETURN TO SAUCEPAN AND COOK OVER MEDIUM HEAT FOR 10 MINUTES, UNTIL THICKENED. LOWER HEAT AND COOK 5 MINUTES LONGER. REMOVE FROM HEAT, STIR IN LEMON JUICE AND BUTTER. SERVE WARM. MAKES ABOUT 1½ CUPS (375 mL).

YEARS AGO, WHEN SOMEONE WORE SNEAKERS, IT OFTEN MEANT THAT HE COULDN'T AFFORD SHOES. TODAY, IF A PERSON IS WEARING SHOES, HE PROBABLY CAN'T AFFORD SNEAKERS.

# VICTORIAN ORANGE 'PEEL' CAKE

ALLOW THE FLAVORS TO MELLOW FOR SEVERAL DAYS. DELICIOUSLY MOIST AND FREEZES WELL.

## CAKE

| | |
|---|---|
| PEEL OF 3 LARGE ORANGES | |
| 1 CUP RAISINS | 250 mL |
| 1 CUP SUGAR | 250 mL |
| ½ CUP BUTTER, ROOM TEMPERATURE | 125 mL |
| 2 EGGS | |
| ¾ CUP BUTTERMILK | 175 mL |
| 2 CUPS FLOUR | 500 mL |
| 1 TSP. BAKING SODA | 5 mL |
| ½ TSP. SALT | 2 mL |
| ½ CUP CHOPPED WALNUTS | 125 mL |

## ORANGE SYRUP

| | |
|---|---|
| 1 CUP FRESH ORANGE JUICE | 250 mL |
| ½ CUP SUGAR | 125 mL |
| 2 TBSP. DARK RUM | 30 mL |

TO MAKE CAKE: REMOVE WHITE PITH FROM PEEL (IT'S THE BITTER PART). PLACE PEEL AND RAISINS IN PROCESSOR AND MIX UNTIL FINELY CHOPPED. PREHEAT OVEN TO 325°F (160°C). CREAM TOGETHER SUGAR AND BUTTER. ADD EGGS AND BUTTERMILK; MIX THOROUGHLY. MIX FLOUR, BAKING SODA AND SALT; STIR INTO BATTER. MIX IN PEEL, RAISINS AND WALNUTS. POUR INTO A WELL-GREASED 9" OR 10" (23 OR 25 cm) SPRINGFORM PAN AND BAKE 45-50 MINUTES, UNTIL CAKE TESTS DONE.

TO MAKE SYRUP: HEAT ORANGE JUICE, SUGAR AND RUM TOGETHER UNTIL SUGAR IS DISSOLVED.

WHEN CAKE IS DONE, LET STAND 10 MINUTES. REMOVE FROM PAN. RE-INVERT; SLOWLY DRIZZLE SYRUP, A SPOONFUL AT A TIME, OVER CAKE.

# POPPY SEED CAKE

THE DAY WE BROUGHT THIS TO THE OFFICE, WE ATE SO MUCH WE HAD TO SKIP LUNCH!

| | |
|---|---|
| ¼ CUP POPPY SEEDS | 60 mL |
| ¼ CUP MILK | 60 mL |
| 18½ OZ. LEMON CAKE MIX | 515 g |
| 4 OZ. PKG. INSTANT VANILLA PUDDING | 115 g |
| 4 EGGS | |
| ½ CUP VEGETABLE OIL | 125 mL |
| 1 CUP WARM WATER | 250 mL |

## SPICE MIXTURE

| | |
|---|---|
| 1 TBSP. COCOA POWDER | 15 mL |
| 1 TBSP. CINNAMON | 15 mL |
| 1 TBSP. WHITE SUGAR | 15 mL |

## GLAZE

| | |
|---|---|
| 3 TBSP. FRESH LEMON JUICE | 45 mL |
| 6 TBSP. ICING SUGAR | 90 mL |

SOAK POPPY SEEDS IN MILK FOR AT LEAST 1 HOUR. MIX TOGETHER CAKE MIX, PUDDING, EGGS, OIL AND WATER. ADD POPPY SEED MIXTURE. IN A SMALL BOWL COMBINE SPICE MIXTURE INGREDIENTS. GREASE AND FLOUR A BUNDT PAN. POUR IN A LAYER OF CAKE MIXTURE AND SPRINKLE WITH SPICE MIXTURE, REPEATING UNTIL ALL IS USED. BAKE AT 350°F (180°C) FOR 1 HOUR. COMBINE GLAZE INGREDIENTS. TURN CAKE OUT AND, WHILE STILL WARM, DRIZZLE GLAZE MIXTURE OVER CAKE.

# SENSATIONAL LEMON ROLL

THIS IS A WINNER! SERVE WITH STRAWBERRIES AND EXTRA COPIES OF THE RECIPE - EVERYONE WANTS IT!

## SPONGE CAKE

| | |
|---|---:|
| 3 EGGS | |
| 1 CUP SUGAR | 250 mL |
| 1 CUP FLOUR | 250 mL |
| 1 TSP. BAKING POWDER | 5 mL |
| ¼ TSP. SALT | 1 mL |
| 1 TBSP. GRATED ORANGE RIND | 15 mL |
| ⅓ CUP FRESH ORANGE JUICE | 75 mL |
| 1 TSP. VANILLA | 5 mL |
| ⅓ CUP ICING SUGAR | 75 mL |

## LEMON FILLING

| | |
|---|---:|
| 2 EGGS | |
| 1 CUP SUGAR | 250 mL |
| 1 TBSP. GRATED LEMON RIND | 15 mL |
| ½ CUP FRESH LEMON JUICE | 125 mL |
| 1 CUP WHIPPING CREAM | 250 mL |
| STRAWBERRIES TO GARNISH | |

TO MAKE SPONGE CAKE: PREHEAT OVEN TO 375°F (190°C). LINE 10" X 15" (23 X 38 cm) EDGED COOKIE SHEET WITH PARCHMENT PAPER OR WAXED PAPER. IN LARGE BOWL, BEAT EGGS UNTIL FROTHY. GRADUALLY BEAT IN SUGAR AND CONTINUE BEATING UNTIL THICK AND PALE YELLOW, AT LEAST 1 MINUTE. MIX TOGETHER FLOUR, BAKING POWDER AND SALT; ADD TO EGG MIXTURE. THEN ADD ORANGE RIND, ORANGE JUICE AND VANILLA. BEAT ON LOW SPEED UNTIL

# SENSATIONAL LEMON ROLL

CONTINUED FROM PAGE 302.

COMBINED. SPOON ONTO PAN (BE SURE AND PUSH BATTER INTO CORNERS); BAKE 15 MINUTES, UNTIL GOLDEN BROWN AND SPRINGY TO TOUCH. DON'T OVERBAKE! PLACE A CLEAN TEA TOWEL ON THE COUNTER. DUST WITH ICING SUGAR. WHEN CAKE IS DONE, LOOSEN FROM EDGES OF PAN WITH A KNIFE AND INVERT OVER TOWEL. REMOVE PAPER AND TRIM OFF CRUSTY EDGES. STARTING FROM THE SHORT END, ROLL UP CAKE AND TOWEL TOGETHER; PLACE ON WIRE RACK TO COOL. (DON'T PANIC IF IT CRACKS OR SPLITS). YOU CAN DO THIS THE NIGHT BEFORE BUT COVER THE COOLED CAKE (STILL ROLLED IN THE TOWEL) WITH PLASTIC WRAP.

TO MAKE LEMON FILLING: IN A DOUBLE BOILER, USE A WHISK TO COMBINE EGGS, SUGAR, LEMON RIND AND JUICE AND COOK UNTIL THICKENED, ABOUT 15 MINUTES. COOL. WHIP CREAM AND FOLD INTO LEMON MIXTURE. COVER AND REFRIGERATE UNTIL READY TO ASSEMBLE.

TO ASSEMBLE: CAREFULLY UNROLL CAKE; REMOVE TOWEL. RESERVE ½ CUP (125 mL) OF LEMON MIXTURE FOR DECORATION. SPREAD REMAINING MIXTURE AND GENTLY ROLL UP CAKE. PLACE SEAM SIDE DOWN ON SERVING PLATTER. DECORATE WITH RESERVED FILLING AND STRAWBERRIES. REFRIGERATE AT LEAST 4 HOURS. SERVES 10 GRATEFUL GUESTS.

# CHOCOLATE ROLL

| | |
|---|---|
| 5 EGGS | |
| ½ TSP. CREAM OF TARTAR | 2 mL |
| 1 CUP SUGAR (DIVIDED) | 250 mL |
| ¼ CUP FLOUR | 60 mL |
| 3 TBSP. COCOA POWDER | 45 mL |
| 1 TSP. VANILLA | 5 mL |
| 2 CUPS WHIPPING CREAM, WHIPPED | 500 mL |
| ICING SUGAR | |

SEPARATE THE EGGS. BEAT WHITES WITH CREAM OF TARTAR UNTIL STIFF. GRADUALLY BEAT IN ½ CUP (125 mL) SUGAR. SET ASIDE.

SIFT TOGETHER REMAINING ½ CUP (125 mL) SUGAR, FLOUR AND COCOA POWDER. BEAT YOLKS UNTIL THICK. FOLD FLOUR MIXTURE INTO YOLKS AND ADD VANILLA. THIS WILL BE VERY STIFF. CAREFULLY FOLD YOLK MIXTURE INTO BEATEN WHITES. PREHEAT OVEN TO 325°F (160°C). LINE A 10" x 15" (25 x 38 cm) EDGED COOKIE SHEET WITH WAXED PAPER, LEAVING AN OVERLAPPING EDGE. GREASE AND FLOUR PAPER. SPREAD BATTER EVENLY ON PAPER. BAKE FOR 20 MINUTES. PLACE ON A RACK AND COOL FOR 5 MINUTES. PLACE A CLEAN TEA TOWEL ON COUNTER, GENEROUSLY SPRINKLE WITH ICING SUGAR AND TURN CAKE ONTO TOWEL. CAREFULLY PEEL WAXED PAPER OFF THE TOP. CUT OFF ANY DRIED EDGES. ROLL UP CAKE AND TOWEL TOGETHER, BEGINNING AT SHORT END. COOL COMPLETELY - NO MORE THAN A HALF AN HOUR. UNWRAP ROLL AND SPREAD WHIPPED CREAM

# CHOCOLATE ROLL

CONTINUED FROM PAGE 304.

OVER SURFACE. ROLL UP CAKE AGAIN BUT THIS TIME - LEAVE OUT THE TOWEL! SPRINKLE WITH ICING SUGAR. SERVE WITH FUDGE SAUCE OR FOAMY BUTTER SAUCE. SERVES 8. FOR COMPANY WHY NOT ADD SOME RUM OR LIQUEUR TO THE WHIPPING CREAM?

## FOAMY BUTTER SAUCE

| | |
|---|---|
| ½ CUP BUTTER | 125 mL |
| 1 EGG | |
| 1 CUP ICING SUGAR | 250 mL |

COMBINE ALL INGREDIENTS IN TOP OF DOUBLE BOILER. COOK, STIRRING, UNTIL IT FORMS A SMOOTH SAUCE. SERVE WARM OVER CHOCOLATE ROLL.

## FUDGE SAUCE

| | |
|---|---|
| 1 TBSP. BUTTER | 15 mL |
| 1 SQUARE UNSWEETENED CHOCOLATE | 30 g |
| ⅓ CUP BOILING WATER | 75 mL |
| 1 CUP SUGAR | 250 mL |
| 2 TBSP. CORN SYRUP | 30 mL |
| ½ TSP. VANILLA | 2 mL |

MELT BUTTER AND CHOCOLATE IN MEDIUM SAUCEPAN. ADD BOILING WATER AND BRING TO A BOIL. ADD SUGAR AND SYRUP. BRING TO BOIL AGAIN AND STIR FOR 5 MINUTES. STIR IN VANILLA. SERVE JUST WARM OVER CHOCOLATE ROLL.

# A "GRAND" CAKE

THIS RECIPE CAN BE MADE THE DAY AHEAD IF COVERED AND REFRIGERATED.

## CAKE

| | |
|---|---|
| 1¾ CUPS FLOUR | 425 mL |
| 1 TSP. BAKING SODA | 5 mL |
| ½ TSP. BAKING POWDER | 2 mL |
| 1 TSP. SALT | 5 mL |
| ½ CUP COCOA POWDER | 125 mL |
| ½ CUP BUTTER, ROOM TEMPERATURE | 125 mL |
| 1⅔ CUPS GRANULATED SUGAR | 400 mL |
| 3 EGGS | |
| 1 TSP. VANILLA | 5 mL |
| 1⅓ CUPS WATER | 325 mL |
| ¼ CUP GRAND MARNIER | 60 mL |

## FILLING

| | |
|---|---|
| ¾ CUP FROZEN ORANGE JUICE CONCENTRATE | 175 mL |
| ¾ CUP SUGAR | 175 mL |
| 1 TBSP. GELATIN (1 PKG.) | 15 mL |
| COARSELY GRATED PEEL OF 2 ORANGES | |
| ¼ CUP GRAND MARNIER | 60 mL |
| 2 CUPS WHIPPING CREAM | 500 mL |
| ¾ CUP ICING SUGAR | 175 mL |

TO MAKE CAKE: PREHEAT OVEN TO 350°F (180°C). GREASE 2, 8" (20 cm) ROUND CAKE PANS. LINE WITH WAXED PAPER AND GREASE AGAIN. MEASURE FLOUR, BAKING SODA, BAKING POWDER, SALT AND COCOA INTO A BOWL AND SIFT TOGETHER. CREAM BUTTER USING ELECTRIC BEATER. GRADUALLY ADD SUGAR, BEATING UNTIL

# A "GRAND" CAKE

CONTINUED FROM PAGE 306.

LIGHT AND FLUFFY. BEAT IN EGGS 1 AT A TIME. ADD VANILLA. AT LOW SPEED, BEAT IN 1/3 OF FLOUR MIXTURE, THEN 1/2 OF THE WATER, BEATING ONLY UNTIL MIXED AFTER EACH ADDITION. BEAT IN ANOTHER 1/3 FLOUR, REMAINING WATER AND REST OF FLOUR. POUR INTO PANS AND BAKE FOR 30-35 MINUTES, OR UNTIL CENTER OF CAKE SPRINGS BACK WHEN LIGHTLY TOUCHED. LET CAKES COOL 5 MINUTES, THEN TURN OUT. REMOVE WAXED PAPER AND COOL THOROUGHLY ON RACKS.

1-2 HOURS BEFORE ASSEMBLING, SLICE EACH CAKE IN HALF HORIZONTALLY TO MAKE 4 LAYERS. PLACE LAYERS CUT SIDE UP AND SPRINKLE EACH WITH 1 TBSP. (15 mL) GRAND MARNIER.

TO MAKE FILLING: COMBINE JUICE, SUGAR AND GELATIN IN A SAUCEPAN; COOK OVER MEDIUM HEAT, STIRRING CONSTANTLY UNTIL SUGAR AND GELATIN ARE DISSOLVED, ABOUT 5 MINUTES. REMOVE FROM HEAT AND STIR IN ORANGE PEEL AND GRAND MARNIER. PRESS A SHEET OF WAXED PAPER ON SURFACE AND REFRIGERATE UNTIL COOL, ABOUT 20 MINUTES. WHIP CREAM UNTIL SOFT PEAKS FORM. GRADUALLY BEAT IN ICING SUGAR, THEN FOLD IN GRAND MARNIER MIXTURE.

TO ASSEMBLE: PLACE 1 LAYER OF CAKE, CUT SIDE UP, ON SERVING PLATE. SPOON ON 1/4 OF FILLING AND SPREAD. TOP WITH ANOTHER LAYER AND CONTINUE UNTIL ALL ARE USED, ENDING WITH FILLING. REFRIGERATE IMMEDIATELY, LET SET AT LEAST 4 HOURS TO BLEND FLAVORS. (PICTURED ON PAGE 258.)

# CHOCOLATE RASPBERRY TORTE

GOD MADE CHOCOLATE AND THE DEVIL THREW THE CALORIES IN!

## CAKE

| | |
|---|---|
| 2 CUPS FLOUR | 500 mL |
| 2 TSP. BAKING SODA | 10 mL |
| ½ TSP. SALT | 2 mL |
| ½ TSP. BAKING POWDER | 2 mL |
| 3 SQUARES UNSWEETENED CHOCOLATE | 85 g |
| ½ CUP BUTTER | 125 mL |
| 2 CUPS BROWN SUGAR, PACKED | 500 mL |
| 3 EGGS | |
| 1½ TSP. VANILLA | 7 mL |
| ¾ CUP SOUR CREAM | 175 mL |
| ½ CUP STRONG COFFEE | 125 mL |
| ½ CUP COFFEE-FLAVORED LIQUEUR (KAHLÚA) | 125 mL |

## FILLING

| | |
|---|---|
| 1 CUP WHIPPING CREAM | 250 mL |
| 2 TBSP. ICING SUGAR | 30 mL |
| 12 OZ. JAR RASPBERRY OR STRAWBERRY JAM | 340 mL |

## FROSTING

| | |
|---|---|
| 1½ CUPS CHOCOLATE CHIPS | 375 mL |
| ¾ CUP SOUR CREAM | 175 mL |
| DASH OF SALT | |
| CHOCOLATE CURLS | |
| FRESH RASPBERRIES OR STRAWBERRIES | |

THE PROBLEM WITH BUCKET SEATS IS THAT NOT EVERYONE HAS THE SAME SIZE BUCKET.

# CHOCOLATE RASPBERRY TORTE

CONTINUED FROM PAGE 308.

NOW TO BUILD IT!

PREHEAT OVEN TO 350°F (180°C). GREASE AND FLOUR 2-9" (23 cm) LAYER CAKE PANS. MIX FLOUR, BAKING SODA, SALT AND BAKING POWDER. MELT CHOCOLATE AND LET COOL. IN A LARGE BOWL BEAT BUTTER, BROWN SUGAR AND EGGS AT A HIGH SPEED UNTIL MIXTURE IS LIGHT AND FLUFFY, ABOUT 5 MINUTES. BEAT IN MELTED CHOCOLATE AND VANILLA. AT LOW SPEED, BEAT IN FLOUR MIXTURE (IN FOURTHS), ALTERNATING WITH SOUR CREAM (IN THIRDS). ADD COFFEE AND LIQUEUR, BLENDING UNTIL SMOOTH. POUR BATTER INTO PANS AND BAKE 30-35 MINUTES, OR UNTIL SURFACE SPRINGS BACK. COOL IN PANS FOR 10 MINUTES, THEN REMOVE FROM PANS AND COOL ON WIRE RACKS.

TO MAKE FILLING: BEAT CREAM UNTIL IT BEGINS TO THICKEN. SPRINKLE IN ICING SUGAR AND BEAT UNTIL STIFF. REFRIGERATE. SLICE CAKE LAYERS IN HALF HORIZONTALLY TO MAKE 4 LAYERS. (CAKE LAYERS CUT MORE EASILY IF FROZEN FIRST). PLACE 1 LAYER, CUT SIDE UP, ON CAKE PLATE. SPREAD WITH ½ CUP (125 mL) RASPBERRY JAM AND ½ CUP (125 mL) WHIPPED CREAM MIXTURE. REPEAT WITH REMAINING LAYERS, ENDING WITH TOP LAYER, CUT SIDE DOWN.

CONTINUED ON PAGE 310

# CHOCOLATE RASPBERRY TORTE

## CONTINUED FROM PAGE 309.

TO MAKE FROSTING: MELT CHOCOLATE CHIPS IN TOP OF DOUBLE BOILER. ADD SOUR CREAM AND SALT AND BEAT UNTIL FROSTING IS CREAMY AND SMOOTH. FROST TOP AND SIDES OF CAKE. GARNISH WITH CHOCOLATE CURLS AND FRESH BERRIES. (FOR PERFECT CHOCOLATE CURLS, HEAT A CHOCOLATE SQUARE IN MICROWAVE FOR 10 SECONDS AND SHAVE WITH VEGETABLE PEELER.)

# SUPER CHOCOLATE CAKE

THIS IS DARN GOOD!

| | |
|---|---|
| 1 CUP WHITE SUGAR | 250 mL |
| 3 TBSP. BUTTER, ROOM TEMPERATURE | 45 mL |
| 1 EGG, BEATEN | |
| ½ CUP COCOA, FILL WITH BOILING WATER | 125 mL |
|     TO MAKE 1 CUP OF (250 mL) LIQUID | |
| ½ TSP. BAKING SODA | 2 mL |
| ½ CUP BOILING WATER | 125 mL |
| 1 CUP FLOUR | 250 mL |
| 1 TSP. BAKING POWDER | 5 mL |

CREAM TOGETHER SUGAR AND BUTTER; ADD EGG AND COCOA LIQUID. MIX SODA AND BOILING WATER. ADD THIS, FLOUR AND BAKING POWDER, MIX WELL. POUR INTO GREASED 9" (23 cm) SQUARE PAN (THE BATTER WILL BE THIN). BAKE AT 350°F (180°C) FOR 30 MINUTES, OR UNTIL A TOOTHPICK INSERTED IN CENTER COMES OUT CLEAN. (THIS CAKE DOUBLES WELL. BAKE IN A 9 X 13" (23 X 33 cm) PAN OR A BUNDT PAN FOR 40-50 MINUTES.)

# CHOCOLATE ZUCCHINI CAKE

*A BEST OF BRIDGE FAVORITE.*

| | |
|---|---|
| ¼ CUP BUTTER | 60 mL |
| ½ CUP VEGETABLE OIL | 125 mL |
| 1¾ CUPS SUGAR | 425 mL |
| 2 EGGS | |
| 1 TSP. VANILLA | 5 mL |
| ½ CUP BUTTERMILK OR SOUR MILK | 125 mL |
| 2½ CUPS FLOUR | 625 mL |
| ¼ CUP COCOA POWDER | 60 mL |
| ½ TSP. BAKING POWDER | 2 mL |
| 1 TSP. BAKING SODA | 5 mL |
| ½ TSP. CINNAMON | 2 mL |
| ½ TSP. CLOVES | 2 mL |
| 2 CUPS GRATED ZUCCHINI | 500 mL |
| ¼ CUP CHOCOLATE CHIPS | 60 mL |

CREAM TOGETHER BUTTER, OIL, SUGAR, EGGS, VANILLA AND BUTTERMILK. SIFT DRY INGREDIENTS AND ADD TO CREAMED MIXTURE. MIX IN ZUCCHINI AND CHOCOLATE CHIPS. BAKE IN A GREASED AND FLOURED BUNDT PAN OR A 9 X 13" (23 X 33 cm) GREASED PAN AT 325°F (160°C) FOR 45 MINUTES. DELICIOUS!

A DAY WITHOUT SUNSHINE IS LIKE, NIGHT.

# CHOCOLATE ANGEL FOOD CAKE

| | |
|---|---|
| 12 EGG WHITES, AT ROOM TEMPERATURE | |
| 2 TSP. CREAM OF TARTAR | 10 mL |
| 1 CUP SUGAR | 250 mL |
| 2 TSP. VANILLA | 10 mL |
| 3/4 CUP SUGAR | 175 mL |
| 1/4 TSP. SALT | 1 mL |
| 1 CUP FLOUR | 250 mL |
| 1/4 CUP COCOA POWDER | 60 mL |
| 1 1/2 TSP. BAKING SODA | 7 mL |
| SPRINKLING OF ICING SUGAR | |

PREHEAT OVEN TO 350°F (180°C). IN A LARGE BOWL USING MEDIUM SPEED, BEAT EGG WHITES UNTIL FROTHY. ADD CREAM OF TARTAR; INCREASE MIXER SPEED TO HIGH. GRADUALLY ADD 1 CUP (250 mL) SUGAR AND VANILLA. BEAT UNTIL STIFF, GLOSSY PEAKS FORM. IN ANOTHER BOWL, COMBINE SUGAR, SALT, FLOUR, COCOA AND BAKING SODA. SIFT AND FOLD INTO EGG WHITES 1/3 AT A TIME. SPOON BATTER INTO UNGREASED ANGEL FOOD PAN. BAKE 40 MINUTES, OR UNTIL PICK INSERTED COMES OUT CLEAN. TO COOL CAKE, INVERT PAN. COOL 30 MINUTES. USING KNIFE, RELEASE SIDES AND MIDDLE OF CAKE FROM PAN. INVERT ONTO PLATE. SPRINKLE WITH ICING SUGAR. SERVE WITH FROZEN YOGURT. SERVES 16.

NOTE: TO USE THE EGG YOLKS, MAKE CRÈME BRÛLÉE (PAGE 277) OR AFTER ANGEL FOOD COOKIES (PAGE 249).

*I BASE MOST OF MY FASHION TASTE ON WHAT DOESN'T ITCH!*

# KARROT'S CAKE

SO GOOD FOR YOUR EYESIGHT, NEVER MIND YOUR TASTE BUDS!

## CAKE

| | |
|---|---|
| ¾ CUP CORN OIL | 175 mL |
| 1 CUP SUGAR | 250 mL |
| 3 EGGS | |
| 1½ CUPS FLOUR | 375 mL |
| ½ TSP. SALT | 2 mL |
| 1⅓ TSP. BAKING SODA | 6.5 mL |
| 1½ TSP. CINNAMON | 7 mL |
| 2 CUPS FINELY GRATED CARROTS (4-5) | 500 mL |

## ICING

| | |
|---|---|
| 8 OZ. PKG. CREAM CHEESE, ROOM TEMPERATURE | 250 g |
| ¼ CUP BUTTER, ROOM TEMPERATURE | 60 mL |
| 2½ CUPS ICING SUGAR | 625 mL |
| 2 TSP. VANILLA | 10 mL |

TO MAKE CAKE: BEAT TOGETHER OIL AND SUGAR. ADD EGGS, 1 AT A TIME, BEATING WELL AFTER EACH ADDITION. COMBINE DRY INGREDIENTS AND ADD TO EGG MIXTURE. BEAT ALL TOGETHER UNTIL WELL BLENDED. FOLD IN RAW CARROTS. BAKE 1 HOUR AT 300°F (150°C) IN A GREASED 9 X 13" (23 X 33 cm) PAN. (THIS CAN ALSO BE MADE IN A BUNDT PAN).

TO MAKE ICING: SOFTEN CHEESE AND BUTTER; BEAT WELL. ADD SUGAR AND VANILLA AND BEAT AGAIN. SPREAD ON COOLED CAKE.

# INDEX

YOUR FAVORITES

YOUR FAVORITES

YOUR FAVORITES